W9-ARE-227

BLACK FAMILIES

SAGE FOCUS EDITIONS

BLACK FAMILIES

Edited by
Harriette Pipes McAdoo

 SAGE PUBLICATIONS   Beverly Hills   London

To my parents, Anna Howard Russell Pipes
and William Harrison Pipes

For information address:

SAGE Publications, Inc.
275 South Beverly Drive
Beverly Hills, California 90212

SAGE Publications Ltd
28 Banner Street
London EC1Y 8QE, England

Printed in the United States of America

Library of Congress Cataloging in Publication Data

Main entry under title:

Black families.

(Sage focus edition ; 41)
Bibliography: p.
1. Afro-American families–Addresses, essays, lectures. I. McAdoo, Harriette Pipes.
E185.86.B525   305.8'96073   81-14442
ISBN 0-8039-1741-4   AACR2
ISBN 0-8039-1742-2 (pbk.)

FIRST PRINTING

CONTENTS

ACKNOWLEDGMENTS

Many people have been involved in the process of developing this book. The contributors are the key ingredients that have made this volume. All are people whose work I respect and who I feel are making important contributions to the study of Black family life. Their writings and diversity of beliefs and orientations accurately reflect the diversity of the field. Some of them were friends before this project began and others I knew only through their writings. Through our letters, calls, and scribblings back and forth in the margins, I feel that I have come to know each of them well. We have become acquainted with the family changes and the births, illnesses, deaths, retirements, funding crises, and activities of each other's family members. Those are the joys and sorrows of being a part of families.

My graduate students at Howard University and their questions and their need for Black family information was the final push that helped me decide to produce this edition. The impetus grew out of the frustration of not being able to find a volume of original works that focused on Black families and having to teach courses at Howard from a pile of reprints. Many good people were doing excellent work, but it was scattered all over and difficult to access in one spot.

This volume also grew out of the workshops and symposia I have organized and participated in at conferences over the past few years, where several of us have tried to pull together the best minds in one area of Black family research for a particular conference. Excitement was generated at these meetings of the National Council on Family Relations (NCFR), the Society for Research in Child Development, Groves Conference on Marriage and the Family, the Association of Black Psychology, Empirical Conferences on Black Psychology, and the Ethnic Minorities Section of NCFR. The hard work of many fellow researchers has provided me with the background materials from our cooperative efforts. All of this increase in activities has given those of us in this field needed support, as sometimes we were working in isolation.

However, the real impetus for writing about Black families has been provided by my own experiences as I have lived within my family of orientation, Pipes and Russells, and within my family of procreation. My husband, John, has been totally supportive, and my children—Michael, John, Julia, and David—have been patient and curious about what this book is really all about.

I want to express appreciation for the partial support provided by the Center for Minority Health of the National Institute of Mental Health. Additional support was provided by the Columbia Research Systems and its staff, who were intimately involved at all stages. Elsie Zdanis was especially instrumental in maintaining the overall organization of the process and in preparing many of the final papers. She was assisted by Judi Yahyavi, who helped in the preparation of some difficult papers. They, along with John McAdoo, Gayle Weaver, Grace Mack, Mary Lee, and Sharon Williams, read all of the papers and made suggestions. Faye Aker and Renee Mayfield were the editors who helped me in many ways in making suggestions to the authors. Other friends, to remain unnamed, did blind reviews of some of the papers. I also thank Sage Publications for allowing me complete freedom to include the content I felt was necessary to this volume. Without all of this help, this book never could have been produced.

PREFACE

The study of Black family life has been an area that has gone through periods of intense activity and then periods of quiescence. At one point it was possible to indicate the one expert in the field and later three or four, but the infusion of researchers has increased the production of research studies, books, and positions on the Black family. This increase in activity has been helpful for the field. It does make it more difficult when one is asked to make a definitive statement about "the Black family." The diversity of Black families, their value systems, and their lifestyles, make it impossible to be "the expert" on Black families. This is as it should be.

This book addresses some unresolved issues regarding Black families. No attempt was made in this volume to represent all sides of each issue, nor were all writings selected to promote any one prevailing view, interest group, or socio-political orientation. A careful reading of the chapters will reveal fundamental unresolved—and some probably unresolvable—differences in frames of reference of Black families represented by the authors.

This lack of consensus keeps the field of Black families lively, volatile, and continuously open to new interpretations as new and old data are incorporated by those writing in the field and those of us living it. The diversity of schools of thought is reflective of the diversities of Black life experiences and is reflected in the title of this book: Black Famil*ies* rather than *The Black Family*.

This diversity is also reflected in the manner in which the racial labels were handled in the various chapters. Conformity in usage is customary in an edited book, but the readers will note variations. The use of racial labels and whether or not to capitalize "black " and "white," during periods of flux, become more than just editorial style; they often become political statements or expressions of personal racial pride or individuality. The histories of our own life experiences, professional training, and ideological stances have affected all our perceptions of families. Conformity would have violated these expressions. Therefore, reflecting the diversity within the field of Black families, the decision was made to let each author decide whether Black, African-American, Afro-American, black, or Negro was to be used within their own chapter.

Some of the best thinkers on the American Black families were selected and asked to prepare chapters that would tie together the major issues, theories, and empirical findings in their area. These contributors were carefully selected from a variety of disciplines, regardless of their philosophical orientation, race, or agreement with my own biases.

This is the third in a series of books published by Sage Publications that began with La Frances Rodgers-Rose's *The Black Woman* and was followed by Lawrence Gary's *Black Men. Black Families* ties the male and female together into the family unit as they attempt to survive economically, develop their relationship in order to procreate and raise their children, and move as advocates for their children and families.

DEMYTHOLOGIZING BLACK FAMILIES

As interdisciplinary researchers we have been able to go beyond the negative stereotypical views that had been held as the position on Black families. Unfortunately the wider society has not made this journey, and many of us are continually called upon to speak against the negative images that are held about Black families—held by those who are often in the position to make policy and programmatic decisions that have a direct impact on the lives of Black families. Therefore some of our creative energies are continually channeled into reactionary activities when we would prefer to concentrate upon the more creative theoretical and empirical examinations of Black family life.

The demythologization of negative images about the Black family is an ongoing process that will probably continue for generations, for the ethnocentric concepts held by the mainstream social science literature about Black families will persist. The one main change that has occurred is that fewer writers are able to make blatant conjectures about Black families and remain unchallenged. Publishers and editors of professional journals, the "gatekeepers" of much of the literature on Blacks, have become more sensitized to these issues. While the process of putting myths to rest is essential, we must not truncate all of our efforts to achieve this one objective. This volume is a move to continue the examination of Black families on a conceptual level and to test some of the theories that have been brought forth on the families. It also was an effort to give a complete review within each chapter of the relevant works and to gather the most current facts and figures known about Black families.

DIVERSE CONCEPTUALIZATIONS

There have been major divisions within the field of Black family studies. The major disagreement has focused on whether or not Black families differ from non-Black families in any way other than the formers' greater level of poverty. One view has held that Black families are what they are simply because they are poor; if poverty was removed, then there would be a convergence of values and structure between all families. Another view is that poverty, plus the experience of slavery and Reconstruction, have left an indelible mark on families that has existed to the present. Still another view is that Black families are unique because of the remnants of African culture that have been maintained and have adapted to discrimination. These divisions found among Black scholars are now evolving into the "Africanist" and the "Empiricist" schools, with a growing personal polarity between the two.

The chapters that are included in this volume reflect both points of view and should move us closer to the answer to some of the age-old debates about the Afro-American family. The real "truth" will probably be found to be an amalgamation of all of these views.

There is no denying the soul-satisfying comfort that identification with a known ethnic lode of culture brings, whether it is retained directly from the old country or recreated in part within the new country. Too often the emotional pull of desiring a base of ethnic identification has caused many writers to go far beyond their data or knowledge to create cultural links that may be tenuous. While this performs a needed grounding in an emotional place of origin, it often is not based on a clear understanding of history.

The works of Herskovits (1941), Nobles (1976), Pipes (1951), Semaj (1980), Sudarkasa (1980), and Walker (1980) have contributed to the study in this direction. The link between African and American Black families has become more obvious as scholars have refined their analyses and as more writers join the effort with skills and expertise in cross-cultural analysis. The only danger in this is to avoid the romantic belief that a return to Africanism will somehow eradicate the problems that beset the contemporary Black family, such as plural marriages within a society that do not allow adequate support of even one average Black family. There may be few, if any, one-to-one direct carryovers, but the common patterns that have been found in non-Western families on the African continent, in the Caribbean, and in isolated areas of rural America would make it impossible not to acknowledge that there are some cultural continuities.

At the same time, one must support the view of those who feel that poverty and discrimination are the major factors impinging on Black families. It is a view that attempts to focus on the variables of Black family life in the here and now. Since we can only reconstruct what may have been retained from Africa or acquired during enslavement, emphasis should only be on what we can measure now. This pragmatic approach says that historians and those in literature will eventually be able to piece together more of the patterns that are now only speculation. Meanwhile we can focus on doing good descriptive studies and move into doing more theoretical pieces.

There is so much value that can and will result from the investigations of these two schools of emphasis that there is no need for antagonism between the two. Yet this tension may be the impetus that will generate even greater endeavors. Serious scholars will have to keep abreast of the dynamic debates and explorations that will come from the concentrations on cultural continuities and from the separate approaches.

KEY SCHOLARSHIP OF THE FIELD

This volume on Black families continues in the same vein as the work of DuBois in *The Negro American Family* (1967) and Robert Staples in his volume *The Black Family: Essays and Studies* (1971). In both of these editions the authors brought together what they felt reflected the best work done at that time on Black families. This volume will not give a historical portrayal of Black families but will concentrate on the contemporary family. The history of Black families has been succinctly presented elsewhere by noted writers and should be familiar to readers: DuBois (1967), Quarles (1964), Blassingame (1972), Lammermeier (1973), Bennett (1975), Gutman (1976), Pleck (1979), Haley (1976) and Drake (1980). In addition, there are large-scale studies with which the reader should also be familiar: Scanzoni (1971) and Heiss (1971), and the forthcoming work of James Jackson et al. at the University of Michigan Institute of Social Research.

Following the beginning made by DuBois, Frazier remains the undisputed leader in the social science study of Black families. While there is not total agreement with some of his analyses about family life, the clearness of his methodology, observations, and analyses, and the vacuum that existed before him, place him in a position that even his opponents have had to respect. The next wave of works was spearheaded by the key writers in the field: Billingsley with his *Black Families in White America* and Hill and his *Strengths of Black Families*. These were works that articulated the essence of where we were and where we hoped to go in the field. While not the only voices of that period, these two became the main spokesmen on Black families. Their theoretical and descriptive works provided a springboard for many of the writings on Black families during the 1960s and '70s.

SOURCE OF BLACK FAMILY RESEARCH DATA

There is one problem in highlighting the traditional leaders, for at the same time there were other scholars in different fields who were making similar observations but whose works were never picked up in the popular professional press. A review of many of the earlier Negro journals, newspapers, and writings in literature, anthropology, religion, education, and social organizations leads one to an awareness of the masses of beautifully documented works that exist scattered over the country and are therefore lost to scholars.

Even today dissertations are being written that are breaking new ground, but for a variety of reasons these findings are not being made known to others in the field. The doctoral and Master's dissertations that are found in the Howard University library, and materials in its Moreland Room, are probably the richest untapped source of information on Black life. Many of the works that were done on a Master's level in the first half of this century are far superior to doctoral dissertations that are now done in the major universities. This is the result of the striving for excellence and the Ivy League-trained professors who came to Howard, attracted by the caliber of minds on the campus and because of the racism that would not allow them positions on the non-Black campuses. They demanded and received a level of scholarship that would be difficult to replicate today with few exceptions.

Across the country are resources on Black family research that are being tapped only slightly: Atlanta and Fisk Universities are two others. Much of the archival work is being done at the larger universities that are able to provide resources that archivists, historians, and oral historians need. The Smithsonian has become another focal point during the present period.

The one continuing resource for data on Black family life has been the Black publications that are put out by professional organizations and a dedicated group of scholars (*Journal of Black Psychology, Black Scholar, Journal of Behavior and Social Scientist, The Western Journal of Black Studies*). The problems are the costs and energy required to maintain these efforts, without the needed university or institutional support. Graduate students' works may not be exposed, and their professors are not familiar with them. These sources of data, in essence, have not been "validated" by the mainstream profession and thus are denied to graduate students, Black and white, who want to use them as their main theoretical bases. The lack of validation limits the use by students but frees writers and editors to take directions that are supportive of scholarly examination unhindered by acceptability of organized mainstream scholarship.

It would be myoptic to indicate that only Black institutions and Black researchers are making inroads in advancing Black family studies. Several professional organizations have supported the efforts on scholarship on Black families. The National Council on Family Relations' *Journal of Marriage and the Family* took leadership with their Decade Reviews written by Robert Staples et al. and the groundbreaking special edition on Black families edited by Marie Peters. Black families had been so ignored in the major professional social science journals that this one edition significantly increased the number of articles published on Black families. The National Association of Social Workers has done likewise with their special edition, edited by June Hopps, on People of Color. Several other "special editions" have further disseminated the work on Black families.

While these target editions have made special contributions, it is unfortunate that Black family studies and papers are not regularly included in the ongoing editions of all major journals. For a variety of ethnocentric reasons, and lack of knowledge about the myriad of work done in this field, editors have not routinely included work on or by Blacks. This situation may be improved in the future with a more active participation of Blacks and other minorities in professional organizations and the professional publication processes. Meanwhile, the reality is that many social scientists do not value the diversity that is found in Black families, so the attitudes that are often encountered by Black researchers require that an active participation and support of the Black-oriented publication efforts must be continued. It will be necessary to continue actively giving energies on both fronts for the foreseeable future.

ROLES PLAYED BY PROFESSIONAL MEETINGS
IN BLACK FAMILY RESEARCH

The major professional organizations often are the validators of the field and control the academic and professional futures of young researchers and, indirectly, the funds for their research efforts. Therefore, a continuation of the integration of knowledge of Black family life is required to make it into the mainstream literature that will be available to all researchers. At the same time, the freedom to take unpopular positions and exploratory thrusts will not be allowed within mainstream journals. These efforts are only possible within journals or institutions that have gone beyond such debates as "Are Black families really a valid subject area?" "Are these really just polemic exercises?" "Are we giving too much emphasis to minorities?" "Can't we just focus on 'good research' and forget about all of this race business?"

There have been other points where the needed dialogue has become traditional. The annual meetings of the Association of Black Psychologists have become a rallying point for many researchers to expend and refresh their own concepts on Black families. The annual conferences that are held at the University of Louisville on Black families have become another point of excitement for those of us immersed in the field. Their selected themes each year have allowed attendees to become up-to-date on many unknown activities that are going on across the country. These meetings allow the "older" researchers in the field to come together and speak to each other, meet younger researchers, and return home to continue their concentration on families.

In past years symposia have been presented at the National Council on Family Relations by some of the contributors to this volume (Staples, Peters, Nobles, McAdoos, Hill, Johnson) on Black families. At each biennial meeting of the Society for Research on Child Development, contributors to this volume (Harrison, Peters, and the editor) have organized and presented information on the Black family and child. There has been a definite effort in these two organizations to bring together those who are doing work on the Black family and those who are working with Black children, for the problems and concerns with one will indirectly affect the other.

Similar efforts have continued over the years at other major professional meetings. Seminars have been organized by Peters and McAdoo at Groves Conference on Marriage and the Family for five years, which have brought together some of the key Black and other minority researchers to focus on one theme each year. The cross-fertilization that has grown out of these efforts has been widespread. These have allowed researchers and writers from all races to come together and share information. They have had some impact on those who are writing the textbooks to be used in college classrooms throughout the country and have brought together researchers for the first time from different disciplines who may never attend the same professional conferences. Similar efforts have been made by the contributors to this book and others at the American Educational Research Association, the National Association of Education for Young Children, American Sociological Association, and American Psychological Association. In addition, the Black and minority caucuses, sections, special interest groups, and other subdivisions of these professional organizations are contributing to the professional socialization of Black professionals and the dissemination of information on Black family life.

There was a period when a poor piece of research was heard and then quietly ignored, for a researcher who focused on Black families often came under so much attack from those in the profession that it was considered contrary to "the code" to also speak out against poor work (Welsing, 1970). We are no longer within the reactionary frame of reference when it was felt unwise to differ with the "leaders." We have to be able to give and receive criticisms within the field on any piece of research that is presented. Efforts at internal critiques have been found in the past six years among a small group of researchers who come together each year to present and to be critiqued in closed sessions at the Conference on Empirical Black Psychology. Papers have been presented and critiqued, and have become stronger as a result. This process supports younger researchers who feel they are unable to get this type of support at their diverse academic institutions and agencies.

In addition to the sometimes esoteric dialogues that are held at professional meetings, the real-world problems of families are continuing to be addressed by those in the community who are providing the leadership in the family advocacy organizations. At their seminars, annual meetings, during media briefings, and in publications, they are acting as watchdogs over the erosion of the Black family resources. They have made evaluations and designed programs and public education efforts in order to allow community persons and parents to take an effective active part in bettering the condition of their family life.

Organizations such as the Urban League, Children's Defense Fund, the National Black Child Development Institute, the NAACP, and the National Council of Negro Women are the major groups. Representatives from the key organizations have presented areas where efforts should be targeted and agendas that could be followed in each community.

PERSONAL REFLECTIONS

One of my special delights in this book was the in-depth study I was able to make of my father's book that led to the excerpt that is presented herein. I had quickly read the book for interest in high school and as an undergraduate, mostly looking for good references, so I felt I knew its contents. But it was only after going over the book repeatedly to select one of the sermons for this volume that I really had a chance to see all of the richness that was included in *Say Amen, Brother!* The Georgia sermons are a vivid reminder of the central role the rural "Black belt" churches played throughout the South. With the growing interest developing in oral history of the Black experience, several persons and major libraries have made copies of these now rare sermons, for mobility, education, and "sophistication" have gradually changed this sermon style, a direct link to the religious patterns found immediately after and probably during enslavement.

When I was a child, my parents, Bill Pipes and Anna Russell Pipes, would take me, their Victor recording machine, and a Brownie box camera down old dusty roads to the little churches to participate in the all-day church meetings, in order to make the recordings that are included in this chapter. I have vague memories of the recordings, and I grew up with the pictures and recordings of these sermons.

It is typical that children take their parents' works for granted and do not pay them the attention they deserve, since these books have always been around on our bookshelves. My oldest sons are having that experience now in college. They paid no attention to the stacks of papers and books all over the house as they grew up, until they were in a class and saw their parents' articles in a bibliography. They are amazed that anyone would bother to read them, let alone think that the papers that they had to eat around on the dining room table were worth their effort to read. They, as I pleasantly was, were surprised and delighted when they finally sat down and really began to understand what their parents had been doing all those years. This process was particularly poignant for me because my father died during the last stages of the production of this book.

Harriette Pipes McAdoo

REFERENCES

ASCHENBRENNER, J. (1973) "Extended families among Black Americans." Journal of Comparative Family Studies 4.

BENNETT, L. (1975) The Shaping of Black America. Chicago: Johnson.

BILLINGSLEY, A. (1968) Black Families in White America. Englewood Cliffs, NJ: Prentice-Hall.

BLASSINGAME, J. (1972) The Slave Community Plantation Life in the Ante-Bellum South. New York: Oxford University Press.

CLARKE, J. H. (1975) "The Black Family in historical perspective." Journal of Afro-American Issues 3, Nos. 3 & 4.

DRAKE, St. C. (1980) "Anthropology and the Black experience." Black Scholar 11, No. 7: 2-31.

DuBOIS, W. E. B. (1967) The Philadelphia Negro: A Social Study. New York: Schocken.

——— (1908) The Negro American Family. Cambridge: Massachusetts Institute of Technology.

FOGEL, R. and S. ENGERMAN (1974) Time on the Cross. Boston: Little, Brown.

FRAZIER, E. F. (1939) The Negro Family in the United States. Chicago: University of Chicago Press.

GURMAN, H. (1976) The Black Family in Slavery and Freedom, 1750-1925. New York: Pantheon.

HALEY, A. (1976) Roots: The Saga of an American Family. New York: Doubleday.

HEISS, J. (1971) The Case of the Black Family: A Sociological Inquiry. New York: Columbia University Press.

HERSKOVITS, M. J. (1941) The Myth of the Negro Past. New York: Harper.

HILL, R. H. (1972) The Strengths of Black Families. New York: Emerson-Hall.

LAMMERMEIER, P. J. (1974) "The urban Black family of the nineteenth century: A study of Black family structure in the Ohio Valley, 1850-1880." Journal of Marriage and the Family 35: 440-456.

NOBLES, W. (1976) "A formulative and empirical study of Black families." DHEW Publication (OCD-90-C-255). Washington, DC: Office of Child Development, Department of Health, Education and Welfare.

PIPES, W. H. (1951) Say Amen, Brother! New York: William-Frederick Press.

PLECK, E. H. (1979) Black Migration and Poverty: Boston 1865-1900. New York: Academic Press.

QUARLES, B. (1964) The Negro in the Making of America. New York: Collier Books.

SCANZONI, J. (1971) The Black Family in Modern Society. Boston: Allyn & Bacon.

SEMAJ, L. (1980) "Meaningful male/female relationships in a state of declining sex ratio." Black Books Bulletin 6.

SHIMKIN, D. B., G. J. LOUIE, and D. A. FRATE (1978) "The Black extended family: a basic rural institution and a mechanism of urban adaptation," in D. B. Shimkin, E. M. Shimkin, and D. A. Frate (eds.) The Extended Family in Black Cities. The Hague: Mouton.

STAPLES, R. [ed.] (1971) The Black Family: Essays and Studies. Belmont, CA: Wadsworth.

SUDARKASA, N. (1980) "African and Afro American family structure: A comparison." Black Scholar, Journal of Black Studies and Research 11, No. 8: 37-60.

WALKER, S. (1980) "African Gods in America: the Black religious continuum." Black Scholar, Journal of Black Studies and Research 11, No. 8: 25-36.

WELSING, F. (1970) The Cress Theory of Color Confrontation and Racism. Washington, DC: Welsing.

PART I

DIVERSE CONCEPTUALIZATIONS OF BLACK FAMILIES

The analyses of the diverse concepts that are held on the Black family begin with the reflective analyses of Jualynne Dodson, in which she reviews the writers in the three major schools of thought: pathological or dysfunctional; cultural relativity; and social class as main determinant. For each school she gives an in-depth review of the major writers and the chief beliefs held by those in each school. This is presented within a historical context. This analysis is invaluable because it sets the stage for the chapters that follow: some were written by authors who represent one of the three identified schools of thought. She stresses the need for further empirical research before we are able to make a definitive statement about the cultural origins of Black family life. A schema is given within the reflective analyses of the minimum requirements needed to effectively evaluate the Black family.

Niara Sudarkasa's work on African and Afro-American family organization brings knowledge from an anthropological view and succinctly critiques, refutes, and sometimes supports the earlier works of Black and non-Black writers on the Black family. Sudarkasa gives an excellent overview of African family structure in an attempt to shed light on the forms and function of Black American family structure as developed within the context of slavery. The enslaved Africans were seen as placing consanguinity or biological kinship (by blood) over that kinship based on affinity (by law) or conjugality (by marriage). This emphasis is seen as the major difference between European and African families. This cultural-historical basis is the origin of Black family organizational differences, even when political and economic differences are held constant. In contrast to Gutman, Sudarkasa does not see the family structure as an adaptation to enslavement. She differs in part with Herskovits and supports Frazier in the formation of female-as-head domestic units that developed during slavery, an unknown permanent unit within western African culture. After enslavement, the extended family became the focus, not the households, with the kin networks having many of the features of the continental African extended family, built around the consanguine kin. Some of the corporate functions of lineages reemerged within the extended families.

The Africanist versus culture of poverty debate is continued in the Pipes chapter. The amazing contrast about the Sudarkasa and Pipes chapters is that the works were done 40 years apart, yet they were addressing, in part, the same issues and arguments: the sources of Black American family and religious or cultural values. Although their fields of emphasis differ—one in anthropology and the other in speech and literature—their conclusions are the same. This shows one that we are still arguing the same arguments. More recent writers are not familiar with the writings that were done by the Negro intellectuals before the turn of the century and during the first half of this century. The fact that certain issues are still introduced in 30-year cycles reflects the importance of these issues to Black life and identity. The review of authors whose works are often unavailable today will add much to the present literature.

Pipes looked at the religious practices that are in essence lost today but were practiced from slavery through the first half of this century. The old-time sermons, the rhythm, the pulse, intensity, and call and response that occurred in these rural Negro churches convey a sense of the cultural southern base that was an integral part of most present-day Black families. The role of the sermon in coping with the pressures of Black life was a key element in families' survival. The leadership of the minister and the tension released during services performed an essential part of their lives. The sermon excerpts and the prayers included in this chapter, which are analyzed with respect and humor, provide a picture of Black life that no longer exists in this pure form.

The chapter by Wade Nobles focuses on the importance of the parent-child relationship and the need for the family to be geared to prepare the child for a unique type of existence in a hostile, racist societal environment. With a strong Afrocentric view, it gives a sound background for the scientific racism that formed the groundwork that allowed one group to receive preferential treatment over another. Nobles explores the changes that have occurred in social scientists' coverage of the Black family and the seminal work of Billingsley, Hill, and Staples. He uses the analogy of the centuries-long enslavement of Africans as an analogy to the existence of Blacks today. The supportive network of the extended family has been used to protect the child; and three domains are outlined that must receive attention if the children are to realize their potential: a sense of history, a strong sense of family, and a sense of the need and power of spiritual beliefs. It ties neatly into the chapters of Sudarkasa on the extended family and that by Pipes on the importance of religious participation. Nobles ends his chapter with the assertion that if the family is able to perform these responsibilities, then it is imperative that the state be supportive of the family. Nobles adds an element of spirituality that one does not often find in the family literature. He presents the cultural base but also supports the chapters by Hill, Edelman, and Moore on the importance of the parents operating within knowledge of the political system in providing for the children, but not at the expense of leaving the spiritual or cultural components of their lives to chance.

Johnson effectively rounds out the discussion on diverse conceptualizations with her empirical study of the theoretical frameworks that have been presented in the sociology and social work journals with the widest circulation during the period 1965-1978. She first presents two conceptual frameworks on the value orientations reflected about the Black family, as presented by Walter Allen and Robert Staples, that are similar to those of Dodson's reflective analysis. Allen's three stages show the changes in orientation that the literature has taken as it has gone from a deviant view, to an equivalent view, and finally to a cultural relative view of the Black family and its function. Staples presented four trend stages that relate to the change in emphasis from looking at families as only victims of poverty, to pathological, to the reactionary stances of the 1960s, and finally to the emphasis on functionality of families, regardless of structure. In each is the clear value that one should put on the later stages, in preference for the earlier stages. Johnson took all the articles that related to the Black family from the ten journals and applied both typologies to each. This extremely useful analysis indicated that less than one percent of all empirical studies related to the Black family, and most of those were in special issues edited by Blacks or Black journals. Social work journals during that time were found to be surprisingly negligent in their coverage of Black families. Earlier articles tended to stress deviance and the later ones, especially those by Black researchers, tended to focus on Black uniqueness without the comparison with white family norms. Johnson lists each of the articles surveyed and provides a rating on each of the value orientations and the topics covered. This should be potentially useful for other researchers who would want to avoid those articles that have been rated as using the cultural deviant or pathological framework.

1

CONCEPTUALIZATIONS OF BLACK FAMILIES

JUALYNNE DODSON

CONTRASTING APPROACHES TO
THE STUDY OF BLACK FAMILIES

The pathological and dysfunctional view of black families has been primarily related to the cultural ethnocentric approach and associated with the work of E. Franklin Frazier (1939) and Daniel P. Moynihan (1965). The works of these scholars have culminated in the adaptation of social policies predicated on the assumption that the black family is unstable, disorganized, and unable to provide its members with the social and psychological support and development needed to assimilate fully into American society.

The cultural relativity school, on the other hand, begins with the assumption that black American culture and family patterns possess a degree of cultural integrity that is neither related to nor modeled on white American norms. Most members of this school trace the origins of these cultural differences back to black American's African cultural heritage, and all tend to focus on the "strengths" of black families rather than their weaknesses.

The cultural relativistic view, developed primarily as a reaction to the deficit view, maintains that the black family is a functional entity. This conceptualization is designed to challenge the theories and social policies emanating from the ethnocentric approach.

Underlying the theoretical and empirical arguments of the two schools is the common assumption that black families and white families are qualitatively different culturally. The schools diverge from each other, however, in their interpretation and explanation of the causes of these differences. The cultural ethnocentric school, operating on the assumption that America is culturally homogeneous and that there are universal norms for American cultural behavior to which all groups must conform, points to certain presumed inadequacies in black people to account for the differences. Similarly, it places a negative value judgment on the fact that black families deviate from the American norm. The cultural relativity school, on the other hand, assumes that America is a multicultural society and concludes that differences are largely accounted for by the variation in the cultural backgrounds and experiences of black and white Americans.

The assumption that black and white families are qualitatively different culturally is not shared by all students of black family life, however. A third set of studies that can be said to fall outside the two schools noted above emphasize the role of social class in determining family patterns and characteristics. The scholars of this perspective maintain that when you control for social class, no appreciable differences exist between black and white families. In-depth discussions of each of the two contrasting major approaches to the study of black family life follow. I will then consider some of the limitations of using social class as a variable in analyzing black family structure and functioning.

THE CULTURAL ETHNOCENTRIC SCHOOL

E. Franklin Frazier (1894-1962) was the leading twentieth-century exponent of the cultural ethnocentric school. He and W. E. B. DuBois pioneered in the study of the black family as a social phenomenon, but, unlike DuBois, one of Frazier's major concerns was understanding the process through which the black family became culturally assimilated into American life. It is important to note that Frazier's works, according to Lyman (1972), were influenced by his determination to (a) refute the argument advanced by Melville Herskovits (and DuBois) that much of black life is a continuation of African cultural forms and (b) empirically demonstrate Robert E. Park's race relations cycle. Frazier believed that black American marriage and family patterns, customs, and structures were the consequence of slavery and American culture, not African cultural transfers. He did not accept Herskovits's conclusion that black family structure, marital customs, and sexual practices were derived from African cultures. Rather, for example, Frazier (1939) interpreted "indiscriminate" and extramarital sexual behavior among blacks as being a product of slavery and unrelated to customs and practices in traditional polygamous African cultures.

Researchers attempting to discover possible African cultural transferences to the New World focused on the slavery period. At the time Frazier began his work, leading authorities on the history of American Negro slavery shared

Frazier's rather than Herskovits's position. Frazier's assertion that as "a result of the manner in which the Negro was enslaved, the Negro's African cultural heritage has had practically no effect on the evolution of his family in the United States" (1939: 66) reflected the views of both U. B. Phillips (1929), and, subsequently, Stanley Elkins (1959). Both concluded that while significant African cultural traits, such as names and folklore, did survive initially, they were eventually lost or distorted. Accordingly, Uncle Remus stories were altered to reflect the new animals and surroundings of the storytellers (Phillips, 1929: 195). If the culture of the African slaves was destroyed, then it is hopeless to expect that the evolution of the black family was influenced by that culture. So begins the logic of the cultural ethnocentric school.

The stability of the black family during slavery was controlled, they maintain, by the plantation owners. If a family arrangement failed to produce offspring, some slaveowners matched the couple, usually the woman, with other mates. Additionally, slave families were frequently broken up, its members sold individually. In spite of the slaves' unstable formal or legal marital and familial life, these authorities believed that blacks accepted and attempted to conform to the social norms of the majority society.

Frazier viewed blacks as an assimilation-oriented minority following the race-relations cycle as predicted and outlined by Ezra Parks (1926-1950). Indeed, Frazier saw the black family's assimilation toward the dominant American norms as part of the process by which it evolved from slavery and servitude toward freedom. In his study of blacks living in Chicago, Frazier found that as they moved outward from the inner city, black families appeared more culturally and physically assimilated, based on the proportion of interracial marriages (1939). It was his faithfulness to Park's race relations cycle which seemingly motivated Frazier to interpret black masses as assimilative and to ignore evidence to the contrary.[1] Although the race relations cycle has yet to be empirically validated, Frazier earnestly attempted to do so. It is, in a sense, a tragic conclusion to his intellectual career that he was forced to observe on the last page of one of his last books, *Black Bourgeoisie: The Rise of a New Middle Class in the United States,* that when blacks achieve "middle-class status their lives generally lose both content and significance" (1957: 238).

The line of research as pursued by Frazier was followed by a number of investigators and culminated in proposals for social policy. In 1965, the Office of Policy Planning and Research of the United States Department of Labor issued a 78-page document prepared by the assistant secretary, Daniel P. Moynihan, under the title, *The Negro Family–The Case for National Action.* This report repeatedly cited Frazier as support for its conclusions that the black community was characterized by broken families, illegitimacy, matriarchy, economic dependency, failure to pass armed forces entrance tests, delinquency, and crime. Moynihan placed the cause of these problems on a supposedly broken and unstable black family. Following his trend-making step, other investigators began to concentrate on the pathologies of black families.

In 1966, Elliot Liebow conducted a participant-observation study of 24 streetcorner black men. He concluded that the men had internalized the American norms for family roles, but that the oppressive conditions of their societal environment prevented their fulfilling these expectations. Lee Rainwater (1968), examining the matrifocal character of black American and Caribbean families, concluded that matriarchal families were pathological and detrimental to the personality development of black children. He also suggested that such families interfered with the ability of black males to develop normal heterosexual roles.

Jessie Bernard (1966) traced the evolution of the black family's stability from 1880 to 1963 and reported that the decrease in the proportion of black infants born out of wedlock was related to two distinct lifestyles independent of social class. One lifestyle was oriented toward the pursuit of pleasure and material consumption, while the other adhered to a firm belief in and acceptance of the Protestant ethic. This hedonistic orientation accounts for the decline in legitimate births among blacks. Having failed to internalize the marital norms of the American society, it is suggested that this subgroup ignores their responsibility when adherence becomes too difficult. The matrifocal family is seen as an outgrowth of the failure of black men to fulfill their paternal roles.

Parker and Kleiner (1966) contrasted the adjustment and attitudes of mothers in broken and intact families and examined the possible impact of these characteristics of their children. They found that mothers in broken family situations had poorer psychological adjustment and were less concerned about goals for their children. It was suggested that children raised in female-headed households would not have the psychological support of their mothers. Such research advances the argument that matriarchy and female-headed households are pathological and undermine any male-female relationship in the family (Blood and Wolfe, 1969; Duncan and Duncan, 1969; Bracey et al., 1971; Parker and Kleiner, 1966).

Other investigators have reported that the data supporting Moynihan's matriarchal concept are conclusive (Hyman and Reed, 1969). Investigators who focused on the validity of the female role in the black family have generally concluded that matrifocal families are not produced by values of the black community but by structural factors in the society which necessitate that males frequently abandon their roles (Yancy, 1972; Staples, 1974). Tenhouten (1970) was unable to substantiate the dominant role attributed to black mothers as implied in the Moynihan Report. Further, King (1967, 1969) found that black fathers were not perceived by their children as passive in decision making, and black mothers were perceived as less dominant than as reported in earlier studies. Delores Mack (1971) examined social class and racial differences in the distribution of power attributable to race. And Heiss (1972) found that instability in the black family does not necessarily lead to instability in future generations.

Studies which concentrated on the dysfunctional and disorganized aspects of black family life have deduced that the typical black family is fatherless, on welfare, thriftless, and overpopulated with illegitimate children. Inevitably, they have recommended economic reforms for "saving" black families from their own pathology (see, for example, Moynihan, 1965; Rainwater, 1965; Rodman, 1968). However, Andrew Billingsley (1968) challenged these stereotypes, pointing out that two-thirds of black families living in metropolitan areas are headed by husbands with their wives: Half have managed to pull themselves into the middle-class and nine-tenths are self-supporting.

There remains, then, considerable controversy among researchers concerning the ability of nonwhite Americans to establish and maintain viable marital and familial relations. Particularly, there are a large number of studies that underscore the dysfunctionality of black families. Implicit in the dichotomous conceptualization of functional versus dysfunctional capacities of black families is an assumption regarding normative model families. The belief that a statistical model of the American family can be identified and used to ascertain the character of the families of all American cultural groups is mythical at best. Further, such an assumption contradicts the ideals of a democratic society and the realities of a culturally plural one.

THE CULTURAL RELATIVITY SCHOOL

The cultural relativity view, primarily in reaction to the cultural ethnocentric view, advocates that the black family is a functional entity. This conceptualization is largely advanced and supported by Andrew Billingsley (1968), Virginia Young (1970), Robert Hill (1972), Wade Nobles (1974), and others. The perspective has been buttressed with old and new investigations which see black Americans' culture as different from that of whites (Valentine, 1968; Young, 1974) and possibly related to their African heritage (Herskovits, 1941; Nobles, 1974; Dodson, 1975, 1977). Although not all proponents of the cultural relativistic school agree on the degree to which African culture influenced the culture of black Americans, they do concur that black Americans' cultural orientation encourages family patterns that are instrumental in combating the oppressive racial conditions of American society.

American studies of the black family, and of blacks in general, have long ignored the works of Melville Herskovits (1885-1963), one of the first scholars to recognize similarities in African cultural patterns and those of African descendants living in the United States, the West Indies, and Brazil. Herskovits (1966) found what he considered to be authentic African cultural patterns reflected in language, music, art, house structure, dance, traditional religion, and healing practices. To many students of the black family, Herskovits's research raises the possibility that other aspects of "Africana" could have influenced the nature of the black family in the United States. Herskovits's works deal only limitedly with such possible relations. However, one of his major contributions was a truer conceptualization of family life in traditional African societies, which are characterized by unity, stability, and security (Herskovits, 1938).

Other writers have since reexamined the unity and stability of African families to refute any assertion that chaos and problems of African families paralleled the problems of contemporary black American families. From such studies, Billingsley concluded:

> Thus the men and women who were taken as slaves to the New World came from societies every bit as civilized and "respectable" as those of the Old World settlers who mastered them. But the two were very different types of society [sic] for the African family was much more closely integrated with the wider levels of kinship and society [1968: 48].

In examining the American black family, proponents of cultural relativism in North America point out that slavery did not totally destroy the traditional African base of black family functioning (Blassingame, 1972; Nobles, 1974; Turnbull, 1976). To these scholars, the black family represents a continuing fountain of strength and endurance built on, and issuing from, its African cultural heritage.

The field research of Young reflects that blacks are not merely versions of white Americans impoverished by lack of access to many of the rewards of American culture. She found that southern rural black families were culturally distinct from white families and demonstrated retention of African forms. This closely paralleled Herskovits's (1941) contentions. Her findings were especially supportive in the areas of interpersonal behavior and deep-level communication.

Similar to Charles Johnson (1934) and Hortense Powdermaker (1939), but contrary to Frazier (1939) and Moynihan (1965), Young did not find black families disorganized or dysfunctional. Young (1970) observed patterns of high illegitimacy rates and frequent marital dissolutions, which are usually associated with disorganization; however, she interpreted these patterns as natural to the emotional underpinnings of the family system and, thus, functional.

Nobles (1974, 1975) has indicated that the black community is oriented primarily toward extended families, in that most black family structures involve a system of kinship ties. This idea has been supported by Hayes and Mendel (1973), Billingsley (1968), Hill (1972), Stack (1974), and others. The extended family system is assumed to provide support for family members, either as assistance for protection or for mobility. It is argued that the extended family in the black community consists not only of conjugal and blood relatives, but of nonrelatives as well. Additionally, the prevalence of extended families, as compared with nuclear families, is held as another cultural pattern which distinguishes whites and blacks. However, the extent to which such families are characteristic of the black community has not been adequately substantiated.

Hayes and Mendel (1973) demonstrated that the extended family is a more prominent structure for black families and that blacks differ from whites in intensity and extent of family interaction. Their study of midwestern urban families, however, included a sample of only 25 complete and incomplete black and white families. The findings show that, with the exception of parents, blacks interact with more of their kin than do whites. Black families also receive more help from kin and have a greater number and more diversified types of relatives living with them than do white families. It is suggested by Hayes and Mendel that minority status in a hostile society strengthens kinship ties.

In a related study, Dubey (1971) examined the relationship between self-alienation and extended family using black, white, and Puerto Rican subjects. His data supported the hypothesis that subjects with a high degree of powerlessness were significantly more oriented toward the extended family. Dubey's study raises the question of whether the extended family is used as a buffer between oppression of the dominant society and the unmet needs of the family. Stack (1974) proposed that the extended family is, in part, a strategy for meeting physical, emotional, and economic needs of black families, and involves a reciprocal network of sharing to counter the lack of economic resources. Mc-Adoo (1978) found that the reciprocal extended family-help patterns transcended economic groups and continued to be practiced even when families had moved from poverty to the middle-income level.

Nobles (1974) believes that the black kinship pattern was derived from African cultures not destroyed in the "Middle Passage" or in slavery; this suggests that perhaps the survival of "Africana" among black American families is not as remote as Elkins (1959) and Frazier (1939) have argued. Blassingame (1972) stated that not only did African cultural patterns survive American slavery, but new cultural patterns unique to black Americans were created. Even Frazier (1963) has noted indisputable non-Western religious practices in the black church. A more recent advocate of this view, Colin Turnbull, sums it succinctly: "(T)he slaves who were exported to the Americas were Africans before they were slaves and Africans afterwards, and *their descendants are still Africans today*" (1976: 242; emphasis added).

According to Turnbull, it is interesting to note that in some cases African cultural patterns were developed and preserved in the western hemisphere while they were lost in Africa. A case in point is Surinam (South America), where slaves escaped and recovered their independence. Although some of the ethnic cultures resemble original African cultures, Turnbull cautions that the Surinam cultures (comprising six "tribal" groups) could not have remained totally in isolation. With the exception of clearly identifiable African cultural patterns in islands along the Georgia coast, Turnbull stated that the splintering of ethnic clans during slavery, along with enforced acceptance of language and Western values, did much to repress African cultures in the United States.

A model that may prove useful for a further understanding of the New World "Africana" culture and black American families has been developed by Smith (1962). Equally important to the clarification of these issues is Nobles's work currently being conducted on African orientations in American families. However, we must await further research findings from the cultural relativistic perspective before determining the cultural origin of black family life.

AN ISSUE FROM BOTH SCHOOLS:
SOCIAL CLASS

Research on racial differences in black family structure and function has been contaminated by methodological problems that make it difficult to conceptualize clear differences within and between groups. Social class has been widely employed as a variable in social science research. It is primarily used for classifying individuals into categories above or below one another on some scale of inferiority and superiority. The scale is intended to denote one's position in terms of social and economic prestige and/or power.

The most popular measure of social class in the United States is an occupation-scaled measure that is commonly used to reflect prestige. Other types of class measurement consist of single variables, such as education, income, and possessions. A number of multiple indices also exist. It has been questioned whether such measures can be applied equitable to all groups in an oppressive, pluralistic, and fluid society such as the United States. This is especially critical, since most measures of social class were developed by and for whites, and there is little convincing evidence that they accurately measure social class for black Americans.

A number of investigators, among them Drake (1965) and Jencks (1972), have demonstrated that education and income are less related for blacks compared to whites than may be expected. It has been shown that blacks are more frequently underemployed, in that they often have more education, training, or skills than their jobs require. Consequently, they receive salaries and wages disproportionate to their preparation. Since an underemployed black person has a lower income than a white with equivalent years of education, the former cannot afford the same standard of living as the latter. This lower standard of living requires the black person to adopt a different lifestyle than his or her status, as measured by education, would indicate.

Neither does occupation tend to indicate the same social classification for blacks as for whites. The owner of a small business in a black shopping area, for example, might not have nearly the same income as the owner of a similar business located in a white shopping area. However, according to the occupation categories of the Hollingshead-Redlich scale (1968), both persons would be designated in a middle-income social classification. Another problem with occupational ranking is that disparities exist within occupations as well as between them.

Jencks (1972) contends that one limitation to the definition of occupation as the indicator of social class is that it refers only to occupations, not to specific jobs within them. Accordingly, some jobs are more attractive and rewarding than others, even though they are classified together as a single occupation.

Billingsley's assertion that current indicators of social class are relatively more reliable when used for white ethnic groups than when used unmodified with black groups has never been adequately refuted. He believes that such indicators have resulted in an overestimation of the number of lower-class blacks and that this obscures rather than clarifies the variety of social class and behavior among black Americans (1968: 123). Although Billingsley accepts the utility of social class, he claims that current measures are mostly indicators of economic and social positions in the wider white community, not accurate descriptions of which blacks associate with whom and why.

It should be pointed out that social classification depends primarily on the degree to which an individual or individuals are held in esteem by their fellow group members. Social class, therefore, depends on the cultural values of the group. Deference is awarded according to what the group cherishes as being noble or worthy. Hence, social class could be based on such characteristics as age, wisdom, heredity, or economic power, and it could vary from one cultural group to another. Since the cultural distinctiveness of black Americans still warrants investigation, measures of social class also await clearer determination. The extent to which blacks possess different values regarding what is worthy in an individual determines their different orientation to family, to their community, and to the wider white community.

Cultural relativity becomes an important, yet complicated, factor when attempting to make social class comparisons of heterogenous groups within a single society. It appears logical to assume that different ethnic groups within the same society can be compared using the same social class criterion. However, this is not the empirical reality for the United States. The logical but incorrect assumption that because both peoples live within the same societal geography (nation), social class is perceived the same way in white and black communities is misleading.

I concur with Billingsley that the importance of social class is that the higher the social class of an individual, the greater will be his or her ability to survive with integrity in a hostile society. For a historically subjugated group such as black America, survival and dignity may be invaluable social qualities. Furthermore, given the nature of the historical and material experiences of, and relationship between, blacks and whites in North America, the extent to which they can be compared using similar social indicators is dubious. To ignore these fundamentally different realities and classify them into common social classes is to commit serious historical, methodological, and theoretical errors.

TOWARD REFLECTIVE ANALYSIS

This examination of major schools of thought in studies of the black family in the United States has been done to help direct thinking regarding prerequisite components of a "reflective analysis." Admittedly, this has been a limited review. For example, individual roles of family members have not been addressed. These are seen primarily as intertwined with the sociocultural patterns of marriage and family in contemporary black communities. For those who desire a more thorough and complete review of literature on black American families, there are at least three substantive sources: Allen (1976), Staples (1974, 1978), and Peters (1978). The particular approach I have taken has emphasized the ideological assumptions undergirding researchers' definitions of and approaches to research of black family life. This perspective was used because it is assumed that the ideological debate has indeed created the current impasse in black family research. Given the review of the debate, Walter Allen's conclusions about the status of studies on black family life is accurate:

> The literature on black families is characterized by inconsistent findings, poor problem conceptualization, overly simplistic research designs, questionable inferences from data and general disagreement over the relative appropriateness of competing perspectives of black family life. The question to be addressed now is: How might researchers go about the business of reconciling some of these problems and in the process strengthening the literature? To begin, theory construction/codification activities should be intensified. . . .
>
> The area of black family studies would also benefit from a change in focus of empirical research.

Any attempt to bring theoretical clarity to human phenomena must be informed by an understanding of the sociocultural, economic, and political contexts in which the phenomena occur. This axiom applies especially when exploring questions related to contemporary black family life in the United States.

In recommending the following components for a "reflective analysis" of black family life, my conceptualizations have been developed in concert with Ruth Dennis, Harriette McAdoo, Art Mathis, and Howard Dodson. This group of black scholars and researchers met and worked together from 1974 through 1977 to develop "Toward a Reflective Analysis" of black family life.

Drawing from the strengths and weaknesses of previous studies, a "reflective analysis" would minimally include the following:

(a) focus on socialization of black families as the process which brings together individual, cultural group(s), and society in a dynamic interactive process;

(b) account for the impact—positive and/or negative—of the relative unavailability of maximum social, economic, and political societal resources to black families and;

(c) account for the environmental reality that black families are forced to use relatively minimal resources to effect a socialization process and product which allows individuals to function in two social realities of the United States—a nonblack world of consistent, sufficient social support and a black world of fluctuating scarcity of resources.

Using these minimal components as a guide, a schema for evaluating black family socialization can be suggested. Positive evaluations can be placed on socialized behavior which allows the individual to interact with any segment of the society and maintain a sense of self-worth. However, because the realities of black family life are often contradictory, socialized behavior that may be evaluated as positive within one level of social functioning may be evaluated as negative within another. Black families must be able to socialize individuals who are able to participate in and yet protect self from the negative social attitudes and actions impinging on self-esteem, feelings of self-worth, and human evolutionary development.

NOTE

1. For example, the widespread support among black Americans for Marcus Garvey's Universal Negro Improvement Association (Cronon, 1964).

REFERENCES

ALLEN, W. R. (1976) Private correspondence in response to "Reflective Analysis" manuscript. Atlanta, Georgia.

_____ (1978) "Search for applicable theories of Black family life." Journal of Marriage and the Family 40: 117-129.

AUSUBEL, D. P. and P. AUSUBEL (1963) "Ego development among segregated Negro children," in A. H. Passow (ed.) Education in Depressed Areas. New York: Bureau of Publications, Teachers College, Columbia University.

BERNARD, J. (1966) Marriage and Family Among Negroes. Englewood Cliffs, NJ: Prentice-Hall.

BETTELHEIM, B. (1964) Review of B. S. Bloom's Stability and Change in Human Characteristics. New York Review of Books 3: 1-4.

BILLINGSLEY, A. (1968) Black Families in White America. Englewood Cliffs, NJ: Prentice-Hall.

BLASSINGAME, J. W. (1972) The Slave Community: Plantation Life in Antebellum South. New York: Oxford.

BLAUNER, R. (1970) "Internal colonialism and ghetto revolt," in M. Westheimer (ed.) Confrontation. Glenview, IL: Scott, Foresman.

_____ (1972) Racial Oppression in America. New York: Harper & Row.

BLOOD, R. and D. WOLFE (1969) "Negro-white differences in blue collar marriages in a northern metropolis." Social Forces 48: 59-63.

BRACEY, J. H., A. MEIER and E. RUDWICK [eds.] (1971) Black Matriarchy: Myth or Reality. Belmont, CA: Wadsworth.

BRONFENBRENNER, U. (1967) Paper read at Conference on Poverty, University of Wisconsin, Madison.

CLOWARD, R. A. and J. A. JONES (1962) "Social class: Education attitudes and participation," in A. H. Passows (ed.) Education in Depressed Areas. New York: Bureau of Publications, Teachers College, Columbia University.

CRONON, E. D. (1955) Black Moses: The Story of Marcus Garvey. Madison: University of Wisconsin Press.

DAVIS, A. and J. DOLLARD (1940) Children of Bondage. New York: Harper & Row.

DAVIS, A. and R. J. HAVIGHURST (1946) "Social class and color differences in childrearing." American Sociological Review 11: 698-710.

DODSON, J. (1975) Black Stylization and Implications for Child Welfare. Final Report (OCD-CB-422-C2). Washington, DC: Office of Child Development.

_____ (1977) Afro American Culture: Expressive Behaviors. Atlanta: Atlanta University.

DRAKE, S. C. (1965) "The social and economic status of the Negro in the United States," in T. Parsons and K. B. Clark (eds.) The Negro American. Boston: Beacon.

DUBEY, S. N. (1971) "Powerlessness and orientation toward family and children: a study in deviance." Indian Journal of Social Work 32: 35-43.

DUNCAN, B., and O. D. DUNCAN (1969) "Family stability and occupational success." Social Problems 16: 273-285.

ELKINS, S. W. (1959) Slavery. Chicago: University of Chicago Press.

FOGEL, R. W. and S. L. ENGERMAN (1975) Time on the Cross, Volumes I and II. Boston: Little, Brown.

FRAZIER, E. F. (1932) The Negro Family in Chicago. Chicago: University of Chicago Press.

_____ (1939) The Negro Family in the United States. Chicago: University of Chicago Press.

_____ (1949a) "The Negro family in America," in R. W. Anshen (ed.) The Family: Its Function and Destiny. New York: Harper & Row.

_____ (1949b) The Negro in the United States. New York: Macmillan.

_____ (1957) Black Bourgeoisie: The Rise of a New Middle Class in the United States. New York: Free Press.

_____ (1963) The Negro Church in America. New York: Schocken.

HAYES, W. and MENDEL, C. H. (1973) "Extended kinship in black and white families." Journal of Marriage and the Family 35: 51-57.

HEISS, J. (1972) "On the transmission of marital instability in black families." American Sociological Review 37: 82-92.

HERSKOVITS, M. J. (1938) Dahomey: An Ancient African Kingdom. New York: J. J. Augustin.

———— (1941) The Myth of the Negro Past. New York: Harper & Row.

HILL, R. (1972) The Strengths of Black Families. New York: Emerson-Hall.

HOLLINGSHEAD, A. B. and F. C. REDLICH (1968) Social Class and Mental Illness. New York: John Wiley.

HYMAN, H. H. and J. S. REED (1969) "Black matriarchy reconsidered: evidence from secondary analysis of sample survey." Public Opinion Quarterly 33: 346-354.

INKLES, A. (1966) "A note on social structure and the socialization of competence." Harvard Educational Review 36: 265-283.

JENCKS, C. (1972) Inequality. New York: Basic Books.

JOHNSON, C. S. (1934) Shadow of the Plantation. Chicago: University of Chicago Press.

KARDINER, A. and L. OVESEY (1951) The Mark of Oppression. New York: World.

KATZ, I. (1969) "A critique of personality approaches to Negro performance, with research suggestions." Journal of Social Issues 25: 12-27.

KING, K. (1967) "A comparison of the Negro and white family power structure in low-income families." Child and Family 6: 65-74.

———— (1969) "Adolescent perception of power structure in the Negro family." Journal of Marriage and the Family 31: 751-755.

LIEBOW, E. (1967) Tally's Corner: A Study of Negro Streetcorner Men. Boston: Little, Brown.

LYMAN, S. M. (1972) The Black American in Sociological Thought. New York: Capricorn Books.

MACK, D. E. (1971) "Where the black-matriarchy theorists went wrong." Psychology Today 4: 24, 86-87.

McADOO, H. P. (1974) The Socialization of Black Children: Priorities for Research in Social Research and the Black Community: Selected Issues and Priorities.

———— (1978) "Factors related to stability in upward mobile black families." Journal of Marriage and the Family 40: 761-766.

McCLELLAND, D. C. (1961) The Achieving Society. New York: Van Nostrand.

MOYNIHAN, D. P. (1965) The Negro Family—The Case for National Action. Washington, DC: Office of Policy Planning and Research, U.S. Department of Labor.

NOBLES, W. W. (1974) "Africanity: its role in black families." The Black Scholar 5: 10-17.

———— (1975) A Formulative and Empirical Study of Black Families. Publication No. OCD-90-C-255. San Francisco: Westside Community Mental Health Center.

PARK, R. E. (1939) "The nature of race relations," in E. T. Thompson (ed.) Race Relations and the Race Problem. Durham, NC: Duke University Press.

PARKER, S. and KLEINER, R. (1966) "Characteristics of Negro mothers in single-headed households." Journal of Marriage and the Family 28: 507-513.

PETERS, M. F. [ed.] (1978) Special issue of Journal of Marriage and the Family, Vol. 40, No. 4, November.

PETTIGREW, T. F. (1964) A Profile of the Negro American. Princeton, NJ: D. Van Nostrand.

PHILLIPS, U. B. (1929) Life and Labor in the Old South. Boston: Little, Brown.

POWDERMAKER, H. (1939) After Freedom: The Portrait of a Negro Community in the Deep South. New York: Viking.

RAINWATER, L. (1965) Family Design. Chicago: AVC.

———— (1968) "Crucible of identity: the Negro lower-class family." Daedalus 95: 258-264.

RIESSMAN, F. (1962) The Culturally Deprived Child. New York: Harper & Row.

RODMAN, H. (1968) "Family and social pathology in the ghetto." Science 161: 756-762.

SMITH, M. G. (1962) West Indian Family Structure. Seattle: University of Washington Press.

STACK, C. B. (1974) All Our Kin. New York: Harper & Row.

STAPLES, R. E. (1974) "The black family revisited: a review and a preview." Journal of Social and Behavior Sciences Spring: 65-77.

———— (1978) The Black Family: Essays and Studies. Belmont, CA: Wadsworth.

TENHOUTEN, W. (1970) "The black family: myth and reality." Psychiatry 33: 145-173.

TURNBULL, C. M. (1976) Man in Africa. Garden City, NY: Doubleday.

VALENTINE, C. A. (1968) Culture and Poverty. Chicago: University of Chicago Press.

WARNER, W. L., M. MEEKER, and K. EELLS (1949) Social Class in America. Chicago: Science Research Associates.

WILLIE, C. V. [ed.] (1970) The Family Life of Black People. Columbus, OH: Charles E. Merrill.

YANCEY, W. (1972) "Going down home: family structure and the urban trap." Social Science Quarterly 52: 893-906.

YOUNG, V. H. (1970) "Family and childhood in a southern Negro community." American Anthropologist 72: 269-288.

YOUNG, V. H. (1974) "A black American socialization pattern." in American Ethnologist 1: 405-413.

2

INTERPRETING THE AFRICAN HERITAGE IN AFRO-AMERICAN FAMILY ORGANIZATION

NIARA SUDARKASA

INTRODUCTION

Many of the debates concerning explanations of Black family organization are waged around false dichotomies. The experience of slavery in America is juxtaposed to the heritage of Africa as *the* explanation of certain aspects of Black family structure. "Class" versus "culture" becomes the framework for discussing determinants of household structure and role relationships. Black families are characterized either as "alternative institutions" or as groups whose structures reflect their "adaptive strategies," as if the two viewpoints were mutually exclusive.

Just as surely as Black American family patterns are in part an outgrowth of the descent into slavery (Frazier, 1939 [1966]), so too are they partly a reflection of the archetypical African institutions and values that informed and influenced the behavior of those Africans who were enslaved in America (Herskovits, 1941 [1958]). With respect to "class" and "culture," it is indeed the case that the variations in historical and contemporary Black family organization cannot be explained without reference to the socioeconomic contexts in which they developed (Allen, 1979). But neither can they be explained without

AUTHOR'S NOTE: I wish to thank Tao-Lin Hwang for his assistance with the research for this chapter, and Bamidele Agbasegbe Demerson for his helpful comments.

reference to the cultural contexts from which they derived (Nobles, 1974a, 1974b, 1978). Whereas Black families can be analyzed as groups with strategies for coping with wider societal forces (Stack, 1974), they must also be understood as institutions with historical traditions that set them apart as "alternative" formations that are not identical to (or pathological variants of) family structures found among other groups in America (Aschenbrenner, 1978).

After more than a decade of rethinking Black family structure (see, for example, Billingsley, 1968; Staples, 1971, 1978; Aschenbrenner, 1973; English, 1974; Sudarkasa, 1975a; Allen, 1978; Shimkin et al., 1978), it is still the case that a holistic theory of past and present Black family organization remains to be developed. Such a theory or explanation must rest on the premise that political-economic variables are *always* part of any explanation of family formation and functioning, but that the cultural historical derivation of the formations in question helps to explain the nature of their adaptation to particular political-economic contexts.

Obviously, it is beyond the scope of this chapter to try to set forth such a holistic explanation of Black family organization. Its more modest aim is to take a step in this direction by laying to rest one of the false dichotomies that stand in the way of such an explanation. This review seeks to show how an understanding of African family structure sheds light on the form and functioning of Black American family structure as it developed in *the context of slavery* and later periods. It seeks to elucidate African institutional arrangements and values that were manifest in the family organization of Blacks enslaved in America, and suggests that some of these values and institutional arrangements continue to be recognizable in contemporary formations.

The relationships of causality, correlation, and constraint that exist between the political-economic sphere and that of the family cannot be dealt with here. What the chapter seeks to clarify is why Black familial institutions embrace certain alternatives of behavior and not others. It suggests a cultural historical basis for the fact that Black family organization differs from that of other groups even when political and economic factors are held relatively constant.

Thus, it is suggested that it cannot suffice to look to political and economic factors to explain, for example, the difference between lower-class Anglo- or Italian-American families and lower-class Afro-American families. One has to come to grips with the divergent culture histories of the groups concerned. In other words, one is led back to the institutional heritage stemming from Western Europe on the one hand and from West Africa on the other. Knowledge of the structure and functioning of kinship and the family in these areas helps to explain the structure and functioning of families formed among their descendants in America.

It might appear that this is too obvious a point to be belabored. However, when it comes to the study of Black American families, the scholarly community has historically taken a different view. Whereas it is generally agreed that the history of the family in Europe is pertinent to an understanding of European-derived family organization in America (and throughout the world), many—if not most—scholars working on Black American families have argued or assumed that the African family heritage was all but obliterated by the institution of slavery. This view has retained credence, despite the accumulation of evidence to the contrary, in large measure because E. Franklin Frazier (1939), the most prestigious and prolific student of the Black American family, all but discounted the relevance of Africa in his analyses.

This chapter takes its departure from W.E.B. DuBois (1908[1969]), Carter G. Woodson (1936), and M. J. Herskovits (1958), all of whom looked to Africa as well as to the legacy of slavery for explanations of Afro-American social institutions. Herskovits is the best-known advocate of the concept of African survivals in Afro-American family life, but DuBois was the first scholar to stress the need to study the Black American family against the background of its African origins. In his 1908 study of the Black family, DuBois prefaced his discussions of marriage, household structure, and economic organization with observations concerning the African antecedents of the patterns developed in America.

> In each case an attempt has been made to connect present conditions with the African past. This is not because Negro-Americans are Africans, or can trace an unbroken social history from Africa, but because there is a distinct nexus between Africa and America which, though broken and perverted, is nevertheless not to be neglected by the careful student [DuBois, 1969: 9].

Having documented the persistence of African family patterns in the Caribbean, and of African derived wedding ceremonies in Alabama, DuBois noted:

> Careful research would doubtless reveal many other traces of the African family in America. They would, however, be traces only, for the effectiveness of the slave system meant the practically complete crushing out of the African clan and family life [p. 21].

With the evidence that has accumulated since DuBois wrote, it is possible to argue that even though the constraints of slavery did prohibit the replication of African lineage ("clan") and family life in America, the principles on which these kin groups were based, and the values underlying them, led to the emergence of variants of African family life in the form of the extended families which developed among the enslaved Blacks in America. Evidence of the Africanity to which DuBois alluded is to be found not only in the relatively few "traces" of direct *institutional transfer* from Africa to America, but also in the numerous examples of *institutional transformation* from Africa to America.

No discussion of the relevance of Africa for understanding Afro-American family organization can proceed without confronting the issue of the "diversity" of the backgrounds of "African slaves" (read "enslaved Africans") brought to America. Obviously for certain purposes, each African community or each ethnic group can be described in terms of the linguistic, cultural, and/or social structural features which distinguish it from others. At the same time, however, these communities or ethnic groups can be analyzed from the point of view of their similarity to other groups.

It has long been established that the Africans enslaved in the United States and the rest of the Americas came from the Western part of the continent where there had been a long history of culture contact and widespread similarities in certain institutions (Herskovits, 1958: chs. 2 and 3). For example, some features of kinship organization were almost universal. Lineages, large co-resident domestic groups, and polygynous marriages are among the recurrent features found in groups speaking different languages, organized into states as well as "segmentary" societies, and living along the coast as well as in the interior (Radcliffe-Brown, 1950; Fortes, 1953; Onwuejeogwu, 1975).

When the concept of "African family structure" is used here, it refers to those organizational principles and patterns which are common to the different ethnic groups whose members were enslaved in America. These features of family organization are known to have existed for centuries on the African continent and are, therefore, legitimately termed a part of the African heritage.

AFRICAN FAMILY STRUCTURE: UNDERSTANDING THE DYNAMICS OF CONSANGUINITY AND CONJUGALITY

African families, like those in other parts of the world, embody two contrasting bases for membership: *consanguinity,* which refers to kinship that is commonly assumed or presumed to be biologically based and rooted in "blood ties," and *affinity,* which refers to kinship created by law and rooted "in-law." *Conjugality* refers specifically to the affinal kinship created between spouses (Marshall, 1968). Generally, all kinship entails a dynamic tension between the operation of the contrasting principles of consanguinity and affinity. The comparative study of family organization led Ralph Linton (1936: 159-163) to observe that in different societies families tend to be built either around a conjugal core or around a consanguineal core. In either case, the other principle is subordinate.

According to current historical research on the family in Europe, the principle of conjugality appears to have dominated family organization in the Western part of that continent (including Britain) at least since the Middle Ages, when a number of economic and political factors led to the predominance of nuclear and/or stem families built around married couples. Certainly for the past three or four hundred years, the conjugally based family has been the ideal and the norm in Western Europe (Shorter, 1975; Stone, 1975; Tilly and Scott, 1978). Whether or not the European conjugal family was a structural isolate is not the issue here. The point is that European families, whether nuclear or extended (as in the case of stem families), tended to emphasize the conjugal relationship in matters of household formation, decision making, property transmission, and socialization of the young (Goody, 1976).

African families, on the other hand, have traditionally been organized around consanguineal cores formed by adult siblings of the same sex or by larger same-sex segments of patri- or matrilineages. The groups which formed around these consanguineally related core members included their spouses and children, and perhaps some of their divorced siblings of the opposite sex. This co-resident *extended family* occupied a group of adjoining or contiguous dwellings known as a compound. Upon marriage, Africans did not normally form new isolated households, but joined a compound in which the extended family of the groom, or that of the bride, was already domiciled (Sudarkasa, 1980: 38-49).

African extended families could be subdivided in two ways. From one perspective, there was the division between the nucleus formed by the consanguineal core group and their children and the "outer group" formed by the in-marrying spouses. In many African languages, in-marrying spouses are collectively referred to as "wives" or "husbands" by both females and males of the core group. Thus, for example, in any compound in a patrilineal society, the in-marrying women may be known as the "wives of the house." They are, of course, also the mothers of the children of the compound. Their collective designation as "wives of the house" stresses the fact that their membership in the compound is rooted in law and can be terminated by law, whereas that of the core group is rooted in descent and is presumed to exist in perpetuity.

African extended families may also be divided into their constituent conjugally based family units comprised of parents and children. In the traditional African family, these conjugal units did not have the characteristics of the typical "nuclear family" of the West. In the first place, African conjugal families normally involved polygynous marriages at some stage in their developmental cycle. A number of Western scholars have chosen to characterize the polygynous conjugal family as several distinct nuclear families with one husband/father in common (Rivers, 1924: 12; Murdock, 1949: 2; Colson, 1962). In the African conception, however, whether a man had one wife and children or many wives and children, his was *one* family. In the case of polygynous families, both the husband and the senior co-wife played important roles in integrating the entire group (Fortes, 1949: chs. III and IV; Sudarkasa, 1973: ch. V; Ware, 1979). The very existence of the extended family as an "umbrella" group for the conjugal family meant that the latter group differed from the

Western nuclear family. Since, for many purposes and on many occasions, *all* the children of the same generation within the compound regarded themselves as brothers and sisters (rather than dividing into siblings versus "cousins"), and since the adults assumed certain responsibilities toward their "nephews" and "nieces" (whom they term sons and daughters) as well as toward their own offspring, African conjugal families did not have the rigid boundaries characteristic of nuclear families of the West.

The most far-reaching difference between African and European families stems from their differential emphasis on consanguinity and conjugality. This difference becomes clear when one considers extended family organization in the two contexts. The most common type of European extended family consisted of two or more nuclear families joined through the parent-child or sibling tie. It was this model of the stem family and the joint family that was put forth by George P. Murdock (1949: 23, 33, 39-40) as the generic form of the extended family. However, the African data show that on that continent, extended families were built around consanguineal cores and the conjugal components of these larger families differed significantly from the nuclear families of the West.

In Africa, unlike Europe, in many critical areas of family life the consanguineal core group rather than the conjugal pair was paramount. With respect to household formation, I have already indicated that married couples joined existing compounds. It was the lineage core that owned (or had the right of usufruct over) the land and the compound where families lived, farmed, and/or practiced their crafts. The most important properties in African societies— land, titles, and entitlements—were transmitted through the lineages, and spouses did not inherit from each other (Goody, 1976).

Within the extended family residing in a single compound, decision making centered in the consanguineal core group. The oldest male in the compound was usually its head, and all the men in his generation constituted the elders of the group. Together they were ultimately responsible for settling internal disputes, including those that could not be settled within the separate conjugal families or, in some cases, by the female elders among the wives (Sudarkasa, 1973, 1976). They also made decisions, such as those involving the allocation of land and other resources, which affected the functioning of the constituent conjugal families.

Given the presence of multiple spouses within the *conjugal* families, it is not surprising that decision making within them also differed from the model associated with nuclear family organization. Separate rather than joint decision making was common. In fact, husbands and wives normally had distinct purviews and responsibilities within the conjugal family (Sudarkasa, 1973; Oppong, 1974). Excepting those areas where Islamic traditions overshadowed indigenous African traditions, women had a good deal of control over the fruits of their own labor. Even though husbands typically had ultimate authority over wives, this authority did not extend to control over their wives' properties (Oppong, 1974; Robertson, 1976; Sudarkasa, 1976). Moreover, even though women were subordinate in their roles as wives, as mothers and sisters they wielded considerable authority, power, and influence. This distinction in the power attached to women's roles is symbolized by the fact that in the same society where wives knelt before their husbands, sons prostrated before their mothers and seniority as determined by age, rather than gender, governed relationships among siblings (Sudarkasa, 1973, 1976).

Socialization of the young involved the entire extended family, not just the separate conjugal families, even though each conjugal family had special responsibility for the children (theirs or their relatives') living with them. It is important to note that the concept of "living with" a conjugal family took on a different meaning in the context of the African compound. In the first place, husbands, wives, and children did not live in a bounded space, apart from other such units. Wives had their own rooms or small dwellings, and husbands had theirs. These were not necessarily adjacent to one another. (In some matrilineal societies, husbands and wives resided in separate compounds). Children ordinarily slept in their mothers' rooms until they were of a certain age, after which they customarily slept in communal rooms allocated to boys or girls. Children usually ate their meals with their mothers but they might also eat some of these meals with their fathers' co-wives (assuming that no hostility existed between the women concerned) or with their grandmothers. Children of the same compound played together and shared many learning experiences. They were socialized by all the adults to identify themselves collectively as sons and daughters of a particular lineage and compound, which entailed a kinship, based on descent, with all the lineage ancestors and with generations unborn (Radcliffe-Brown and Forde, 1950; Uchendu, 1965; Sudarkasa, 1980).

The stability of the African extended family did not depend on the stability of the marriage(s) of the individual core group members. Although traditional African marriages (particularly those in patrilineal societies) were more stable than those of most contemporary societies, marital dissolution did not have the ramifications it has in nuclear family systems. When divorces did occur, they were usually followed by remarriage. Normally, all adults other than those who held certain ceremonial offices or who were severely mentally or physically handicapped lived in a marital union (though not necessarily the same one) throughout their lives (for example, Lloyd, 1968). The children of a divorced couple were usually brought up in their natal compound (or by members of their lineage residing elsewhere), even though the in-marrying parent had left that compound.

Several scholars have remarked on the relative ease of divorce in some traditional African societies, particularly those in which matrilineal descent was the rule (for example, Fortes, 1950: 283). Jack Goody (1976: 64) has even suggested that the rate of divorce in precolonial Africa was higher than in parts of Europe and Asia in comparable periods as a corollary of contrasting patterns of property transmission, contrasting attitudes toward the remarriage of women (especially widows), and contrasting implications of polygyny and monogamy. If indeed there was a higher incidence of divorce in precolonial Africa, this would not be inconsistent with the wide-ranging emphasis on consanguinity in Africa as opposed to conjugality in Europe.

Marriage in Africa was a contractual union which often involved long-lasting companionate relationships, but it was not expected to be the all-encompassing, exclusive relationship of the Euro-American ideal type. Both men and women relied on their extended families and friends, as well as on their spouses, for emotionally gratifying relationships. Often, too, in the context of polygyny women as well as men had sexual liaisons with more than one partner. A woman's clandestine affairs did not necessarily lead to divorce because, in the absence of publicized information to the contrary, her husband was considered the father of all her children (Radcliffe-Brown, 1950). And in the context of the lineage (especially the patrilineage), all men aspired to have as many children as possible.

Interpersonal relationships within African families were governed by principles and values which I have elsewhere summarized under the concepts of respect, restraint, responsibility, and reciprocity. Common to all these principles was a notion of commitment to the collectivity. The family offered a network of security, but it also imposed a burden of obligations (Sudarkasa, 1980: 49-50). From the foregoing discussion, it should be understandable that, in their material form, these obligations extended first and foremost to consanguineal kin. Excepting the gifts that were exchanged at the time of marriage, the material obligations entailed in the conjugal relationship and the wider affinal relationships created by marriage were of a lesser magnitude than those associated with "blood" ties.

AFRO-AMERICAN FAMILY STRUCTURE: INTERPRETING THE AFRICAN CONNECTION

Rather than start with the question of what was *African* about the families established by those Africans who were enslaved in America, it would be more appropriate to ask what was *not* African about them. Most of the Africans who were captured and brought to America arrived without any members of their families, but they brought with them the societal codes they had learned regarding family life. To argue that the trans-Atlantic voyage and the trauma of enslavement made them forget, or rendered useless their memories of how they had been brought up or how they had lived before their capture, is to argue from premises laden with myths about the Black experience (Elkins, 1963: 101-102; see also Frazier, 1966: ch. 1).

Given the African tradition of multilingualism and the widespread use of lingua francas (Maquet, 1972: 18-25)—which in West Africa would include Hausa, Yoruba, Djoula, and Twi—it is probable that many more of the enslaved Africans could communicate among themselves than is implied by those who remark on the multiplicity of "tribes" represented among the slaves. As Landman (1978: 80) has pointed out:

> In many areas of the world, individuals are expected to learn only one language in the ordinary course of their lives. But many Africans have been enculturated in social systems where multiple language or dialect acquisition have been regarded as normal.

The fact that Africans typically spoke three to five languages also makes it understandable why they quickly adopted "pidginized" forms of European languages as lingua francas for communicating among themselves and with their captors.

The relationships which the Blacks in America established among themselves would have reflected their own backgrounds *and* the conditions in which they found themselves. It is as erroneous to try to attribute what developed among them solely to slavery as it is to attribute it solely to the African background. Writers such as Herbert Gutman (1976), who emphasize the "adaptive" nature of "slave culture" must ask what it was that was being adapted as well as in what context this adaptation took place. Moreover, they must realize that adaptation does not necessarily imply extensive modification of an institution, especially when its structure is already suited (or "preadapted") to survival in the new context. Such an institution was the African extended family, which had served on that continent, in various environments and different political contexts, as a unit of production and distribution; of socialization, education, and social control; and of emotional and material support for the aged and the infirm as well as the hale and hearty (Kerri, 1979; Okediji, 1975; Shimkin and Uchendu, 1978; Sudarkasa, 1975b).

The extended family networks that were formed during slavery by Africans *and their descendants* were based on the institutional heritage which the Africans had brought with them to this continent, and the specific forms they took reflected the influence of European-derived institutions as well as the political and economic circumstances in which the enslaved population found itself.

The picture of Black families during slavery has become clearer over the past decade, particularly as a result of the wealth of data in Gutman's justly heralded study. Individual households were normally comprised of a conjugal pair, their children, and sometimes their grandchildren, other relatives, or nonkin. Marriage was usually monogamous, but polygynous unions where the wives lived in separate households have also been reported (Gutman, 1976: 59, 158; Blassingame, 1979: 171; Perdue et al., 1980: 209).

Probably only in a few localities did female-headed households constitute as much as one-quarter of all households (Gutman, 1976: esp. chs. 1-3). The rarity of this household type was in keeping with the African tradition whereby women normally bore children within the context of marriage and lived in monogamous or polygynous conjugal families that were part of larger extended families. I have tried to show elsewhere why it is inappropriate to apply the term "nuclear family" to the mother-child dyads within African polygynous families (Sudarkasa, 1980: 43-46). In some African societies—especially in matrilineal ones—a small percentage of previously married women, or married women living apart from their husbands, might head households that were usually attached to larger compounds. However, in my view, on the question of the origin of female-headed households among Blacks in America, Herskovits was wrong, and Frazier was right in attributing this development to conditions that arose during slavery and in the context of urbanization in later periods (Frazier, 1966; Herskovits, 1958; Furstenberg et al., 1975).

Gutman's data suggest that enslaved women who had their first children out of wedlock did not normally set up independent households, but rather continued to live with their parents. Most of them subsequently married and set up neolocal residence with their husbands. The data also suggest that female-headed households developed mainly in two situations: (1) A woman whose husband died or was sold off the plantation might head a household comprised of her children and perhaps her grandchildren born to an unmarried daughter; (2) a woman who did not marry after having one or two children out of wedlock but continued to have children (no doubt often for the "master") might have her own cabin built for her (Gutman, 1976: chs. 1-3).

It is very important to distinguish these two types of female-headed households, the first being only a phase in the developmental cycle of a conjugally headed household, and the second being a case of neolocal residence by an unmarried female. The pattern of households headed by widows was definitely not typical of family structure in Africa, where normally a widow married another member of her deceased husband's lineage. The pattern of neolocal residence by an unmarried woman with children would have been virtually unheard of in Africa. Indeed, it was also relatively rare among enslaved Blacks and in Black communities in later periods. Before the twentieth-century policy of public assistance for unwed mothers, virtually all young unmarried mothers in Black communities continued to live in households headed by other adults. If in later years they did establish their own households, these tended to be tied into transresidential family networks.

The existence during slavery of long-lasting conjugal unions among Blacks was not a departure from African family tradition. Even with the relative ease of divorce in matrilineal societies, most Africans lived in marital unions that ended only with the death of one of the spouses. In the patrilineal societies from which most American Blacks were taken, a number of factors, including the custom of returning bridewealth payments upon the dissolution of marriage, served to encourage marital stability (Radcliffe-Brown, 1950: 43-54). Given that the conditions of slavery did not permit the *replication* of African families, it might be expected that the husband and wife as elders in the household would assume even greater importance than they had in Africa, where the elders within the consanguineal core of the extended family and those among the wives would have had major leadership roles within the compound.

When the distinction is made between family and household—and, following Bender (1967), between the composition of the co-resident group and the domestic functions associated with both households and families—it becomes apparent that the question of who lived with whom during slavery (or later) must be subordinate to the questions of who was doing what for whom and what kin relationships were maintained over space and time. In any case, decisions concerning residence per se were not always in the hands of the enslaved Blacks themselves, and space alone served as a constraint on the size, and consequently to some extent on the composition, of the "slave" cabins.

That each conjugally based household formed a primary unit for food consumption and production among the enslaved Blacks is consistent with domestic organization within the African compound. However, Gutman's data, and those reported by enslaved Blacks themselves, on the strong bonds of obligation among kinsmen suggest that even within the constraints imposed by the slave regime, transresidential cooperation—including that between households in different localities—was the rule rather than the exception (Gutman, 1976: esp. 131-138; Perdue et al., 1980: esp. 26, 256, 323). One might hypothesize that on the larger plantations with a number of Black families related through consanguineal and affinal ties, the households of these families might have formed groupings similar to African compounds. Certainly we know that in later times such groupings were found in the South Carolina Sea Islands and other parts of the South (Agbasegbe, 1976, 1981; Gutman, 1976; Johnson, 1934: ch. 2; Powdermaker, 1939: ch. 8).

By focusing on extended families (rather than simply on households) among the enslaved Blacks, it becomes apparent that these kin networks had many of the features of continental African extended families. These Afro-American groupings were built around consanguineal kin whose spouses were related to or incorporated into the networks in different degrees. The significance of the consanguineal principle in these networks is indicated by Gutman's statement that "the pull between ties to an immediate family and to an enlarged kin network sometimes strained husbands and wives" (1976: 202; see also Frazier, 1966: pt. 2).

The literature on Black families during slavery provides a wealth of data on the way in which consanguineal kin assisted each other with child rearing, in life crisis events such as birth and death, in work groups, in efforts to obtain freedom, and so on. They maintained their networks against formidable odds and, after slavery, sought out those parents, siblings, aunts, and uncles from whom they had been torn (Blassingame, 1979; Genovese, 1974; Gutman, 1976; Owens, 1976). Relationships within these groups were governed by principles and values stemming from the African background. Respect for elders and reciprocity among kinsmen are noted in all discussions of Black families during slavery. The willingness to assume responsibility for relatives beyond the conjugal family and selflessness (a form of restraint) in the face of these responsibilities are also characteristics attributed to the enslaved population.

As would be expected, early Afro-American extended families differed from their African prototypes in ways that reflected the influence of slavery and of Euro-American values, especially their proscriptions and prescriptions regarding mating, marriage, and the family. No doubt, too, the Euro-American emphasis on the primacy of marriage within the family reinforced conjugality among the Afro-Americans even though the "legal" marriage of enslaved Blacks was prohibited. As DuBois noted at the turn of the century, African corporate lineages could not survive intact during slavery. Hence, the consanguineal core groups of Afro-American extended families differed in some ways from those of their African antecedents. It appears that in some of these Afro-American families membership in the core group was traced bilaterally, whereas in others there was a unilineal emphasis without full-fledged lineages.

Interestingly, after slavery, some of the corporate functions of African lineages reemerged in some extended families which became property-owning collectivities. I have suggested elsewhere that "the disappearance of the lineage principle or its absorption into the concept of extended family" is one of the aspects of the transformation of African family organization in America that requires research (Sudarkasa, 1980: 57). Among the various other issues that remain to be studied concerning these extended families are these: (1) Did members belong by virtue of bilateral or unilineal descent from a common ancestor or because of shared kinship with a living person? (2) How were group boundaries established and maintained? (3) What was the nature and extent of the authority of the elder(s)? (4) How long did the group last and what factors determined its span in time and space?

CONCLUSION

At the outset of this chapter it was suggested that a holistic explanation of Black family organization requires discarding or recasting some of the debates which have framed discussions in the past. I have tried to show why it is time to move beyond the debate over whether it was slavery *or* the African heritage which "determined" Black family organization to a synthesis which looks at institutional transformation as well as institutional transfer for the interplay between Africa and America in shaping the family structures of Afro-Americans.

Obviously, Black families have changed over time, and today one would expect that the evidence for African "retentions" (Herskovits, 1958: xxii-xxiii) in them would be more controvertible than in the past. Nevertheless, the persistence of some features of African family organization among contemporary Black American families has been documented for both rural and urban areas. Although this study cannot attempt a full-scale analysis of these features and the changes they have undergone, it is important to make reference to one of them, precisely because it impacts upon so many other aspects of Black family organization, and because its connection to Africa has not been acknowledged by most contemporary scholars. I refer to the emphasis on consanguinity noted especially among lower-income Black families and those in the rural South. Some writers, including Shimkin and Uchendu (1978), Agbasegbe (1976; 1981), Aschenbrenner (1973; 1975; 1978; Aschenbrenner and Carr, 1980) and the present author (1975a, 1980, 1981) have dealt explicitly with this concept in their discussions of Black family organization. However, without labelling it as such, many other scholars have described some aspects of the operation of consanguinity within the Black family in their discussions of "matrifocality" and "female-headed households." Too often, the origin of this consanguineal emphasis in Black families, which can be manifest even in households with both husband and wife present, is left unexplained or is "explained" by labelling it an "adaptive" characteristic.

In my view, historical realities require that the derivation of this aspect of Black family organization be traced to its African antecedents. Such a view does not deny the adaptive significance of consanguineal networks. In fact, it helps to clarify why these networks had the flexibility they had and why they, rather than conjugal relationships, came to be the stabilizing factor in Black families. The significance of this principle of organization is indicated by the list of Black family characteristics derived from it. Scrutiny of the list of Black family characteristics given by Aschenbrenner (1978) shows that 12 of the 18 "separate" features she lists are manifestations of the overall strength and entailments of consanguineal relationships.

Some writers have viewed the consanguineally based extended family as a factor of *instability* in the Black family because it sometimes undermines the conjugal relationships in which its members are involved. I would suggest that historically among Black Americans the concept of "family" meant first and foremost relationships created by "blood" rather than by marriage. (R. T. Smith

[1973] has made substantially the same point with respect to West Indian family organization.) Children were socialized to think in terms of obligations to parents (especially mothers), siblings, and others defined as "close kin." Obligations to "outsiders," who would include prospective spouses and in-laws, were definitely less compelling. Once a marriage took place, if the demands of the conjugal relationship came into irreconcilable conflict with consanguineal commitments, the former would often be sacrificed. Instead of interpreting instances of *marital* instability as prima facie evidence of family instability, it should be realized that the fragility of the conjugal relationship could be a consequence or corollary of the *stability* of the consanguineal family network. Historically, such groups survived by nurturing a strong sense of responsibility among members and by fostering a code of reciprocity which could strain relations with persons not bound by it.

Not all Black families exhibit the same emphasis on consanguineal relationships. Various factors, including education, occupational demands, aspirations toward upward mobility, and acceptance of American ideals concerning marriage and the family, have moved some (mainly middle- and upper-class) Black families toward conjugally focused households and conjugally centered extended family groupings. Even when such households include relatives other than the nuclear family, those relatives tend to be subordinated to the conjugal pair who form the core of the group. This contrasts with some older type Black families where a senior relative (especially the wife's or the husband's mother) could have a position of authority in the household equal to or greater than that of one or both of the spouses. Children in many contemporary Black homes are not socialized to think in terms of the parent-sibling group as the primary kin group, but rather in terms of their future spouses and families of procreation as the main source of their future emotional and material satisfaction and support. Among these Blacks, the nuclear household tends to be more isolated in terms of instrumental functions, and such extended family networks as exist tend to be clusters of nuclear families conforming to the model put forth by Murdock (1949: chs. 1 and 2).

For scholars interested in the heritage of Europe as well as the heritage of Africa in Afro-American family organization, a study of the operation of the principles of conjugality and consanguinity in these families would provide considerable insight into the ways in which these two institutional traditions have been interwoven. By looking at the differential impact of these principles in matters of household formation, delegation of authority, maintenance of solidarity and support, acquisition and transmission of property, financial management, and so on (Sudarkasa, 1981), and by examining the political and economic variables which favor the predominance of one or the other principle, we will emerge with questions and formulations that can move us beyond debates over "pathology" and "normalcy" in Black family life.

REFERENCES

AGBASEGBE, B. (1976) "The role of wife in the Black extended family: perspectives from a rural community in Southern United States," pp. 124-138 in D. McGuigan (ed.) New Research on Women and Sex Roles. Ann Arbor: Center for Continuing Education of Women, University of Michigan.

———— (1981) "Some aspects of contemporary rural Afroamerican family life in the Sea Islands of Southeastern United States." Presented at the Annual Meeting of the Association of Social and Behavioral Scientists, Atlanta, Georgia, March 1981.

ALLEN, W. R. (1978) "The search for applicable theories of Black family life." Journal of Marraige and the Family 40 (February): 117-129.

———— (1979) "Class, culture, and family organization: the effects of class and race on family structure in urban America." Journal of Comparative Family Studies 10 (Autumn): 301-313.

ASCHENBRENNER, J. (1973) "Extended families among Black Americans." Journal of Comparative Family Studies 4: 257-268.

———— (1975) Lifelines: Black Families in Chicago. New York: Holt, Rinehart & Winston.

———— (1978) "Continuities and variations in Black family structure," pp. 181-200 in D. B. Shimkin, E. M. Shimkin, and D. A. Frate (eds.) The Extended Family in Black Societies. The Hague: Mouton.

———— and C. H. CARR (1980) "Conjugal relationships in the context of the Black extended family." Alternative Lifestyles 3 (November): 463-484.

BENDER, D. R. (1967) "A refinement of the concept of household: families, co-residence, and domestic functions." American Anthropologist 69 (October): 493-504.

BILLINGSLEY, A. (1968) Black Families in White America. Englewood Cliffs, NJ: Prentice-Hall.

BLASSINGAME, J. W. (1979) The Slave Community. New York: Oxford University Press.

COLSON, E. (1962) "Family change in contemporary Africa." Annals of the New York Academy of Sciences 96 (January): 641-652.

DuBOIS, W. E. B. (1969) The Negro American Family. New York: New American Library. (Originally published, 1908).

ELKINS, S. (1963) Slavery: A Problem in American Intellectual Life. New York: Grosset and Dunlap. (Originally published, 1959).

ENGLISH, R. (1974) "Beyond pathology: research and theoretical perspectives on Black families," pp. 39-52 in L. E. Gary (ed.) Social Research and the Black Community: Selected Issues and Priorities. Washington, DC: Institute for Urban Affairs and Research, Howard University.

FORTES, M. (1949) The Web of Kinship among the Tallensi. London: Oxford University Press.

———— (1950) "Kinship and marriage among the Ashanti," pp 252-284 in A. R. Radcliffe-Brown and D. Forde (eds.) African Systems of Kinship and Marriage. London: Oxford University Press.

———— (1953) "The structure of unilineal descent groups." American Anthropologist 55 (January-March): 17-41.

FRAZIER, E. (1966) The Negro Family in the United States. Chicago: University of Chicago Press. (Originally published, 1939).

FURSTENBERG, F. , T. HERSHBERT, and J. MODELL (1975) "The origins of the female-headed Black family: the impact of the urban experience." Journal of Interdisciplinary History 6 (Autumn): 211-233.

GENOVESE, E. D. (1974) Roll Jordan Roll: The World the Slaves Made. New York: Random House.

GOODY, J. (1976) Production and Reproduction: A Comparative Study of the Domestic Domain. Cambridge: Cambridge University Press.

GUTMAN, H. (1976) The Black Family in Slavery and Freedom: 1750-1925. New York: Random House.

HERSKOVITS, M. J. (1958) The Myth of the Negro Past. Boston: Beacon. (Originally published, 1941).

JOHNSON, C. S. (1934) Shadow of the Plantation. Chicago: University of Chicago Press.

KERRI, J. N. (1979) "Understanding the African family: persistence, continuity, and change." Western Journal of Black Studies 3 (Spring): 14-17.

LANDMAN, R. H. (1978) "Language policies and their implications for ethnic relations in the newly sovereign states of Sub-Saharan Africa," pp. 69-90 in B. M. duToit (ed.) Ethnicity in Modern Africa. Boulder, CO: Westview Press.

LINTON, R. (1936) The Study of Man. New York: Appleton-Century-Crofts.

LLOYD, P. C. (1968) "Divorce among the Yoruba." American Anthropologist 70 (February): 67-81.

MAQUET, J. (1972) Civilizations of Black Africa. London: Oxford University Press.

MARSHALL, G. A. [Niara Sudarkasa] (1968) "Marriage: comparative analysis," in International Encyclopedia of the Social Sciences, Vol. 10. New York: Macmillan/Free Press.

MURDOCK, G. P. (1949) Social Structure. New York: Macmillan.

NOBLES, W. (1974a) "African root and American fruit: the Black family." Journal of Social and Behavioral Sciences 20: 52-64.

———— (1974b) "Africanity: its role in Black families." The Black Scholar 9 (June): 10-17.

———— (1978) "Toward an empirical and theoretical framework for defining Black families." Journal of Marriage and the Family 40 (November): 679-688.

OKEDIJI, P. A. (1975) "A psychosocial analysis of the extended family: the African case." African Urban Notes, Series B, 1(3): 93-99. (African Studies Center, Michigan State University)

ONWUEJEOGWU, M. A. (1975) The Social Anthropology of Africa: An Introduction. London: Heinemann.

OPPONG, C. (1974) Marriage among a Matrilineal Elite: A Family Study of Ghanaian Senior Civil Servants. Cambridge: Cambridge University Press.

OWENS, L. H. (1976) This Species of Property: Slave Life and Culture in the Old South. New York: Oxford University Press.

PERDUE, C. L., Jr., T. E. BARDEN, and R. K. PHILLIPS [eds.] (1980) Weevils in the Wheat: Interviews with Virginia Ex-Slaves. Bloomington: Indiana University Press.

POWDERMAKER, H. (1939) After Freedom: A Cultural Study in the Deep South. New York: Viking.

RADCLIFFE-BROWN, A. R. (1950) "Introduction," pp. 1-85 in A. R. Radcliffe-Brown and D. Forde (eds.) African Systems of Kinship and Marriage. London: Oxford University Press.

———— and D. FORDE [eds.] (1950) African Systems of Kinship and Marriage. London: Oxford University Press.

RIVERS, W. H. R. (1924) Social Organization. New York: Alfred Knopf.

ROBERTSON, C. (1976) "Ga women and socioeconomic change in Accra, Ghana," pp. 111-133 in N. J. Hafkin and E. G. Bay (eds.) Women in Africa: Studies in Social and Economic Change. Stanford: Stanford University Press.

SHIMKIN, D. and V. UCHENDU (1978) "Persistence, borrowing, and adaptive changes in Black kinship systems: some issues and their significance," pp. 391-406 in D. Shimkin, E. M. Shimkin, and D. A. Frate (eds.) The Extended Family in Black Societies. The Hague: Mouton.

SHIMKIN, D., E. M. SHIMKIN, and D. A. FRATE [eds.] (1978) The Extended Family in Black Societies. The Hague: Mouton.

SHORTER, E. (1975) The Making of the Modern Family. New York: Basic Books.

SMITH, R. T. (1973) "The matrifocal family," pp. 121-144 in J. Goody (ed.) The Character of Kinship. Cambridge: Cambridge University Press.

STACK, C. (1974) All Our Kin. New York: Harper & Row.

STAPLES, R. (1971) "Toward a sociology of the Black family: a decade of theory and research." Journal of Marriage and the Family 33 (February): 19-38.

———— [ed.] (1978) The Black Family: Essays and Studies. Belmont, CA: Wadsworth.

STONE, L. (1975) "The rise of the nuclear family in early modern England: the patriarchal stage," pp. 13-57 in C. E. Rosenberg (ed.) The Family in History. Philadelphia: University of Pennsylvania Press.

SUDARKASA, N. (1973) Where Women Work: A Study of Yoruba Women in the Marketplace and in the Home. Anthropological Papers No. 53. Ann Arbor: Museum of Anthropology, University of Michigan.

———— (1975a) "An exposition on the value premises underlying Black family studies." Journal of the National Medical Association 19 (May): 235-239.

———— (1975b) "National development planning for the promotion and protection of the family." Proceedings of the Conference on Social Research and National Development, E. Akeredolu-Ale, ed. The Nigerian Institute of Social and Economic Research, Ibadan, Nigeria.

———— (1976) "Female employment and family organization in West Africa," pp. 48-63 in D. G. McGuigan (ed.) New Research on Women and Sex Roles. Ann Arbor: Center for Continuing Education of Women, University of Michigan.

———— (1980) "African and Afro-American family structure: a comparison." The Black Scholar 11 (November-December): 37-60.

———— (1981) "Understanding the dynamics of consanguinity and conjugality in contemporary Black family organization." Presented at the Seventh Annual Third World Conference, Chicago, March 1981.

TILLY, L. A. and J. W. SCOTT (1978) Women, Work, and Family. New York: Holt, Rinehart & Winston.

UCHENDU, V. (1965) The Igbo of South-Eastern Nigeria. New York: Holt, Rinehart & Winston.

WARE, H. (1979) "Polygyny: women's views in a transitional society, Nigeria 1975." Journal of Marriage and the Family 41 (February): 185-195.

WOODSON, C. G. (1936) The African Background Outlined. Washington, DC: Association for the Study of Negro Life and History.

3

OLD-TIME RELIGION
Benches Can't Say "Amen"

WILLIAM HARRISON PIPES

Preaching and churches have traditionally been a mainstay of Black families. Among Blacks in the United States today, old-time preaching (the uneducated Black man's emotional type of preaching that came from slavery) is still a vital element. The fundamental reason why the Black man clings to the old-time religion is that he has been without a means of normal outward expression, due to his domination by powers beyond his control—in Africa, under colonial control; in America before the Civil War, the institution of slavery; in America today (especially in the "Black Belt" and to a lesser degree in other parts of the United States), the plantation system and/or "divine white right." In Africa and in America many Blacks have made their adjustment to an "impossible world" by means of an emotional escape—the frenzy and shouting of old-time religion.

To explain the preaching of this old-time religion, the author (1) investigated the African and slavery time characteristics of this type of preaching, and (2) compared and contrasted these findings with the characteristics of the preaching that was recorded in Macon County, Georgia.

Besides the religious motive, the chief purpose of old-time Black preaching appears to be to "stir up," to excite the emotions of the audience and the minister

AUTHOR'S NOTE: This chapter is condensed and adapted from the author's book, *Say Amen, Brother!* (New York: William-Frederick Press, 1951). Copyright by William Harrison Pipes.

as a means for their escape from an "impossible world." The old-time purpose of persuading people to come to Jesus is still present in varying degrees, but the emphasis here seems to be a secondary one.

EARLY AMERICAN AND AFRICAN HERITAGES

It cannot be overstressed that the "real" old-time Black preaching—undiluted by education and freedom—existed in America only during the days of slavery. Preaching in Macon County is merely its most immediate descendant. The rhythmical preaching of some sermons is illustrative. Indeed, it should be, for the preacher is a living example of the sudden crossing of two religious cultures.

This section seeks to show that the mixing of American and African backgrounds of religious practices produced old-time Black preaching. This was done by (1) considering the very earliest American background and the coming of enslaved Africans; (2) considering the African religious background of the slaves; (3) showing the actual mixing of the cultures; and (4) observing actual preaching of the Black church.

THE AMERICAN HERITAGE

It appears that there was Christian civilization in America, on the Island of Greenland, as early as the twelfth century (O'Gorman, 1895). But America had little pulpit eloquence until the sixteenth century, although it is said that Columbus's first act, in 1492, of kneeling to thank God for a safe journey might be considered preaching of a sort. It is known that, on returning to America in 1494, Columbus brought with him twelve priests. In the sixteenth century, Spanish Catholic priests wrote America's first real chapter in preaching, a chapter of humble missionary teaching.

It was the seventeenth century that marked the significant period in the development of the American heritage of preaching, especially as it was to influence Black preaching. Africans were first brought to America in large numbers in 1619 (Bacon, 1898). In this century there were two centers of preaching in America: Virginia and New England. Preaching activities in Jamestown, Virginia (settled in 1607) are very important, because this state fell within the "Black Belt" section, where there were many newly arrived enslaved Africans. "'About the last of August (1619),' says John Rolfe in John Smith's *Generall Historie,* 'came in a Dutch man of warre, that sold us twenty Negars.' These Blacks were sold into servitude, and Virginia . . . ; and thus slavery gained a firm place in the oldest of the colonies" (Brawley, 1921).

The Black slave faced a severe type of colonial religion in the beginning. But he had his own African religious heritage. The author is not unaware of Frazier's (1939) insistence that "African traditions and practices did not take root and survive in the United States" (pp. 7-8). Frazier attempted to destroy the contentions that Black religious practices in the United States may be attributed to African sources, but his attempts are feeble. For example, he stated:

> Of the same nature is the claim of Herskovits (1935, pp. 256-57) that the practice of baptism among Negroes is related to the great importance of the river-cults in West Africa, particularly in view of the fact that, as has been observed, river-cult priests were sold into slavery in great numbers. It needs simply to be stated that about a third of the rural Negroes in the United States are Methodists and only in exceptional cases practice baptism.

Frazier's refutation is fallacious for two reasons. First, he simply made a statement about the proportion of Blacks: who are Methodists without proof or documentation. The author knew from experience that some Methodists do baptise; but even if one accepted his unsupported implication that a third of the Blacks in the rural South do not practice baptism, Herskovits's contention that the American Black man's practice of baptism is related to the river-cults in West Africa may still stand. Over a period of 320 years, without contact with African religious practices, the American Blacks naturally have lost much of the African traditions and heritage. It is possible that they could have lost entirely the practice of baptism, but it is also possible that the continuity still remains. Frazier ignored these lines of reasoning, and labelled as "uncritical" and "absurd" the assertions of Herskovits, Woodson (1936), and others. Even if Africans were not allowed to bring actual religious practices to America, they certainly did bring with them their religious memories and their temperaments. As Park (1919) concluded, the tradition may have been American, but the temperament was African.

Contrary to John Hope Franklin (1947), Turner (1949), in an examination of the extent of Africanisms in the Gullah dialect, uncovered the use of 4000 African words, names, and numbers used by Blacks in the United States today. Good (1926) spoke even more specifically:

> Negroes have not lived in this country long enough to destroy the customs of the race developed in Africa. They hand down from generation to generation many of the customs and superstitions of the race, though most of them are greatly modified by life in the United States.

DuBois (1903) pointed out very definitely that the American Black's religion was influenced by African practices:

It [the Negro church] was not at first by any means a Christian Church, but a mere adaptation of those heathen rites which we roughly designate by the term Obe Worship, or "Voodooism." Association and missionary effort soon gave these rites a veneer of Christianity, and gradually, after two centuries, the Church became Christian . . . , but with many of the old customs still clinging to the services. It is this historic fact that the Negro Church of today bases itself upon the sole surviving social institution of the African fatherland, that accounts for its extraordinary growth and vitality.

It is significant that Herskovits (1930) said that the African influence in America was strongest in the South and especially in Georgia.

It does seem reasonable that these Africans who were brought to America retained something of their African background. It cannot be denied that time and American influences modified and even eliminated some of this background. But it is inconceivable that a people could suddenly lose all of their religious practices. As Park (1919) said, "It is in connection with his [the Black man's] religion that we may expect to find, if anywhere, the indications of a distinctive Afro-American culture."

A STUDY OF BLACK PREACHING

This study was concerned with the preaching of the Black church, furthermore, because this phase of the creations of the American Black has not been studied extensively. As James Weldon Johnson (1932) pointed out, "A good deal has been written on the folk creations of the American Negro: his music, sacred and secular; his plantation tales, and his dances; but that there are folk sermons, as well, is a fact that has passed unnoticed." Since Johnson made this statement, some interest has been shown in old-fashioned preaching. The moving picture industry, newspapers, and radio have given attention to the subject. However, in almost every instance, the Black man's religion is used for entertainment; it is not considered seriously.

The fact that Black preaching has not been studied thoroughly in this field might not justify this investigation if it were not also true that for Black families within the Black man's most important institution (the church), the preacher (and his preaching, of course) is most important. "The Negro ministry is still the largest factor in the life of this [the Black] race" (Woodson, 1921). W. E. B. DuBois (1903), the eminent sociologist, evaluated the Black minister in these terms:

The preacher is the most unique personality developed by the Negro on American soil. A leader, a politician, an orator, a "boss," an intriguer, an idealist—all these he is, and ever, too, the center of a group of men, now twenty, now a thousand in number.

It should be stressed here that the old-fashioned (old-time) Black is the unique personality referred to, for the more educated, unemotional Black ministers preach much the same as ministers of other races. But the

> old-time Black preacher has not yet been given the niche in which he properly belongs. He has been portrayed only as a semi-comic figure. He had, it is true, his comic aspects, but on the whole he was an important figure, and at bottom a vital factor. . . . It was also he who instilled into the Negro the narcotic doctrine epitomized in the Spiritual, 'You May Have All Dis World, But Give Me Jesus.' This power of the old-time preacher, somewhat lessened and changed in his successors, is still a vital force; in fact, *it is still the greatest single influence among the colored people of the United States.* The Negro today is, perhaps, the most priest-governed group in the country [Johnson, 1932].

STUDY APPROACH

The purpose of this work was to make an interpretive study of old-time Black preaching as it was reflected during the late 1930s and early '40s in Macon County, Georgia, using the recordings of seven sermons.

Old-time Black preaching is important without a doubt, but James Weldon Johnson declared, "the old-time Negro preacher is rapidly passing." And this fact leads to the distinctive nature of this project: the recording of the sermons. Although the type of preaching under consideration is passing out of existence, students of American homiletics, of Black dialect, of public speaking, social sciences, and the general public may use the recordings made for this study as a basis for further study and understanding.

Without taking cognizance of the recording machine, Johnson (1932) declared of Black sermons: "There is, of course, no way of recreating the atmosphere—the fervor of the congregation, the amens and hallelujahs, the undertone of singing which was often a soft accompaniment to parts of the sermon." The recordings, even though they are unable to capture all of these aspects, go a long way toward a true presentation of these characteristics.

CHOICE OF MACON COUNTY

Throughout, the study had been confined to Macon County because conclusive proof had been given by Arthur Raper, an able sociologist, that among Blacks the closest parallel to pre-Civil War days (during which time old-fashioned Black preaching flourished on the big slave plantations) was to be found in the "Black Belt." The "Black Belt" is the name given to some 200 counties which stretch, crescent-like, from Virginia to Texas. The name has no reference to the color of the many Blacks who live in this section of the country, but to the

rich, black soil of these counties. During slavery days, the large slave plantations, on which were found most of the Blacks in the United States, were to be
found in the Black Belt (Raper, 1936).

It became a formidable task to record representative Black sermons which
are delivered in almost every part of the country. Because the vast majority of
Blacks live in the South, the problem became one of finding a typical Southern
locality.

Since Reconstruction, and up to the present time, the Black Christian has
become more and more like the white man; the former belief in the sinfulness of
dancing and card-playing, for example, is being discarded. The author knew
this to be true from actual experience as a member of a Black family in the Black
Belt. In the course of this work, he often drew upon this experience but only
when there was no better source of information available. His grandfather,
Harrison Shaffer, a former slave, furnished much information concerning the
days of slavery in the Black Belt.

Only in the Black Belt do we still have situations that are very close to the
Black man's slavery days: the slave plantations with master and slaves become
plantations with landlord and croppers; here alone have the Black man's earliest
(old-time) religious practices been kept almost intact (Powdermaker, 1939).
Macon County is typical of that part of the Black Belt which has clung most to
the conditions of the old days. Macon County was acceptable as the "Middle-
town" of Black society.

These churches usually "hold services" (with preaching) on one regular
Sunday in each month—every first Sunday, for example. This situation exists
because one church alone is unable to pay a preacher a full salary. Consequently, a minister usually pastors four churches and preaches one Sunday a
month at each church.

METHODOLOGY

The initial survey uncovered much interesting information on the Black man
and many allusions to Black preaching; but, more significant to the investigator, it revealed that no detailed study with recordings had been made of genuine
old-fashioned preaching among Blacks. From the beginning, it was felt that
only by means of the recording machine could these sermons be put down
accurately. Shorthand could not be depended upon. Yet, the sermons had to be
taken down as delivered because this type of minister does not (often cannot)
write his sermon. It was agreed, then, that the recording machine had to be
used.

The following plan was followed:

(1) Study literature pertaining to the folkways, religion, beliefs, etc. of the audiences in the Black churches in Macon County.

(2) Attend church services to
    (a) record a representative number of sermons;
    (b) observe the practices of each preacher as to gestures, etc.
(3) Confer with each preacher and some of his members to learn the minister's training, preparation for a particular sermon, etc.
(4) Make the interpretation of Black preaching on the basis of accumulated data.

The original plan of procedure was followed closely, despite many difficulties. The Fort Valley State College purchased a Victor recording machine, and the college president kindly made the equipment available for recording Negro sermons over a period of three months.

Fortunately, Macon County is only a few miles from Fort Valley State College, where the author, during the summer of the recordings, was teaching a class in the Summer School's English Workshop. The students in this group were teachers from the high schools and grade schools of Georgia, and many of them came from Macon County. They knew where the churches were located, whether or not the churches had electricity, when preaching was "held," the denominations of the various churches, the ministers' names, and other information. This was very important, but even more important was the fact that these summer school teachers were known in the various communities in Macon County. Having them as members of the visiting party made it less likely to destroy the normalcy of the preaching situation. Rural teachers in Georgia often attend church services regularly; therefore, these teachers from Macon County were a part of the church audiences and were not considered strangers or outsiders.

Caution along this line was most important. An outsider has a difficult time learning anything about the inner thoughts and beliefs of Blacks in the Black Belt. They smile and act "nice" and the outsider thinks he has the facts. But the truth is often concealed. There are numerous sociological "investigations" which are supposed to reveal facts about the Black man; many of them only confuse the facts. As a Black who was born on a cotton plantation in the heart of the Black Belt and who grew up picking cotton and plowing as a typical "Black Belt" Black before leaving for Tuskegee Institute, the author knew this to be true from experience. It would be all but impossible for a white man to record sermons in Macon County without destroying the normalcy of the situation. (To make a successful study of the county, Raper, a white man, had to live in the county for the greater part of a year.) It was fortunate for this study that the author was able to joke with the people before church, talk their language in church and Sunday School, sing and pray and, in general become one of them.

The English Workshop Group and the author's wife, Anna Howard Russell Pipes, became the planning board for the recordings; Black preaching in Macon County became their project. First, it was agreed that, since of the 130 or more Black churches in Macon County, 78 were Missionary Baptist, 20 were Primitive Baptist, and 15 or 20 were Methodist, the six sermons to be recorded might be: 3, Missionary Baptist; 2, Primitive Baptist and 1, Methodist. We became known as the "Preaching Group."

The group left Fort Valley early on Sunday mornings and journeyed to the chosen church in time for Sunday School. Usually the investigator had to teach Sunday School (not a new experience for him) and the other members of the "Preaching Group" mixed with the church people and made friends. After these preliminaries, it was generally an easy matter to obtain permission to make the recording. Then the apparatus was set up outdoors and out of sight; only the microphone was visible to the audience during the recording. When there was a minister's study near the pulpit, it was used to house the apparatus; when it rained, the apparatus was set up inside the group automobile, which was parked close to the rear of the church.

The greatest difficulty in carrying out the recording project was due to the war and was beyond the power of this board: (1) recording discs (because of their rubber base) became almost unobtainable; the regular price doubled and tripled and then were not obtainable at any price; (2) gasoline rationing had come to Georgia. The four gallons per week would hardly take the group to some places in Macon County and back to Fort Valley. One student in the group was a minister himself and had an "X" card; thus he saved the project.

After the sermon was recorded, invariably the recorder was asked to play back the services and the sermon. The minister and the audience (now no longer religiously emotional) laughed and enjoyed hearing themselves. Frequently someone remarked, "Dat's jest whut he sed!" Others considered it "wonderful" that a member of their race could make records.

It is not likely that the recording tended to destroy the normalcy of the preaching situation to any great degree. Once or twice there was some artificiality at first, but the ministers and the audiences always accepted us or forgot about our presence when the "spirit" touched them. The recordings caught the spontaneity of the preaching and the reaction of the audience.

SERMONS[1]

SERMON III: "JOHN THE BAPTIST—A VOICE CRYING IN THE WILDERNESS"

It's very pleasant to be present here with you all today. Short service if possible. Got me kinda run-up; Communion at Smith Chapel, to preach Anniversary Sermon. Not feeling good. Ben on road, two weeks of service. Journeyed all night to git home. Don't feel good; got headache. You all peach-struck[2]; you all tired; been "gwine to it." Since you been "gwine to it" and am tired and I been "gwine to it" and am tired, don't 'spect too much. Omitted

Sunday School. Kinda late; hafta bear with you 'cause I know you ti'ed. *(Reads from the Bible in such a manner that one hardly can understand a word.)*

"In those days came John Baptist, preaching in the wilderness—*(of Judea).*[3] And saying, Repent ye: for the kingdom of heaven is at hand. For this is he that was spoken of by the prophet Esaias, saying, *The voice of one crying in the wilderness, Prepare* ye the way of the Lord, make his paths straight . . . (Matthew 3:1-17.)

"Then was Jesus led up of the spirit into the wilderness to be tempted of the devil. And when he had fasted forty days and forty nights, he was afterward an hungered. And when the tempter came to him, he said, If thou be the Son of God, command that these stones be made bread. But he answered and said, It is written, Man shall not live by bread alone, but by every word that proceedeth out of the mouth of God."[4] (Matthew 4:1-4.)

John was a preacher, baptizing folks. John the Baptist *(Loud cry of a baby in the audience.)*—and he was preaching to folks telling them about repentance of sin. Men don't lack you to tell them that.

Revival meeting about here. Been helping a man who gwine to help us. Gave me swell time down there. Only one thing: didn't have the spirit you got. *(Amens.)* I knocked 'round there. He will help us. We don't want to treat him no way but royal. If you want to be helped, have to help somebody. We wont to put him on a good revival. He got a home right there at home next to mine. If he don't treat me right, he's right there where I can hear what he say. *(Chuckles.)* We start now to make our aim. Five dollars or eight dollars ain't gwine to speak to no good preacher. Ten dollars ain't gwine to speak to no preacher. He gwine to preach! Every time I bring a man here, he better preacher'n me. *("No, he ain't," from the audience.)*

John was a preacher; preach 'pentance of sins. I *(have taken in a)* number of devils since I been here. Whether they converted or not, I don't know. I like that they sit down. But you'll do. Talk to me now. *(Asking for audience response.)* Them little black places dere ain't no good if you can just sit down. *(Humor; refers to the black faces of the audience.)* Consecrate myself now. *(Get serious.)* Get fair with you. I ain't got no need to come here; no one's a Christian here. Benches can't say, "Amen." You all can hear, can't yer? But John was a preacher and he went down there by himself. Wasn't no crowd down dere when he got dere.

Jesus said, "Lift Me up from the earth and I draw all men unto Me. And I draw all men unto Me." In the life you live—some us lives mighty—lift Him up. We live it while we at the church, in the church, in your songs, your moans, and your groans. Lift Him up. Let's see—er—John went down there and lift Him up. Jesus came to him and talked to him and when the Tempter came to Him, "If Thou the Son of Man, turn these rocks to bread."

He answered, "Man shall not live by bread alone." Testing Jesus, showing Him all the good things, calling Him in question. Ef he done got hungery, "Then make bread outta them stones lying around the mountain, jest like yer see 'em. Look at 'em!"

Then He got hungry, and they say to Him, "If Thou be the Son of God, command that these stones be made bread." Ain't that what he say? Preach it out there with me. I know what I'm talkin' 'bout; you too!

They thought that a fast change Him and carry Him their way. Some folks, if dey carry you their way, it's all right; ain't got nothin' to do for you if dey can't. After done been to wilderness, fast and pray. "Fast" mean don't eat, don't drink. After that, at a certain time, He got hungry. He thought *(The Tempter did.)* dat a fine time, fine time, fine chance to change Him—change His idea, change His mind—and he didn't stay 'way! You know, some folks belong to the church; long's dey can't carry you dey way, dey have nothin' for you to do. Ain't dat right? Now dat's de Lawd's turf! But as long as dey git you to do what dey want, dey wid you.

After he'd taken Him on the pinacke of dat temple, then He got hungry. He got—let me tell you, He don't eat, don't drink—after that, at a certain time, He got hungry, see? He got hungry. Then he[5] say that "this is my time." We're on our way. "Hungry; got nothin' to eat, but He says He's the Son of God." He said, "If you Christ, you outta prove it! You talk and don't prove it. Doing! He said that He God's Son; He always been with His Father; He hungry; got nothin' to eat and got no money and, quite natural, He'll yield to it." (You know, sometimes a fellow take things off people he wouldn't do it, but it's conditions.) Conditions make you do things that you wouldn't do. If conditions didn't have us so 'tight', have us going, don't you know you wouldn't work all day and all night Saturday? *(Amens.)*[6] Our conditions! Conditions! You look right at yer God sometime folks. God! Jesus look right at that rock. Rocks! Rock's something hard; something you can't bite; danger to swallow (Conditions make you do things that you wouldn't do, don't you know.) Rock's hard; bust fellow's brains out. "Turn to bread; make bread out of these" . . . .

John, forerunner of Jesus Christ, born of Elisha, come before Jesus Christ advertising Jesus Christ. One hundred years before His coming, Ezekiel—David say likewise. Daniel says he saw Him as a stone tore out of a mountain. "I'll give him all power." Ezekiel saw Him as a wheel; Ezekiel saw Him as a wheel comin' from—teeming. One Ezekiel saw Him; kept spying things—spectacle of force. Wheel in a wheel, little in big, Matthew—Luke—John—He's coming. John then grew up; maturity come up.

Don't know how much done in a run of a day. Lotta cussin' done in a run of a day; lotta disaster done in a run of a day; so much disaster done in a run of a day; no end to lying in the run of a day. Here's a day; another day. Grow—one day—days seem—. John Baptist preached in wilderness; say he go there by himself, holding up Jesus. Preached only one text. I'm got to git 'nother text every time I come here. Give up world; give 'self to God. Then you see Him, shall find the kingdom of Heaven at hand. He talk about Jesus; he talk about Jesus.

I know what I's telling you 'bout. "The Rose of Sharon, Knight of the Mornin' Star, come down to be ruler of the day. Kingdom of Heaven is at hand; Jesus not far off; always there to come to your need." That was spoke about by the prophet, the one crying in the wilderness: "Prepare ye the way of the Lord; make His paths straight; prepare the way for Him." Oh, brother, we ought to walk in such a life that somebody else ought to be prepare' through you for the Kingdom of God, the Kingdom of Heaven.

Heaven! I feel like it's a very splendid place. Heaven! I feel like it's the best place ever I have known. Wherever you at—in your state, in your field—when dat spirit of God hit you, you feel like you in Heaven right dare. You—ain't you never got happy? By yourself? You just done forgot everything and—and God knows you just feel like you in Heaven right then and there. *(Amens.)* Heaven is a spiritual place, spirit place. And Heaven make His paths straight—er—first why—.

Some folks say, "I'm a straight man myself; I'm a straight woman." Oh-oh-oh-oh, just follow on down the line; you just go her way; you'll find out whether she's straight or no. You'll find out whether she's straight or no, brother. You just deal with a man; you'll find out; you'll find out he's crooked as can be. Don't make 'em no crookeder'n him. He—. A straight man or woman don't care what time, when or where they are, they want to do right, want to walk out-right, plain before the world. Not ashamed of their lives; "I'm living straight." I ain't talking about walking straight and calmly, but your life! Straight! Straight! I ain't talkin. . . .

Forty days, forty nights—I told yo' what fasting mean. They got hungry. Bible said they tempted them. They—call Son of God, commanded stone be made bread. Testing—Jesus said, "Man, man shall not live by bread alone." Ain't dat true, man? *(The audience chants: "Man shall not live by bread alone.")* Man, God's word good. Hungry soul, hear somebody sing and pray. Certain, man can't get filled till he harken.

Uncle Sam calling for me; mighty war on calling for me. Dis last remark to you. Sit on a high hill, sit on a high hill—East and West—Lilly of the Valley—. Things of the world, things of the world, things of the world. This world—. Yes—oh, Jesus! Oh, Jesus! Sundown—. Pinackle of temple—. Lily of the Valley—. Beautiful things. "All this is mine, all this is mine. It is mine, it is mine, it is mine." Oh, Lord! "I tell you what you do now, if you just fall down and worship me."

"Get behind!" My Lord! God got His eyes on you. See all you do. Midnight! Save Jesus,[7] Save Jesus. Died on Calvary Hill. Save Jesus, save Jesus, save Jesus. Hint to the wise. Save Jesus. Get free. Save Jesus. Leper—save Jesus— take up your bed and go home. Save Jesus. Writing on the ground. Save Jesus, Man to depend on when trouble come. Put truth to him *(Devil)*and he go away. Truth breaks down things; truth washes down things. Last day—disciples— this Friday—took Him this night, took Him this night—all night long—now before Pilate. Judas, as he betrayed—little money—Judas as he betrayed, told 'em with a kiss. (Kiss ain't so good.) Judas, as he betrayed Jesus, betrayed with a kiss. Mighty man.

Hold it *(the spirit,)* hold it! Sometimes makes you cry, sometimes makes you cry, sometimes makes you pray, sometimes makes you moan, sometimes makes you right-living. If it makes you cry, I'll be with you, will not forsake you. Mother cry. Father fine. Everybody thinks you git it. Hold it. *(Moaning.)* Go with you to graveyard. He makes you your dying bed. Mercy! Hold it. *(Sings.)* I been had hold Him a long time; He ain't never let me down.

'Tis on cross, Friday evening. Lord! Right there Sunday morning soon, Sunday morning soon *(Christ)* rose out of the grave. Soon, soon, *(Sings it.)* soon *(Shouting in the audience–climax begins)*; watches 'round grave; felt like dead man on to himself. Oh—oh, knocked off dying smile; put back in one corner of grave. Angel sitting on Heavenly grave holding God's hand. Sat right there; nobody in the grave; saw it standing gaping open. He not there; somebody done stole Him away. I see Him go back. John go down to grave, go down to grave, go down to grave, go down to grave. Look-a-yonder, look-a-yonder; who do you see? Who you see? Jesus! Jesus! "I looked for Jesus, but shook and tremble." Jesus! Rocks began to roar. Jesus! "Got to tell my brother." Jesus! "I'm going before day."

Ahhhhhhh! Ahhhhhhh! *(Climax! General confusion.)*

Got my *(Pause.)* . . . in your soul. Got to cry sometime. Know I been born again. Git off by 'self and cry. My soul, *(Audience moans, "My soul.")* My soul have Savior. Have trouble and tribulation; sometimes afflicted; have to crawl into your home. Farewell; Farewell! *(Uniformed ushers come to administer to the shouting ladies.)* For motherless child, nowhere to go, nobody to go to. Fatherless child . . . *(Leaves pulpit and comes down to the audience.)* My! My! Don't you feel lonely sometime in world by yourself? Give me your hand. *(Picks up a tune on "Give me your hand." Audience joins in singing.)* Lord, give me your hand. Won't He lead you? *(Talking now.)* Won't He take care of you, chillun? Be consolation for you? My, my Lord! I done tried! I know He *do* care of you, preserve your soul, and den what I like about You, carry you home. Here rain wouldn't fall on you. Beautiful land. Gwine to sing and open de doors of the church.

OLD-TIME PREACHING

People listen attentively to a speaker if they feel that his message vitally concerns them. Are the speaker's ideas worthy of their sincere considerations? If they are, the speaker may be assured of their interest and goodwill. The emotions and the basic beliefs—friendship, duty, honor, fear, shame, emulation, patriotism, compassion—are the stuff of which emotional or pathetic appeal is made. These are the elements of emotional proof. Stripped of the unparalleled emphasis upon this appeal, old-time Black preaching is not unique. But, as James Weldon Johnson (1932) declared, the old-time Black preacher "had the power to sweep his hearers before him; and so himself was often swept away." This was the original old-time Black preacher. Do the original elements of pathetic proof appear in Macon County sermons? What is the nature of the new influence?

This question suggests the role of pathetic (emotional) appeal with the old-time Black audience. Blacks keep this emotional light burning within themselves constantly—in their moans, in their spirituals, and in their prayers; as they work the fields or walk the roads; as they shy down the streets of the country town or bow into some country store (always fearful of the Lords of the South and of Judge Lynch). They come to church with this emotional spark already within them; they only want the minister to fan it into a flame—to encourage them to let this light set them on fire with shouts and groans. This is their emotional escape from an impossible world; this action of shouting and moaning and laughing and crying relieves them. Therefore, a consideration of pathetic appeal with such people resolves itself into a determination of the methods the Black minister employs to fan these emotional sparks into flames. The audience's knowledge of the Bible (the chief source of information) equalled that of the speaker; the congregation and the minister share the same religious ideas. Therefore, this is not an intellectual occasion; this is not a time for thinking. The problem becomes one of arousing the emotions, of helping the tired, subdued Black man to associate his trials, sorrows, and joys with those of the Biblical characters.

The genuine old-time preacher knows that his mission in part is to fan emotions into flames. He accomplishes this by leading the audience to concentrate upon "getting happy" by suggestion (directly or indirectly)—through action, by the audience and by the minister (delivery). This initial action suggests the climactic emotional state which the audience and the minister seek.

The old-time Black preacher, although a master hypnotist, follows in the footsteps of great orators when he appeals to his audience's basic beliefs—Biblical ideas which have been adjusted to fit the descendants of Africans and of American slaves. The conception of God is at the center of these beliefs; to the

Black man, God is mysterious and all-powerful. The Black man's attitude toward God makes the congregation susceptible to certain emotional appeals. This preacher appeals to his audience's great *admiration* and *joy over* the power of God. Revealing how vital to them was his subject, ministers dwell on the audience's *love* for God and their *hope* for a new life to come.

The *fear* of God is another emotion to which the old-time Black preacher appeals:

"My Lord! God got His eyes on you! See all you do."
"Have mercy now; oh, Jesus, have mercy now."

Fear has consistently dogged the footsteps of the Black man—as an African, as an American slave, and now as a second-class citizen. Observe how a minister produces shouting by appealing to the *fear* of God:

"Yonder He come. . . . God Almighty. . . . Thunder, your conscience; lightning in Your hand. . . . Everybody is gwine ter pray now!" *(Audience shouts wildly.)*

There is suggestion too in the last statement:

"You may be too proud *(Suggests the preacher.)* to pray now; too proud to shout now, but you *will* shout and pray when God comes, so why not now?"

The people agree, and they do shout and pray. The audience's *fear* of God often approaches *awe* under the spell of the preacher's description of God's work.

But unadulterated *fear of death* is the emotion to which a minister appeals. The minister, even when not striking directly at fear-producing descriptions of death, likes to talk about things with which *death* has some connection. Any mention of the grave or of death serves the purpose—to produce shouting. Jesus' triumph over the great mystery, *death,* is most effective. The Biblical story of the strange death of Almighty God's Son is used frequently:

Christ "kept on dying *(on the cross)*. He never stopped dying."

The preacher often stimulated the emotions of his audience by telling of his "call" to preach. In all instances, when the members of the audience are excited and open to the mildest suggestion, they are thinking of their own trials, joys, and sorrows, and their emotional condition is heightened by the rhythmical delivery and their own actions. For example, when the minister, after telling the Biblical story of Joseph the Dreamer, says:

"I seed Him . . ., a shield over here one Sunday mornin'. He was takin' on board. . . . And I *dream, chillun,*" *(Sings the last two words; the audience joins in. Shouting.)*

he unlocks the door of his audience's world with the words *"dream, chillun,"* as did Martin Luther King in his "I Had a Dream" sermon. They too had trials and problems (like Joseph); they too were *dreaming* and hoping for a better day to come. When the preacher says "dream, chillun," he stimulates thoughts and emotions within the audience which lie too deep for words. The people understand; they shout. "How long" is the unlocking key to the door of frustration when a minister moans:

> *"How long?* How long must I work in the vineyard?"

The words "how long" suggest to the Black his apparently endless chain of trials. How often he has wondered *how long* the Lord would permit his chosen servant to be mistreated in this world below. *"How long."* Pent up emotions overflow. Shouting.

WHEN IT COMES OUR TIME TO DIE[8]

The Black man's old-time religious prayer is not confined to the church. Outside the church, it keeps the emotional flame alive. It replaces the sermon at home, at the sick-bed, and at "wakes." Blacks in the Black Belt still observe the old custom of sitting up all night with the dead. Friends and relatives visit the house of the deceased on the night of the "wake"; the body is in plain view, and the night is spent in talking of death, of the dead person (especially, how the "end"—death—came), and in drinking coffee or something stronger.

This prayer given at a wake in the Black Belt is not unusual—and demonstrates too the new influences, which fight against the prayer's old-time emotional appeal:

> "Oh, Gawd, we come this evenin' beared down wid the sorrows of this worl.' We come as paupers to Thy th'one o' grace. We been down in the valley o' the shadder, an' our hearts is heavy this evenin,' Lord. Thou's done thundered fo'th Thy will. Thou's done took from out our mist one o' Yo' lambs. Thou's done took a good brother who's done lived his 'lotted time an' died, Gawd, like we all mus' die. Ummmmmmmmmmmm. Thou's done come into this house o' sons an' wid Yo' own han', Yo' own grat han', Gawd—Ummmmmmmmmmmmm—Thou's done dashed down the vessel outa what Yo' po'ed life into them. Thou's done took a father an' a gran'-father. Thou's done beared down hearts. Thou's done put burdens on 'em. Thou's done whupped 'em wid stripes. 'Member dese hearts, great Lawd. Relieve 'em. You know when t' suns's been a-shinin' too long an' the earth's all parched an' barren, You sen's Yo' rain, Lord. You relieve the earth. When wars rage, like the one ragin' now, an' mens dies an' makes widders an' orfins, den, in Yo' own good time, Gawd—Yo' precious time Ummmmmmm— You sen's peace. You takes the burden off'n the hearts o' nations. An' You promise', Father, by the sweetflowin' blood o' Jesus, to rescue the perishin', suckle the needy, give health to the ailin' . . ."

> (He did not pause at a piercing scream from Jamie. *She is shouting.* His extended fingers worked spasmodically, as if each had a life, independent of him.)

"An' sen' balm to the hearts o' sufferin'. Sen' it now, Lord. Let it flow like the healin' waters o' Gilead, an' ease the burden o' dese hearts broken by the fulfillin' o' Yo' almighty will. Amen."

(The preacher opened his eyes and looked around as he lowered his arms, shooting his cuffs as he did so. The three brothers stared at spots about six inches beyond their toes. One corner of his thick mouth drawn in a hard snarl, Paul lifted the pitcher *(of whiskey)* from the table and drank. In the other room there was a general snuffling and loosening of throats. Walter was the first to recover.)

"That was a fine prayer, Rev'ren'," he said. "Mighty fine."

"Thank you, brother."

. . . "That's fine. That's jus' fine,' the preacher said pompously. "Uncle Henry's *(Refers to the dead man.)* goin, a smile up there wid Gawd tomorrer. I'm aimin' to do him proud."

With that, he went back into the other room. Neely closed the door.

"He can lay a pow'ful prayer." [Redding, 1942].

The prayer, like the sermon, appeals to the emotions of gratitude to God, compassion, fear of death, fear of God, sorrow, shame; it, too, employs suggestion.

Like the prayer, the singing is important in stimulating the emotions. The hymn (like the spiritual) is really a blending of emotions. The words themselves are unintelligible unless they are "lined." That is, someone states a line or two before the audience sings them; the audience sings and pauses while additional lines are stated; the singing continues in this manner until the end; the audience is seated part of the time and stands part of the time. Even after the song is "lined," the words are so run together in the long-meter fashion that they are not distinguishable. Such singing is an emotional experience, like an instrumental rendition. Spirituals carry the same emotional charge. The singing is so important in setting the stage emotionally that the sermon is almost inconceivable without it.

DuBois (1903) said that "three things characterize the religion" of the Black man: the preacher, the music, and the frenzy. "The music is that plaintive rhythmic melody, which is touching in minor cadences, which, despite caricature and defilement, still remains the most original and beautiful expression of human life and longing yet born on American soil. Sprung from the African forests, where its counterpart can still be heard, it was adapted, changed, and intensified by the tragic soul-life of the slave, until, under the stress of law and whip, it became the one true expression of a people's sorrow, despair, and hope."

The old-time Black man is indeed a master of this art of emotional appeal. Even the order of services builds toward the desired emotional climax of shouting. Observe the order of services for the sermon, "Thou Shalt Love the Lord Thy God:"

1. *Song:* "My Faith Looks Up to Thee."
2. *Prayer:* A deacon thanks the Lord for having permitted *death* to leave them in the world "a little longer." *(The minister did not ordain the use of these exact words, but he knows the content of the average Negro old-time prayer.)*
3. *Song:* "I Love Jesus." *(A perfect selection.)*
4. *Song:* "Come, Thou Fount of Every Blessing."
5. *Hymn:* "Father, I Stretch My Hands to Thee."
6. *Responsive Reading from the Bible.*
7. *Song:* More of "Father, I Stretch My Hands to Thee."
8. *Prayer:* A preacher thanks the Lord for sparing them. The goodness of God is stressed.
9. *Song:* "Where He Leads Me I Will Follow."
10. *Scripture Reading:* "Thou Shalt Love the Lord Thy God."

In the order of services a prominent place is given to the prayer. Much can be said of the importance of prayer in emotional appeal. The prayer (or prayers) precedes the sermon and, using many of the same appeals to the emotions that are to be found in the sermons, serves to prepare the way, to set the mood, for the ultimate emotional frenzy caused by the sermon. The following prayer reveals the importance of the prayer for pathetic appeal:

(The congregation, bowed, hums the last verse of "My Faith Looks Up to Thee" as the deacon moves searchingly and rhythmically into his prayer.) "Dear Lawd, we come befo' Thee and ask Thee ter stand by us. Thank Thee for ev'ry thing Thou's did for us. Christ, essemble between these four walls; git in the hearts uv men and women, boys and girls, Thou art God an' God alone.

"Since the last time we's bowed, we's done things that we ought not uv done, an' we's left things undone what we ought uv done. Rule over Heav'n and earth; rule over these people down here, the sick an' afflicted and weary. And bind us one to another.

"Now, Lawd, when it come our time to *die,* pray You receive us into Thy kingdom an' give us souls a resting place. Amen."

This prayer, given by another minister from the pulpit, revealed the effectiveness of prayer in emotional appeal: They "warm up" the emotions of the audience for the sermon.

THE PREACHER: MAN OF GOD

Some Blacks declared that the magnetism and power of the preacher solely are responsible for a "good meetin'," that the minister's ability to affect the emotions of the audience accounted for the shouting and the frenzy. Few observers accepted logical argument as an important element in old-time Black preaching.

The audience's conception of the Black minister as a "Man of God" is obviously a persuasive element. Even before the preacher speaks, his listeners are in a receptive mood, for the old-time Black preacher does not "just go to school" and then begin preaching; he is "called of God to preach." But what forces and influences develop this "man of God?" What is the nature of being "called?" What character qualities of the preacher make him persuasive? How does the "Man of God" differ from other Christians?

The preparation of the "man of God" often begins before birth, with the dedication of the child to God by a pregnant mother. Others are called after living a life of sin. There are "good" Negroes and "bad" Negroes who become ministers. The background of the "bad" Negro gives him ethical appeal because of the contrast between his new life and his old, "sinful" life. The people reason, "As bad as old Henry was, he surely must have been 'called' or he never would have become a preacher." Both types of preachers are "called" and both have appeal because of what they are.

Booker T. Washington (1924) implied that the Negro preacher is not always sincere in his claim that he has been called to preach. He tells the story of the Negro who, working along in the cotton field one day, suddenly stopped and cried in a pulpit voice:

> De sun am so hot and dis Nigger am so tired, bless my soul, I believe I done been called to preach! Glory!!

A common joke among Blacks is that such-and-such a preacher thought God said, "Go *preach*," when what He really said was, "Go *plow!*"

The character of Black preachers persuades their audiences—despite the moral weakness of some of them. The old-time Black preacher is "a good man." Blacks stress this point: the preacher must not dance, play cards, or drink. Yet some preachers are "the biggest devils" in the church. Members of the church can name the "sweethearts" of such pastors. Occasionally, a "sister's" husband or lover takes a knife or a razor and "cuts up" the minister. Almost every Black knows "dirty jokes" about the minister's lack of morals; it is a common saying that preachers love three things: money, women, and chicken. Yet the old-time Black preacher is respected and honored. (The author knows there are many upright and moral Black ministers. His intention here is not to disparage such ministers or their profession.) His being a "Man of God" is not the full answer. Other elements of his character are important to the understanding of this paradoxical situation.

Perhaps, above all, the old-time Black preacher was superior to his people in intelligence. As James Weldon Johnson (1932) said:

> The old-time preacher was generally a man far above the average in intelligence; he was, not infrequently, a man of positive genius. The earliest of these preachers

must have virtually committed many parts of the Bible to memory through
hearing the scripture read or preached from . . .

Native intelligence gives him leadership, for the old-time preacher lacked
education to give him prestige.

The Black preacher's small income meant that well-educated men did not
pastor these churches. This introduced other characteristics of these ministers.
"Pastoring" three churches, the typical minister received an average $546.60 a
year. He spent about one-sixth for traveling expenses. Even this small amount
was not paid as salary. It was charity. The minister had to "take up collection."
This explained two other characteristics of the preacher: first, why he was
extremely money-conscious and, second, why he must please the audience.
Only a burning desire to be a leader could compensate for this situation.

This *desire to lead* is an important element in the preacher's character; it
often accompanied natural leadership. Perhaps "leadership" is not the proper
word, but certainly these old-time preachers tackled any problem. James W.
Johnson tells of an old Black minister who opened his Bible one Sunday and
read from a rather cryptic passage. He did not understand a word of it, but
(always the leader) he removed his eyeglasses, slammed the Bible shut, stared
down at his respectful and expectant congregation, and said: "Brothers and
sisters, this morning—I intend to explain the unexplainable—find out the
undefinable—ponder over the impossible—and unscrew the inscrutable." Intelligence, leadership ability, and the "man of God" conception serve the Macon County preacher well.

SUMMARY

The methods of persuasion of the Macon County preaching demonstrate that
emotional appeal remains dominant; appeal through the character of the
preacher (the "Man of God") runs a close second. Logical argument is not
entirely absent. Especially in the sermons of the more highly educated ministers, there appear evidences of both inductive and deductive reasoning (at the
less emotional points of the sermon.) The method of instructing the audience
unemotionally is being ushered in by the more highly educated Black ministers.
Another modern influence seems to be the underlying purpose of soliciting
money.

The style of Macon County preaching is basically simple: short words which
are familiar to the audience (with a long word thrown in occasionally for
effect). Sentences are often elliptical (without complete subject and predicate).
Such sentences, however, are joined by conjunctions, to help maintain the
speaker's rhythmical flow of words. Slang and Black dialect (the language of
the audience) form the level of expression. But the style is figurative, with the

use of metaphor, based on the experiences of the audience or drawn from the Bible, taking the lead. The style is narrative—for the listener rather than for the reader. The amount of poetic, Biblical prose is decreasing, perhaps because education (newspapers, magazines, radio) is bringing in new expressions—a condition which is unlike the original complete dependency upon the Bible.

The delivery of the Macon County sermon is most characteristic of earlier old-time Black preaching. Entirely impromptu, it is rhythmical—which helps to heighten the emotions of the minister and the audience. It gains effect by the change from conversational to rhythmical speaking. The delivery is also made more effective by the preacher's appearance, his sincerity, his bombastic gestures, and his many movements in the pulpit. Possibly most important, the preacher's delivery is aided by his masterful modulation and control of his excellent voice. The recorded Macon County sermons indicate that old-time Black preaching today is still a vital part of the Black man's existence. Preaching is still the soul of a frustrated people.

The background of this study of American Blacks, A People in Bondage (from Africa, to American slavery, and to present-day second-class citizenship), explains old-time Black preaching partly as an escape mechanism for a frustrated people. This study also points up two conclusions: (1) the Black race in the United States has made unparalleled progress in normal adjustment (against odds), but the Black man should not expect to exercise first-class American citizenship immediately—unless America herself decides (probably beginning with a Supreme Court decision) to practice true democracy *for all people:* to remove from the American scene the half-century-old concept (based on a ruling of the United States Supreme Court) of "separate-but-equal"; (2) the crying need of the Black race in the United States is for improved leadership, regardless of the time-table of democracy: first-class citizenship for the Black man *now* as his American right.

First-Class Citizenship for the Black Man Now. If the masses of U.S. Blacks are to have their frustration-producing condition eliminated permanently in the near future, America must somehow come to realize the menace to the nation of racial prejudice in a nuclear age; she must realize in deed as well as in word that it is the American creed and law that no man deserves second-class citizenship because of race, color, or previous condition of servitude; she must realize that the best *preparation* for the Black man's wise use of first-class citizenship is to be found in the Black man's *practice* of first-class citizenship.

Long-range first-class citizenship will come to the Black man mainly through the unity of effort on the part of the Blacks themselves; this unity of effort must be used to prepare the race to exercise wisely his rights as a citizen and to prepare the minds of Southern white people to permit such democracy. If the Black man is frustrated because of persecution, the mind of the white man is warped because of the un-American practices of enslaving and degrading the

Black man; Booker T. Washington stated it in this manner: "You cannot hold a man down in a ditch without remaining there yourself."

Freedom for the Black man through unity of effort on the part of Blacks themselves? Is this not the blind leading the blind? Certainly, united action on the part of the Black Belt Blacks is in the distant future, for the Black man (due to his background of bondage) is far from belonging to a race that has solidarity. Old-time Black ministers often declare, "Negroes just won't stick together." As Gunnar Myrdal (1944) shows, however, the masses of a people *must* have education and some degree of economic security before they can unite to improve themselves permanently in a social, economic, and political way. The Black man as a group is still a semi-illiterate proletariate and, hence, cannot be expected to unite to improve the masses of his people until a sizable group of Blacks are both more highly educated and more economically secure. The Black man himself cannot make this a fact within the near future, nor is the white man likely to clear his mind of prejudice voluntarily within the near future. American democracy never had a greater command—for when the Black man is denied first-class citizenship, American democracy as a whole is debased.

Undoubtedly, the old-time Black preacher is *the* Black leader today; it is to him that the great majority of Blacks in this country look for guidance. The degreed and trained Black educators, ministers, writers, et al., should not delude themselves into thinking that they are the true Black leaders. The masses of Blacks seldom get to know these "leaders" and even when the opportunity does bring the highly trained leader into contact with the average Black the latter either does not understand the "highbrow" leader or distrusts his motives—and not always unjustly. But the old-time preacher is "one of the flock." He is trusted, listened to, and understood. Therefore, the crying need in improving the Black masses (whether first-class citizenship comes immediately or in the distant future) is for improved Black leadership.

As Richardson (1947) pointed out in his study, improvement of the Black ministry can do much to improve the condition of the Black masses, but the author is dubious of the leadership of any Black who is economically dependent on the goodwill of the prejudiced white persons (which eliminates many college presidents and teachers) or who is economically dependent upon the masses of Blacks (which seems to minimize the effectiveness of the leadership of the average Black minister, who is dependent upon Blacks for his income).

Without a feeling of despair or pessimism (but trying to read the timetable correctly, which is essential for the Black race in making the journey himself to first-class citizenship), the author does not conceive of Blacks possessing within the immediate future the educational and economical improvement necessary to wrest first-class citizenship from a reluctant country—and the country will be reluctant for some time to come. Will the greatest democracy on earth meet the challenge? Will the "Land of the Free" return to *her* old-time religion, *freedom for all people:* "All men are created equal and from that equal creation they derive rights inherent and unalienable, among which are the preservation of life and liberty and the pursuit of happiness?"

If America really wants to return to *her old-time* religion of freedom for all people, then let her say in deed—"Amen, Brother!" ("Benches can't say 'Amen.' You all can hear, can't yer?")

NOTES

1. Complete transcriptions of each of the sermons may be found in Say Amen, Brother! (Pipes, 1951).

2. It was peach-packing season in Georgia and most of the audience had worked until very late Saturday night, really until Sunday morning.

3. These words, like many others in this passage, he omitted. He often mumbled. It was discovered later that he could not read very well.

4. It appeared that the minister read on and on until he struck something in the Bible that appealed to him, something that would serve as his subject; entirely extemporaneous.

5. The Tempter.

6. He means the sermon, the emotional part, is getting underway.

7. Observe how "Save Jesus" becomes a refrain.

8. The minister, closing Sermon IV: "May the Lord bless us, may He help us, and may He save us when it comes our time to die. Amen."

9. Sermon III.

REFERENCES

BACON, L. W. (1898) A History of American Christianity. New York: Scribner.

BRAWLEY, B. (1921) A Short History of the American Negro. New York: Macmillan.

DUBOIS, W. E. B. (1903) Souls of Black Folk. Chicago: McClurg.

FRANKLIN, J. H. (1947) From Slavery to Freedom. New York: Alfred Knopf.

FRAZIER, E. F. (1939) The Negro Family in the United States. Chicago: University of Chicago Press.

GOOD, A. (1926) Sociology and Education. New York: Harper.

HERSKOVITS, M. (1930) "The Negro in the new world." American Anthropologist 32 (November).

JOHNSON, J. W. (1932) God's Trombone, Seven Negro Sermons in Verse. New York: Viking.

MYRDAL, G. (1944) An American Dilemma. New York: Harper.

O'GORMAN, T. (1895) A History of the Roman Catholic Church in the United States. New York: Christian Literature.

PARK, R. (1919) "The conflict and fusion of cultures with special reference to the Negro." Journal of Negro History 4, 2 (April).

PIPES, W. H. (1951) Say Amen, Brother! New York: William-Frederick Press.

POWDERMAKER, H. (1939) After Freedom. New York: Viking.

RAPER, A. A. (1936) Preface to Peasantry: A Tale of Two Black Belt Counties. Chapel Hill: University of North Carolina Press.

REDDING, J. S. (1942) No Day of Triumph. New York: Harper.

RICHARDSON, H. (1947) Dark Glory. New York: Friendship Press.

TURNER, L. D. (1949) Africanisms in the Gullah Dialect. Chicago: University of Chicago Press.

WASHINGTON, B. T. (1924) Up from Slavery. New York: Doubleday.

WOODSON, C. (1921) The History of the Negro Church. Washington, DC: Associated Publishers.

———— (1925) Negro Orators and Their Orations. Washington, DC: Associated Publishers.

———— (1936) The African Background Outlined. Washington, DC: Associated Publishers.

4

AFRICAN-AMERICAN FAMILY LIFE
An Instrument of Culture

WADE W. NOBLES

INTRODUCTION

Given the critical importance of child-rearing practices and orientation in shaping the personalities, behaviors, and values of future citizens in any society, the parent-child relationship should be viewed as one of the major points at which the family's obligation to the state and the state's obligation to the family is crystallized. Unfortunately, a clear understanding of African-American parent-child relationships and their subsequent importance in our understanding of the African-American family's obligation to the state and the state's obligation to the African-American family has been clouded by racism.

A proper understanding of the strengths of African-American families, the difficulties they face, and the ways in which they are affected by public policy is confused and clouded by several co-mingling issues, among which the most prominent is racism. The issue of racism totally masks the understanding of African-American culture itself, to say nothing of the family as an instrument of culture.

It has been racism, primarily, that has allowed the guiding assumption of the "innate" inferiority of African people to go almost completely unchallenged in over 200 years of research and scientific investigation. It has been primarily the research guided by this assumption that has resulted in the examiners of African-American family life consistently offering evidence, information, theory, and analyses that focused solely on the so-called problems inherent in African-American family systems. Blinded by this racist assumption, these researchers have created what is the overwhelming historical character of the field: that the African-American family system was (is) an organization inherently laden with problems and inadequacies. Similarly, though far more subtle and sophisticated, the new thrust toward highlighting and examining only the African-American middle-class, well-to-do family creates the false image that the socioeconomic gap between African-Americans and white Americans has closed, that African-Americans are no longer victims of poverty and racism, and that all African-American people have benefited from the civil rights struggle. The basis of this false image is just as racist as the false image that all African-American families were on welfare. In a very sophisticated way, by overprojecting the image that there is nothing "wrong" with the African-American family, contemporary scientific researchers have participated in a scheme to simultaneously take away the gains of the 1960s and/or misdirect the blame for the concrete condition of African-American family life. The actuality is that generally there has been a perpetual state of disadvantage for most African-American families, yet the literature or data defines the condition of the African-American family as progressively more advantaged.

One need simply to recognize that our country is still a racist country (ergo: the continued popularity of KKK and Nazi parties) and that to be African-American in a white racist society is problematic by definition. Consequently, the family life of African-American people would be and is characterized by real and definite problems and conditions associated with racism and oppression.

Although a great deal of research has been done, the gap in useful, usable knowledge remains just as wide. In fact, the legacy of white-dominated research and racist scientific investigations has totally prevented us from understanding the nature of African-American family life; and, consequently, as a result of racist research, the understanding of African-American family life has been, in a very real way, held hostage by the intellectual instruments of the socioeconomic, political establishment.

DISCRIMINATION OR SCIENTIFIC COLONIALISM

AFRICAN-AMERICAN FAMILY LIFE HELD HOSTAGE BY WHITE-DOMINATED THINKING

There are two concepts that must be recognized if one is to see the pervasive and insidious nature of the phenomena that negatively affect African-American families. First, one must recognize that discrimination is an act designed to separate individuals or people for the purpose of allowing one group to receive preferential treatment and/or advantage; and second, that in a system characterized by racism and oppression, almost every element or process managed by the racist system is designed primarily to continue and secure the status of the "advantaged" by guaranteeing in all arenas their preferential treatment.

It is not difficult to equate the racist system with the act of holding a thing or a person hostage. The latter is an act designed to keep under one's control the person or thing held in order that the "hostage" can be used to bargain with or in exchange for one's own safety, benefit, or freedom. Combined, the almost total misrepresentation of African-American family life and the almost absolute control of the scientific understanding of African-American family life by non-African thinkers suggests that the African-American family has been and is being held hostage by white-dominated research and scientific studies. Some would argue that African-American families are not being held hostage physically; and, if anything, it is the understanding of African-American family life which is being held hostage. Given the concrete condition of African-American family life, this distinction is debatable.

Given that the first Africans came to these shores as enslaved captives in the mid-1700s, we could legitimately say that African-American families have been held hostage for over 87,000 days. From this historical perspective, one is able to see that the exploitation, domination, and control of African people in this country has been its most constant feature. Hence, it is fair to say that the state of African-American family life has been held hostage while other segments benefited from the disadvantage experienced by African people.

If, for example, one simply notes that white researchers from the early 1700s have consistently argued for and supported (without proof) the notion of African-American family inferiority (see Von Linnaes, 1735; Burmeister, 1835; Galton, 1969; Spencer, 1884; Hall, 1904; Thorndike, 1940; and Terman, 1916), then one is compelled to ask why. Given the prevalence of institutionalized racism in all areas of American life—politics, job opportunities, and education are three of the most noted areas—such a concerted effort suggests that science also was (is) being used as a tool of oppression and control and that indeed the creation of these findings were (are) beneficial, if no more than psychologically, to non-African people in this country. Of course, such information placed African-American people at a decided disadvantage. The African-American family as an area of investigation, for instance, has been examined from almost every conceivable orientation, and in almost every case it has been found to be less than viable (see Frazier, 1932; Bernard, 1966; Jeffers, 1967; Chilman, 1966; Willie, 1970; and Scanzoni, 1971). One cannot, in this regard, dismiss the relationship between the "results" of this line of research and the treatment of African-American families in the society at large.

It is in fact the case that, guided by the assumption that blackness is intrinsically inferior, racist models, theories, and/or orientations coupled with unsophisticated scientific treatments and analyses of African-American family life have not only led to mass confusion and an unusable body of knowledge, they have also translated to the direct maltreatment of African-American families (for example, forced sterilization).

Unfortunately, as long as this country remains racist, the need to hold African-American families hostage will exist and, with it, the continued uncritical adoption of non-African interpretations and/or analytical frameworks which will invariably result in both misdirected analyses of African-American life and blind acceptance of erroneous assumptions and "meanings" that "define" the reality of African-American family life.

This, in effect, is the legacy which we bring to the analyses of African-American life; and this is the legacy from which we must free ourselves as we go forward with the study and understanding of African-American family life.

PARENT-CHILD RELATIONSHIPS HELD HOSTAGE

THE 87,965TH DAY

The analogy of African-American families being held hostage is, of course, designed to refocus our attention on the real condition of African-American life in America and to the fact that, like those who were earnestly concerned about the Americans being held hostage in Iran, we know very little about what happened to them. The knowledge gap we face is extremely wide, even though a huge amount of data has accumulated over the years. The major gap is in studies that honestly reflect the condition of African-American family life and are not guided by various racist assumptions of African inferiority and negativity. The lack of a substantial body of studies (of all types) which from conceptualization to methods, from procedures to analyses, and from conclusions to interpretations, respect and reflect the cultural integrity of African-American family dynamics is the major gap in the field.

Despite this dilemma, there exist several classical contributions (Billingsley, 1968; Staples, 1976; Hill, 1971) which have addressed the mandate to find "What are the strengths?" Though none focused on the more narrow issue of parent-child relationships exclusively, the important works of Robert Hill, Andrew Billingsley, and Robert Staples have served as the cornerstones for the understanding of African-American family strengths. However, one must keep in mind, as did these authors, that to talk only about the strength of the African-American family without simultaneously recognizing that, without this dogged strength and resilience, African-American families would have been shattered and torn apart long ago is tantamount to closing one's eyes to the full complexity of the problem at hand. Given the continued and historical concrete conditions of racism and oppression, it is, in fact, a testimony to our humanity and a miracle of the human spirit that we even have an African-American family left to talk about.

Strengths and Interpersonal Relationships. The benchmark work on African-American family strength is Hill's classic documentation, *The Strength of African-American Families.* The focus of this discussion is interpersonal relationships, particularly parent-child, and the associated family strength found in that arena.

Traditionally, the analyses of parent-child relationships centered on understanding how parents instill in their children particular behavior repertoires, attitudes, and beliefs in their childhood training, child-rearing practices, and socialization strategies. Seldom did the attention turn to an examination of strengths implicit in the parent-child relationship. Though some researchers examined the psychological dispositions and/or behavioral or personality styles that emerged from the parent-child interaction, seldom did they turn their attention to an examination of the strengths and support implicit in the interpersonal relationships (parent-child and others) found in the family.

In his study of the African-American family system, Shimkin et al. (1974) isolated five critical elements of African-American family life that distinguish it from the family structure of other ethnic/racial groups. They noted that the traditional African-American family is a unique cultural form enjoying its own inherent resources. It is comprised of several individual households, with the channels of authority reaching beyond the household units that compose it. In periods of crises and at times of ceremony, the extended family is most visible and provides needed emotional support for its members. The family may (and often does) perform many ritual, social (and psychological) functions, including the education of its young and the adjudication of the family's internal conflicts. Even though some features of the African-American family can be explained "situationally" (that is, are adaptive responses to certain pressures of the moment), or through "borrowing," the underlying structure of the African-American extended family is ultimately traceable to Africa.

Almost ten years prior to Shimkin's work, Billingsley (1968) pointed out that the African-American family unit is itself an element embedded in a larger network of mutually interdependent relationships with the African-American community and the wider (white) society. Billingsley went on to point out that, even though the African-American family system is one institution in a complex of various American institutions, the African-American family cannot be totally understood or interpreted from a general (white) analytical framework. The limits of using a general analytical framework can be seen through an earlier study (Nobles et al., 1976) in which we found that a critical aspect of the parent-child relationship was that parents prepared their children to deal with racism. In fact, the unique child-rearing techniques found in African-American families seem to be geared to prepare the child for a *particular* kind of existence in a hostile racist environment. Children were in effect prepared to take on the appropriate sex and age roles as well as the racial role.

Consistent with Billingsley's conception of interlocking systems, Staples's (1976) work offers a valuable insight into the relation between African-American families and the wider society. Staples suggests that the African-American family has been a sanctuary that protected individuals from the pervasiveness of white racism and provided needed support systems that were unavailable in other majority group institutions. Consequently, the processes in the African-American family promoted and maintained the emotional well-being of its individual members in spite of the wider society.

In *A Formulative and Empirical Study of Black Families* (Nobles et al., 1976), we found that African-American parent-child interactions were characterized by an "atmosphere" or attitude that emphasized strong family ties or orientations, unconditional love, respect for self and others, and the assumed natural goodness of the child. Child-rearing techniques associated with the parent-child bond centered on the unconditional expression of love. That is, parents seldom made their love for their children a reinforcement contingency. The interpersonal relationship between parent and child could, therefore, be characterized by parent anger, punishment, and disappointment as well as the child's mistakes, failure, and misbehavior without canceling out the love associated with the parental-child bond.

A family strength, like the support network or system in which it operates, is any process or network of interactions that aid or help individuals in anticipating, addressing, interpreting, managing, and otherwise successfully responding to their concrete condition or situation. Within this definition, the kinds of elements or features mentioned previously are African-American families' strengths.

Upon further analyses of the interpersonal dynamics of African-American family styles and mental health support systems (see Nobles et al., 1979), five additional strengths were identified, classified, and defined.

Legitimation of Beingness. Through the parent-child (sibling and other familial relationships), the family provides its members with a source of connection, attachment, validation, worth, recognition, respect, and legitimacy. If one is secure in one's own personal meaning, then one is more capable of addressing and responding to complex, vague, and unfamiliar experiences confronted outside the home.

Provision of a Family Code. By providing its members with a "family code" (guidelines for behaving in novel and/or confusing situations), the family, via interpersonal relations, aids its members in interpreting, managing, and responding to both known and undefined situations.

Elasticity of Boundaries. Legitimation of Beingness and the provision of a family code produces an elasticity in African-American family interpersonal relationships. The unbreakable bond and associated rules of conduct give African-American family members the latitude and opportunity to stretch out and develop their own sense of "specialness" without fear of violating the familyhood. In a sense, the phrase or label, "the elasticity of boundaries," is indeed a literal interpretation of this phenomenon, in that family boundaries stretch to accommodate the various expressions of individual styles, personalities, and/or conditions. The sense of almost unconditional permanence or undeniable belonging strengthens family members' ability to respond to their unique concrete condition in ways that satisfy or are peculiar to their individual and personal needs.

The Provisions of Information/Knowledge. This feature gives members the benefit of shared insights and experiences and by so doing strengthens their ability to interpret and understand the events and happenings that affect their lives. The transgenerational mutual sharing of knowledge and experience heightens the individual member's (young and old) ability to address, manage, and respond to the rapidly changing as well as constant conditions in their reality.

Mediation of Concrete Conditions. The family kinships' ability to mediate the conflicts and other concrete conditions affecting its members provides a strength or support so obvious that it barely warrants explication. Clearly, the family's ability to provide its members with concrete aid and pragmatic help and to engage in interpersonal relations around problem solving and decision making (in response to both external and internal issues) while constantly buffering and repairing the damage resulting from racism and oppression directed at its members is a critical strength.

AFRICAN-AMERICAN FAMILY PARENT-CHILD RELATIONSHIP AND OUR OBLIGATION TO THE STATE

Given that African-American children must become adults during a period in which racism, discrimination, and oppression will change disguises and will not simply go away, the family parent-child relationship will have to center on the creation and maintenance of three senses: the sense of history, the sense of family, and the sense of the ultimate supreme power (God).

The sense of history will tell African-American children that they are first and foremost Africans and that we are Africans because of our common cultural orientation which gives us the same sense of the natural universe and human condition that characterizes all African peoples, and we have a common history of racial oppression which resulted in shared victimization. The sense of history will help African-American children to recognize that as Africans they must and will continue to struggle for the liberation of the human condition from oppression and racism. The sense of history will help them understand that the natural human condition is one of freedom and growth, and that any person, people, or invention which denies their freedom and potential to grow should be opposed and fought against. History will tell them that to resist and struggle against such a force is the only natural human response. To do otherwise is to conspire in the creation of their own dehumanization. The sense of history will also tell them that "the struggle" is by definition a human struggle and not an individual, personalized battle. Finally, the sense of history will tell African-American children that the enemies of human growth and freedom, wherever they are found in the world, are easily recognized by their behavior and attitude. History will show them that the historical enemy of our people is still our enemy today and that until that enemy changes its basic response to other human beings, it will always remain our enemy.

The sense of family is really the specific application of the sense of history previously defined. The sense of family will explicitly give African-American children the understanding that their identity and being is in the family—that, unlike the families of other groups, our family is a source of strength. It is not a burden to individual aspirations. In fact, in understanding the sense of family, African-American children will also understand that they will expand in personal strength as the family expands in size. The sense of family will give them the security of knowing that no matter what happens, the family love and protection will be unconditional and ever-present. The sense of family will help them realize that in their people (and not necessarily things) they will find a common meaning (definition) and a common ground.

The final sense that should emerge from the parent-child interaction is a sense of supreme being (God). The importance of formalized religion is in its ritual, which helps to replenish the necessity and the belief in the supreme force. It is important that African-American children engage in the religious ritual. It is even more important that African-American children understand, respect, and obey the supreme spirit which makes them human. The sense of the supreme being will help African-American children realize that there is a power and a will that is greater than all else. The sense of the force will tell them that the power is in us all and that its natural laws must be obeyed. Knowing that the force is in them will help them realize that in being the manifestation of the supreme force, they have no limitation—as long as they obey the natural (God's) laws of the universe. The sense of the supreme being will help them realize that just as the natural path of living plants is to grow toward the sun, our natural path is to grow (in understanding) toward the supreme force.

THE AFRICAN-AMERICAN FAMILY'S
OBLIGATION TO THE STATE

Ultimately, the African-American family parent-child relationship must become the focal point to which the African-American family's obligation to the state and the state's obligation to the African-American family is crystalized. For human beings, and especially those who are being oppressed and discriminated against, the parent-child relationship should make clear that the state's obligation to every family within its domain and jurisdiction is to guarantee each and every family a level of existence or a quality of life which ensures and guarantees the family's ability to advance and affirm the life and well-being of its members. In turn, and in tandem with the state's obligation, the human family's obligation to the state is to support the state in its correctness (in deed and action) and to never allow the state as the agent and instrument of the people to infringe upon or allow to continue in any form the dehumanization and degradation of its citizenry or in any way diminish, discriminate, or disallow the growth of the human potential.

REFERENCES

BERNARD, J. (1966) Marriage and Family Amongst Negroes. Englewood Cliffs, NJ: Prentice-Hall.

BILLINGSLEY, A. (1968) Black Families in White America. Englewood Cliffs, NJ: Prentice-Hall.

BURMEISTER, H. (1853) The Black Man: The Comparative Anatomy and Psychology of the African Negro. New York: W. C. Bryant.

CHILMAN, N. C. (1966) Growing Up Poor. Washington, DC: U.S. Department of Health, Education and Welfare.

FRAZIER, B. F. (1932) The Negro in Chicago. Chicago: University of Chicago Press.

GALTON, F. (1969) Hereditary Genius. London: Macmillan.

HALL, G. S. (1904) Adolescence. New York: Appleton-Century-Crofts.

HILL, R. (1971) The Strength of Black Families. New York: Emerson Hall.

JEFFERS, C. (1967) Living Poor. Ann Arbor, MI: Ann Arbor Publishers.

NOBLES, W. W. et al. (1976) A Formulative and Empirical Study of Black Families. Washington, DC: U.S. Department of Health, Education and Welfare.

———— (1979) Mental Health Support Systems in Black Families. Washington, DC: U.S. Department of Health, Education and Welfare.

SCANZONI, J. (1971) The Black Family in Modern Society. Boston: Allyn & Bacon.

SHIMKIN, D. et al. (1974) The Black Extended Family: A Basic Rural Institution and a Mechanism of Urban Adaptation. Cited in Ebony, March 1974.

SPENCER, H. (1884) The Man Versus the State. Baltimore: Penguin.

STAPLES, R. (1976) Introduction to Black Sociology. New York: McGraw-Hill.

TERMAN, L. M. (1916) The Measurement of Intelligence: An Explanation of and a Complete Guide for the Use of the Stanford Revision and Extension of the Binet-Simon Intelligence Scale. Boston: Houghton Mifflin.

THORNDIKE, E. L. (1940) Human Nature and the Social Order. New York: Macmillan.

VON LINNAES, C. (1735) Systema Natural. Luyduni: Butavurum.

WILLIE, C. (1970) The Family Life of Black People. Columbus, OH: Charles E. Merrill.

5

PERSPECTIVES ON BLACK FAMILY
EMPIRICAL RESEARCH: 1965-1978

LEANOR BOULIN JOHNSON

INTRODUCTION

Guided by different perspectives while using the same data, Black and White social scientists often differ on the nature of Black family life and the direction social policies should take. The works of Moynihan (1965) and Hill (1972) demonstrate the critical link between data and interpretive frameworks (see Johnson, 1978). Although both analyzed the same U.S. Census data, they employed different theoretical perspectives and arrived at divergent conclusions. Moynihan reported a deteriorating Black family and recommended social policies that would encourage changes in the Black family's structure and values. Hill observed the resilience of Black families and recommended social policies that could build on the strengths of Black family values and structure. Without arguing the validity of either conclusion, the importance of studying perspectives governing Black family research should be evident. Yet, too often when trying to create a fit between scientific data and social needs, researchers argue over apparent discrepancies in the data or debate the merit of various statistical methods while ignoring another possible culprit—the subjective frame of reference (Gouldner, 1970; Van den Berghe, 1967; Mills, 1959; Mannheim, 1936).

AUTHOR'S NOTE: The author is indebted to Tony Haynes of Florida State University, whose original conceptualization contributed greatly to this chapter.

Recognizing both the limitations of scientific objectivity, particularly when racial groups are the target of analysis, and the tendency for policymakers to use social science research to guide policies on Black families, Staples (1974) and Allen (1978; Allen and Stokes, 1981) identified major theoretical and value frameworks that either impede or facilitate a fuller understanding of Black families and the social policies that govern their lives. Notwithstanding these researchers' valuable contributions, they failed to document empirically the frequency of these frameworks and their occurrence over time. Further, their methodology prevents a systematic identification of changing perspectives in empirical Black family research. Thus, this chapter proposes to extend Staples's and Allen's studies by identifying journals that fostered empirical Black family studies: determining the frequency of their frameworks over time and identifying topics studied within each framework.

THEORETICAL PERSPECTIVES

The more than 500 Black family articles that appeared in the 1960s and '70s represent five times more such literature than was produced during the preceding century (Staples and Mirande, 1980). With the exception of Allen (1978) and Staples (1974), social scientists have not categorized the various frameworks represented in this growing body of literature. Allen identifies three theoretical perspectives or value orientations: "Cultural Deviant" (CD), "Cultural Equivalent" (CE), and "Cultural Variant" (CV). The first framework views Black families as pathological; the second depicts Black families as legitimate when they adapt the lifestyle and norms of middle-class White families; and the third views Black families as different but functional family forms. Using a time typology, Staples identifies four eras through which Black family research has progressed: "Poverty/Acculturation," "Pathologists," "Reactive," and "Black Nationalist Family Studies." According to Staples, studies focusing on the pathological nature of Black families appeared during the thirties, forties, and sixties (that is, during the poverty/acculturation and pathologists eras). During the poverty/acculturation period—the thirties and forties—DuBois, Frazier, and others believed that the solution to Black family disorganization and poverty was conformity to White family norms. The pathologists differed from the poverty/acculturation approach in that pathologists' views emerged in the sixties and had significant impact on public policy; most scholars taking this view were White; and pathologists blamed Black families for Blacks' inferior social position. Studies reacting to this negative image of Black families emerged during the reactive era (approximately 1966-1977). Most recently, Black Nationalist Family Studies have depicted Black families as unique and functional.

TABLE 5.1   Theoretical Frameworks Used in Studying Black Families:
             Related Typologies

Staples	Allen
Poverty-Acculturated (e.g., Frazier, 1932, 1939; DuBois, 1909)	Cultural Deviant (e.g., Frazier, 1939; Moynihan, 1965)
Pathologist (e.g., Moynihan, 1965; Aldous, 1969)	Cultural Deviant (e.g., Frazier, 1939; Moynihan, 1965)
Reactive (e.g., Liebow, 1966; Billingsley, 1968)	Cultural Equivalent (e.g., Frazier, 1939; Scanzoni, 1971)
Black Nationalist (e.g., Cade, 1970; Hill, 1972)	Cultural Variant (e.g., Rodman, 1971; Ladner, 1971)

Common to both Allen's and Staples's categorization are basic value orientations (see Table 5.1). The cultural deviant perspective recognizes qualities that differentiate Black and White families and gives negative meaning, that is, pathological or dysfunctional attributes—to Black family traits. Both the poverty/acculturation and the pathologists eras manifest orientations similar to the cultural deviant perspective. During the poverty/acculturation era (early 1900s) the massive Black migration from the agrarian setting to the city uprooted a significant group in the Black community. DuBois (1908) and Frazier (1932, 1939) focused on the rate of illegitimacy and the number of female-headed households among this unstable Black group; both concluded that conformity to White middle-class family norms would eliminate family disorganization. Approximately 60 years later, the pathologists extended DuBois's and Frazier's thesis by blaming Black families for the deterioration of the Black community. The 1965 Moynihan report characterized this period.

The reactive era extended from approximately 1966 to 1971. During this period White and Black behavioral scientists reacted to Moynihan's "blame the victim" conclusions. By arguing that economic and racial discrimination victimized Blacks, they concluded that, given the same economic conditions, Black and White families are equivalent. Thus, the perspective of this era parallels Allen's cultural equivalent perspective. However, in addition to including authors of the late sixties and early seventies (such as Scanzoni, 1971; Bernard, 1966), Allen includes Frazier's writings of the thirties (those reports which describe Black families as "Black Puritans" when they adopt White morals). It must be remembered that while the Black Family was not being blamed for the problems it faced, little or no positive value was attributed to the unique traits of Black family structure.

The cultural variant perspective acknowledges certain family functions as universal, but recognizes that various constraints may produce culturally distinct structures and dynamics. Thus, the importance of cultural relativity is stressed. Although differences between Black and White families are noted, unique aspects of Black family life are not necessarily taken as reflections of pathologies (Allen, 1978). Consistent with this approach is the perspective used during the era of Black Nationalists research. In fact, it was the Black Nationalists who first began to delineate the strengths of Black families. Thus, they distinguished themselves from the reactive researchers, who also challenged the pathologists' position, but failed to attach positive value to the unique aspects of Black family life (Staples, 1974). Black Nationalists contend that if social scientists desire to report on the behavior of a culture other than their own, they must not use their own cultural framework and definitions to explain that behavior. Consequently, Black values cannot be used to explain White cultural patterns, nor can White values be used to explain Black cultural patterns (Johnson, 1978).

METHODOLOGY

In analyzing the treatment of Black families in the research literature of the 1965-1978 period, we first employ Allen's trichotomized typology which is free from a time sequence idea, yet captures the orientations underlying the stages presented by Staples. However, when focus is given to trends, Staples's stages will be the referent.

In some cases there appeared to be more than one perspective represented. An effort was made to label according to the most dominant theme. Since a clear distinction was not always possible, the reader may disagree with a particular interpretation. For the reader's benefit we have labeled each article by perspective (see Bibliography notes).

Articles were classified according to three criteria. Reports are labeled:

- *Cultural Equivalent* (CE) if emphasis is given to White middle-class family norms as the referent to which Black families are compared; and if similarities between the two groups are explicitly or implicitly interpreted as support for shared cultural values (for example, Scanzoni, 1971);
- *Cultural Deviant* (CD) if emphasis is given to White middle-class norms as the referent to which Black families are compared; and if deviation from these norms by Black families is explicitly or implicitly interpreted as pathological (Aldous, 1969); and

- *Cultural Variant* (CV) if White middle-class norms are not the primary referent and Black cultural patterns are primarily explained by use of Black values and experiences (Jackson, 1971).

The reliability of this content analysis was maintained by consistently applying this classification criteria (see Lantz, 1968). In order to minimize the sampling error, our list of articles was randomly checked against articles cited in the *International Bibliography of Research in Marriage and the Family, Vol. II.*

We carefully scanned the table of contents in each periodical for titles and/or abstracts which involved aspects of Black family life (the unit of analysis). If after reading the first few and the last paragraphs the article appeared relevant, we examined the entire article and made the appropriate classifications.

Journals from two fields were selected: sociology, because of its focus on social institutions and relationships, and social work, for its traditional concern with the welfare of families. From sociology we selected five journals; two specialized in family research and three were among the most widely circulated. From social work we selected the five most widely circulated journals.[1] The following list of ten journals was examined, and lengthy journal titles are abbreviated in the text.

Sociology: *Journal of Marriage and the Family (JMF)*
             Journal of Comparative Family Studies (JCFS)
             American Journal of Sociology (AJS)
             American Sociological Review (ASR)
             Social Forces

Social Work: *Child Welfare*
             Social Casework
             Social Service Review
             Public Welfare
             Social Work

In order to include representation from "established" Black periodicals, that is, journals in circulation for at least ten years—three additional journals were included: *Black Scholar, Journal of Social and Behavioral Sciences* (JSBS), and *Phylon*. We selected only those empirical articles which explicitly discussed some aspect of Black families.

FINDINGS

Although Moynihan's 1965 attack on Black families stimulated a plethora of articles on Black families, our selected journals reflect few empirical articles.

Of the 7017 articles published during the 13-year period, 3547 (51 percent) were empirical family studies. Empirical articles on Black families represented .01 percent (92) of all articles and .03 percent (107) of all empirical studies. The *JMF* special issue on Black families, edited by a Black scholar, and the Black journals accounted for 38 percent of all Black articles. Considering only the nonspecialized journals (that is, excluding *JMF* and *JCFS*) the Black journals contributed 57 percent of the empirical Black family studies. Although *JSBS* did not specialize in family articles, it devoted a slightly higher percentage of its articles to Black families than did *JMF* (6.0 percent versus 4.9 percent). Obviously, special issues and Black journals play an important role in publicizing the data from Black family research (see Table 5.2).

In the 1960s, 60 percent of the Black family studies were published by *JMF* and the remainder appeared in five other journals. In contrast, during the first five years of 1970, *JMF* published only 31 percent of the articles; the others were distributed among seven other journals, including two new journals— *Black Scholar* and *JCFS*. Even when we exclude the new journals, *JMF* published only 33 percent of the articles. Although *JMF*'s monopoly was weakened during this period, its 1978 special issue on Black families supplied 92 percent of the 12 articles published that year.

Given social work's traditional concern with family welfare, it is surprising that not only did *Social Casework* and *Social Work* each publish only one

TABLE 5.2   Black Family Studies by Periodicals and Year

Periodical	65	66	67	68	69	70	71	72	73	74	75	76	77	78	Total
Journal of Marriage and the Family	1	3	2	3	6	2	0	5	2	2	4	2	3	11	46
*Journal of Social and Behavioral Sciences**	0	0	0	3	2	1	1	1	0	5	0	0	0	0	13
American Sociological Review	0	0	0	0	0	0	2	3	1	0	0	0	0	0	6
*Phylon**	1	0	0	0	0	0	0	1	0	0	0	1	5	1	9
American Journal of Sociology	0	0	0	0	1	0	1	0	2	2	0	0	0	0	6
Social Forces	1	0	0	0	1	1	0	0	0	1	0	0	0	0	4
Journal of Comparative Family Studies	**	**	**	**	**	0	1	0	0	0	2	1	0	0	4
*Black Scholar**	**	**	**	**	0	1	1	0	0	0	0	0	0	0	2
Social Casework	0	0	0	0	1	0	0	0	0	0	0	0	0	0	1
Social Work	0	0	0	0	0	0	0	0	0	0	0	1	0	0	1
Total	3	3	2	6	11	5	6	10	5	10	6	5	8	12	92

* Black journals
**Journal was not published in these years.

article in the 13-year survey period, but no empirical articles appeared in the other three selected social work journals. However, these latter journals did publish a few nonempirical Black family studies.

A greater percentage of articles was published between 1969 and 1972 (35 percent) than in the previous or following four years; 15 percent and 28 percent, respectively. *Social Work,* however, had at least one article in each journal on Black families during this period.

The frequency with which the theoretical perspectives appeared in the periodicals is shown in Table 5.3. Most journals contained studies that interpreted their data through a cultural equivalent framework. The cultural deviant perspective was absent from six of the ten journals. Although *JMF* gave preference to cultural equivalent, cultural deviant was represented in one-quarter of their articles. If we exclude *JMF*'s 1978 special issue on Black families, cultural deviant's representation in *JMF* increases to one-third and the cultural variant decreases from one-third to less than 12 percent. It should be noted that 69 percent of the cultural variant articles appeared in Black-edited journals. Black editors were generally more likely than non-Black editors to publish studies which used the cultural variant perspective; however, they were least likely to publish articles which used the cultural deviant perspective.

In tabulating Table 5.3 the three perspectives were evenly distributed among the six articles appearing in *ASR,* while all articles appearing in *Social Forces, JCFS,* and *Social Casework* used the cultural equivalent perspective.

Staples's unilinear evolutionary typology implies that each era will lead to and culminate in the next—poverty-acculturation to pathologists (both equiva-

TABLE 5.3   Black Family Studies by Periodical and Theoretical Perspectives, 1965-1978

Periodical	Total Reports	Theoretical Perspectives*		
		CE	CD	CV
Journal of Marriage and the Family	46	21	11	14
Journal of Social and Behavioral Sciences	13	8	1	4
American Sociological Review	6	2	2	2
Phylon	9	5	0	4
American Journal of Sociology	6	3	1	2
Social Forces	4	4	0	0
Journal of Comparative Family Studies	4	4	0	0
Black Scholar	2	0	0	2
Social Casework	1	1	0	0
Social Work	1	0	0	1
Total	92	48	15	29

*CE = Cultural Equivalent
CD = Cultural Deviant
CV = Cultural Variant

lent to cultural deviant), to reactive (cultural equivalent) to Black Nationalist (cultural variant). Figure 5.1 gives moderate support to Staples's time typology: Although the cultural deviant perspective was present throughout the sixties and early seventies, it disappeared after 1974. Throughout the 13-year period, cultural equivalent tended to dominate the literature. No doubt this reflects America's long-standing commitment to the various forms of Anglo-conformity. The cultural variant perspective emerged in 1968, when Edwards, a Black researcher, published his *JMF* article, "Black Muslims and Negro Christian Relationships." Throughout the 1960s and continuing through 1976, this perspective maintained a low profile; its most recent two-year prominence resulted primarily from the *JMF* special issue.

Most writings of the sixties referenced Frazier's works, not Moynihan's. The first major response to Moynihan appeared in 1968, when Geismar and Gerhart published their *JMF* article, "Social Class, Ethnicity and Family Functioning: Exploring Some Issues Raised by the Moynihan Report." This article and Aldous's (1969) represent the most policy-oriented research of the sixties. Although both these articles appeared within the reactive era noted by Staples, the response to Moynihan appeared throughout the seventies (for example, Bould, 1977, Balkwell et al., 1978).

The conceptual framework of the areas studied is shown in Table 5.4. The cultural variant perspective was used in interpreting one-third of the family roles and structure articles, while approximately two-fifths and one-fifth were interpreted through the cultural equivalent and cultural deviant frameworks, respectively. Forty-four percent of the data on family roles, structure, and function were interpreted through the cultural equivalent perspective. In contrast, family roles, structure, and function represented 29 percent and 27 percent of the cultural deviant and cultural variant perspective, respectively. The cultural variant framework was absent in family function studies, and the cultural deviant perspective did not appear in studies on housing and mate selection and premarital sexual patterns.

Although a vast amount of literature on minority families and housing appears in economic journals, housing and its sociopsychological effects on minority families received insignificant attention in our selected journals. Only two studies (two percent of all reports) were published in the 13-year survey period.

One-half of the studies focused on family structure and roles—for example, role aspiration, attitude, and performance. Although not shown in Table 5.4, nearly two-fifths of these studies were published in the 1960s. More importantly, these two areas represented 75 percent of the studies published in that decade. During the next nine years the diversity of areas increased—the other five areas represented 55 percent during the 1970-1975 period; thereafter their representation increased an average of one percent each year. Focusing only on

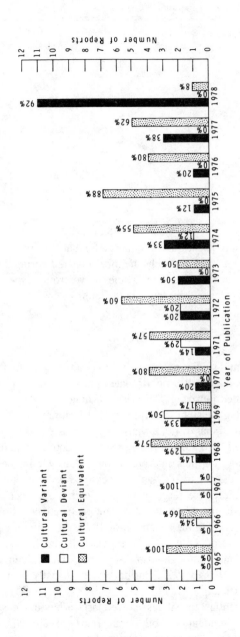

FIGURE 5.1   Changes in Theoretical Perspective by Year, 1965-1978

TABLE 5.4   Area Studied, by Theoretical Perspectives

Area Studied	Total Reports	Theoretical Perspectives*		
		CE	CD	CV
Family roles	27	11	7	9
Family structure	18	8	3	7
Mate selection and premarital sexual patterns	12	8	0	4
Family functions	18	9	8	1
Fertility	8	4	1	3
Marital stability	7	5	1	1
Housing	2	1	0	1
Total	92	46	20	26

*CE = Cultural Equivalent
CD = Cultural Deviant
CV = Cultural Variant

the categories of "Marital Selection or Premarital Sexual Pattern" and "Fertility," we find that only one study in each category appeared during the sixties. By the end of 1978, an additional ten articles (five from a special issue) appeared in the former category and seven in the latter.

CONCLUSIONS

Empirical Black family studies represent less than one percent of all empirical family studies. Although a disproportionate number of these studies were published in Black-edited journals, *JMF* was the major source of Black articles, particularly during the sixties. Surprisingly, Black family articles were virtually absent from the social work journals.

Our analysis revealed variations in theoretical perspective by journals and across time. While most journals interpreted their data within the cultural equivalent perspective, the cultural deviant perspective was least likely and the cultural variant most likely to emerge in journals edited by Black scholars. Generally, the cultural deviant and cultural variant perspectives followed Staples's typology. However, with the exception of 1978, the cultural equivalent framework was strong throughout the 13-year period, and reactions to the Moynihan Report continued throughout the seventies. The golden years for empirical studies were 1969 to 1972, during which virtually every journal published at least one article.

In contrast to the seventies, the sixties showed less variety in areas studied. Housing received the least attention (both publications appeared in the seventies). The emphasis given to roles and structure perhaps reflects the preoccupation with the stability of the Black family and its presumed inability to fulfill societal prerequisites—for example, the socialization of children. This concern, sparked by Frazier and revisited by Moynihan, has resulted in a narrow research agenda. While the Black matriarchy and its role in socializing children and marriage stability received enormous attention, no study focused on the interaction between cultural values, demographic factors (for example, Black sex ratio) and family organization. Furthermore, given the tradition of mul-tiearners within Black families, low family income, and the high number of large families and Black youth, there exists a conspicuous absence of studies on dual job-career families, sibling relationships, dating and courtship, and hous-ing and social policies (particularly social security and tax laws). All these areas are of vital concern to Black families and represent tasks for future research.

Now that researchers appear to have abandoned the cultural deviant perspec-tive and cultural variant is gaining prominence, many more culturally relevant empirical studies should emerge. It appears that Black researchers must take major responsibility for identifying the unique aspects of Black families.

NOTE

1. Based on Ulrich's International Periodical Directory, 1977-1978, these journals were among the most widely circulated:

Journal of Marriage and the Family	(Est. 1939/Cir. 11,000)
American Journal of Sociology	(Est. 1895/Cir. 10,892)
American Sociological Review	(Est. 1936/Cir. 15,000)
Social Forces	(Est. 1922/Cir. 5,000)
Child Welfare	(Est. 1922/Cir. 9,600)
Social Casework	(Est. 1920/Cir. 17,000)
Social Service Review	(Est. 1927/Cir. 6,736)
Public Welfare	(Est. 1943/Cir. 12,000)
Social Welfare	(Est. 1956/Cir. 85,000)

REFERENCES

ALLEN, W. (1978) "The search for applicable theories of Black family life." Journal of Marriage and the Family 40 (1): 111-129.

―――― (1977) The Effects of Government Policies on Black Families. Division on Education and Research: Public Education, The Ford Foundation (October).

―――― and S. STOKES (1981) "Black family life styles and mental health of Black Americans," in R. Endo and F. Munoz (eds.) Perspectives on Minority Group Mental Health. Chicago: Charter House.

DuBOIS, W. E. B. (1908) The Negro American family. Atlanta: Atlanta University Press.

FRAZIER, E. F. (1932) The Negro Family in Chicago. Chicago: University of Chicago Press.

―――― (1939) The Negro Family in the United States. Chicago: University of Chicago Press.

GOULDNER, A. (1970) The Coming Crisis of Western Sociology. New York: Avon Books.

HILL, R. (1972) The Strength of Black Families. New York: Emerson Hall.

JOHNSON, L. (1978) "The search for values in Black family research," pp. 26-34 in R. Staples (ed.) The Black Family: Essays and Studies. Belmont, CA: Wadsworth.

JONES, M. (1976) "Scientific method, value judgments, and the Black predicament in the U.S." Review of Black Political Economy 7 (1): Fall.

LANTZ, H., R. SCHMITT, M. BRITTON, and E. SNYDER (1968) "Pre-industrial patterns in the colonial family in America: a content analysis of colonial magazines." American Sociological Review 33 (3): 413-426.

MANNHEIM, K. (1936) Ideology and Utopia. London: Routledge & Kegal Paul.

MILLS, C. W. (1959) The Sociological Imagination. New York: Grove Press.

MOYNIHAN, D. (1965) The Negro Family: The Case for National Action. Washington, DC: Office of Policy Planning and Research, U.S. Department of Labor.

NOBLES, Wade W. (1978) "Toward an empirical and theoretical framework for defining Black families." Journal of Marriage and the Family 40 (November): 679-688.

SCANZONI, J. (1971) The Black Family in Modern Society. Boston: Allyn & Bacon.

STAPLES, R. (1974) "The Black family revisited: a review and a preview." Journal of Social and Behavioral Sciences 20 (Spring): 65-78.

_____ and A. MIRANDE (1980) "Racial and cultural variations among American families: a decennial review of the literature on minority families." Journal of Marriage and the Family 42 (4): 887-903.

Ulrich's International Periodical Directory (1978) New York: R. R. Bowker.

VAN DEN BERGHE, P. (1967) Race and Racism. New York: John Wiley.

BIBLIOGRAPHY

SELECTED RESEARCH REPORTS AND ASSIGNED CLASSIFICATIONS

(First parenthetical designation following the citation refers to area studied and the second to theoretical perspective: CE = Cultural Equivalent; CD = Cultural Deviant; CV = Cultural Variant.)

AMERICAN JOURNAL OF SOCIOLOGY

EPSTEIN, C. F. (1973) "Positive effects of the multiple negative explaining the success of Black professional women." 78 (4): 151-173. (Role: CV)

GOLDSCHIEDER, C. and P. R. UHLENBERG (1969) "Minority group status and fertility." 84 (4): 361-372. (Fertility: CE)

KANDEL, D. B. (1971) "Race, maternal authority, and adolescent aspiration." 76 (6): 999-1020. (Family functions: CE)

LOPATA, H. A. (1973) "Social relations of Black and White widowed women in a northern metropolis." 78 (4): 241-248. (Role: CE)

ROBERTS, R. E. and E. S. LEE (1974) "Minority group status and fertility revisited." 80 (2): 503-523. (Fertility: CD)

UDRY, J. R., K. E. BAUMAN, and C. CHASE (1971) "Skin color, status, and mate selection." 76 (4): 722-733. (Mate selection: CV)

AMERICAN SOCIOLOGICAL REVIEW

CENTERS, R., B. H. RAVEN, and A. RODRIGUES (1971) "Conjugal power structure: a re-examination." 36 (1): 1-17. (Role: CD)

HEISS, J. (1972) "On the transmission of marital instability in Black families." 37 (1): 82-92. (Marital stability: CV)

HERMES, G. (1972) "The process of entry into first marriage." 37 (2): 173-182. (Mate selection: CE).

REYNOLDS, F. and A. I. HERMALIN (1971) "Family stability: a comparison of trends between Blacks and Whites." 36 (1): 1-17. (Marital stability: CD)

ROLAND, J. and J. E. MARBLE (1972) "Family disruption and delinquent conduct: multiple measures and the effect of subclassification." 37 (1): 93-99. (Family functions: CE)

SAMPSON, W. A. and P. H. ROSSI (1975) "Race and family social standing." 40 (2): 201-214. (Role: CV)

BLACK SCHOLAR

JACKSON, J. (1971) "But where are the men?" 3 (4): 34-41. (Mate selection: CV)

REED, J. (1970) "Marriage and fertility in Black female teachers." 1 (3-4): 22-28. (Fertility: CV)

JOURNAL OF COMPARATIVE FAMILY STUDIES

MONAHAN, T. P. (1971) "Interracial marriage and divorce in Kansas and the question of instability of mixed marriages." 2 (1): 107-120. (Mate selection: CE)

——— (1976) "The occupational class of couples entering into interracial marriages." 7 (2): 176-192. (Mate selection: CE)

JACKSON, R. N. (1975) "Some aspirations of lower class Black mothers." 6 (2): 171-181. (Family functioning: CE)

TOBIN, P. L., W. B. CLIFFORD, R. D. MUSTIAN, and S. C. DAVIS (1975) "Value of children and fertility behavior in a triracial rural county." 6 (1): 46-53. (Fertility: CE)

JOURNAL OF MARRIAGE AND THE FAMILY

AGRESTI, B. F. (1978) "The first decades of freedom: Black families in a southern county, 1870 and 1885." 40 (4): 697-706. (Family structure: CV)

ALDOUS, J. (1972) "Children's perception of adult role assignment: father absent, class, race, and sex influences." 34 (1): 55-65. (Role: CD)

——— (1969) "Wives' employment status and lower-class men as husbands-fathers: support for the Moynihan thesis." 31 (3): 469-476. (Role: CD)

AXELSON, L. J. (1970) "The working wife: differences in perception among Negro and White males." 32 (3): 457-464. (Role: CE)

BALKWELL, C., J. BALEWICK, and J. W. BALKWELL (1978) "On Black and White family patterns in America: their impact on the expressive aspect of sex-role socialization." 40 (4): 743-747 (Role: CV).

BARTZ, K. W. and E. S. LEVINE (1978) "Childrearing by Black parents: a description and comparison to Anglo and Chicano parents." 40 (4): 709-719. (Family functions: CV)

BAUMAN, K. E. and J. R. UDRY (1972) "Powerlessness and regularity of contraception in an urban Negro male sample: a research note." 34 (1): 112-114. (Role: CE)

BERNARD, J. (1966) "Note on educational homogamy in Negro-White and White-Negro marriage, 1960." 28 (3): 274-276. (Mate selection: CE)

BOULD, S. (1977) "Female-headed families: personal fate control and the provider role." 39 (2): 339-349. (Family structure: CE).

BRODERICK, C. (1965) "Social heterosexual development among urban Negroes and Whites." 27 (2): 200-212. (Role: CE)

BROWN, P., L. PERRY, and E. HARBURG (1977) "Sex role attitudes and psychological outcomes for Black and White women experiencing marital dissolution." 39 (4): 549-561. (Role:
CE)

CHRISTENSEN, H. T. and L. B. JOHNSON (1978) "Premarital coitus and the southern Black: a
comparative view." 40 (4): 721-732. (Premarital sexual patterns: CV)

CROMWELL, V. L. and R. E. CROMWELL (1978) "Perceived dominance in decision making
and conflict resolution among Anglo, Black, and Chicano couples." 40 (4): 749-759. (Family
functions: CV).

DICKINSON, G. E. (1975) "Dating behavior of Black and White adolescents before and after
desegregation." 37 (3): 602-608. (Mate selection CE)

DIETRICK, K. T. (1975) "A reexamination of the myth of Black matriarchy." 37 (2): 367-374.
(Role: CE)

EDWARDS, H. (1968) "Black Muslim and Negro Christian relationships." 30 (4): 604-611. (Role:
CV)

FISCHER, A., J. D. BEASLEY, and C. L. HARTER (1968) "The occurrence of the extended
family at the origin of the family of procreation: a developmental approach to Negro family
structure." 30 (2): 290-300. (Family structure: CD)

GEISMAR, L. L. and U. C. GERHART (1968) "Social class, ethnicity, and family functioning:
exploring some issues raised by the Moynihan Report." 30 (3): 480-487. (Family functions:
CE)

HANEY, C. A., R. MICHIELUTTE, C. M. COCHRANE, and C. E. VINCENT (1975) "Some
consequences of illegitimacy in a sample of Black women." 37 (2): 359-366. (Role: CE)

HARRISON, A. O. and J. H. MINOR (1978) "Interrole conflict, coping strategies, and satisfaction
among Black working wives." 40 (4): 799-805. (Role: CV)

HEER, D. M. (1966) "Negro-White marriage in the U.S." 28 (3): 262-273. (Mate selection: CE)
———— (1974) "The prevalence of Black-White marriage in the U.S., 1960 and 1970." 36 (2):
246-258. (Mate selection: CE)

HOBBS, D. F. and J. M. WIMBISH (1977) "Transition to parenthood by Black couples." 39 (4):
677-689. (Family functions: CE)

KAMI, C. and N. L. RADIN (1967) "Class difference in the socialization practice of Negro
mothers." 29 (2): 302-310. (Role: CD)

KING, C. A., T. J. ABERNATHY, and A. H. CHAPMAN (1976) "Black adolescents' views of
maternal employment as a threat to the marital relationship: 1963-1973." 38 (4): 733-737.
(Role: CE)

KING, K. (1969) "Adolescent perception of power structure in the Negro family." 31 (4): 751-755.
(Role: CD)

KUVLESKY, W. and A. OBORDO (1972) "A racial comparison of teen-age girls' projections for
marriage and procreation." 34 (1): 75-84. (Role: CD)

LAMMERMEIER, P. J. (1973) "Urban Black family of the nineteenth century: a study of Black
family structure in the Ohio Valley, 1950-1980." 35 (3): 440-456. (Family structure: CE)

LANDRY, B. and M. P. JENDICK (1978) "Employment of wives in middle class Black families."
40 (4): 787-797. (Family functions: CV)

McADOO, H. P. (1978) "Factors related to stability in upwardly mobile Black families." 40 (4):
761-776. (Family functions: CV)

MELTON, W. and D. L. THOMAS (1976) "Instrumental and expressive values in mate selection of
Black and White college students." 38 (3): 509-517. (Mate selection: CE)

MIAO, G. (1974) "Marital instability and unemployment among Whites and nonwhites, the
Moynihan Report revisited—again." 36 (1): 77-86. (Marital stability: CE)

MERCER, C. V. (1967) "Interrelations among family stability, family composition, residence, and
race." 29 (3): 456-460. (Family structure: CD)

NOLLE, D. (1972) "Changes in Black sons and daughters: a panel analysis of Black adolescents' orientations toward their parents." 34 (3): 443-447. (Family functions: CE)

PARKER, S. and R. KLEINER (1966) "Characteristics of Negro mothers in single-headed households." 28 (4): 507-513. (Family structure: CD)

PARKER, S. and R.J. KLIENER (1969) "Social and psychological dimensions of the family role performance of the Negro male." 31 (3): 500-511. (Role: CE)

POPE, H. (1969) "Negro-White differences in decisions regarding illegitimate children." 31 (4): 756-764. (Family structure: CV)

REED, F.W., J.R. UDRY, and M. RUPPERT (1975) "Relative incomes and fertility." 37 (4): 799-805. (Fertility: CE)

RODMAN, H., F.H. NICHOLS, and P. VOYDANOFF (1969) "Lower class attitudes toward 'deviant' family patterns: a cross-cultural study." 31 (2): 315-321. (Family structure: CV)

SAVAGE, J.E., A.V. ADAI, and P. FRIEDMAN (1978) "Community-social variables related to Black parent-absent families." 40 (4): 779-785. (Family structure: CV)

SCANZONI, J. (1975) "Sex roles, economic factors, and marital solidarity in Black and White marriages." 37 (1): 130-144. (Marital stability: CE)

STAPLES, R. (1978) "Race, liberalism, conservatism and premarital sexual permissiveness: a bi-racial comparison." 40 (4): 733-742 (Premarital sexual patterns: CV)

VINCENT, C.E., C.A. HANEY, and C.M. COCHRANE (1969) "Familial and generational patterns of illegitimacy." 30 (4): 659-667. (Family structure: CD)

WILLIAMS, J.A. and R. STOCKTON (1973) "Black family structure and functions: an empirical examination of some suggestions made by Billingsley." 35 (1): 39-49. (Family structure: CV)

WILLIE, C.V. and S.L. GREENBLAT (1978) "Four 'classic' studies of power relationships in Black families: a review and look to the future." 40 (4): 691-694. (Family functions: CE)

JOURNAL OF SOCIAL AND BEHAVIORAL SCIENCES

BILLINGSLEY, A. and M.G. GREENE (1974) "Family life among the free Black population in the 18th century." 20 (2): 1-18. (Family structure: CV)

EPPS, E.G. (1968) "Parent social status and personality characteristics of Negro high school students." 13 (2): 27-33. (Roles: CE)

HARRISON, A.E. (1974) "Dilemma of growing up Black and female." 20 (2): 28-40. (Role: CV)

JACKSON, J.J. (1974) "Ordinary Black husbands: the truly hidden man." 20 (2): 19-27. (Role: CE)

———— (1970) "Kinship relations among older Negro Americans." 16 (1-2): 5-17. (Family Structure: CE)

KENNEDY, E.J. (1968) "The relationship of maternal emotionality to obstetric complications and childbirth abnormalities." 13 (2): 3-8. (Family functions: CE)

KREPTAL, E.R. and E.G. EPPS (1968) "The 'father absence' effect aspirations: myth or reality." 13 (3): 9-17 (Family roles: CE)

KUTNER, N.G. (1974) "Differential adaptation among lower-class Black homemakers in a rural urban community." 20 (3): 55-65. (Role: CE)

LADNER, J. (1974) "Black women in poverty." 20 (2): 41-50. (Role: CV)

RHODES, E.C. (1969) "Family structure and the achievement syndrome among students at Tennessee A&I State University." 14 (1): 55-59. (Family functions: CD)

SHERMAN, E.G. (1969) "Urbanization and the Negro family: a case study in Florida." 14 (1): 36-41. (Family structure: CE)

SMITH, R. (1971) "Family life and environment in the Lincoln neighborhood community." 18 (1): 80-89. (Housing: CV)

STAPLES, R. (1972) "The influence of race on reactions to a hypothetical premarital pregnancy." 18 (3): 32-35. (Premarital sexual patterns: CE)

PHYLON

ANDERSON, J. E. (1977) "Planning of births: difference between Black and White in U.S." 38 (3): 323-296. (Family structure: CE)

BABCHUCK, N. and J. A. BALLWEG (1972) "Black family structure and primary relations." 33 (4): 334-347. (Family structure: CE)

CATES, W. (1977) "Legal abortion: are American women healthier because of it?" 38 (3): 267-281. (Fertility: CV)

HAWKINS, H. C. (1976) "Urban housing and the Black family." 37 (1): 73-84. (Housing: CE)

KOVAR, M. G. (1977) "Mortality of Black infants in the U.S." 38 (4): 378-397. (Fertility: CV)

LEE, A. S. (1977) "Maternal mortality in the United States." 38 (3): 259-266. (Fertility: CV)

SCHWARTZ, M. (1965) "The Northern U.S. Negro matriarchy: status vs. authority." 26 (1): 18-24. (Family structure: CE)

SIMON, R. (1978) "Black attitudes towards transracial adoption." 39 (2): 135-142. (Family functions: CV)

STOKES, C. S., K. W. CROKER, and J. C. SMITH (1977) "Race, education, and fertility: a comparison of Black-White reproductive behavior." 38 (2): 160-169. (Fertility: CE)

SWEET, J. A. and L. L. BUMPASS (1970) "Differentials in marital instability of the Black population: 1970." 34: 323-331. (Marital stability: CE)

SOCIAL CASEWORK

BILLINGSLEY, A. (1969) "Family functioning in the low-income Black community." 50 (1): 563-572. (Family structure: CE)

SOCIAL FORCES

BACON, L. (1974) "Early motherhood, accelerated transition, and social pathologies." 52 (3): 333-341. (Marital stability: CE)

BELL, R. R. (1965) "Lower class Negro mothers' aspirations for their children." 43 (4): 493-500. (Family functions: CE)

BLOOD, R. O. and D. M. WOLFE (1969) "Negro-White differences in blue-collar marriages in a northern metropolis." 38 (1): 59-64. (Role: CE)

MONAHAN, T. P. (1970) "Are interracial marriages really less stable?" 48 (4): 461-473. (Marital stability: CE)

SOCIAL WORK

BECKETT, J. O. (1976) "Working wives: a racial comparison." 21 (5): 463-471. (Role: CV)

PART II

DEMOGRAPHIC CHARACTERISTICS, ECONOMICS, AND MOBILITY

Poverty has been the lot of most Blacks, as Glick indicated in his chapter on the demographic characteristics and as Hill, Moore, and Edelman pointed out in their chapters on social policy and advocacy. The goal of many Blacks has been to move from poverty to a more secure economic status. In spite of severe economic and occupational isolation and the lack of role models for many of the children, some Black families and individuals *have* managed to master the necessary skills, education, and jobs that allow them to move to a comparatively more secure situation. However, this situation is not secure—it is tenuous, and because there is so little inherited wealth among Black families, it tends to depend totally on wage earnings in service fields. This requires that each generation of a Black family must recreate the effort needed to climb the mobility ladders itself, unlike majority families where the status of the father can be transferred to that of the sons and future generations. The major contribution that Black families have traditionally been able to bestow on their children has been the drive to succeed and the motivation to achieve within the school setting. Ogbu pointed out the futility dreams sometimes meet: the child wants to succeed, but the society has decided that it is hopeless and transmits this to the child, who then turns away from the goal of academic excellence.

Glick documents the changes that have occurred in Black family life. He reemphasizes the reality that there is no such thing as "the Black family," for different forms exist at different classes and levels. Three areas are covered in detail in the chapter: family compositions, marriage and divorce, and employment and income. Within this chapter he points to the fact that Black families tend to have more younger children; that there is short joint survival of the unit after the children leave the home; that one-half of Black children now live only with their mothers; and that Black men tend to be less educated than their wives, although the level of education as a whole is increasing. Other trends highlighted are that the number of children in one-parent homes grew at a slower rate than in non-Black homes and that more adult children now remain in the family because of the inability to maintain separate households. The notorious imbalanced sex ratio is predicted to decline by the mid-1990s. Glick recognizes the centrality of children in Black families and predicts that there will be a decrease in the differences between Black and other families in the future, if there is less stratification by race.

Glick's chapter is packed with demographic background data that effectively pull together sources from multiple locations and will prove to be of great value to other writers in the field. This clear presentation is deceptive of the complexity of the mass of information covered. Glick presents the most current analyses and portrayal of the Black family one could possibly find and will be the source for current figures until the 1980 census results are released in two or three years.

Davis's analysis of the rapid flow of funds out of the Black community, without the multiple turnover that is found elsewhere to be beneficial in communities, clearly points to a major weakness in the economic development of Black business and economic base. Davis reemphasizes some of Glick's points about the economic situation of Blacks and goes on to point to the economic inequality and the growing trend toward even greater inequality of economic resources. Glick describes what exists in the community and Davis offers an explanation of why these factors exist.

Davis describes the economic models that operate within the Black inner cities and proposes theories that would redevelop the flow of money into and out of the central city. Funds enter the community from service-related labor earned by those with limited training and lower productivity and also in the form of governmental transfer payments. These funds quickly leave the central city and afford no investment or development of local resources. Davis believes that to reduce Black poverty, this income distribution should be rechanneled, or the substantial wealth that exists will be lost. In other communities the money changes hands, or is turned over, several times before it leaves the community, allowing more to benefit from it. The need for some modifications within the private sector is highlighted by the fact that one-half of young Blacks are unemployed and one-third of the families are below poverty and every sign indicates that more will join them. Davis's theories on the underutilization of savings, investment, and labor offer an alternative for those in family studies who are concerned about the economic level of the families. While the economic presentation may not be easy reading for those accustomed to sociology or psychology reports, it offers an understanding from an economist that is needed for those concerned with families.

Ogbu also offers an explanation for why the educational level of young Blacks is low, an explanation that is counter to some well-accepted theories. His main thesis is that Black youth and their educators and parents are all locked into a caste-like status from which there is no exit. Ogbu's work has shown the futility of a nature-nurture argument on lower Black school achievement by clearly articulating the effect of being in a caste-like minority. Black youth, upon receipt of deliberate inferior education, correctly perceive the lack of comparable payoff of advanced education and are molded by both Black and white to enter and remain in their lower-status position.

Ogbu rejects the four major excuses that have been put forward for the lack of Black academic achievement: home environment, school environment, genetics, and different cultural values that reinforce different skills utilized in school. He finds all of the above faulty. They do not adequately compare data and they do not perceive the role that racial discrimination plays in the situation of Blacks. Most theories of poor achievement, and the policies that are implemented to overcome the differences, are color-blind and see that the life experiences of Blacks and non-Blacks are alike. This is a false assumption, for Blacks and other poor minorities are unable ever to escape their caste-like positions. The achievement of Blacks is compared to that of other "immigrant minorities" with an explanation of the differences that exist in their perceptions of job opportunities and thus are provided a different motivation to prepare themselves for these jobs.

Ogbu points to the collective historical experience of discrimination, the structural barriers that have a reciprocal influence on the employer and students' perceptions of their ability to get jobs. This circular interaction of perceptions and actual barriers results in a job ceiling that is obvious to youth, who then stop attempting to move out of their castes. Schools play their part in reinforcing children in the directions that would ensure that they remain in this status, making them the victims of the "double stratification of class and race caste."

Ogbu's analyses are refreshing and are free of the customary defenses or negative explanations that often appear in explanations of Black schooling. As a Nigerian, trained as an anthropologist, he may have the objectivity that many of us may lack, allowing him to clearly analyze the downward spiral within which Black youth find themselves caught.

Harriette McAdoo presents a theoretical discussion of the role the extended family has played in assisting Black family members to avoid the destructive cycle outlined by Ogbu and become upwardly mobile. The educational achievements were found to be the result of personal perseverence, strong support, and often sacrifice by other family members. They did not have to cut themselves off from the reciprocal obligations of the kin support network in order to be mobile. This network was not felt to be only a coping strategy of poverty, but evolved into a cultural pattern that tended to transcend social class. The barriers to mobility were so great that it took more than one generation to move from abject poverty to middle-income status. One mobility pattern was found to have families who appear to be operating with a minimum amount of stress, with the highest educational, occupational, and economic rewards. These were families who had been upwardly mobile in three generations, from poverty status and into middle-income status. Family members were found to remain in the supportive network even after mobility, for cultural/family reasons. Those who had been middle class tended not to remain at that level but to gradually slip back down through the succeeding generations, falling victims to their own lowered academic attainments and discrimination within the labor market.

6

A DEMOGRAPHIC PICTURE OF
BLACK FAMILIES

PAUL C. GLICK

Among the many well-recognized differences between Black and other families, some have been converging, some diverging, and others simply persist. These differences can be overemphasized, however, because all families tend to share in the periodic changes that occur in economic opportunities and in other aspects of the cultural environment, although the sharing is not always equal. During periods of economic expansion, Black families have tended to improve their well-being especially rapidly because a larger proportion of their adults were available to fill expanding vacancies. But during the last few decades, the pursuit of greater personal freedom has been on the increase, even if it results in the diminished economic well-being that is usually associated with marital dissolution.

This chapter will throw light on changes in the diversity of family life in the United States during the 1970s, with special reference to comparisons between the family patterns of the Black population and the population of all races combined. The presentation will confirm that "'the' Negro family is itself a fiction. Different family forms prevail at different class and income levels throughout our society" (Willie, 1970). The treatment is organized around three major demographic areas: family composition, marriage and divorce, and em-

AUTHOR'S NOTE: I wish to thank my colleagues Arthur J. Norton, James A. Weed, and Steve W. Rawlings for their helpful comments on this chapter.

ployment and income. The chapter will conclude with a discussion of some implications of the outstanding demographic features of Black family life.

FAMILY COMPOSITION

According to the traditional norm, families are formed through marriage, and those who marry remain married until one spouse dies. The extent to which current marital behavior differs from this norm will be examined in this section, along with some of the implications for the living arrangement of children, when children leave home and establish new families, and the composition of households as distinct from families.

VARIETY OF FAMILY TYPES

Most of the families in the United States are maintained by a married couple or by one parent and one or more of the parent's sons and/or daughters. Fully 86 percent of Black families in 1980 were of these two types, and the corresponding proportion for all families without regard to race was 93 percent (Table 6.1). Thus, although the vast majority of families consist of one of these types, twice as large a proportion of Black families as other families (as defined by the Census Bureau) were not of these types (14 versus 7 percent). Many of the families of the latter type consist of grandparents providing homes for grandchildren whose parents live elsewhere or have died, or consist of such combinations as brothers and sisters living together apart from their parents.

One distinguishing feature of Black families is that they continue to be more likely than other families to include young children. By 1980, 62 percent of the Black families, as compared with 52 percent of the families of all races, included one or more sons and/or daughters under 18 in the home. The larger proportion of Black families with young children reflects, among other things, the higher birth rate of Black women and the shorter joint survival of Black marriages after the children leave home. There was little change during the 1970s in the proportion of Black families with young children present because the substantial increase in one-parent families was nearly offset by a decrease in married-couple families with children.

In 1980, one-half of the Black families with children present were one-parent families (31 percent), and one-half were married-couple families (31 percent). At the same time, less than one-fifth of the families of all races with children were maintained by one parent. As far back as 1950, 9 percent of the Black families were one-parent families, but at that time only 4 percent of the families of all races were one-parent families. Therefore, this is one aspect of family life in which the gap between Black families and other families has persisted.

TABLE 6.1   Families by Type, Race, and Presence of Own Children Under
                      18 Years Old: United States, 1980 and 1970

Type of Family and Presence of Own Children under 18	1980		Percent Black	1970		Percent Change 1970 to 1980	
	All Races	Black		All Races	Black	All Races	Black
All families							
(thousands)	58,426	6,042	10.3	51,586	4,887	13.2	23.6
Percent	100.0	100.0	—	100.0	100.0	—	—
With own children	52.2	61.8	12.2	55.9	61.1	5.8	25.0
No own children	47.8	38.2	8.3	44.1	38.9	22.5	21.4
Married-couple families	82.5	55.5	7.0	86.7	68.0	7.6	0.9
With own children	42.0	31.2	7.7	49.5	40.9	−3.9	−5.9
No own children	40.5	24.3	6.2	37.2	27.1	22.9	11.1
Parent-child families	10.2	30.6	31.1	6.4	20.2	81.7	87.7
Mother and own children	9.2	28.9	32.7	5.7	18.7	82.4	91.6
Father and own children	1.0	1.7	16.7	0.7	1.5	76.5	39.7
Other families	7.3	13.9	19.3	6.9	11.8	20.5	44.9
Female householder	5.4	11.3	21.4	5.2	9.6	19.8	45.3
Male householder	1.9	2.6	13.3	1.7	2.2	22.5	43.1

SOURCES: U.S. Bureau of the Census, 1980a, 1980b, and unpublished Current Population Survey data.

TYPE OF FAMILY AND EDUCATIONAL LEVEL

The great majority of children under 18 years of age live with parents who are under 45 years old. Moreover, close to nine-tenths of all families maintained by adults under 45 have young children among their family members. Among Black adults of this age who were maintaining families in 1980, a substantial minority—30 percent of those who were married men and 20 percent who were unmarried women—had completed at least one year of college. These figures represent an approximate doubling of the corresponding figure for the married men, and more than a fivefold increase for the unmarried women, during the preceding decade. Further analysis shows that only a small part of this improvement can be accounted for by the increase in the educational level of all adults under 45. Corresponding but smaller increases were made at the high school graduation level.

Therefore, it is correct to infer that Black children currently live in the homes of much better-educated adults than did Black children a decade earlier. Also, the rate of improvement in the education of Black parents under 45 has been about twice as large as the corresponding rate for other parents. The fact remains, however, that the average educational level of Black persons maintaining families is substantially lower than that of their counterparts of other races. Thus, the gap between the educational levels of Black parents and other parents has been narrowing, but differences still persist.

Another kind of racial difference is found in the gap between the educational attainments of husbands and their wives: Black women are more likely than other women to be married to men with less education than they have, and this situation is particularly associated with women in second and subsequent marriages (Spanier and Glick, 1980). This situation is related to the much smaller proportion of Black husbands than other husbands who are college educated. Again, this differential has been decreasing.

LIVING ARRANGEMENTS OF CHILDREN

Even though the number of one-parent *families* increased at a faster rate among Black families than other families during the 1970s, the number of *children* in one-parent families actually grew at a slower rate among Black families than in other families (Table 6.2). This tendency toward convergence is attributable primarily to the smaller rate of increase in the already quite high proportions of Black children living with separated or never-married parents. A closely related change has been a smaller rate of increase between 1970 and 1978 in the proportion of births to unmarried Black women than to unmarried women of all races (41 percent increase as compared to 52 percent increase). Nonetheless, in 1978, 53 percent of Black births, but only 16 percent of births of all races, were to women who were not currently married; corresponding figures for 1970 had been 38 percent and 11 percent, respectively.

In both 1980 and 1970, a majority of children in one-parent families regardless of race were living with a divorced or separated mother. During the 1970s the proportion of Black children living with a divorced parent increased much more rapidly than did the proportion living with a separated parent. This fact suggests that more of the parents with serious marital problems were resolving them by becoming divorced and therefore eligible to remarry if that option seemed better than remaining unmarried.

The median age of Black children under 18 living with a divorced parent in 1979 was 11.6 years, about two years older than the median age for all Black children under 18. Moreover, the average age of children under 18 increased by about one year during the 1970s because of the declining birth rate. This change must have made it easier for women to obtain a divorce and maintain a home without a husband, at least to the extent that fewer of them had very young children requiring close supervision.

A declining proportion of children have been living with a widowed parent, as the mortality rates for adults of child-rearing age have continued to fall. On the other hand, an increasing proportion of children have been living apart from either parent, but the great majority of these children live with grandparents or other relatives. The most recent information on children under 18 living with grandparents apart from their parents was obtained in 1970; it showed that such

TABLE 6.2 Living Arrangements of Noninstitutional Children Under 18 Years Old by Race: United States, 1980 and 1970

Living Arrangements	1980			1970		Percent Change, 1970 to 1980	
	All Races	Black	Percent Black	All Races	Black	All Races	Black
All children under 18 (thousands)	61,744	9,290	15.2	69,162	9,406	-10.7	-1.2
Percent	100.0	100.0	—	100.0	100.0	—	—
Living with:							
Two parents	76.6	42.2	11.5	85.2	57.8	-19.7	-28.1
One parent	19.7	45.8	25.7	11.9	33.3	48.3	36.0
Mother only	18.0	43.8	25.6	10.8	30.3	49.4	42.8
Divorced	7.5	10.9	10.2	3.3	5.0	101.9	113.1
Married	5.7	16.1	38.9	4.7	14.6	8.8	9.3
Separated	4.9	15.0	39.4	3.4	12.6	29.3	17.3
Widowed	2.0	4.0	34.5	2.0	4.6	-9.5	-14.2
Never married	2.8	12.8	33.5	0.8	6.1	224.7	108.2
Father only	1.7	2.0	26.8	1.1	2.9	38.0	-33.9
Divorced	0.8	0.6	5.1	0.3	0.3	185.3	119.2
Married	0.5	0.6	50.7	0.4	1.5	-1.0	-58.3
Separated	0.4	0.6	63.9	0.2	0.6	56.6	—
Widowed	0.3	0.4	38.0	0.4	0.7	-32.7	-47.7
Never married	0.1	0.3	58.3	—	0.4	140.0	-26.2
Other relatives only	3.1	10.7	36.4	2.2	7.4	23.4	43.3
Nonrelatives only	0.6	1.3	34.1	0.7	1.5	-14.0	-7.9

SOURCES: U.S. Bureau of the Census, 1973, and unpublished Current Population Survey data.

children constituted 5 percent of all Black children, about three times the percentage (1.5) of children of other races (Glick, 1976). Another 5 percent lived with one or both parents in the home of the children's grandparents. In these circumstances, many of the mothers must have left their children in the care of grandparents while they—being younger, better educated, and more employable—earned a living.

A rapidly increasing, but still small, minority of Black children live in the suburbs of metropolitan areas. During the 1970s this number increased three times as rapidly for the Black population as for persons of all races (45 percent as compared to 14 percent). In 1980, 21 percent of the Black population, as compared to 40 percent of the entire population, lived in metropolitan suburbs.

CHILDREN LEAVING HOME

The departure of young adults from their parental home is generally a critical period for all persons involved and most often occurs in the early 20s. The proportion of Black persons 20 to 24 years of age who were still living with their parents (or had returned to their parental home) declined from 45 percent in 1940, near the end of the Depression, to 39 percent by 1960, after a couple of decades of more prosperous times. Nevertheless, by 1970, the direction had changed; at that time 42 percent were living with their parents. Although statistics are not available from the 1980 census on this subject, they are expected to show further increases in this proportion during the latter part of the 1970s because of the relatively high unemployment rates and divorce rates and because more young adults during recent years have been able to remain in their parental homes while they delay marriage and attend the growing number of community colleges.

CHILDBEARING

Most of the young adults who leave their parental homes rather soon establish separate households at the time of marriage and before childbearing. Historically, Black families have had more children than other families as a whole, but there are some signs that the average number of children born to mothers in the two racial groups may be currently in a phase of convergence. This impression is based partly on answers to questions the Census Bureau asked in 1979 about how many children they had borne and how many more they expected to have. Among women 18 to 34 years of age regardless of marital status, Black women had already had an average number of children that was 32 percent above that for women of all races combined. However, the average number of "lifetime births expected" by Black women was only 8 percent higher than that for all women. Recent studies have shown that married women during the 1970s tended to overestimate the total number of children they will have.

Childlessness is another measure of fertility, which generally varies inversely with the average number of children per woman and which is often analyzed for women 45 to 49 years of age because almost all of them have ended their childbearing. Women of this age in 1960 had been at the height of childbearing during the Depression of the 1930s, and fully 28 percent of the Black women of this age had borne no children; for all races the figure was 18 percent. During the two following decades, these childlessness rates declined dramatically, so that by 1979 only 9 percent of the Black women and 7 percent of the women of all races 45 to 49 reported they had had no children. These women had been at the crest of childbearing during the baby boom period of the 1950s. When the women in 1979 were asked how many children they expected to have during their lifetime, 9 percent of the Black women 30 to 34 years old reported they expected to have none; this level was actually lower than that—11 percent—for women of all races. Here, the trend for the two racial groups not only converged but crossed.

Poorly educated Black women tend to have especially high birth rates, and highly educated Black women tend to have especially low birth rates. For example, Black women age 35 to 44 in 1979 with less than 8 years of school had borne 4.6 children, on the average, as compared to 3.8 children for women of all races of this age and educational level. But corresponding rates for women with some college education were 2.4 children for Black women and 2.3 for all women. Still sharper contrasts at the upper educational level are available from the 1970 census, which revealed that Black women 35 to 39 years old with graduate school training had even lower fertility than women of all races of the same age and education—1.9 children versus 2.2 children ever born, on the average.

These differentials suggest, among other things, that Black women with little education may be more inclined than other women to have several children as a primary source of personal and family enjoyment, or that they tend to use less effective means of family limitation, or both. The differentials also suggest that Black women with advanced college education may tend to find it necessary to limit their family size especially severely in order to be competitive in the world of work.

FAMILY HOUSEHOLDS AND OTHER HOUSEHOLDS

The term "family household" is defined as a household maintained by a person who shares living quarters with one or more relatives. This type of household has been growing more slowly than other types of households, among Blacks and others alike, as young adults delayed marriage and had rising divorce rates, and as women increasingly outlived their husbands. In 1980, 7 of every 10 of the 8.4 million Black households were maintained by families. During the 1970s, Black family households increased only about one-third as fast as nonfamily households (24 percent as compared to 77 percent). Most of the 2.4 million households of the latter type consisted of Black persons living alone; Black persons living alone under 35 years old were almost twice as numerous in 1980 as in 1970. Moreover, Black persons 65 and over were half again as numerous in 1980 as in 1970. Evidently an increasing number of adults today find it financially feasible to keep up a home alone who would have shared the home of someone else in earlier times. Although this home may have relatively few accommodations, it provides a shelter from the irritations that often arise while living in another person's home.

Unmarried-couple households are still not very numerous, but they increased three times as fast during the 1970s as other types of households among Blacks and eight times as fast as among persons of other races. In 1980, 3.5 percent of all Black households included a man and a woman not related to each other and no other adults; 2.0 percent of all households, or about 1.5 million households maintained by adults regardless of race, were of this type. Although Blacks maintained 11 percent of all households in 1980, they maintained 19 percent of all unmarried-couple households. Thus, nearly twice as large a proportion of Black households as other households were of this type, but the gap between Blacks and others in this respect has been narrowing. The number of Black unmarried couples was only about 300,000 in 1980, according to the Census Bureau's Current Population Survey, and that number is rather small to show significant racial differences in the social and economic characteristics of unmarried couples. Much more can be learned from 1980 census data on this subject, which are scheduled to become available in 1982 and 1983.

Despite the foregoing developments, the fact remains that one-half of the Black people in the United States live in households maintained by a married couple—despite the sharp increases in one-parent households, one-person households, and unmarried-couple households. Yet, the corresponding proportion for persons of all races living in households maintained by a married couple is significantly higher still—namely, three-fourths. Within this context, the most common living arrangement of the population is a home containing both a married couple and one or more children under 18 years of age; one in every three Black persons lives in such a home, whereas one in every two other persons does. These facts imply that close to one-sixth of all Black persons are members of married-couple households with no children under 18. The remaining half of all Black persons are about equally divided between those in one-parent households and those in "other" households. One-third of the Black persons in "other" households (8 percent of all Black persons) live entirely alone. That leaves 3 percent living in unmarried-couple households and 16 percent in a variety of household types (usually including two or more related persons) or in institutions or other group quarters.

MARRIAGE AND DIVORCE

The most meaningful analysis of marital status depends strongly on classification by age. Yet attention cannot be given to the full distribution of marital status by age in the space to which the subject must be limited in this chapter. Consequently, the following treatment of each marital status category focuses on the age range that is most relevant.

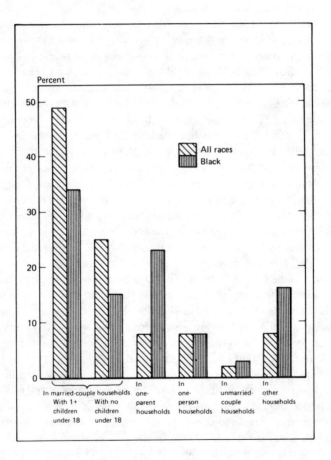

FIGURE 6.1   Living Arrangements of the Noninstitutional Population by Race: United States, 1980

DELAY OF MARRIAGE

During the 1960s and 1970s, young adult Blacks had a consistent pattern of postponing marriage longer than their White counterparts (Table 6.3). However, this difference became much more apparent by 1980 than it had been in either 1970 or 1960 among those 20 to 24 years of age, the period of life when the median ages for first marriage occur for both men and women. Contributing factors were the higher unemployment rates and more rapidly increasing college enrollment rates among Blacks.

A strictly demographic factor in the large amount of marriage postponement during the last two decades has been the "marriage squeeze." In the context that women are usually two or three years younger than men at marriage, the marriage squeeze developed as a consequence of the upward trend of births during the baby boom. Thus, a woman born in 1947 when the birth rate had risen was likely to expect to marry a man born in 1944 or 1945 when the birth rate was still low. The result, about 20 years later, was an excess of women in the primary ages for marriage, and this phenomenon continued for the length of time that the baby boom lasted. Therefore, by 1970, the number of Black men 20 to 26 years of age was only 82 percent of the number of women 18 to 24. The corresponding figure for persons of all races was 93 percent.

TABLE 6.3   Marital Status of the Noninstitutional Population in Selected Age
             Groups by Race and Sex: United States, 1980, 1970, and 1960

| Marital Status, | Men | | | Women | | |
Age, and Race	1980	1970	1960[a]	1980	1970	1960[a]
Percent never married, 20 to 24 years old						
All races	69	56	53	50	36	29
Black	79	57	56	69	43	36
Percent separated or divorced, 25 to 34 years old						
All races	9	5	4	14	8	6
Black	13	9	8	28	20	17
Percent in intact marriage, 35 to 44 years old						
All races	81	84	84	84	79	80
Black	61	69	71	49	58	62
Percent widowed, 55 years old and over						
All races	9	11	12	37	38	38
Black	14	16	16	45	44	47

[a]Races other than White for 1960.

SOURCES: U.S. Bureau of the Census, 1972, 1966, and unpublished Current Population Survey data.

Thus, by 1970, for young adults regardless of race, there was a shortage of men in the primary marriageable ages for women. By 1980, these percentages had risen somewhat, to 89 percent for Blacks and 98 percent for all races. And by 1995, the corresponding figures are expected to rise to 96 percent and 108 percent, respectively, as the declining birth rates of the 1960s and early 1970s cause a reversal of the marriage squeeze phenomenon. Incidentally, the consistently lower figures for Blacks is a consequence of both a smaller proportion of boys among Blacks than others at birth and to the larger undercount of young Black men than of other young men in the census.

SEPARATION AND DIVORCE

An acceleration in marital disruption (separation and divorce), as well as in the delay of marriage, occurred during the 1970s among Blacks as well as others (Table 6.3). The racial difference in the level of disrupted marriages is more marked among women than men, primarily because of the especially large minority of Black women who are reported as separated. To some extent this discrepancy may be the result of many never-married mothers incorrectly reporting themselves as separated. Another consideration is the greater tendency for persons in the lower economic strata to use separation as the "poor person's divorce." An alternate hypothesis is that Black women are more likely than other women to experience a period of married life before deciding to maintain themselves in an unmarried state.

Among adults of all races combined, currently divorced persons in 1980 were about 10 percent as numerous as persons in intact marriages. The corresponding proportion has doubled since 1970 for Blacks as well as those of other races. By 1980, there were 15 percent as many Black divorced men as Black married men and 26 percent as many Black divorced women as Black married women.

Divorce and income tend to be negatively correlated for men of all races 35 to 44 years old, according to 1970 census data for this age group, by which most marriages and divorces have occurred. But for Black men, the smallest proportion of divorces occurs among those in the middle income range, above which the proportion increases. An explanation for the deviation of Black men from the general pattern does not readily occur to this writer. However, the proportion of Black men in the upper income range where the anomaly occurs is relatively small.

Women college graduates with no graduate school training tend to have the most stable first marriages, regardless of race. Black women with an incomplete college education have the greatest likelihood of divorce; and those with graduate school education also have relatively high divorce probabilities, as do women of other races. Women with advanced college degrees, regardless of race, are probably the most likely to have career interests that compete with the desire to maintain a permanent marriage.

INTACT MARRIAGES

As first marriages have been delayed and marital disruption has become more frequent, the proportion of persons in the middle adult years who are in intact marriages has been declining. Again, both the general trend and the race differential were accelerated during the 1970s, as is evident from the data on persons age 35 to 54 shown in Table 6.3. During both the 1960s and the 1970s, the extent to which marital stability was affected by changes in the proportion widowed was very slight; widowhood continues to be far more prevalent among women than men above the mid-50s, partly because of lower death rates among women and higher remarriage rates among men, regardless of race.

As the income level of men increases, the proportion of men with intact first marriages tends to increase, among both Black men and men of other races, according to 1970 census data. Evidently for men there is a positive relation, on the average, between their degree of success in their field of work and in the continuation of their experience as a partner in an intact marriage, but this relationship is strongest at the lower end of the income distribution. This fact suggests that marital permanence for men depends less on being well-to-do than it does on not being poor.

The pattern for women is generally in the opposite direction: The more income women earn, the less likely they are to remain in their first marriage. Women with high incomes often find that the demands of their work interfere with their marital adjustment, and such a situation has a likelihood of being made worse if the wife earns more than her husband.

The lesser degree of marital stability among Black men and other men can be explained in part by the differences between their socioeconomic statuses. This generalization can be documented by 1970 census data for men 45 to 54 years old, who were essentially in the prime of life (U.S. Bureau of the Census, 1972: table 6). From this source the percentage currently married can be derived for two contrasting groups of men according to their socioeconomic status: those ranking simultaneously in the highest strata of education, occupation, and income, and those ranking simultaneously in the lowest strata. The results show that the differences between Black men and White men with respect to the percentage married by the time of middle age are greatly reduced if comparisons are made within such well-controlled socioeconomic levels. Some of the remaining differences may be attributable to such factors as the lower average quality of education at a given grade level for Blacks and a greater proportion of

Black men in the lower range of a particular occupational group. Similar relationships may be expected in the 1980 census results when they become available.

REMARRIAGE

The most recent information available from Census Bureau surveys on remarriage is that collected in June 1975. At that time, 20 percent of the Black men and 19 percent of all Black women who had ever married were reported as remarried (Glick, 1980). The corresponding proportion of divorced persons who remarry is higher among Whites than among Blacks at each interval since divorce (Eckhardt et al., 1980). This apparent contradiction is a result of the different socioeconomic levels of Blacks and Whites, on the average. There has been a historic tendency for Black couples to have lower average incomes than White couples, for their divorce rates to be relatively high, and yet for remarriage rates after divorce to be relatively low among men of low income.

Among divorced women, however, remarriage rates are higher for those with less than a full high school education than they are for those with more education, regardless of race. This generalization suggests that poorly educated women tend to remarry rather quickly because they have more difficulty in finding employment that would sustain them and their children, especially in view of the comparatively high fertility and dependency rates among women without a high school education.

Early marriage, regardless of race, is associated with twice as much likelihood of divorce and remarriage within three to five years after first marriage as marriage at more "preferred" or intermediate ages, according to 1970 census data. Early marriage refers to persons 14 to 17 years of age for women and 14 to 19 years for men. Intermediate ages refers to women 20 to 24 years and to men 25 to 29; these are the ages at which college graduates are most likely to marry. The 1975 study mentioned previously demonstrated that remarriage is more likely to be followed by redivorce among Black women age 35 to 44 than among other women of the same age. It also showed that Black women 35 to 44 with no children were more likely to become redivorced than those with children, especially those with preschool-age children; this result no doubt reflects the greater ease of childless women than mothers to be self-sustaining.

INTERMARRIAGE

A special tabulation of 1977 data from the Current Population Survey showed that there were 421,000 interracial married couples in the United States, or about one-third more than the number in 1970 (U.S. Bureau of the

Census, 1980d). The reported number had approximately doubled during the 1960s; some of the increase may have resulted from more willingness to report accurately. The 125,000 Black/White couples in 1977 were close to twice the number in 1970: 65,000. Three-fourths (74 percent) of the Black/White couples in 1977, as compared to close to two-thirds (63 percent) in 1970, had a Black husband and a White wife. Altogether, the Black/White married couples in 1977 represented about 3.6 percent of all Black couples and 0.3 percent of all White couples. Thus, the number of interracial married couples has continued to grow, and the predominant proportion of Black/White couples that include a Black husband and a White wife is evidently increasing.

Interracial married couples have a greater probability of having a short marriage than married couples with the husband and wife of the same race, whether both are Black or both are White. Perhaps the best evidence is found in census data reported by Heer (1974) concerning first marriages contracted in the 1950s that were still intact in 1970. The results show that 90 percent of the couples with a White husband and wife, both in their first marriage, were still living together and that 78 percent of the couples with a Black husband and wife were also still together; however, smaller proportions—63 percent—of the couples with a Black husband and a White wife and only 47 percent of those with a White husband and a Black wife had continuing first marriages. Presumably the current proportion of couples with a Black husband and a White wife is larger than that for couples with a White husband and a Black wife, not only because more couples of the former type become married but also because the former type tend to have a longer duration of marriage than the latter type.

Unmarried couples are more likely than married couples to be interracial. Although the numbers involved are quite small, the 1975 survey mentioned previously shows that 2 percent of unmarried couples, but only about 0.5 percent of married couples, were combinations of a Black adult and a White adult of opposite sex (Glick and Spanier, 1980).

EMPLOYMENT AND INCOME

WORKING WIVES AND MOTHERS

Most of the Black husbands as well as husbands of other races are in the labor force, but the proportion of men in the labor force has been declining as the population has been aging and as more men choose to retire at an earlier age. Thus, 84 percent of the Black husbands were in the labor force in 1970, but the percentage decreased to 80 percent in 1979 (U.S. Bureau of the Census, 1973b; U.S. Bureau of Labor Statistics, 1981). The corresponding change for husbands of all races was from 86 percent to 81 percent. By contrast, the worker rate for wives rose sharply during the 1970s.

The labor force participation rate for Black wives as well as other wives rose by 9 percentage points between 1969 and 1979. However, at both dates the rate for Black wives was about 11 percentage points higher than that for wives of all races. Specifically, 51 percent of Black wives in 1969 and 60 percent in 1979 were in the labor force, as compared to 40 percent and 49 percent, respectively, for wives of all races. This growth in the proportion of wives in the labor market reflects many other social and economic changes, including the extensive increase in education and therefore the employability of young women and the expansion of employment opportunities for the performance of clerical and professional work.

Young wives with no children have continued to include a relatively high and increasing proportion in the labor force. Childless Black wives 16 to 34 years of age in 1970 had a worker rate of 64 percent, and by 1979 the rate had risen to 72 percent, a few percentage points below the rates for women of all races—68 percent and 82 percent, respectively. A more detailed analysis of the differences by race would show, among other related things, that the Black wives have higher unemployment rates and a somewhat lower average educational level than other wives; both of these factors must discourage some other women from even looking for work.

By contrast, Black wives under 35 years of age with one or more of their children under 18 in their home have had worker rates 16 percentage points higher than the corresponding rates for wives under 35 of all races in both 1970 and 1979. For Black wives the respective rates were 49 percent in 1970 rising to 65 percent in 1979, whereas for wives of other races the rates were 33 percent rising to 49 percent. These shared increases in the worker rates for young mothers are no doubt related to both the falling birth rate and the increasing proportion of children in the home who are of school age.

In 1979, more than half (57 percent) of the Black married couples had both the husband and wife in the labor force. This compares with 51 percent for all married couples. But between 1970 and 1979, the increase in this type of two-worker family was twice as large for Black couples as for all couples (up 11 percentage points versus 5 percentage points). As a consequence, the median income of Black married-couple, two-earner families rose especially sharply during the 1970s, consistent with the discussion in the next section.

EMPLOYMENT AND INCOME BY TYPE OF FAMILY

Changes in family income by race during the 1970s have been profoundly affected by the changing mix of families by type as well as by the changing proportion of families with both the husband and the wife in the labor force. The lowest pair of rows in Table 6.4 shows that the median income of Black families in 1979 was 54 percent as large as that for families of all races combined, not very different from the corresponding figure for 1969, 53 percent. However, for each type of family, shown in the table, there was an appreciable improvement in the family income of Blacks as compared with that for families of all races. The greatest improvement was that for Black families with the wife in the paid labor force, which shows that by 1979 the median income of these Black families was about 83 percent as large as that for families of all races; it had been only 69 percent as large in 1969.

An important reason for the relative position of Black families with the wife in the paid labor force is the much larger proportion of Black wives than wives of all races who worked year-round full-time (42 percent as compared to 31 percent). Moreover, the median income of Black wives who worked year-round full-time in 1979 ($9,300) was almost as high as that for all wives ($9,483). Consequently, the median income for all Black wives in 1979 was 29 percent,

TABLE 6.4   Type of Family in 1980 and 1970 and Median Family Income in 1979 and 1969 by Race: United States

| Year and Race | All Families | Married-Couple Families | | Male Householder, No Wife Present | Female Householder, No Husband Present |
		Wife in Paid Labor Force	Wife Not in Paid Labor Force		
PERCENT					
All races:					
1980	100.0	40.7	41.8	2.9	14.6
1970	100.0	34.1	52.6	2.4	10.9
Black:					
1980	100.0	32.8	22.7	4.3	40.2
1970	100.0	36.3	31.8	3.7	28.3
MEDIAN FAMILY INCOME					
All races:					
1979	$21,521	$24,973	$17,791	$16,888	$9,933
1969[a]	$18,677	$23,025	$17,580	$16,513	$9,547
Black:					
1979	$11,648	$20,704	$11,616	$12,497	$6,907
1969[a]	$ 9,916	$15,099	$ 9,277	$10,287	$5,523
Black as percent of all races:					
1979	54.1	82.9	65.3	74.0	69.5
1969	53.1	65.6	52.8	62.3	57.9

[a]In terms of 1979 dollars.

SOURCES: U.S. Bureau of the Census, 1970, 1980d, and unpublished Current Population Survey data.

considerably higher than that for all wives regardless of race ($5,128 as compared to $3,973). Meantime, Black men were less likely to work full-time and had lower average incomes than other men. These are among the main reasons why the median income of Black families with the wife in the labor force was "only" 83 percent as large as that for families of all races with the wife in the labor force.

Incidentally, Black wives had the same or more income than their husbands in 25 percent of the families in 1978 as compared to 15 percent for wives of all races. In addition, Black wives with earnings contributed 33 percent of the family income in 1979 as compared to 26 percent for wives of all races with earnings (U.S. Bureau of Labor Statistics, 1981).

WOMEN WITHOUT HUSBANDS AT HOME

Another significant development during the 1970s affecting the relative income level of Black families was the much more rapid growth in the proportion of Black families that were maintained by a woman with no husband in the household. These families have consistently the lowest average incomes, and by 1980 fully 40 percent of all Black families were of this type as compared to 28 percent in 1970. And as the proportion of all Black families that were maintained by women increased, the proportion with the wife in the paid labor force became smaller among all Black families, as did the proportion of Black families with two or more earners. Meantime, among the families of all races, both of these proportions increased during the 1970s.

For this complex set of reasons, the net effect was a consistent increase in the relative income position of Black families of each type but practically no overall change in the position of Black families as a whole. A much fuller exposition of this situation is presented in chapter 9 of *Social Indicators III* (U.S. Bureau of the Census, 1980e).

The poverty rate for Black families in 1979 was 28 percent, the same as in 1969. Meantime, the poverty rate for all families declined from 10 to 9 percent. Accordingly, the overall poverty rate has continued to be about three times as high for Black families as for all families. However, for each type of family the poverty rate was less than three times as high for Black families, because the poverty rate for Black families maintained by women was so much higher than that for all families (49 percent as compared to 30 percent) and because that type of family was found in nearly three times as large a proportion of Black families as in all families (40 percent as compared to 15 percent). Even though the poverty rate for Black families was quite high during the last decade, it was still higher a decade earlier; in 1959, the poverty rate for all Black families was 48 percent and that for families maintained by Black women was 65 percent. Comparable rates for families of all races were much lower—19 percent and 43 percent, respectively.

PER CAPITA INCOME

This measure provides a basis for assessing the comparative income standing of the Black population independent of differences in family structure that change from one time to another. Recent information from the Current Population Survey shows that the average annual income per Black person in 1979 was $4,414, and that the average for persons of all races was $7,061; thus, per capita income for Blacks in 1979 was 63 percent of that for persons of all races. In 1970, per capita income for Blacks had compared somewhat less favorably, when it was 60 percent of that for persons of all races ($1,922 as compared to $3,183 in terms of 1970 dollars).

CHILD SUPPORT AND ALIMONY

According to a recent study conducted by the U.S. Bureau of the Census (1980c), in 1979 only 29 percent of the Black women who had sole custody of young children, as compared with 59 percent for similar women of all races, were awarded child support payments. And not quite as large a proportion of Black women as women of all races who were supposed to receive child support payments actually received the payments (five-eighths as compared to three-fourths). But the amount of child support actually received constituted about as small a proportion of the mothers' total income, on the average, for both Black mothers (18 percent of $7,270 total income) and mothers of all races (20 percent of $8,940 total income). Black mothers, as well as other mothers, who received child support payments had larger total incomes, on the average, than those who received none. A substantial proportion of those 2.5 million mothers of all races and 260,000 Black mothers who received such support probably had absent husbands who had higher incomes and were more effective in their attempts at obtaining the payments that had been awarded than their counterparts who did not receive child support from their husbands.

Very few ever-divorced Black women are awarded alimony, but the likelihood of receiving it is about the same for them as it is for other women to whom it is awarded. Only 7 percent of Black women and 14 percent of women of all races in 1979 who had been divorced had been awarded alimony, and about 7 of every 10 of those who were supposed to receive alimony, regardless of race, actually did receive it.

DISCUSSION

This chapter represents the author's attempt to add to the growing number of "works on Black families that tend to view them from a positive rather than a negative perspective" (Wilkinson, 1978). From a balanced viewpoint, Black families are regarded as "an important subculture of American society, different in many ways from White families, but possessing a value system, patterns of behavior, and institutions which can be described, understood, and appreciated for their own strengths and characteristics" (Peters, 1978).

A strength, as well as a liability, that is prominent among Black families is "the centrality of children," to borrow an apt expression from Cazenave (1980). As Table 6.1 demonstrated, a larger proportion of Black families than families of other races include young children among their members. Another distinguishing feature of Black families has been the large and continually growing proportion maintained by women. These prevailing Black family lifestyles have been interpreted, in part, as adaptations to the special circumstances in which many Black persons find themselves and, in part, as preferences for certain values that often differ from those of members of other races. Yet Black families vary widely in the personal and social characteristics of their members; moreover, Black family members tend to be concentrated somewhat more in selected parts of the range of these characteristics than family members of other races because of differing circumstances or matters of choice.

Some of the apparent differences between Black and other families are probably the result of unequal amounts of misreporting in censuses and surveys on such subjects as the absence of the husband from the household. Most likely many poor couples, regardless of race, yield to the temptation to report that the husband is absent if they believe that doing so will improve their chances of receiving welfare benefits; if such reporting is more likely to occur among Black families, it could be at least in part because a larger proportion of Black families than other families are poor. Also, Black husbands are more likely than other husbands to live apart from their wives because larger proportions of them are serving in the Armed Forces or are residing in an institution.

Some of the signs of diminishing differences between Black and other families also deserve to be mentioned. For example, even though a larger proportion of Black children live in one-parent families, the rate of increase in this proportion has been less rapid since 1970 among Black children than children of other races. Therefore, this gap has been narrowing. Other demonstrations of converging tendencies since 1970 include the more rapid increase in the (generally lower) average educational level of Black than other women who maintain homes; the less rapid increase in the (generally higher) proportion of households maintained by unmarried Black than other couples; and the more rapid increase in the (generally lower) median incomes of Black than other families of each type. In some respects these developments are evidence that "Black families have managed to sustain their families under pressures that are now being shared by a growing number of non-black families" (McAdoo, 1978).

Many of the racial differences in family characteristics persist but are demonstrably smaller within socioeconomic levels than they are for all levels combined. If racial differences in socioeconomic stratification should diminish during coming years, one might reasonably expect that more of the residual differences in family characteristics will become matters of choice to fulfill aspirations rather necessary to cope with their unique problems of adjustment.

REFERENCES

CAZENAVE, N. A. (1980) "Alternate intimacy, marriage, and family lifestyles among low-income black Americans." Alternative Lifestyles 3 (November): 425-444.

ECKHARDT, K. W., W. R. GRADY, and G. E. HENDERSHOT (1980) "Expectations and probabilities of remarriage: findings from the National Survey of Family Growth, Cycle III." Unpublished manuscript.

GLICK, P.C. (1976) "Living arrangements of children and young adults." Jounral of Comparative Family Studies 7 (Summer): 321-333.

———— (1980) "Remarriage: some recent changes and variations." Journal of Family Issues 1 (December): 455-478.

———— and G. B. SPANIER (1980) "Married and unmarried cohabitation in the United States." Journal of Marriage and the Family 42 (February): 19-30.

HEER, D. M. (1974) "The prevalence of black-white marriage in the United States, 1960 and 1970." Journal of Marriage and the Family 36 (May): 246-258.

McADOO, H. P. (1978) "Factors related to stability in upwardly mobile black families." Journal of Marriage and the Family 40 (November): 761-776.

PETERS, M. F. (1978) "Black families: notes from the guest editor." Journal of Marriage and the Family 40 (November): 655-658.

SPANIER, G. B. and P.C. GLICK (1980) "Paths to remarriage." Journal of Divorce 3 (Spring): 283-298.

U.S. Bureau of the Census (1966) Marital Status. 1960 Census, II: 4E. Washington, DC: Government Printing Office.

———— (1970) "Income in 1969 of families and persons in the United States." Current Population Reports, Series P-60, No. 75. Washington, DC: Government Printing Office.

———— (1972) Marital Status. 1970 Census, II: 4C. Washington, DC: Government Printing Office.

———— (1973a) Persons by Family Characteristics. 1970 Census, II: 4B. Washington, DC: Government Printing Office.

———— (1973b) Employment and Work Experience. 1970 Census, II: 6A. Washington, DC: Government Printing Office.

———— (1978) "Perspectives on American husbands and wives." Current Population Reports, Series P-23, No. 77. Washington, DC: Government Printing Office.

———— (1980a) "Population profile of the United States: 1979." Current Population Reports, Series P-20, No. 350. Washington, DC: Government Printing Office.

———— (1980b) "Households and families, by type: March 1980." Current Population Reports, Series P-20, No. 357. Washington, DC: Government Printing Office.

———— (1980c) "Child support and alimony." Current Population Reports, Series P-23, No. 106. Washington, DC: Government Printing Office.

———— (1980d) "Money income and poverty status of families and persons in the United States: 1979." Current Population Reports, Series P-60, No.125. Washington, DC: Government Printing Office.

———— (1980e) Social Indicators III. Washington, DC: Government Printing Office.
U.S. Bureau of Labor Statistics (1981) "Marital and family characteristics of the labor force, March 1979." Special Labor Force Report 237. Washington, DC: Government Printing Office.
WILLIE, C. V. (1970) The Family Life of Black People. Columbus, OH: Charles E. Merrill.
WILKINSON, D. Y. (1978) "Toward a positive frame of reference for analysis of black families: a selected bibliography." Journal of Marriage and the Family 40 (November): 707-708.

7

ECONOMICS AND MOBILITY
A Theoretical Rationale for
Urban Black Family Well-Being

FRANK G. DAVIS

INTRODUCTION

The black family in the United States represents an economic and social sub-group in terms of income, education, and employment; further, the black family is struggling to survive under tragic conditions of economic inequality (Davis, 1978: 24-26), where economic and social stratification constitute a permanent feature of the economy (Tussing, 1975: 16-17). Whereas the goal of American society, as expressed in the legislation of the sixties, is to dele-gitimize inequality, the facts of the seventies seem to deny any significant economic progress for the black masses. And if there is a trend for the eighties and beyond, it is clearly toward further inequality (Davis, 1978: ch. 4). The new administration, whose doctrinaire approach to economic policy reawakens a time-worn and challenged doctrine of economic individualism and self-inter-est, has begun to legitimize inequality.

Since a political reaffirmation of self-regulation and self-interest means unleashing previously regulated institutionalized market forces, which restrict the economic mobility of black labor, a basic question is: What can be done in terms of a new approach to policies designed to counteract a continuous decline in black family well-being[1] and central-city decline? Since the problem of black economic well-being is concentrated in central cities, we may ask what can be done in central cities that will reduce the decline in black family well-being and help reduce the decline in central-city prosperity. This question forms the subject matter of this chapter.

OBJECTIVE

The objective of this chapter is to develop a new approach to inner-city poverty.[2] We wish to show that inner-city poverty can be reduced if we link the policies of reducing poverty in the inner city to the economic processes of inner-city economy—namely, production, income distribution, and consumption. To show how this can be done, an attempt is made to establish the theoretical and policy rationale for recognizing the validity of the capital transfer approach, rather than the income transfer approach, in the economics of poverty; particularly inner-city poverty, where there exists substantial income and wealth differences between two economic groups, the poor and the well-off, existing side by side in the same economy; and where one group, the poor group, represents a substantial proportion of the inner-city population and may be delineated as an economic subsector or subeconomy. The basis for the distinction between the two groups is mainly differences in the market structure (Davis, 1972: ch. 3, 38ff) of firms between the two groups, and differences in inner-city market behavior with respect to employment and income distribution between two groups.

In the four sections which follow, a brief account is given of the problem of reducing poverty in terms of a new policy approach; the assumptions and underlying theory; and the choice between two economic models of the black family and their implications—one model accelerating black family economic decline and one model showing black family economic growth. Finally, we outline a theory of black family mobility and central-city prosperity.

THE PROBLEM AND A NEW POLICY APPROACH
TO POVERTY

A basic economic problem of the declining inner-city economy—and, with it, declining black family well-being—is the absence of an economic policy that (a) recognizes the essentiality of developing and linking the economic processes of the urban economy with the market potential of a concentrated mass of poor consumers located in the heart of the city, and (b) takes steps to increase the production, distribution, and consumption possibilities of the black community as a means of improving the purchasing power deficiencies of the urban economy. One of the key problems in inner-city decline is the exodus of higher-income groups and the declining purchasing power of a large concentration of low-income receivers left behind, which has nothing to sell but unskilled labor at low wages.

If, somehow, part of this mass of low-productivity, unskilled black labor could be converted to high-productivity capital, the black community could produce something more to sell, and thereby receive, in addition to wages, the returns to capital such as profits, rents, interest, and dividends, making up some of the purchasing power deficiencies of low wages. As it is now, the purchasing power deficiencies stemming from low wages and unemployment are partly made up out of social welfare receipts, which are now threatened to be reduced, thus accelerating a general decline in inner-city trade.

Our new approach involves the exchange of black community labor for white community capital, which we designate as a capital transfer policy for meeting the problem of poverty in the inner city. This new approach to poverty policy is designed to increase the productivity and income distribution to the poor by capitalizing on their own labor. This stands in sharp contrast to existing policies of income maintenance programs (Haveman, 1977: 55-56), which tend to maintain a poverty class as a permanent institutional outcome of the structural deficiencies in the economy (1977: 4). But it is just because of these structural deficiencies which restrict the income mobility of large segments of the inner-city population that a new policy approach is necessary. It is necessary for the prosperity of the inner-city economy because the existing inner-city market demand fails to generate sufficient consumption, investment, and employment. The market demand for black labor is circumscribed by institutional restrictions (Davis, 1978: 22-36), such as technological change, structural changes in industry, and the rise in human capital as an important factor in production, racism, and classism. These institutional restrictions are manifested by excessive unemployment, poverty, and limited economic opportunities and impose a serious fixity upon black family income mobility. Currently, almost half of the younger black family workers are unemployed; and at least one-third or more of all black families are below the poverty line. And under current conditions of stagflation, the proportion below the poverty line is increasing.

Technological change in industry reallocates black family labor out of high-productivity and higher-paying manufacturing industries (Davis, 1978: ch. 3). It forces those who can find a job into lower-paying and lower-productivity service-producing industries, where black workers have been traditionally concentrated. Structural changes in industry have generated what is known as "structural unemployment" and the rising hard-core unemployed. Combined with racism, shifts in technology and the rising demand for human capital (Averett, 1968: 149-150) development reduce the economic opportunity for a rise in black family income; classism tends to perpetuate the restrictions of racism.

ASSUMPTIONS AND UNDERLYING THEORY

BASIC ASSUMPTION

Our basic assumption is that prosperity in central-city and black family economic well-being are endogenously two sides of the same economic coin. It is assumed that a rise in the level of induced investment in the inner city depends on a rise in the level of consumption. Here, we assume an open system on the grounds that the accelerator by itself determines the behavior of consumption and income (Goodwin, 1948). And without a rise in the level of investment, there would be no rise in the level of employment. Thus, a rise in total consumption, investment, and employment in inner cities depends heavily on a rise in the large aggregate black family income and potential demand which are concentrated in inner cities, and where aggregate consumption spending of U. S. black families and individual households amounted to an aggregate of $33.1 billion in 1969 and $125.5 billion in 1980 (Brimmer and Co., n. d.),[3] an increase of 3.8 times over an 11-year period. It is therefore assumed that a rise in such a large aggregate black purchasing power is essential to a rise in consumption and investment in the inner city, where black families are concentrated.

THE UNDERLYING THEORY AND HYPOTHESIS

Our underlying theory is underutilization of saving, investment, and employment in the inner city due to serious inequality in the distribution of both income and productive assets between the two groups. The result is that one group in the city has declining consumption because of previous rises in aggregate income but reduces investment because of the fall in purchasing power of the poor group. So the economic situation is that one urban group has experienced a falling ratio of consumption to profits but refuses to invest its previously rising proportion of profits to income in the inner city because the very process of a rise in the ratio of profits to aggregate income reduces the ratio of wages to aggregate income. This transfer of income from wages to profits because of the relative fixity of low wages compared with profits (Sherman, 1964: 82-86, esp. 82 on interaction of income distribution and consumption function) generates savings, much of which will not be consumed or invested in the inner city, and a failure of a rise in consumption among the low-income group due to lack of income. Hence, we have a situation of declining central-city income, consumption, and investment and rising poverty of a large segment of the central-city population, due primarily to a failure of both consumption and investment in the inner city.

Our hypothesis is that the concentration of black families in central cities under prevailing institutional constraints on black family income creates an imbalance in the rate of the circuit flow of goods and money among high- and low-income receivers in the urban economy. This creates a demand gap between overall urban production and overall urban consumption, causing a fall in consumption and investment. This demand gap must be made up through either income transfers to the black subeconomy, as under present conditions, or through income-earning wealth transfers in the form of black community capital formation sufficient to raise the productivity, income, and consumption of the black community.

There are two crucial concepts in our hypothesis—the demand gap concept and the capital transfer concept—involving, as we shall show later, the swap of black labor for white capital. Both concepts are illustrated below in our black family models. In the meantime, we define our demand gap concept as the differential between factor costs and factor returns going to the ghetto community. As we shall see later, this differential which we may call profits goes mainly to households outside the ghetto economy and is not reinvested in new net capital growth in the ghetto.

The demand gap and our capital transfer approach to poverty policy, along with the underlying theory of the acceleration principle and certain aspects of the underconsumption theory, including investment demand, permit the use of a model of swapping black labor for white capital. This model links the inner-city processes of production, distribution, and consumption to the reduction of inner-city poverty. This also remedies an important deficiency in the existing literature on the economics of poverty, which basically links poverty policy to changes in the level of overall production in the economy as a whole, together with some programs of government transfer payments in cash and in-kind which may raise some persons over the poverty line (Plotnick, 1975: 109).

By linking the reduction of poverty to the market processes which generate poverty in the first place, we are able to see the deficiencies in the circuit flow of resources in the inner-city economy and take steps to offset these deficiencies with a system of ghetto capital growth which raises the income and purchasing power of the poor.

BLACK FAMILY MODELS

DEFINITION

Our models view black families as a subeconomy carrying on an exchange with the general central-city economy, where the purchasing power of a concentrated black population is essential to the solvency of the major cities. That is, a rise or fall in the level of income and purchasing power of the subeconomy, amounting in the aggregate to $125 billion—most of which is concentrated in inner city—constitutes a balancing factor in the profit and loss of important business establishments in the central city. The low purchasing power in the subeconomy has resulted in an exodus of business establishments, which have relocated in the suburbs, further reducing the level of income, consumption, investment, and employment in the central city.

THE TRADITIONAL BLACK
FAMILY MODEL

The traditional and current black family model consists of the following elements: (1) aggregate ghetto factor costs and returns; (2) aggregate ghetto income and purchases; and (3) a demand gap created by the fact that the bulk of ghetto factor returns and savings go to the enclave sector households that neither purchase goods in the ghetto nor increase aggregate net investment in the ghetto. This demand gap is now partly supplied from goods purchased in the ghetto out of earnings of unskilled black labor employed outside the ghetto economy, and partly by government (relief and welfare) expenditures. A graphic illustration of this model is shown in Figure 7.1.

It should be noted that the emphasis of this model is on showing the process of the flow of ghetto factor costs into ghetto incomes and incomes into ghetto expenditures. It should also be noted that the business receipts, including profits from existing black consumer expenditures earned outside the ghetto, go back to the enclave sector (businesses owned by whites) and flows to the outside economy. These profits include savings which do not generate any net new investment in the ghetto.

We have represented the costs of black capital and labor as constituting a relatively small proportion of aggregate ghetto factor costs and, accordingly, as a small proportion of black consumer demand as costs become incomes and incomes become black consumer expenditures. It is this limited proportion of aggregate ghetto factor costs, represented by the employment of black capital and labor, and the consequent limited conversion of ghetto factor costs into ghetto incomes and expenditures that define the economic limits of the ghetto domestic sector.

We have represented the white capital and labor of the enclave sector as receiving the bulk of ghetto factor returns to households where savings occur. The aggregate savings of these white enclave households, however, flow directly to the outside economy rather than to new capital investments in the ghetto. Hence, we have represented aggregate gross investment in the white-owned sector as equal only to aggregate capital replacement demand. Simi-

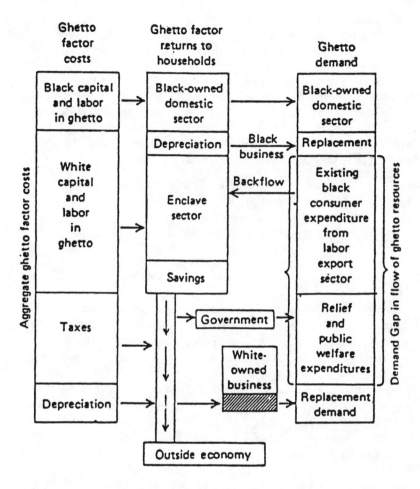

FIGURE 7.1   Flow of Ghetto Factor Costs, Incomes, and Employment

larly, we have represented the black-owned sector as having zero aggregate net investment, largely because there are no aggregate net savings. Thus, there is only a capital replacement demand in the ghetto economy insofar as business investment is concerned.

The significance of this model is that the ghetto economy will remain a depressed area as long as a substantial demand gap exists between aggregate ghetto factor returns (income) to ghetto households and aggregate ghetto factor costs.

A NEW BLACK FAMILY MODEL OF
CAPITAL GROWTH AND RISING INCOME

Our new model is designed to link the black family model with the central-
city economy whereby we may capitalize on the economic mutuality between
black family well-being and central-city prosperity. This model substitutes the
transfer of capital investment to the black community for the current transfer of
income in the form of public welfare payments. The model uses labor exports
from the ghetto to pay for the import of white capital. In this case, the production function of the ghetto would be written as:

$$Y = (L_B, L_K, L_D)$$

where

Y = total ghetto output
L_B = labor exported to white capital
L_K = exported labor converted to white
        capital imports invested in the ghetto
L_D = labor employed in the local black ghetto.

In applying this production function to the ghetto economy, we assume the
beginnings of three economic subsectors in the ghetto community: a capital
goods sector, consisting of manufacturing operations based on the import of
machines, equipment, and raw material from outside the ghetto economy; a
consumer goods sector, consisting of wholesale and retail operations generated
by manufacturing in the capital goods sector; and a labor export sector, representing otherwise unemployed ghetto labor employed outside the ghetto community by white capital. The intersectoral flow of resources between these
three sectors is shown in Table 7.1.

The following is observed:

1. The total output of the economy (GNP) was 7,000.

2. The capital goods sector (manufacturing operations) bought its machines and raw materials from outside the black economy.

3. The value of imports of machines and raw materials (2,000) was paid for
by the export of 2,000 worth of labor.

4. The capital goods sector is vertically integrated with the consumer
goods sector (wholesale and retail operations).

5. The money value of the purchases of the wholesale operations in the
consumer goods sector must equal the output of the manufacturing operations
in the capital goods sector, and the purchases of the retail operations of the
consumer goods sector must equal the output of the wholesale operations of the
consumer goods sector.

6. There is no producer goods sector. All producer goods are imported and

TABLE 7.1   Intersectoral Flow of Resources in a Three-Sector Labor-Intensive Ghetto Economy

	Capital Goods Sector	Consumer Goods Sector		Labor Export Sector	
	Manu-facturing opera-tions	Whole-sale opera-tions	Retail opera-tions	Labor employed outside the black community	Value of Output
Capital imports					
Borrowed capital					
a. Machines	1,000				1,000
b. Raw material	1,000				1,000
c. Stock, merchandise		(3,000)*	(4,000)*		
Wages	700	700	700	2,000	4,100
Profits	300	300	300		900
Value of output (Sales)	3,000	1,000	1,000	2,000	7,000
Payments for imports				(2,000)	−2,000
Net value of output in the black community					5,000

*Excluded to avoid double counting.

paid for out of earnings from otherwise unemployed labor exported to the white community.

7. The export sector is the balancing factor for general equilibrium. Since this ghetto economy does not produce its own machines and raw materials for manufacturing, it runs a deficit in its trade balance and would have to cut back 2,000 on capital purchase or make up the deficit by exports that do not require machines for its production. Export of labor bringing in wages of 2,000 would wipe out the import deficit and the economy would be in equilibrium.

8. In terms of the ghetto production function, it is observed that:

$$Y = L_E (2,000) + L_K (2,900) + L_D (2,100) = 7,000$$

9. The total value added in the ghetto community (wages + profits) at all stages was 3,000.

10. The 2,000 earned outside the ghetto and converted to capital within the ghetto generated a net value of output of 5,000. Thus the output/capital ratio 5,000/2,000 = 2.5—that is, $1.00 of borrowed capital—would yield $2.50 in net value of output in this hypothetical model.

Our new model explicitly shows that the balancing factor for equilibrium in a model of capital transfers to the black community is the labor export sector. In the illustration of the model it was noted that the transfer of capital to the ghetto economy would incur a deficit in its trade balance and would have to cut back 2,000 on capital purchases or make up the deficit by exports that do not require machines for its production. The export of labor bringing in 2,000 of wages would wipe out the import deficit and the model would be in equilibrium. Thus the rise in capital transfers under community ownership becomes the means of increasing the productivity of the community in the form of additional income such as profits, rent, interest, and dividends.

In the current traditional model, the export of labor from the ghetto generates additional wages which go to the enclave sector (white-owned enterprises such as food stores), but the profits, interest, dividends, and rents go to outside owners who do not incur net capital investment or consumption in the ghetto. This creates a demand gap in both consumption and investment. The primary focus of our capital transfer model is the replacement of the enclave sector, which inhibits a rise in black community income, and in its stead to develop community-owned manufacturing operations and wholesale and retail operations.

A THEORY OF BLACK FAMILY MOBILITY
AND CENTRAL-CITY PROSPERITY

The thrust of our model of capital transfers to the black community is to raise the income level and economic mobility of a large mass of low-income black families who now receive only low wages. The theory of the model is that under conditions of community ownership it is economically feasible to generate profits for the community as a whole, which now has only unskilled labor to sell; and that, by way of a change in the capital structure of the black community as indicated in the three sectors of the model, unskilled black labor can be swapped for white capital. This exchange will stimulate a rise in capital growth and a rise in family mobility and purchasing power of the black community as well as the urban economy as a whole.

Our thesis of the imbalance in the circuit flow of goods and money between low- and high-income receivers sets limits beyond which consumer spending cannot rise, even including consumer credit. In terms of the acceleration principle,[4] consumer spending cannot level off without having a downward effect on capital expansion. Thus, a large and growing community of poor black people in the heart of the central city creates conditions of economic distress because of the slow rate of rise in low incomes, which further accelerates conditions of unemployment and poverty.

Our model of capital transfers is designed to develop and capitalize on the economic potential of an increase in black family mobility. The underlying theory of our model is that the income class immobility of the black family and the income inequality between the black and white populations in the central city create deficiencies in the circuit flow of goods and money in the urban economy. This causes a fall in income, consumption, investment, and employment in the inner city.

These deficiencies in the rate of rise in black purchasing power can be made up out of profits earned in the black ghetto. This could be achieved by transferring to the black community as a whole community ownership of all private capital resources located in the black ghettos. This would give the black community as a whole a right to the whole product of their community.

The black ghetto's right to the whole product of its community means that profits would go directly to the black ghetto as a result of employing its own resources, rather than through transfer payments in the form of welfare receipts. These welfare payments represent an attempt to make up deficiencies in the aggregate wage bill through the redistribution of higher incomes and profits from the more affluent of the population to the poverty-stricken black community. This is a socially more costly way of maintaining the level of spending and income in urban communities. Everyone would be better off if all privately owned capital resources of the black ghettos were purchased outright and transferred to the black ghettos; this would be a business transfer payment rather than a social transfer in the form of welfare payments. Furthermore, it would be infinitely more economical and socially more significant if, instead of making piecemeal loans in the black community to initiate small marginal and peripheral (Averett, 1968) firms, one huge loan were made to a holding company operation with controlling interest in all capital resources in the black ghettos. The risk would be spread over all enterprises operating in the black ghettos, and uneconomic and marginal enterprises would be replaced with more efficient and optimum-sized units. Furthermore, high-caliber management could be sought for the top positions in one big corporation owned by the black community in each of the major cities throughout the United States.

The economic justification for maximizing total output and profits in the black community, under conditions where the people of the black community receive the whole product, is based on our hypothesis that the relationship between family consumption and total value of output (net of depreciation and taxes) will depend on the rate of growth of family income relative to the growth of total output. If the total value of output in the urban community as a whole grows faster than family income in the black ghetto sector, overall consumption will fall relative to total output. Overall consumption will fall because, under conditions of income inequality between the black and the white community, self-sustaining output or maintainable consumer spending depends heavily on the income class mobility of all sectors of the urban community. And since income class mobility is directly associated with the mobility rate of labor, which is associated directly with changes in the aggregate wage bills, the income class immobility in the black ghetto of the urban community holds down the aggregate bill in relation to total output. This reduces effective demand in the midst of poverty. This deficiency in effective demand in relation to total output must either be made up out of social welfare payments to the black community from the white community, or the black community must be allowed to own and organize the private capital resources in the black ghettos and make up the deficiency in the aggregate wage bill out of community receipts of profits, rent, interest, and dividends.

NOTES

1. "Well-being" is here taken as a positive function of the ability of low-income receivers to consume goods and services. It is assumed that increases in family consumption is positively correlated with an increase in family welfare.

2. "Poverty" is here defined according to the "official" party lines, adopted in 1969. See U. S. Bureau of the Census (1969).

3. Estimates and projections are based on historical data from U. S. Commerce, Bureau of Economic Analysis and Bureau of the Census.

4. The accelerated effect of a change in consumption on investment levels. Consumption has to keep increasing in order for investment to stand still. A fall in the rate of consumption reduces the level of net investment.

REFERENCES

AVERETT, R. T. (1968) The Dual Economy. New York: W. W. Norton.

Brimmer and Co. (1981) Statistical Profile of Black Economic Development. Cited in Black Enterprise Magazine, Vol. II, April, p. 68.

DAVIS, F. G. (1972) The Economics of Black Community Development. Chicago: Markham.

———— (1978) The Black Community's Social Security. Washington, DC: University Press of America.

GOODWIN, R. M. (1948) "Secular and cyclical aspects of the multiplier and the accelerator," in Income, Employment and Public Policy: Essays in Honor of Alvin H. Hansen. New York: W. W. Norton.

HAVEMAN, R. G. (1977) A Decade of Federal Anti-Poverty Programs: Achievements, Failures and Lessons. New York: Academic Press.

PLOTNICK, R. D. (1975) The Effect of Macroeconomic Conditions on the Poor in Progress Against Poverty: A Review of the 1964-1974 Decade. New York: Academic Press.

SHERMAN, H. J. (1964) Growth, Unemployment and Inflation. New York: Appleton-Century-Crofts.

TUSSING, D. (1975) Poverty in a Dual Economy. New York: St. Martin's Press.

U. S. Bureau of the Census (1969) Revision in Poverty Statistics, 1959 to 1968. Current Population Reports, Special Studies, Series P-23, No. 28 (August 12). Washington, DC: Government Printing Office.

8

BLACK EDUCATION
A Cultural-Ecological
Perspective

JOHN U. OGBU

INTRODUCTION

In this chapter I will attempt to explain why black children do less well in school than other children. The chapter will also discuss the effects of these perceptions and academic efforts on black upward mobility. I want to explore how black school performance is related to black perceptions of social and occupational opportunity structure as well as educational opportunity structure.

The chapter is divided into four parts. The first outlines the problem and some of its current explanations; the second examines the structural context of the problem; the third describes the cultural-ecological framework and the mechanisms of maintaining the disproportionately high rate of school failure; the concluding part of the chapter considers some of the policy implications of the cultural-ecological perspective.

THE PROBLEM AND
SOME CURRENT EXPLANATIONS

One baffling educational problem in the United States is the persistence of low academic performance among Black Americans and other caste-like minorities with similar features—Chicanos, Indians, Native Hawaiians, and Puerto Ricans. These minorities not only do less well in school than white Americans, they also do less well than other minorities, including Chinese Americans and Japanese Americans. It is true that children from poor families of all groups do less well in school than children from affluent families; it is also true that a disproportionate number of black children come from poor families. However, differences between blacks and whites in academic achievement remain when children from similar socioeconomic backgrounds are compared (Jensen, 1969: 81-82; Baughman, 1971: 5-8; Jencks, 1972: 154; Mayeske et al., 1973; CEMREL, 1978; Haskins, 1980).

Since the sixties special efforts have been initiated to help "disadvantaged" black and other children improve their school performance. These efforts have had some positive results; but they have not significantly changed the relative academic position of black children, especially those of the inner city (CEMREL, 1978; Ogbu, 1978).

The failure of these efforts lies, in part, in the theories undergirding the rationale with which they are approached. Social scientists assumed in the sixties that school performance depends on three factors: home environment, school environment and genetic endowment (Bloom et al., 1965; Coleman, 1966; Jensen, 1969; Guthrie et al., 1971). Given these assumptions, it follows that blacks are relatively unsuccessful in school because they come from homes or attend schools or have genetic endowment less conducive to school success. Social scientists continue to argue about the relative weight of each of these three factors in influencing school performance. Policymakers have generally been more sympathetic to theories emphasizing the deficiencies of the home or school. Consequently they have based their programs for change on such theories.

In more recent years a cultural difference or cultural discontinuity perspective has emerged to explain the disproportionately high rate of school failure among blacks and other caste-like minorities. This perspective argues that blacks have their own culture with its own child-rearing practices through which distinctively black instrumental competencies are inculcated; and that black children probably fail in school because schools do not recognize and utilize black children's competencies for teaching, learning, and testing (Wright, 1970; Gibson, 1976; Boykin, 1980).

Elsewhere I have analyzed the strengths and weaknesses of these explanations (Ogbu, 1978, 1980a, 1980b, 1981a). Here I will briefly summarize three issues most relevant to the present chapter. First, these explanations are not based on adequate comparative data. They are based on data from one type of minority group, *caste-like minorities*, and fail to explain why other types of minorities with similar features of poverty and cultural differences succeed in the same schools. Second, although proponents of these views want to assist black children to improve their school performance in order to better their chances of obtaining good jobs with good wages after graduation, they do not usually consider the possible effects of job discrimination against black parents on their children's education. They do not, for example, ask how black perceptions of job discrimination influence their perceptions of and responses to schooling. On the whole, current explanations generally neglect the reciprocal influence of employment opportunities and schooling. Third, some of the explanations erroneously assume that the educational and economic problems of Black Americans are the same as those of lower-class whites. In reality this is a false assumption, because blacks occupy more or less a caste-like position in a racial stratification system. Other weaknesses of these explanations will become apparent when we consider the structural position of Black Americans as the context for understanding their lag in school performance. Traditional educational research has considered neither the collective historical experience of blacks nor the structural barriers of the wider society.

The term "caste-like" minorities is used for two reasons. It contrasts this type of minority with "immigrant minorities" in terms of both structural and school experiences. Many wonder why some minorities do well in school and others do not. The term is also used in reference to some minority groups which are not racially different from the dominant group and yet are doing poorly in school. Chicanos, for instance, cannot as a group be racially defined as different from whites; many of them call themselves "white" and are officially defined as "white" or "Caucasian." However, in my analysis in terms of structural barriers and school experiences, they qualify as a "caste-like" minority group.

RACIAL STRATIFICATION AS
A STRUCTURAL CONTEXT OF
SCHOOL FAILURE

Social scientists concerned with the problem of lower school performance among blacks have long recognized "race" as a variable but not "racial stratification." If they consider American society stratified at all, their preferred model is class stratification (Coleman, 1966; Jensen, 1969; Jencks, 1972; Mosteller and Moynihan, 1972; Ogbu, 1977, 1981b). They have ample data on parental education, occupation, and income to show that a disproportionate number of black children come from "lower-class" backgrounds. From this classification they argue that school performance among blacks is class-related. But this class model is only one of several that can be constructed for American society, and it is probably not the one that most accurately reflects the position of blacks, who are a racial caste. However, I am using the concept of caste or caste-like advisedly, as a methodological tool to emphasize the structural legacy of black subordination. I am not suggesting that Black Americans are a caste in the classical Hindu sense. One of the questions, then, is: How does the stratification of racial castes differ from class stratification?

CLASS VERSUS RACIAL CASTE STRATIFICATION

In general, stratification of racial castes differs from class stratification with regard to closure, affiliation, status summation, social mobility, and cognitive orientation.

Closure and Affiliation. Class stratification is based on economic relations, an acquired characteristic, whereas racial stratification is based on "status honor," regarded as an inborn quality (Berreman, 1977). Social classes are more or less permanent entities but have no clear boundaries; nor is their membership necessarily permanent, because people are continually moving in and out of them. Furthermore, children of interclass marriage can affiliate with the class of either parent. Racial castes, on the other hand, are permanently hierarchically organized into more or less endogamous groups, clearly bounded, publicly recognized and named. Interracial/caste marriage is often prohibited, but where it is allowed there is usually a formal or informal rule as to which parent's group the children must affiliate (Berreman, 1967: 279-280). For example, before their emancipation in 1871, the Japanese Buraku outcastes were legally forbidden to intermarry with the dominant Ippan group (Mitchell, 1967); in contemporary South Africa, intermarriage between blacks and whites is legally forbidden (van den Berghe, 1967); and in the United States, "it was not until 1967 that the United States Supreme Court finally declared unconstitutional those statutes (in 16 states at that time) prohibiting interracial marriage" (Higginbotham, 1978: 41; see also Franklin, 1971). In the United States the rule of affiliation has always been that any children of known black-white mating must affiliate with the black. In very rare cases do some "blacks" covertly become "whites" through the painful and noninstitutionalized process of "passing" (Warner et al., 1941; Burma, 1946; Eckard, 1946).

Status Summation. In a class stratification, such as exists among American whites, occupational and other status positions are based on training (for example, on formal education) and ability. This is much less true for racial minorities because of a *job ceiling* and other barriers. A job ceiling is composed of the highly consistent pressures and obstacles that selectively assign minorities (and women) to jobs at the low level of status, power, dignity, and income, while allowing white males to compete more easily and freely for the more desirable jobs above that ceiling on the basis of individual training and ability. The job ceiling and other barriers have been the object of racial minorities' struggle for equal social, economic, and political opportunities (Drake and Clayton, 1970; · Newman et al., 1976; Ogbu, 1978).

Social Mobility. Vertical social mobility is built into class stratification and the means of achieving it are usually prescribed. Mobility from one racial stratum to the next is proscribed.

Cognitive Orientation. Class and racial castes differ also in cognitive orientation (Berreman, 1977). For instance, blacks and other caste-like minorities do not accept their low social, political, and occupational status as legitimate outcomes of their individual failures and misfortunes, whereas lower-class whites often do (Sennett and Cobb, 1972). Blacks see racial barriers in employment and education as the primary causes of their low social status and poverty. Most Black Americans, regardless of their class positions, blame "the system" rather than themselves for their failure to get ahead as individuals and as a group, an orientation which underlies their collective struggle for equal employment and educational opportunity.

In contrast, there is neither a conscious feeling among white Americans of any given class "that they belong together in a corporate unity" nor a feeling that their common interests are different from those of other social classes (Myrdal, 1944). Not even the lower-class whites share a collective perception of their social and economic difficulties as stemming from "the system." *What distinguishes Black Americans and similar minorities from lower-class whites is not that their objective material conditions are different but that the way the minorities perceive and interpret their conditions is different.*

Blacks are, of course, internally stratified by social class, as whites are internally stratified. But the black classes and the white classes differ both in development and attributes. They are unequal in development because historically blacks have had less access to the number and types of jobs and training that facilitate class differentiation and mobility. Black social classes are also qualitatively different because the historical circumstances that created them and the structural forces that sustain them are different from those that created and sustain white social classes. For example, the narrow base of black class differentiation began during enslavement rather than, as among whites, with differences in education, ability, and family background. During enslavement most blacks had no access to schooling and were relegated to slave status, regardless of their individual abilities; among the few free blacks, most were confined to menial jobs and social position through legal and extralegal mechanisms. After enslavement, racial barriers in employment—*the job ceiling*—continued to limit their base of class differentiation and mobility. These collective experiences resulted in the shared perception of the lack of equal opportunity for blacks of any social class; that is, blacks came to believe that it is much more difficult for *any black* than for *any white* to achieve economic and social self-betterment in the mainstream economy *through free competition based on training and ability*. Another reason for the qualitative difference is the forced *ghettoization* of blacks. Until recent decades whites created and maintained clearly defined residential boundaries of the city to which they restricted the black population. Many relatively well-to-do blacks who preferred to live elsewhere were forced to share the ghetto with poorer blacks. This involuntary segregation of blacks further reinforced their shared sense of oppression.

In summary, then, the economic and educational problems of Black Americans, even poor blacks, are not merely those resulting from lower-class status. They are, instead, consequences of the *double stratification of class and racial caste*. As a result, lower-class blacks share certain attributes common to all lower-class people everywhere; but they also have distinctive attributes because they belong to a subordinate racial caste. This additional impact of double stratification is apparent in the black status mobility system described in the next section.

CASTE-LIKE MINORITIES VERSUS OTHER MINORITIES

Some minorities do relatively well in American schools, and it is important to distinguish them from those who do not. Generally, blacks fit into a category I call *caste-like minorities* (Ogbu, 1978). Such minorities are characterized by a greater lag in school performance. They are distinguished from other minorities by four factors. First, they have usually been incorporated into "their country" involuntarily and permanently. Blacks are a classic example, having been brought to America as slaves. As a result, they occupy a more or less permanent place in society from which they can escape only through "passing" or emigration—options not always open. Second, membership in a caste-like minority is acquired permanently at birth. Third, caste-like minorities have limited access to the social goods of society by virtue of their group membership rather than because they lack training and ability. More specifically, *they face a job ceiling*. Finally, having been incorporated into society involuntarily and then relegated to menial status, caste-like minorities tend to focus on their economic and social problems in terms of collective institutional discrimination, which they perceive as more than temporary.

These then, are the structural features that distinguish blacks from whites, poor blacks from lower-class whites, and blacks from such immigrant minorities as Chinese Americans and Japanese Americans, who came to America more or less voluntarily for social and economic self-betterment. The occupational and educational implications of this structural position of blacks are expressed through their unique status mobility system.

STATUS MOBILITY SYSTEM
AND SCHOOL PERFORMANCE

STATUS MOBILITY SYSTEM

A status mobility system is the way of getting ahead in a society or social group. Members of a society or social group usually share a theory about how their status mobility system works or how one gets ahead or "makes it," however "making it" is defined (LeVine, 1967). The theory or folk assumptions generally cover the range of available status positions (for example, types of jobs open to members), rules for eligibility to compete for the available positions, and how to qualify for successful competition. A status mobility system works insofar as the actual experiences of a large proportion of the population confirm the folk beliefs about it. And how the system works influences the values and practices of parents and others entrusted with the upbringing of children as well as how children themselves strive to be as they get older. People's theory of how their status mobility system works is the cognitive basis of their behaviors with regard to child rearing and schooling as well as strategies for subsistence and self-advancement (Ogbu, 1980a, 1980b, 1980c).

In a relatively open class system, such as exists among white Americans, differences in the status mobility systems of the different classes are minor. But for stratified racial castes, such as blacks and whites, the status mobility system of each stratum is unique in many respects. For example, the status mobility system of the subordinate racial caste is distinctive in two ways that have important implications for schooling. First, the minority status mobility system offers access to fewer social goods such as high-paying jobs than the status mobility system of the dominant group; and second, the minority status mobility system embodies two sets of rules of behavior for achievement: one imposed by the dominant group and the other evolved within the subordinate population. In the United States whites "impose" educational credentials on blacks; as a consequence, blacks have developed a number of alternative or "survival" strategies, including collective struggle, clientship, and hustling for making it. Black Americans employ these two sets of rules differentially according to their circumstance.

Caste-like minority schooling reflects these two features of their status mobility system for two reasons. On the one hand, the dominant group's perceptions of how the minorities get ahead or should get ahead influence how it defines and provides for the minorities' educational needs; on the other hand, how the minorities perceive their opportunity structure and the role of schooling within it influences their response to schooling. In this situation caste-like minority schooling generally functions to prepare children to participate as adults in the minority rather than the dominant group's status mobility system. From this point of departure, I would suggest that a clue to the differences in the education and school performance of whites and blacks lies in the nature of their status mobility systems. Specifically, the caste-bound black status mobility system traditionally offers fewer jobs requiring high-level schooling or credentials and also embodies two sets of rules of behavior for achievement. The black status mobility system makes both whites and blacks behave in a manner that promotes black school failure. Perceptions of dominant whites of how blacks ought to get ahead leads them to provide blacks with inferior education. For blacks, their own perceptions of the limited opportunities to get ahead in the conventional economy and their perceptions of inferior education generate attitudes and behaviors that are often not conducive to school success. Among the black responses to the job ceiling and to inferior education discussed below are disillusionment and lack of persevering academic efforts because of low educational payoffs. Other responses are alternative or survival strategies that may require skills and attitudes incongruent with attitudes and skills required for classroom teaching and learning; and hostility and lack of trust toward the public school. Let us briefly examine in more detail how white and black responses to black status mobility systems cause the disproportionately high school failure among blacks.

Inferior Education. Many public and private schools now profess to offer blacks some quality education provided whites and have even established special programs to enable black children to "succeed" like the whites. These are, however, recent developments which must not mask the fact that before the sixties there was no explicit or implicit goal to educate blacks and whites equally for adult occupational and social positions. Also, while it is true that lower-class white education has always been inferior to that of the white middle class (Warner et al., 1944; Hollingshead, 1949; Sexton, 1961), it is equally true that at every class level blacks have been provided still more inferior education. For example, as late as 1972 the money spent by the school district of Washington, D.C., for each child decreased as the proportion of black children in a given school increased (Hughes and Hughes, 1973), a situation also documented for Chicago and other cities (Sexton, 1968: 228).

In general, prior to Emancipation, blacks were systematically excluded by law from formal education. Thereafter they were given an inferior education in segregated schools. Segregation was legal nationwide, though it lasted longest in the South (Pierce, 1955: 35-36; Bond, 1966: 374-384; Bullock, 1970; Weinberg, 1977). In the separate schools the inferiority of black education was maintained through inadequate funding, facilities, and staffing; through a shorter school year and a curriculum which emphasized manual rather than academic training (Pierce, 1955: 234; Bond, 1966: 97-99, 1969: 132, 235-265; Thomas and Noblitt, 1978). Blacks who attended integrated schools received inferior education through more subtle mechanisms—negative teacher attitudes and low expectations (Knowles and Prewitt, 1969; U.S. Senate Select Committee, 1972; Hobbs, 1975); biased testing and classification (Mercer, 1973; Children's Defense Fund, 1974: 101-114; Illinois Advisory Commission on Civil Rights, 1974); tracking or ability grouping (Findley, 1973; Ogbu, 1974: 169); biased textbooks and inferior curriculum (Kane, 1970; U.S. Senate Select Committee, 1972). They also generally received academic and career guidance which reinforced their preparation for inferior positions in adult life (Ogbu, 1974a: 120, 1974: 193). Extracurricular activities were race-typed. These subtle devices were also present in segregated schools. Today, both gross and subtle mechanisms still exist in many schools, as evidenced by many lawsuits for school integration and from protests against testing, tracking, and related matters in many American cities (U.S. Commission on Civil Rights, 1967, 1977).

One subtle mechanism now receiving increasing attention is the disproportionate labeling of black children as having "learning handicaps" and channeling them into special education which prepares them for inferior occupations. In a recent court case brought by blacks against the San Francisco school district, for instance, evidence was presented showing that black children who made up only 31 percent of the school enrollment in the 1976-1977 school year constituted 53.8 percent of all children in the educable mentally retarded classes. In the same year, in 20 California school districts, which enrolled 80 percent of all black children in public schools in the state, blacks constituted 27.5 percent of the school population but 62 percent of the educable mentally retarded population. The judge in the case ruled against the San Francisco school district, noting that the disproportionate placement of blacks in the special education classes could not have occurred by chance (U.S. District Court for Northern California, 1979). The figures for San Francisco are similar to those for other large American cities, including Chicago and New York.

Some evidence suggests that in many instances blacks are provided inferior education deliberately. We find in the South purposive misappropriation of black school funds for white schools, legislation to legalize such misappropriation, and employment of less qualified teachers for black schools, less pay for the teachers, and a disproportionate workload (Pierce, 1955; Bond, 1966; Bullock, 1970).

Even northern philanthropists who helped make public school education more available to blacks and whites in the South endorsed an explicit policy to give whites superior academic education for superior jobs and other adult positions, and to give blacks an "industrial" or manual education. They did, however, make some provision for a few blacks to receive academic training to serve the black community as preachers, teachers, doctors, and lawyers (Harlan, 1968: 76-80; Bullock, 1970: 93-98). Interestingly enough, when industrial education became an asset to acquiring well-paying industrial jobs and attracted state and federal financial support, black participation was curtailed (Pierce, 1955). Myrdal (1944: 877) explains this policy reversal by saying that southern whites believed that blacks should receive an industrial education so long as it did not mean preparing them to compete more effectively with whites for skilled and economically rewarding jobs (see also Frazier, 1957: 439; Bond, 1966: 404).

In the North the policy of differential and inferior education has been more covert and, partly because records are not kept by race, less adequately documented. But it has existed as a deliberate policy in many instances. Evidence presented in various desegregation cases shows the prevalence of inferior education for blacks in the North (Sexton, 1968; U.S. Commission on Civil Rights, 1967, 1977). And many blacks educated in the North who discussed their experiences with me usually recounted how they and other blacks were channeled into "dead-end courses" in segregated and integrated schools.

The possibility of blacks receiving inferior education has also been reinforced by many school personnel sharing the general folk assumptions of whites that blacks are less "intelligent" than whites and therefore apparently not capable of mastering the type of education required for the more desirable jobs and social positions (Johnson, 1930: 224; Pierce, 1955: 20; Conant, 1961). These folk beliefs, which predate the invention of modern psychometric measures of "intelligence" (Bullock, 1970: 68), have had a considerable influence on the type of curriculum school personnel consider appropriate for black children and on perceptions of how black children should be treated. Another factor contributing to the inferior education is that well-meaning school personnel with an awareness of the limited chances of black school leavers obtaining good jobs tended to channel black pupils into those educational programs which prepared them mainly for traditional "Negro jobs."

Black Responses. It would appear from their long history of collective struggle for equal education that blacks see formal education as a means to improve their social and economic status. But their expectations have not been met, partly because their education has not been designed to do this. It appears that this dilemma has caused blacks to appear to respond to both the inferior education and to the job ceiling in some ways that actually promote school failure and preparation for marginal economic participation. These responses are considered next.

Disillusionment and Lack of Effort Optimism. Disillusionment is one of the responses blacks have made to the job ceiling with adverse effects on academic behavior. Blacks do not believe that American society is a land of equal opportunity; they often point out that racial discrimination has historically prevented them from obtaining desirable jobs, good wages, and promotions commensurate with their education and ability; discrimination has also prevented them from owning houses and living in better parts of the community.

One result of this perception of limited opportunity structure is disillusionment about the real value of schooling. Another is lack of perseverance in academic pursuits. The disillusionment is summed up in the maxim, "What's the use of trying?" From my own observations of black children in the classrooms and community of Stockton, California, I would conclude that the children do not take their schoolwork seriously and do not persevere at it, even though they acknowledge that a serious attitude toward school and perseverance or hard work are necessary for doing well in school. Furthermore, interviews with parents suggest that they, too, may be teaching their children ambivalent attitudes toward schooling. On the one hand, parents espouse the need to work hard in school and to get more education than they themselves did. On the other hand, the same parents teach their children verbally and through their own life experiences of unemployment, underemployment, and other discriminations, as well as through gossip about similar experiences among relatives, neighbors and friends—*through the actual texture of life in the home and community*—that even if the children succeed in school they may not make it as adults in the wider society. Eventually black children become disillusioned and "give up"; and they learn to blame "the system" for their school failure as their parents blame "the system" for their own failures.

The historical barriers confronting blacks have restricted educational payoffs. Blacks do not remain passive, but respond actively and creatively to these barriers. The important consideration is if the nature of these responses have facilitated or hindered the successful pursuit of formal education. My observations have been that some reactions have been incongruent with the maximization of school efforts. It is my theses that as structural barriers are removed and as blacks experience and perceive the barriers as eliminated, they will respond with perceptions and behaviors that facilitate a greater degree of school success.

SURVIVAL STRATEGIES AND INCONGRUENT ATTITUDES AND SKILLS

Another response to the job ceiling which has some adverse effects on black school performance is what blacks call "survival strategies." These fall into two categories. One consists of those strategies directed toward increasing conventional economic and social resources of the black community and obtaining conventional jobs and other social rewards. These strategies include *collective struggle* or civil rights activities (Scott, 1976; Newman et al., 1978) and *clientship* or "uncle tomming" (Myrdal, 1944; Dollard, 1957; Farmer, 1968; Powdermaker, 1968; Ogbu, 1981b). The other category includes *hustling* and related means—strategies directed toward exploiting nonconventional economic and social resources or "the street economy" (Heard, 1968; Milner, 1970; Wolfe, 1970; Bullock, 1970; Foster, 1974).

Within the black community success in obtaining conventional jobs and other social resources often requires collective struggle (at least to make them available) and/or clientship, *in addition to educational credentials*. There are also other survival strategies which provide alternative ways of making a living and achieving status to school credentials and conventional jobs. People who succeed in the conventional economy and status system, either through school credentials only, through a combination of school credentials and clientship or other form of survival strategy, or through hustling and related activities in the street economy—all are "legitimately successful" in the eyes of the community. Such people are admired, and they influence the ways others, including children, try to make it.

I suggest that the survival strategies may require knowledge, attitudes, and skills not wholly compatible with those required for white middle-class classroom and school behavior. I also suggest that children probably begin to learn the survival strategies from preschool years as part of their normal "enculturation." As a result, they may begin school with potential dispositions for academic and behavioral difficulties. But whether or not and to what extent they experience learning problems depends on their encounter with school personnel and other children.

CONFLICT AND DISTRUST

A third response to the job ceiling is hostility and distrust toward the public schools, which has grown out of a long history of unpleasant experiences with the schools and with white society in general. Throughout the history of public school education in America blacks have learned to perceive their frequent exclusion and discriminatory treatment as designed to prevent them from qualifying for the more desirable jobs open to whites. Consequently, a significant thrust of black collective struggle has been forcing whites and the schools to provide them with equal education.

Thus, initially we find blacks fighting against total exclusion from the public schools. For over one century they have fought against inferior education in segregated and integrated schools. Where blacks attend segregated schools, these schools are theoretically black schools, so that one might expect blacks to identify with and work with such schools. However, the identification and cooperation of blacks have often been undermined by simultaneous perceptions of segregated schools as inferior to white schools. This results in diverting attention and efforts toward integration and equalization of education. These events frequently generate a feeling that the public schools cannot be trusted to educate black children because of their gross and subtle mechanisms of discrimination. The conflicts also force the schools to treat blacks defensively, often resorting to various forms of control, paternalism, or contest. The schools' responses, too, divert their efforts from educating black children. On the basis of these observations, which can be documented in many American cities, I would suggest that black-school relationship, riddled with conflicts and suspicion, would make it difficult for blacks to accept and internalize the schools' goals, standards, and teaching and learning approaches, and that this situation would contribute to the school performance lag of black children.

POLICY IMPLICATIONS

Given this analysis of the sources of the lag in black school performance, there seem to be three prerequisites for eliminating the lag. These prerequisites are to recognize, first, that stratification of racial castes exists in America, second, that the disproportionately high rate of school failure is a kind of collective adaptation to the job ceiling and other features of the black status mobility system. The adaptation was historically engendered by policies and actions of whites and their institutions and has been maintained by the same; it has also been sustained by black responses to their situation. The third prerequisite for a change is to recognize that *real change* depends on opening up decent jobs and other opportunities to black youths and adults, not just on patching up individuals' supposed past or present "deficiencies." The solution requires both short-range and long-range policies and programs. Short-range remedies may include some current programs to assist the present generation of children experiencing difficulties in school. The long-range goal is, however, to develop policies and programs that will ensure that future generations of black children will not experience a disproportionately high rate of school failure and that the solution is the ultimate destruction of the caste system, particularly the element of the job ceiling.

REFERENCES

BAUGHMAN, E. (1971) Black Americans. New York: Academic Press.
BERREMAN, G. D. (1967) "Caste in cross-cultural perspective: organizational components," in G. DeVos and H. Wagatsuma (eds.) Japan's Invisible Race: Caste in Culture and Personality. Berkeley and Los Angeles: University of California Press.
_____ (1977) "Social inequality: a cross-cultural paradigm." Unpublished manuscript, Department of Anthropology, University of California, Berkeley.
BLOOM, B. S., A. DAVIS, and R. D. HESS [eds.] (1965) Compensatory Education for Cultural Deprivation. New York: Holt, Rinehart & Winston.
BOND, H. M. (1966) The Education of the Negro in the Negro Education in American Social Order. New York: Octagon.
_____ (1969) Negro Education in Alabama. New York: Atheneum.
BOYKIN, A. W. (1980) "Reading achievement and the social cultural frame of reference of Afro

American children." Presented at NIE Roundtable Discussion on Issues in Urban Reading, Washington, D.C.

BULLOCK, H. E. (1970) A History of Negro Education in the South: From 1619 to the Present. New York: Praeger.

BURMA, J. H. (1946) "The measurement of Negro passing." American Journal of Sociology 52: 18-22.

CEMREL, Inc. (1978) Minority Education 1960-78: Grounds, Gains, and Gaps, Vol. 1. Chicago: CEMREL, Inc.

Children's Defense Fund (1974) Children Out of School in America. Washington, DC: Washington Research Project, Inc.

COLEMAN, J. S. (1966) Equality of Educational Opportunity. Washington, DC: Government Printing Office.

COLLINS, T. W. and G. W. NOBLITT (1978) Stratification and Resegregation : The Case of Crossover High School, Memphis, Tennessee. Final Report, NIE Contract Grant 400-76-009. Washington, DC: National Institute of Education.

CONANT, J. B. (1961) Slums and Suburbs. New York: McGraw-Hill.

DOLLARD, J. (1957) Caste and Class in a Southern Town. Garden City, NY: Doubleday.

DRAKE, S. C. and H. CAYTON (1970) Black Metropolis: A Study of Negro Life in a Northern City, Vols. 1 and 2. New York: Harcourt Brace Jovanovich.

ECKARD, E. W. (1946) "How many Negroes pass?" American Journal of Sociology 52: 498-500.

FARMER, J. (1968) "Stereotypes of the Negro and their relationships to his self-image," in H. C. Rudman and R. L. Featherstone (eds.) Urban Schooling. New York: Harcourt Brace Jovanovich.

FINDLEY, W. G. (1973) "How ability grouping fails." Inequality in Education 14: 38-40.

FOSTER, H. L. (1974) Ribbin', Jivin', an Playin' the Dozens: The Unrecognized Dilemma of Inner-City Schools. Cambridge, MA: Ballinger.

FRANKLIN, J. H. (1971) The Free Negro in North Carolina, 1790-1860. New York: W. W. Norton.

FRAZIER, E. F. (1940) Negro Youth at the Crossways. Washington, DC: American Council on Education.

GIBSON, M. A. (1976) "Approaches to multicultural education in the United States." Anthropology and Education Quarterly 7: 7-18.

GUTHRIE, J. W., G. B. KLEINDORFER, H. M. LEVIN, and R. T. STOUT (1971) Schools and Inequality. Cambridge: MIT Press.

HARLAN, L. R. (1968) Separate and Unequal. New York: Atheneum.

HASKINS, R. (1980) "Race, family income and school achievement." Unpublished manuscript.

HEARD, N. C. (1968) Howard Street. New York: Dial Press.

HIGGINBOTHAM, A. L. (1978) In the Matter of Color: Race and the American Legal Process: The Colonial Period. New York: Oxford University Press.

HOBBS, N. (1975) The Future of Children. San Francisco: Jossey-Bass.

HOLLINGSHEAD, A. (1949) Elmtown's Youth. New York: John Wiley.

HUGHES, J. F. and A. O. HUGHES (1973) Equal Education: A New National Strategy. Bloomington: Indiana University Press.

Illinois Advisory Commission on Civil Rights (1974) Bilingual/Bicultural Education—A Privilege or a Right? Washington, DC: U.S. Government Printing Office.

JENCKS, C. (1972) Inequality. New York: Basic Books.

JENSEN, A. R. (1969) "How much can we boost IQ and scholastic achievement?" Harvard Educational Review 39: 1-123.

JOHNSON, C. S. (1930) The Negro in American Civilization. New York: Holt.

KNOWLES, L. L. and D. PREWITT (eds.) (1969) Institutional Racism in America. Englewood-Cliffs, N.J.: Prentice-Hall.

LEVINE, R. A. (1967) Dreams and Deeds. Chicago: University of Chicago Press.

MAYESKE, G. W., T. OKADA, A. E. COHEN, A. E. BEATON, and C. E. WISLER (1973) A Study of the Achievement of our Nation's Students. Washington, D.C.: U.S. Government Printing Office.

MERCER, J. R. (1973) Labeling the Mentally Retarded. Berkeley: University of California Press.

MILNER, C. A. (1970) "Black pimps and their prostitutes." Unpublished Ph.D. dissertation, Department of Anthropology, University of California, Berkeley.

MITCHELL, R. H. (1967) The Korean Minority in Japan. Berkeley: University of California Press.

MOSTELLER, F. and D. P. MOYNIHAN (eds.) (1972) On Equality of Educational Opportunity. New York: Random House.

MYRDAL, G. (1944) An American Dilemma. New York: Harper.

NEWMAN, D. K., B. K. AMIDEI, D. D. CARTER, W. J. KRUVANT, and J. S. RUSSELL (1978) Protest, Politics and Prosperity: Black Americans and White Institutions, 1940-1975. New York: Pantheon Books.

OGBU, J. U. (1974a) The Next Generation. New York: Academic Press.

―――― (1974b) "Learning in Burgherside," in G. M. Foster and R. V. Kemper (eds.) Anthropologists in the City. Boston: Little, Brown.

―――― (1977) "Racial stratification and education: The case of Stockton, California." IRCD Bulletin 12 (3): 1-26.

―――― (1978) Minority Education and Caste. New York: Academic Press.

―――― (1980a) "Caste and IQ in cross-cultural perspective," to appear in D. A. Wilkerson (ed.) Human Diversity and the Assessment of Intellectual Development.

―――― (1980b) "Equalization of educational opportunity and racial/ethnic inequality: A cross-cultural perspective," to appear in P. Altbach, R. Arnove, and G. Kelley (eds.) Comparative Education. New York: Macmillan.

―――― (1980c) "Societal forces as a context of ghetto children's school failure," to appear in L. Feagans and D. Darran (eds.) The Language of Children Reared in Poverty. New York: Academic Press.

―――― (1981a) "Minority schooling and transition to labor force." Paper presented for a seminar Youth Education and Employment: Policy Issues for the 1980s, Madison, Wisconsin.

―――― (1981b) "Schooling in the ghetto: A cultural-ecological perspective on community and home influences." Paper presented at the NIE Conference on Follow Through, Philadelphia, Pennsylvania.

POWDERMAKER, H. (1968) After Freedom. New York: Atheneum.

SCOTT, J. W. (1976) The Black Revolts. Cambridge: Schenkman.

SENNETT, R. and J. COBB (1972) The Hidden Injuries of Class. New York: Random House.

SEXTON, P. C. (1961) Education and Income. New York: Viking Press.

―――― (1967) Racial Isolation in the Public Schools: A Report, Vol. 1. Washington, D.C.: Government Printing Office.

―――― (1968) "Schools: Broken ladder to success," in L. A. Ferman (ed.) Negroes and Jobs. Ann Arbor: University of Michigan Press.

U.S. Commission on Civil Rights (1977) The Unfinished Business. U.S. Government Printing Office.

U.S. District Court for Northern California (1979) Opinion: Larry P. vs Riles. San Francisco, California Mimeo.

U.S. Senate Select Committee on Education (1972) Report: Toward Equal Educational Opportunity. Washington, D.C.: U.S. Government Printing Office.

VAN DEN BERGHE, P. (1967) Race and Racism: A Comparative Perspective. New York: Wiley.

WARNER, W. L., R. J. HAVIGHURST, and M. B. LOEB (1941) Color and Human Nature: Negro

Personality Development in a Northern City. Washington, D.C.: American Council on Educa-
     tion.
———— (1944) Who Shall Be Educated? The Challenge of Equal Opportunity. New York: Harper.
WOLFE, T. (1970) Radical Chic and Mau-Mauing the Flack Catchers. New York: Strauss and
     Giroux.
WEINBERG, M. (1977) A Chance to Learn: A History of Race and Education in the United States.
     New York: Cambridge University Press.
WRIGHT, N. (ed.) (1970) What Black Educators are Saying. New York: Hawthorn Books.

9

PATTERNS OF UPWARD MOBILITY IN BLACK FAMILIES

HARRIETTE PIPES McADOO

Despite the thrust of discrimination and the pall of poverty that lies over so many Black families, some few have managed to acquire the needed education, skills, and achievements that have allowed them to become more economically secure. This security is tenuous and is totally dependent, for the most part, on the good health and employment of wage earners. Blacks who have succeeded have had to overcome the adaptive reaction to the caste-like status of Blacks that leads to the expectation and realization of lowered school achievement that inhibits mobility (Ogbu, 1974). This chapter will explore patterns of upper mobility.

Because of the rigid segregation of Black communities in the past and because of the duality of Black existence, there are criteria of socioeconomic status that are identical to that of the majority society; but there are also unique criteria that are applied within the Black community that are used to differentiate between high- and low-rank status. There is the view that there is only one status for Blacks, that of being low, but that view only leads to the stereotypical view of Blacks that does not give recognition to the diversity within and between Blacks.

TRADITIONAL SOURCES OF
MOBILITY ASSISTANCE

Few Black families have wealth they are able to pass on to the succeeding generation. Each generation of Blacks thus must recreate the mobility cycle and generate effort necessary to succeed and be upwardly mobile again. The greatest gift a Black family in the past has been able to bestow upon its children has been the motivation and the skills necessary to succeed in school.

Only through his or her achievement, with the support of the wider community and extended family help, has an individual Black been able to get the advanced education needed to move into the higher-status jobs and positions. While there may be proclaimed "self-made" persons who are now in high-income positions, a close examination usually reveals that these persons were the recipients of "screens of opportunities" (Billingsley, 1968)—special efforts of relatives, school teachers in segregated school systems, community groups— or they were fortunate to be picked up and protected by a mentor as they worked on their higher degrees or status (Franklin, 1979; Hill, 1971; Martin and Martin, 1978; McAdoo, 1978).

Another source of help that has been downplayed during the preceding period of reactionary writing about Black families has been that provided by non-Blacks. This help may have come in the form of missionaries who went South to set up freedmen's schools, or persons who paid college tuition (Haley, 1976), or unacknowledged white relatives who quietly opened doors in northern schools or found funds for bright young Black students. This latter element was a carryover from miscegenation and the house-field divisions that existed during enslavement. Certain individuals and groups, therefore, were given advantages from these contacts that persisted for generations (Horton and Horton, 1979; Pleck, 1979).

TYPES OF STATUS WITHIN BLACK COMMUNITIES

Frazier (1939) made two divisions within the Black middle class. The first group was well educated, quiet, and closely tied to the Black community, and the second wave became the notorious "Black bourgeois" by conspicuous consumption and with less of an emphasis on education. These two groups have blended in the present-day younger and middle-age groups, along with the newly mobile who fit neither earlier class. The two older groups are clearly evident in the older society of most urban centers.

There has existed within the Black ethnoclass/ethnocaste several forms of demarkation. There is the standard differentiation that comes with advanced educational and occupational status. There is the high status afforded those in the public entertainment and athletic fields who have the recognition factor and finances but not necessarily the education and security most mobile groups have. There is also the status that comes from political and community influences; these may be elected officials or those who live within the outer limits of legal activities. There are also those within the community, independent of their jobs, who wield tremendous influence through leadership in church or social organizations.

Additional differentiation exists based on skin color. This preference was strong in earlier times within and outside the Black community. This is markedly less than in earlier times but is still a viable, though often unspoken, criterion of status leading to certain levels of antagonism between light- and dark-skinned Blacks. Skin color differentiations still exist, to a more limited extent, in preferences for mates or employees. Only within recent generations have some skin color advantages lessened, as Blacks, regardless of SES or skin color, have been able to obtain some of the benefits of higher education in a variety of settings and locations. Skin color is not as important a mobility criterion now as is individual achievement, other than to mark a person permanently within a racial caste in our society.

GEOGRAPHIC MOBILITY

Geographic mobility from the rural South to southern cities, from the South to the industrial North, and from the mid-Atlantic and southern coastal regions to the New York and Boston areas have been Blacks' traditional routes in order to take advantage of better economic conditions. The present pattern appears to be the return of older workers to their native South in search of a slower pace, or the movement of young workers from depressed northern cities to the Sunbelt for immediate employment. Northern urban patterns have often consisted of an urban to inner suburban to outer suburban movement as the families searched for the perceived better life and education for their children. Each wave of migrants hopes that a better economy will result in the provision of greater resources for the family members. Not all are successful, but enough have been able to improve their condition to fuel the continual search for a better place.

Movements to new areas have often been within the sponsorship of the broader extended family members. These "support chains" for geographic mobility often operated when one person moved to the site and became established. This person, in turn, sponsored other relatives, friends, and church members as they relocated to the same area (Pleck, 1979; Horton and Horton, 1979). The support chains resulted in relocation of practically entire youth cohorts of a community. It ensured that a person who moved to an area was not totally isolated, but was met with an existing supportive network that would give assistance until a niche had been found.

UPPER MOBILITY AND RACE

The overall impressions that have been presented in the public media are that a growing number of Black families have become middle class through the opportunities that have been provided through higher education and the affirmative actions. Some now feel that so much improvement has been made that affirmative programs are no longer needed, while the growing impression appears to be that Blacks may have been able to obtain a greater share of economic rewards than they are entitled to. To the contrary, there are now fewer Black middle-class families than there were in the mid-1970s. There has been a steady erosion of the proportion of Blacks who are preparing for and being employed by the traditional professional careers. There has been a loss of earning power per family unit, in relation to all of the other families in the United States (Hill, 1981). More families are being forced to "double up" with other family members as a result of the high unemployment rate and growing inflation. The growing underclass entrapment of Blacks, including the working poor, prevents any consideration of upward mobility (Glasgow, 1980).

One Black subgroup has reached economic parity with non-Blacks of the same age group. This is the "golden cohort" of young male and female professionals, aged 25-35, who have delayed childbearing and are concentrating their energies on their careers (Malveaux, 1981). They have left college and are now employed at a salary level that is equal to that of whites. This new element has led some writers to believe that race is no longer an important element in employment for these select people who have been able to obtain advanced education (Wilson, 1978). While it is true that racial differences are minimal in this younger professional group, there are no data on what differential changes will occur as the two racial groups attempt to climb the occupational ladder. Initial employment and increases may be on a par while employees are in their early professional and occupational careers. However, it is anticipated that, with time, the solidarity and racial preferential patterns will become more evident as promotions, salary increases, and transfers into managerial positions are not equally distributed, but continue to reinforce the older patterns that are built on racial group membership.

When looking at income mobility, it becomes obvious that factors other than simple ability are at play. Blacks get a lower dollar return for their education in general and on the proportional basis of the number of years spent in school (Schwartz and Williams, 1977). Regardless of test scores, similarity of background, or length of time spent in getting advanced education, the data clearly show that employers hire and promote on the basis of the race of the person, regardless of what factors are controlled in statistical calculations (Corcoran, 1977). They unfailingly become victims of the Black job ceiling (Ogbu, this volume).

To concentrate only upon those Blacks who have been privileged to gain the higher level of education, and who have the enthusiasm of youth, is misleading, for the vast majority of Blacks not in that age cohort do not have those resources. The elimination of affirmative action programs will also work to truncate the career mobility of those who are fully qualified but who may not be provided the opportunity to realize their potentials fully. Only time will tell.

THEORETICAL CONSIDERATIONS RELATED TO BLACK MOBILITY

Three theoretical considerations must be examined when focusing on mobility within Black families. The first relates to the disagreement within the field of Black family studies about the relative merits of the African-linked cultural patterns. Some writers feel that no such links exist and that any deviations from the mainstream are the result of class, race, and poverty (Heiss, 1975; Hill, 1981). Existing family forms are thus seen as an adaptation of individuals within a poverty status to the mainstream family structures and organization (Shimkin et al., 1978; Aschenbrenner, 1973). This view is also supported by the belief that nonpoor Black families are indistinguishable from nonpoor non-Black families (Heiss, 1975).

Some writers prefer to use ethnicity to focus on Black families, combining class level and caste-like status (Scanzoni, 1971; Ogbu, 1974). Others have posited that to look at class only without some cultural framework is to view the families within a vacuum, even when extensive assimilation had occurred (Herskovits, 1941; Nobles, 1976; Sudarkasa, 1980). This last group has placed emphasis on the cultural continuity of Black family patterns. The position writers tended to take on this issue often was a reflection of their academic disciplines; sociologists relied more on income and class data, and anthropologists, along with some psychologists, leaned toward the cultural data.

The second theoretical consideration was whether the kin support networks helped or hindered upward mobility. Some writers have stressed the draining aspect of this mutual aid because of the lack of support from community institutions (Pleck, 1979; McQueen, 1971). Most have indicated that this mutual aid was essential, in that it extended the economic reach of all the family members (Hill, 1971; Stack, 1975; McAdoo, 1978). The inherent reciprocity of the obligation requires family members to keep their resources fluid and open to the emergencies of those within the extended circle. While this prevents an individual from focusing his or her resources only on the family of procreation, the assurances of available help they provide are deemed to far outweigh the negative aspects of involvement within the kin insurance network.

The third theoretical consideration is that extended patterns are only an element of sheer poverty. The lack of resources that exists for poor Blacks requires a continuation of kin-help patterns as a coping strategy. This point of view predicts that the extended kin help patterns would no longer exist when the family was above poverty. This view states that there is no basis in fact for the belief that some continuity of present Afro-American families and distant African family patterns were lost during and after enslavement. All of these varying views are discussed in detail in other chapters.

In the examination of the mobility patterns that have existed in a representative sample of Black families, it was impossible to articulate support or rejection of the source of the cultural patterns that were predicted to exist. Rather, it was an examination of whether or not some of the traditional "strengths" of Black families actually did exist and could be empirically examined. However, this study was able to examine whether the involvement within the extended family support network was a help or a hindrance to its upper mobility. The theories related to the value of support networks as a coping strategy of poverty and not of culture could be addressed through this study.

HYPOTHESES

In addition to the theoretical considerations, literature reviews indicated that there was a void of good descriptive material on mobile Black families. Several questions on these families had simply not been answered. Therefore, the primary purpose was to obtain good descriptive data on upwardly mobile Black families.

The secondary purpose of the present examination was to test the hypothesis that certain family cultural patterns are a viable element within Black family life and that these patterns would be present even after mobility had occurred. One pattern that was selected was the extended family support networks, operationally defined as close and frequent interactions between kin and the frequent exchange of emotional support, goods, and services.

The second hypothesis was that active extended support patterns would be found in all mobility patterns, and that they would be similar regardless of the length of time the family had been at this economic level, either newly mobile or middle class for two or more generations. It was anticipated that the extended family patterns were more than a coping mechanism of poverty, to be discarded when they were no longer poor, and that the family members would not have discarded their cultural pattern of close involvement with the kin and fictive kin.

In order to test these hypotheses and to examine some of the mobility patterns of Blacks, it was decided to select a group of currently middle-class persons and trace with them the geographic, educational, and occupational mobility their families had followed over the past three generations. This study was designed to answer the following questions:

(1) What are the characteristics and mobility patterns of upwardly mobile Black families?
(2) Are currently middle-class Black families involved in the extended family support patterns?
(3) Are the family support patterns different for those of families who were born poor from those who were born middle class?
(4) Is the reciprocity inherent in support networks felt to be excessive?
(5) Are there differences in the family characteristic between families in each of the three mobility patterns that exist?

METHODS

The family data used to answer these questions were obtained from surveys of an urban and suburban sample of middle-income Black families, whose parents had some college education, were above the age of 25, and who had school-aged children in the home. Suburban families were randomly selected, with replacement, from a list of all Blacks living in the town. Once they were interviewed, their educational and occupational levels were matched with a comparative sample from a nearby mid-Atlantic city.

Families were interviewed for about five hours each. Attempts were made to control as many external variables as possible. Each parent was interviewed by Black, college-educated adults, with the fathers interviewed by males and the mothers by females. The interviewing was done only after the questions had been field-tested twice and extensively modified to be sensitive to the race-related and personal topics that were covered.

To avoid the difficulties of applying standardized SES scales to Blacks, five different procedures were used: the modified scoring of the Hollingshead-Redlich scale, self-ratings of social class status, educational rankings, occupational rankings, and the standard Hollingshead-Redlich scale. For this study, only the modified SES will be used, in which education was given a higher factor loading than occupation. Income was obtained but not used in SES classifications because of the lower incomes of Blacks in spite of their occupations.

RESULTS

FAMILY DESCRIPTIONS

Data obtained from 178 domestic units included 305 parents, 131 fathers, and 174 mothers. While no control was made for family type (one/two-parent families), 28 percent were one-parent homes, a close approximation of the proportion of single-parent homes in current census reports. Ninety-three percent of the families were nuclear in structure, comprised of either one or two parents. Only six percent were extended in structure, while two percent were augmented in form, with nonrelatives living in the home. They had an average of 2.37 children each, consistent with the low number of children that have traditionally been born to middle-income families. The average income was $20,000 for fathers and $11,000 for the 85 percent of the mothers who worked. The mean ages were 41 years for the fathers and 37 years for the mothers.

These parents had not moved a great deal during their lives: 85 percent had never moved or moved only once. Almost half had been born in the mid-Atlantic area, and one-fourth were born in the South and had moved North. They were the children of migrants from the South who had moved to this area and had remained geographically close to their kin.

Religion continued to play an important role in the lives of only half of the parents, a direct contrast to the important role that the church played in their parents' and grandparents' lives. One-fourth indicated that religion played no role in their lives. There was a definite move across the three generations from the fundamental denominations as income increased. For example, the Baptists were the largest group in all three generations, but membership declined from over 60 percent in the grandparents' generation to 32 percent in the subjects' generation. Meanwhile, Catholic membership doubled (7 to 15 percent) and Episcopal membership tripled (3 to 9 percent).

Fathers' occupational status was high, but still was not commensurate with their very high educational achievement, as shown by the SES differences when the two status codings were made. The occupational distributions of the mothers who were in positions were much lower than would be expected based on their education. The mobility or financial stability of these families was clearly tied to the occupation and income of the father. The maternal occupation dominance stereotype was not supported for these families. While these mothers had jobs of generally lower status than the fathers, in earlier generations the mothers' families had higher status for both male and female. The males' fathers were skilled workers and the females' fathers held higher clerical positions.

The stereotype of the woman being better educated did not hold in the present generation. In two-parent homes, the fathers were significantly better educated than the mothers (χ^2 (12) = 29.90, p < .003). When their education was compared by their status at birth, no educational difference was found between the fathers who were born middle class and those who were born working class. However, mothers who were born working class had significantly higher educations than those born in middle-class families (χ^2 (4) = 15.69, p < .001). In earlier generations, the mother tended to be better educated than the male. It appears that education peaked at the point of mobility. It was maintained in the second generation and began to decline in the third generation of middle-class status.

SUPPORT NETWORK INVOLVEMENT

The hypothesis that families would be involved in the kin-help exchange network, even after obtaining middle-class status, was supported: Parents indicated an extensive and intensive involvement with the network. The majority tended to live within 30 miles of their family members, a fact that facilitated interaction. They felt that it was relatively easy for them to stay in contact with their kin.

Family members were seen as the most important source of outside help. Eighty percent of the families had a reciprocal involvement with their kin. They gave and received help with child care, financial aid, and emotional support. The reciprocal obligations that were involved with the support network were not felt to be excessive and were part of everyday life. The pressure on the newly mobile to help kin who were less fortunate was significantly stronger than for those who were born middle class. They did not feel that this was a burden, but simply the way that things are done in the family. Many mentioned that their advanced education was possible only because of family help.

When the four mobility patterns were combined into those who were born working class versus those born middle class, there were no significant differences between the two social classes of origin in the amount or kind of help given to or received from family members, nor in the attitudes that were held about the reciprocity. The hypothesis that extended family involvement would extend beyond the point of mobility was supported.

CROSS-GENERATIONAL MOBILITY PATTERNS

We were able to compute four generations of SES status for 128 of the families, going from the children of the subjects (all born middle class) back to the subjects' grandparents. The patterns had three possible points of mobility. The mobility patterns revealed, surprisingly, that no one was able to move from abject poverty into middle-income status in just one generation. Several subjects had said that they went from being poor to where they are now, but a closer examination of the data indicated that their parents may have low incomes but that the parents had higher educations than one would expect. They would not be considered as part of the permanent underclass, but rather as solid working but poor individuals.

The original nine mobility patterns were condensed into four, shown in Table 9.1.

Pattern I: Born Working Class, Newly Mobile. Families in the largest group represented the typical Black who is now of middle-class status. They were born into solid working-class families, poor but self-supporting and indepen-

TABLE 9.1   Four Cross-Generational Mobility Patterns

Patterns	Grandparents	Parents	Subjects	Percent
I	working	working	middle*	62
II	lower*	working*	middle*	23
III	working	middle*	middle	6 ⎫ 15
IV	middle	middle	middle	9 ⎭
				100

*Point of upward mobility.

dent of governmental support. They were able to achieve this status through the acquisition of professional degrees that allowed them to move into higher-status jobs. Seventy-nine percent had college or professional training. As the first generation to move up, they had relatives who were much poorer but with whom they kept in frequent contact.

Their parents usually had grade school or less than high school educations. Their mothers tended to be better educated than their fathers. Their grandparents had grade school educations, although 17 percent of them did attend some college. As a group, the grandparents and the parents were those who had just a little more education than the average Black, and they were able to get solid, respectable working-class jobs within the community.

Pattern II: Upwardly Mobile in Each Generation. Over three generations these families had been in three different levels. Their grandparents had been reared in lower-class poverty families, the parents had moved to working class, and the subjects were mobile into the middle class. Subjects in this group had the highest academic training—almost all had college or advanced degrees. Their fathers had high school and their grandparents had junior high or grade school educations. Again, their mothers were better educated: 14 percent had college degrees and 24 percent had some college training. The mobility in the second generation may have been helped a great deal by the education of the mother. Of all four patterns, this one had the highest educational, occupational, and income levels and the lowest level of stress.

Pattern III: Upwardly Mobile in Parents' Generation. These subjects had all been born into middle-class status, while their grandparents had been born into working-class families. The mobility occurred in their parents' generation. Educational achievement had decreased in the present generation: only 29 percent had graduate or professional training, compared to 63 percent of their fathers and 50 percent of their mothers. The group's second generation was better educated than any of the other four patterns. In the paternal grandparents' generation, one-third of each sex had high school training. In the maternal line, the males had grade school while the females finished high school, and 14 percent of the maternal grandmothers graduated from college. Education clearly was a goal within these families. The small cell size for which we have three generations of information, however, limits the implications that can be drawn from this group.

Pattern IV: Middle Class over Three Generations: For these families, the subjects' grandparents had been middle class and this had been maintained into the subjects' generation. Nine percent of the families were in this group. A subset of this pattern, three percent of all families, had parents and grandparents who were at a higher level than they had reached. This was usually because the subjects had received less education and were earning a much lower salary than had the past two generations. Because these subjects were clearly still middle class, they are included in the fourth group.

An interesting finding for this three-generation middle-class group was that they had the lowest level of education—33 percent had college and only 9 percent had advanced professional degrees. The parent generation had the same level of achievement as the subjects (father, 42 percent; mother, 25 percent). They had maintained their accomplishments but had not moved beyond their parents. However, grandfathers (born in the late 1800s) on both sides were very well educated, even by today's standards. Sixty percent of the paternal grandfathers and 20 percent of the maternal grandfathers had college and advanced degrees.

MATERNAL ROLE IN MOBILITY

While the overall mobility was dependent on the education and income of the father, because of the inequity of pay, the cross-generation data indicate that the point of mobility for the family coincided with employment outside the home of both mother and father. Mobility would not have been possible without the dual income and could not be maintained without the continued employment of both parents.

While the level of maternal employment was high in all patterns, there were some indications that the present level of maternal employment was related to the father's ability to maintain the middle-income lifestyle on one income. More mothers worked when income tended to be low, and fewer worked when the father's income, education, and occupational status were high. When a choice was feasible, more tended not to work and to concentrate on the home and the family.

The role model that was provided by an employed grandmother was not a factor for only 30 percent of the grandmothers who worked in all of the patterns. However, the role model of a working mother may be a salient point for the fathers. The mobility pattern in which almost all of the mothers now work was the one in which the male subject had a mother who worked outside the home.

Sons who were born to families in which the mothers had higher occupations than the fathers are the ones who currently are highest achievers. Their motivation may be attributed, in part, to the drive of the employed mother with limited education who was able to move to a responsible position that was higher than the subject's father.

The most important factor for the mother in deciding to work was the economic necessity for wanting to be mobile and the precariousness of the Black middle-class families who are, because of the dearth of inherited wealth and unearned income, only one paycheck from poverty. Despite their high educational level, Blacks' lower payoff has meant that they have little surplus income that could be invested and used to augment their wage earnings. Families are where they are because of their own effort and not because the financial benefits of earlier generations have been passed on, as is effectively done in non-Black populations.

SOURCES OF STATUS

Because differential skin color and hair type were the traditional status criteria for many Blacks, the parents were asked how important these were in Black life. Physical characteristics that are race-related still appear to be an important element for these adults. One-half felt that higher status was afforded to non-Black characteristics, and one-third felt that it was of less importance now but of serious concern in the past. This becomes operational in mate selection and in job promotions. Parents appear to assume that everyone had internalized a status preference for the characteristics of the majority group but that attitudes were not as important as in Frazier's day. Other than skin color, the status was assigned to families within the community in a manner that is indistinguishable from other groups.

DISCUSSION

MIDDLE-CLASS DECLINE

When the educational levels of each pattern were reviewed over the generations, it was obvious that the level of education peaked at the point of mobility. The level was maintained in the second, and there was a definite decline in the third generation of middle-class status. It seems that these families are unable to pass on the major benefits from one generation to the next, except when they are upwardly mobile. Once mobility occurred, it was difficult to maintain this higher status. The highest levels of education, occupational status, and income were found in the pattern that had been upwardly mobile for each of the three generations.

There are many explanations for this decline. It could be a function of a regression toward the mean in education and achievement. Or it could be that the comparative security these families experienced as the children were growing up tended to sap the achievement of youth. Another alternative may be that since they did not feel the need to be as conscious of selecting a job for basic survival, they were allowed to select occupations on the basis of interest rather than for financial security. Another explanation could be that the parents were both deeply involved in their jobs and may not have given the children the guidance and structure that was needed in order to match successfully the academic excellence of their parents. An indulgent lifestyle may be the middle-class "dream" for which they worked so hard to give to their children, but this may be the same type of environment that would not reinforce the strive toward achievement. Society was not supportive of the maintenance of Black upward mobility. Therefore, unless the drive to achieve remained active and sacrifices were made, that status declined.

SUPPORT NETWORKS AND MOBILITY

This examination of upwardly mobile patterns in Black families has indicated that the education and achievement of the individuals were often impossible without the support of the extended family. Mobility, the result of acquisition of professional training that leads to high-paying jobs, appears to require intensive effort by family members, and without perseverence there is a tendency to experience a decline in status. The employment of both parents is required for initiation and maintenance of mobility, but maternal employment appears to lessen if the husband is able to support the family adequately on his salary. Families with only one parent are at a distinct disadvantage and find it difficult to maintain their hard-earned status. The positions many of the parents held were not as high as would be expected, but the racial "job ceiling" effect becomes evident even within the professions and with people who have special talents.

The continuation of the extended family support system reflects continued cultural patterns, and is a factor of the vulnerability of the Black middle class. Both factors are operational within all of the mobility patterns. The kin support network is still as essential now as it was in earlier generations, for it involves cultural patterns that were created and retained from earlier times that are still functional and supportive of Black family life.

REFERENCES

ASCHENBRENNER, J. (1973) "Extended families among Black Americans." Journal of Comparative Family Studies 4.

BILLINGSLEY, A. (1968) Black Families in White America. Englewood Cliffs, NJ: Prentice-Hall.

CORCORAN, M. (1977) "Who gets ahead: a summary," in C. Jencks (ed.) Who Gets Ahead? The Determinants of Economic Success in America. New York: Basic Books.

FRANKLIN, V. (1979) The Education of Black Philadelphia, The Social and Educational History of a Minority Community, 1900-1950. Philadelphia: University of Pennsylvania Press.

FRAZIER, E. (1939) The Negro Family in the United States. Chicago: University of Chicago Press.

GLASGOW, D. (1980) The Black Underclass, Poverty, Unemployment and Entrapment of Ghetto Youth. San Francisco: Jossey-Bass.

HALEY, A. (1976) Roots. New York: Doubleday.

HEISS, J. (1975) The Case of the Black Family, A Sociological Inquiry. New York: Columbia University Press.

HERSKOVITS, M. (1941) The Myth of the Negro Past. New York: Harper & Row.

HILL, R (1971) Strengths of Black Families. New York: Emerson-Hall.

——— (1981) "The Black family and national policy." Presentation at the University of Wisconsin Black History Week.

HORTON, J. and L. HORTON (1979) Black Bostonians, Family Life and Community Struggle in the Antebellum North. New York: Holmes and Meier.

McADOO, H. (1978) "Factors related to stability in upwardly mobile Black families." Journal of Marriage and the Family 40 (4).

McQUEEN, A (1971) "Incipient social mobility among poor Black urban families." Presented at Howard University Research Seminar, Spring.

MALVEAUX, J. (1981) "Shifts in the occupational and employment status of Black women: current trends and future implications." Paper presented at the Conference on Black Working Women, University of California, Berkeley, May 21.

MARTIN, E. and J. MARTIN (1978) The Black Extended Family. Chicago: University of Chicago Press.

NOBLES, W. (1976) "A formulative and empirical study of Black families." Washington, DC: Department of Health, Education and Welfare.

NOBLES, W. and L. GODDARD (1977) "Consciousness, adaptability and coping strategies: socio-economic characteristics and ecological issues in Black families." Western Journal of Black Studies 1 (2): 105-113.

OGBU, J. (1974) The Next Generation, An Ethnography of Education in an Urban Neighborhood. New York: Academic Press.

PLECK, E. (1979) Black Migration and Poverty, Boston 1865-1900. New York: Academic Press.

SCANZONI, J. (1971) The Black Family in Modern Society. Chicago: University of Chicago Press.

SCHWARTZ, J. and J. WILLIAMS (1977) "The effects of race on earnings," in C. Jencks (ed.) Who Gets Ahead? The Determinants of Economic Success in America. New York: Basic Books.

SHIMKIN, D. B., E. M. SHIMKIN, and D. A. FRATE [eds.] (1978) The Extended Family in Black Societies. The Hague: Mouton.

STACK, C. (1975) All Our Kin: Strategies for Survival in a Black Community. New York: Harper & Row.

SUDARKASA, N. (1980) "African and Afro-American family structure." The Black Scholar, Journal of Black Studies and Research 2 (8).

WILSON, J. (1978) The Declining Significance of Race: Blacks and the Changing American Institutions. Chicago: University of Chicago Press.

PART III

BLACK ATTITUDES TOWARD PAIR-BONDING

This section gives an overview of the roles and attitudes of Black males and Black females, and then examines the parental attitudes that are held by both and their attitudes toward procreation. Cazenave and Harrison point to the void that exists to date in the roles of men in pair-bonding processes and in socialization of children. Gary's volume on *Black Men* should make a real contribution on male roles, as did Rodgers-Rose's *The Black Woman* for women's roles.

Robert Staples gives a brief overview of race and marital status and their impact on Black families. He gives a historical basis to the present relationship between Black males and females and explains some of the unique patterns that are sometimes found. The equalitarian relations, the role overload of women, and the greater independence of women within the families are based on historical and financial reasons and may have implications for marriage relations. Regardless of these pressures, Blacks are heavily committed to marriage in former years, with a postponement occurring in the younger age groups, consistent with other families. The increasing level of singlehood is explained, as are the structural restraints that are faced at the lower- and middle-income levels. The complexity for the relations in the pair-bonding process are begun by Staples and detailed by Cazenave, Heiss, and Harrison.

Noel Cazenave reviews writings on the Black male, and his chapter presents the data on race-by-class-by-gender contributions to families. It includes an analysis of the conceptual frameworks of gender identity and masculine attainment that have been used to examine the Black male. He connects the difficulty in providing adequately for their families with the negative stereotypes that have been drawn about them in the literature.

Jerold Heiss presents a clear articulation of the different points of view that have been presented in the literature in relation to the association of family values and race or SES. He uses a national probability sample to test Ladner's hypothesis that Black women reject society's expectation and create alternative family forms that result in different values. He tackled the difficult task of looking at family and marriage values from three points: Is race associated with values? If race does matter, then what is the impact of the differential SES? Which is greater? And if one controls all other variables, is race still important? He began with the premise that SES, not race or culture, was the key variable, and he found that the racial differences were minor, indicating a divergence projected by Glick of values and structure. The instrumental concerns were more salient for Black women in terms of marriage partners, and SES had less influence on Blacks than on whites. There were no race differences in attitudes toward divorce, and there was an increase in the acceptance by Blacks for out-of-wedlock parentage.

Algea Harrison points to the importance of parental role expectations and how they have changed and how they impact on the procreational attitudes of Black adults. While little was found about the male role in parenting and in procreation planning, there were many studies about the women. Black families were found to provide modeling that would lead the children toward androgynous roles. The importance of the active maternal roles, as noted also by Staples, and the centrality of children in the women's lives often lead to subsequent prioritization of the mother over the wife role. The decline of the fertility levels and the increase in the use of effective birth control, along with the delay in parenting of younger career-oriented women, will have an influence on the pair-bonding and on the attitudes toward procreation in the future.

10

RACE AND MARITAL STATUS
An Overview

ROBERT STAPLES

Relationships between Black men and women have had a peculiar evolution. Unlike the white family, which was a patriarchy and sustained by the economic dependence of the female, the Black dyad has been characterized by more equalitarian roles and economic parity in North America. The system of slavery did not permit Black males to assume the superordinate role in the family constellation, since the female was not economically dependent on him. Hence, relationships between the sexes were ordered along sociopsychological factors rather than economic compulsion to marry and remain married. This fact, in part, explains the unique trajectory of Black male/female relationships.

In the past slavery era, the economic parity of Black men and women continued. Due to the meager wages of most Black males, women were forced to enter the labor market and contribute to the maintenance of the households. Such a strong economic role in the family had certain consequences for the marital relationship. The stability of the white, patriarchal family was based on the economic dependence of the female member, forcing her into the prescribed role of a passive, subordinate female. Because Black females were more economically independent, many developed attitudes of freedom and equality unknown to most women in the nineteenth century. While this trait may be currently perceived as a healthy predecessor to the modern women's liberation movement, it produced tensions in Black marriages that were less prevalent in white marriages. The independent woman, in the past, and present, is more likely to be party to a dissolved marriage than her more reliant and passive counterpart.

Economic factors, however, provide only the foundation for dyadic conflict, which is subject to the interplay of other psychosocial forces. Another cause of male/female conflict is the often ignored consequences of the dual role Black women play in the family: worker and mother. The heavy concentration of Black women in domestic service often meant that they held the unenviable position of caring for two households: their own and that of their employer. It has seldom been questioned that the negative effects of doing double duty in two households has created competition between obligations to the two households and could tear at the fabric of the Black woman's marital relationship. Certainly, it could lead to role overload that might compound the difficulties of prosaic marital interaction. It might be noted that this same role overload continues to be extant, albeit in a slightly different form. Many Black women remain burdened by the multiple roles they must play—worker, mother, and wife. Surely, it partly explains the resultant tension and high rate of marital dissolution among so many Black couples.

Despite the problematic aspects of marriage, Blacks continued to marry in record numbers. When one looks at the marital status of Black women over the age of 65, only 3.5 percent had never married in comparison to 6.5 percent of white women.[1] However, the younger group of Blacks appear to have abandoned marriage as a viable institution. At least, the figures which show only a minority of them married and living with a spouse indicates that to be the case. Upon closer inspection, it seems that the desire to marry and remain married has not diminished, only the conditions for doing so have altered.

One can best understand the high rate of singlehood among Blacks by examining it along class and gender lines. The basic causes are structural constraints and ideological preferences. Among lower-income Blacks, the structural constraints consist of the unavailability and undesirability of Black males in the eligible pool of potential mates. Due to the operational effects of institutional racism, large numbers of Black males are incarcerated, unemployed, narcotized, or fall prey to early death. There may actually be an excess of three million Black women without the opportunity to find an available or desirable mate. As a result, many Black women have children out of wedlock and raise them with the assistance of extended family members and the biological father.

Similar structural constraints are operative among the Black middle class. Assuming a desire for homogeneity in mate selection, it is not possible for every Black female college graduate to find a mate among her peers. In 1975, there were 68,000 more Black female college graduates than males. Overall, the ratio of single college-educated Black women to similar men is two to one. In certain categories the ratio is as low as 38 women to every male. This gap, while currently wide, will continue to widen, as there are 150,000 more Black women than men currently enrolled in college. A very different demographic picture exists among whites, where there are a million more white male college graduates than females. This difference can originally be attributed to the historical practice of Black families sending their daughters to college because the males had a wider variety of occupations open to them. The daughters either went to college and became schoolteachers or went into domestic service, an occupation fraught with risks for young Black women in the postbellum south.

However, it is among this middle-class group that ideological preference—that is, the desire not to marry—is more prevalent. Because the women in this group earn 90 percent of a similar male's income, they do not need to marry for economic support. It is more often the satisfaction of psychological needs that is the dominant reason for entering into marriage. Yet, the satisfaction of psychological needs is not the forte of American males. Moreover, the greater a woman's educational level and income, the less desirable she is to many Black males. While a male's success adds to his desirability as a mate, it detracts from a woman's. Hence, the women in this group are less likely to marry and remain married, if they do marry. It is a classical case of success in the labor market and failure in the marriage arena.

Relationships between Black men and women are probably more complex than spelled out in this brief overview. Certainly the dominant factors are contained in the interplay of institutional racism with individual traits. The problems of Black male/female conflict are ultimately a function of political and economic forces beyond their control. Even within the context of economic and racial oppression, many Black men and women share happy moments with each other. For many of them, the relationship lasts a lifetime. There are also those for whom the tension of living in a racist society filters into their most intimate relationships. Relationships between the sexes is, at best, fragile in a society undergoing such rapid social change as occurs in the United States. Rapid social change, no matter in what direction, can cause dislocation in individuals and institutions. The dyadic relationships of Blacks, America's most vulnerable group, to economic and political change, are most sensitive to those changes.

NOTE

1. All figures used are taken from Staples (1981).

REFERENCE

STAPLES, R. (1981) The World of Black Singles. Westport, CT: Greenwood Press.

11

BLACK MEN IN AMERICA
The Quest for "Manhood"

NOEL A. CAZENAVE

Most of the research on the positions and roles constituting black families has been concerned with the so-called black matriarchy and father absence with a neglect of black men involved in familial roles. As Hannerz (1969: 113) puts it, "In all of these studies . . . the black man—as son, lover, husband, father, grandfather—is a distant and shadowy figure 'out there somewhere." In fact, Jacquelyne Jackson (1974: 19) found this neglect to be so severe five years later that she referred to "ordinary black husband/fathers" as "the truly hidden men from the perpetrators of the 'culture of investigative poverty.'" Still more recently I reviewed 27 popular family texts and readers and discovered no articles, sections, or index references to the "present" black father, and concluded that there is a specter haunting black family research and more than any other figure the black father qualified as the phantom of American family studies (Cazenave, 1979). In brief, for one reason or another, a relatively extensive literature on black families has developed in which the male has been either ignored completely or treated in a very marginal manner. A more complete understanding of the dynamics of black life in America demands a fuller understanding of the familial roles of black American men.

RACE, CLASS, AND GENDER

In fact, an understanding of the dynamics of black masculine attainment provides nothing less than an intellectual unraveling of American society itself. To understand the workings of this society it is essential to delineate the key determinants of "who is" and "who isn't" in America. In large part, status in American social structure is ascribed on the basis of race, sex, and class. Black men are generally assumed to be afflicted with two severe handicaps at birth: race and class. However, it is often assumed that gender is an important advantage that guarantees black men a modicum of relief from the toils of oppression (even if it is at the expense of black women). In order to adequately test this and other assumptions about black American men, it is essential to understand the substance of masculinity in America.

MASCULINITY IN AMERICA

Anthropologists (for example, Mead, 1963) have illustrated that there is no such thing as a "natural" man or woman in any society. What a particular society expects from men or women—rather than inherent sex temperaments—determines both their behavior and how they perceive themselves. Traditionally, femininity in American society has been associated with passivity; and masculinity, prescribed activity. Consequently a woman was more likely to be assured her gender identity as a birthright. That is, provided she followed the appropriate feminine scripts (for example, to marry and bear children) there were (theoretically at least) institutional supports to guarantee her right to *be* feminine, and fewer consequences for gender-inappropriate behavior (Hacker, 1957). However, a male's gender identity—his masculinity—has been and continues to be much more volatile. It has to be earned and proved on a day-to-day basis. A man can't just be masculine, he must constantly "prove" it (Turner, 1970). *Masculine attainment* refers to this persistent, lifelong quest for gender identity among American males.

THE "DOUBLE BIND"

Despite the impact of advocates of men's liberation and more flexible sex roles (Farrell, 1974; Fasteau, 1976), today being a man in America society still means achieving, accomplishing, having a good job, and providing adequately for oneself and one's family. The central question, therefore, in comprehending the behavior and attitudes of black men in America is: What happens to black men who accept society's notions of what it takes to *be a man* but are denied the resources to *"earn"* their masculinity through traditional channels? An awareness of this precarious predicament is the key to understanding the unique psychological and social drudgery which distinguishes black men from other sex/race groups in America. For example, while *objectively* the economic position of black women is worse than that of white men, white woman, and black men, *subjectively* it is black men who are forced into the humiliating "double bind" of proving their manhood while being denied access to the legitimate tools with which to do so (Franklin and Walum, 1972; Walum, 1977). The hopes, aspirations, attitudes, and behaviors of black men are formed in this process of masculine attainment, and its vicissitudes are a major motivating force behind much of the day-to-day interactions and lifestyles of black American males.

In the remainder of this Chapter I will take a close look at how race, class, and gender affect the lives of black American men and those closest to them. I will explore their precarious quest for masculine attainment and its social, psychological, and political consequences.

MERTON'S THEORY OF ANOMIE

One of the most useful theories for studying the behavioral consequences of forcing men to measure up to unattainable standards of "masculinity" is suggested by the work of Robert K. Merton. According to Merton's theory of anomie, socially deviant or unacceptable behavior results for certain groups in American society because, while the majority share the basic *goals* of society, all do not share the *means* of achieving those goals. Consequently, he argues, the very structure of society (especially differential access to the opportunity structure) actually encourages certain individuals to function deviantly to obtain its cultural goals (i.e., the material and social prestige rewards of society). Merton identifies five distinct modes of adaptation that an individual can use in his adjustment to the social structure: conformity, innovation, retreatism, ritualism, and rebellion. As one author sees it, Merton's theory describes a world that is very similar to the operation of a giant fruit dispensing machine, where

> the machine is rigged and only some players are consistently rewarded. The deprived ones then either resort to using foreign coins or magnets to increase their chances of winning (innovation) or play mindlessly (ritualism), give up the game (retreatism) or propose a new game altogether (rebellion) [Taylor, 1971: 48].

In the next section I will explore the dynamics of race, class, and masculine attainment by discussing the *conformist* and *innovator* modes of adaptation in greater detail. In both cases these men have accepted traditional notions of masculinity; but they differ significantly in their ability to implement these ideals.

CONFORMISTS: PATRIARCHS

As early as 1939, E. Franklin Frazier postulated that a black male's involvement in familial responsibilities was associated with his ability to provide for his family. For example, Frazier believed that with Emancipation some black men who managed to obtain property went to extreme measures to secure and maintain familial power which had previously been denied them. That is, given the opportunity, they not only embraced traditional notions of American patriarchy, but they tended to overconform to its mandates. Frazier also recognized that during this same period after Emancipation many black men did not acquire the economic base to secure their position in the family. Frazier envisioned the development of a black proletariat as the key to masculine attainment for the hoards of black men who migrated to the urban North seeking employment. He saw the black industrial worker, having gained the means to provide adequately for his family, as the model for responsible manhood. These themes of responsibility and adequate economic provision are still central in understanding working-class black men today.

BRINGING HOME THE BACON

In a recent study of 54 black fathers employed as letter carriers (Cazenave, 1979), the respondents were asked: "What do you think it means to be a man today?" The largest of six response categories, 41 percent, centered on one key word: responsibility. Other prominent response categories included hard work, ambition, and firm guiding principles. And although the respondents believed they were emotionally closer to their children than their fathers were to them and saw masculinity as a complex, demanding, and changing role, the most salient masculine identity for them was that of economic provider. These men were very much aware that their income and greater job security enabled them to provide for their family to a much greater extent than their fathers, who had lower-status jobs, less stability, and less pay. To them, being a man meant taking care of one's family. They clearly understood this norm, had the resources to execute it, and prided themselves in their adherence to it. As such, they exemplify the (unrealized) aspirations that Frazier had for the masses of black industrial workers in the private sector.

INNOVATORS: VESTIGIAL FAMILY ROLES

Those men who are not able to obtain their "manhood" through the execution of responsible familial roles, anchored in their ability to provide adequately for their families, carry out their husband and father roles in a vestigial manner (Kardiner and Ovesey, 1951) and look to other avenues of masculine demonstration.

EARLY SOCIALIZATION

It appears that among lower-class black men the expectation of only limited involvement in family life starts during their boyhood in their families of orientation. As Schulz (1969: 59) observed in his study of socialization practices among low-income blacks:

> While the feminine role is associated with respectability, dependability, the family, and the home, masculinity is more often associated with the reverse of these and its locus is the street. A boy strives to achieve a "rep" on the street because he perceives that he does not have much status in the home.

In brief, even before an underclass black male inherits the economic problems that have contributed to a low level of involvement for his father in family affairs, he is socialized to expect that men demonstrate their manhood in the streets, not the home. To protect themselves from the denigrating blow that institutional racism deals to their quest for masculine attainment, most become active participants in what Glasgow refers to as a "survival culture." In distinguishing between a survival culture and what other scholars label the "culture of poverty," Glasgow (1980: 25) cautions:

> Notwithstanding its reactive origin, survival culture is not a passive adaptation to encapsulation but a very active—at times devious, innovative, and extremely resistive—response to rejection and destruction.

While acknowledging the positive role of what, in gender identity terms, can be seen as an alternative form of masculine attainment, Glasgow notes that with the internalization of the attitudes, and behaviors appropriate to this adaptive style, many young underclass black males effectively eliminate the likelihood of individual mobility should the opportunity present itself. The cycle is thereby now completed and they are locked into alternative modes of masculine attainment.

ALTERNATIVE MODES OF MASCULINE ATTAINMENT

Hannerz (1969) identifies the following characteristics of what he refers to as the "ghetto-specific male alternative": sexual conquests; concern with expressive styles in speech, dress, and personal appearance; liquor consumption; and toughness and the ability to command respect. Glasgow saw more than one general monolithic pattern and noted that different men tended to choose different strategies for responding to their designation as failures. Some give up and accept whatever label is bestowed upon them (for example, "dope head," "wino," "crazy"). Others maintain hope that they will eventually break into the mainstream. They accept whatever menial employment may be available and hope for some measure of upward mobility. However, Glasgow found that the majority did not retreat or acquiesce. They resorted to an extremely aggressive manipulation of their environment (compare these patterns of adaptation to Anderson's [1978] "Winos," "Regulars" and "Hoodlums," respectively). This is not surprising. Earlier Turner (1970) noted that two major responses of American men to threats to their masculinity are generally rigidity and aggressiveness. Let's look more closely at physical violence as a consequence of such aggression and a vehicle for masculine attainment.

VIOLENCE AND MASCULINE ATTAINMENT

In American society the ultimate resource that a man uses to demonstrate his manhood is his ability to exert, violently, toughness and control over others. That is, violence may be an effective tool for achieving what (such as respect and status) is not otherwise available to a low-status individual. In brief, violence can actually be a form of social achievement. A "tough" guy's reputation can be earned in ghetto streets as well as in corporate suites. This view is consistent with what sociologists refer to as the "resource theory of violence" (Goode, 1974). Violence is seen as a resource that can be used to achieve desired ends when other resources are lacking or are found to be insufficient. For example, whereas a middle-class man may have the resources to maintain his being the "head" of his family, a lower-class man may feel that since he cannot coerce or impress his family with his social status, education, money, prestige or other attributes, the only way for him to maintain his position as "head of the family" is through the use of his superior physical force—the only resource he sees as operating effectively for him. This process is not limited to a "subculture of violence." The neurotic search for masculine attainment is a crucial component of the "cultural apparatus" (Mills, 1963) of the larger society, and violence is a vehicle commonly used for its achievement (Graham and Gurr, 1969). At first an individual may simply try to act out appropriate masculine scripts. If that doesn't work, he asserts himself. If that fails, he becomes aggressive and eventually violent (Wilber, 1975). In the absence of institutionalized means to obtain and maintain a positive masculine identity, the negotiation of masculine identities (with the very real possibility of violent eruptions) becomes a very volatile and precarious undertaking (Anderson, 1978).

BLACK MEN AND SOCIAL PROTEST: INNOVATION OR REBELLION?

The black man's efforts to attain manhood have not been confined to individual acts of what some scholars refer to as "masculine protest." The Black

Liberation Movement of the sixties and early seventies represented, in large part, the collective realization of black men that American society was systematically organized against their efforts at masculine attainment. This movement, therefore, appeared to have been burdened with *two* agendas: Improving the objective conditions of blacks—the manifest objective—and increasing the psychological power of black men in relation to other gender and race groups—the less acknowledged but no less effective motive (Walum, 1977). While there is little controversy as to whether these two objectives were both key motivating forces behind black collective protest efforts, there is considerable controversy as to the effects of this dual agenda. On one hand, there are scholars—among them Nathan Hare (1971: 35)—who, at that time at least, felt that the two were inextricably tied : "there can be no true liberation of the world—indeed of the black race—without the liberation of the black male." More recently, others suggested that it was the black man's inability to distinguish between the black male agenda and the Black Liberation Movement agenda that helped ensure the latter's failure. Journalist Michele Wallace (1978: 54-55) believes the pursuit of manhood was the illusionary "carrot" that white society held out before black men to divert them from initiating more fundamental challenges to the structure of American society.

Regardless of whether black male liberation was the major concern of, or simply a companion issue to, the Black Liberation Movement, it is clear that at that time there was more concern with obtaining manhood using traditional American definitions of masculinity than with substituting new definitions of masculinity and instituting new means toward its achievement.

TOWARD A RECONCEPTUALIZATION
OF MASCULINE ATTAINMENT

A major problem in the conceptualization of black male familial roles is the misconceptualization of white masculine roles. For example, while there has been much written about female-dominated lower-class black households; in controlling for the combined effects of race and class, Tenhouten (1970) found more similarities among black working-class men, white middle-class men, and black middle-class men than differences. All tend toward egalitarian relationships with their wives. It is the extremely patriarchal working-class white male who is atypical and who serves as the standard against which working-class black families are judged.

The failure to study ethnic differences adequately in sex role research has lead to other misconceptualizations as well. For example, the breadwinner role has been characterized as a restrictive form of male familial involvement which excludes the more multidimensional and caring masculine styles (Brenton,

1966; Chafetz, 1974; Fasteau, 1976). In a study of middle-income black fathers, I (1979) challenged this view and demonstrated that adequate economic provision is essential for *all* modes of male familial involvement, especially the more multifaceted and expressive modalities. It was suggested that the provider role may not be a salient role identity for fathers of low socioeconomic status because they cannot develop a realistic expectation of providing for their family. It also may not be a major identity for those men of high socioeconomic status because economic provision is not a problem. The provider role appeared most salient, however, for first generation working-class men who were able to provide adequately for their families and furnish them with the security that their own fathers could not give them. In brief, the ability to provide is a key determinant of how men carry out their masculine role responsibilities and their degree of emotional involvement in family life. In reviewing the literature of black men, I (1977) found that the studies can be placed into four categories based on the degree of male familial involvement. Most of the existing research focuses on father absence (Lincoln, 1965; Biller, 1969; Collier, 1973; compare with Merton's retreatist mode). Another large group focuses on men in vestigial relationships with a minimum of involvement (Liebow, 1967; Blood and Wolfe, 1969; compare with the innovator mode). A smaller number emphasizes men as patriarchs and economic providers (Young, 1970; Scanzoni, 1971; Jackson, 1974; compare with the conformist mode). Finally, the smallest group examines the more complex and emotionally expressive forms of involvement (Gillete, 1962; Tuck, 1971; Daniel, 1975). After finding that adequate economic provision among black men was key for all parenting modalities and that there was a curvilinear relationship between the ability to provide and the emphasis placed on the provider role (Cazenave, 1979), it became clear that these categories were closely associated with the class level of the men studied. Avoidance of familial responsibility and the abandonment of existing commitments is more characteristic of the underclass; vestigial relationships, the working poor; patriarchial styles, the working nonpoor; and multidimensional relationships, the middle and upper classes. This suggests that at the present time economically secure black men have the greatest ability to challenge traditional and repressive masculine roles and to choose and develop the less restrictive forms of gender identity and masculine attainment that are becoming more common among American males generally. More extensive changes in gender definitions, however, will require not only a critique of society's gender role prescriptions, but a critical reevaluation of its basic values of what it takes to "be somebody" (for example, extreme forms of individualism, competitiveness, materialism, and productivity-based achievements).

In brief, eliminating the pitfalls associated with the traditional quest for masculine attainment may mandate nothing less than a new "cultural apparatus" for affirming one's humanity and self-worth.

CONCLUSION

In this chapter I have attempted a social structural level analysis of black male familial roles in American society. Concern was focused on how race, class, and gender determine one's position in American society generally and within families in particular. The concept of masculine attainment was used to explore the correlates of male familial role execution, and the varieties of familial styles when the male is present and functioning in the home.

My major concern was in exploring one possible analytical framework for the study of black men. Consequently I made no attempt to document and describe the full diversity of black male familial life. Additional research is needed to uncover the perceptions that black men at various class levels have of their world, overall, and their family life, specifically. We need to tie in structural variables like those discussed here with more microlevel analyses of the way black men see their various familial roles in terms of what they think is expected of them from others, what they expect of themselves, and what they actually do. Finally, if we are to move past simply describing the sex roles of various categories and groups of black men, we will need cogent conceptual frameworks and analytical theories that will explain the social conditions under which we might expect various gender identities and role modalities to manifest themselves. It is to this end that the preceding analysis is dedicated.

REFERENCES

ANDERSON, E. (1978) A Place on the Corner. Chicago: University of Chicago Press.
BILLER, H. B. (1969) "A note on father absence and masculine development in young lower-class Negro and white boys." Child Development 39: 1003-1006.
BLOOD, R. O. and D. M. WOLFE (1969) "Negro-white differences in blue-collar marriages in a Northern metropolis." Social Forces 48: 59-64.
BRENTON, M. (1966) The American Male. New York: Fawcett.
CAZENAVE, N. A. (1977) "Middle-income Black fathers: family interaction, transaction, and development." Doctoral dissertation, Tulane University. Dissertation Abstracts International, 1978, 38, 6989A-7617A. (University Microfilms No. 78-07647).
———— (1979) "Middle-income Black fathers: an analysis of the provider role." The Family Coordinator 28: 583-593.
CHAFETZ, J. S. (1974) Masculine/Feminine or Human? Itasca, IL: Peacock.
COLLIER, L. (1973) "The effect of the father absent homes on 'lower class' black adolescents." Educational Question 17: 11-14.
DANIEL, J. E. (1975) "A definition of fatherhood as expressed by Black fathers." Unpublished doctoral dissertation, University of Pittsburgh.
FARRELL, W. (1974) The Liberated Man: Beyond Masculinity. New York: Random House.
FASTEAU, M. (1976) The Male Machine. New York: Macmillan.
FRANKLIN, C. W., Jr. and L. R. WALUM (1972) "Toward a paradigm of substructural relations: an application to sex and race in the United States." Phylon 33: 242-253.

FRAZIER, E. F. (1939) The Negro Family in the United States. Chicago: University of Chicago Press.

GILLETE, T. L. (1962) "Maternal employment and family structure as influenced by social class and race." Unpublished doctoral dissertation, University of Texas.

GLASGOW, D. G. (1980) The Black Underclass. San Francisco: Jossey-Bass.

GOODE, W. J. (1974) "Force and violence in the family," pp. 25-43 in S. K. Steinmetz and M. A. Straus (eds.) Violence in the Family. New York: Harper & Row.

GRAHAM, H. D. and T. R. GURR [eds.] (1969) Violence in America. New York: Signet.

HACKER, H. M. (1957) "The new burdens of masculinity." Marriage and Family Living 3: 227-233.

HANNERZ, U. (1969) Soulside: Inquiries into Ghetto Culture and Community. New York: Columbia University Press.

HARE, N. (1971) "Will the real black man please stand up?" The Black Scholar (June): 32-35.

JACKSON, J. J. (1974) "Ordinary black husband-fathers: the truly hidden men." Journal of Social and Behavioral Sciences 20: 19-27.

KARDINER, A. and L. OVESEY (1951) Mark of Oppression. New York: W. W. Norton.

LIEBOW, E. (1967) Tally's Corner: A Study of Streetcorner Men. Boston: Little, Brown.

LINCOLN, C. E. (1965) "The absent father haunts the Negro family." New York Times Magazine (November 28): 61, 172-176.

MEAD, M. (1963) Sex and Temperament in Three Primitive Societies. New York: William R. Morrow.

MERTON, R. K. (1968) Social Theory and Social Structure. New York: Free Press.

MILLS, C. W. (1963) Power, Politics and People. New York: Ballantine.

ROBERTSON, I. (1977) Sociology. New York: Worth Publishers.

SCANZONI, J. (1971) The Black Family in Modern Society. Boston: Allyn & Bacon.

SCHULZ, D. A. (1969) Coming Up Black: Patterns of Ghetto Socialization. Jamaica, NY: Spectrum.

TAYLOR, L. (1971) Deviance and Society. London: Michael Joseph.

TENHOUTEN, W. D. (1970) "The Black family: myth and reality." Psychiatry 23: 145-173.

TUCK, S., JR. (1971) "Working with black fathers." American Journal of Orthopsychiatry 41: 465-471.

TURNER, R. H. (1970) Family Interaction. New York: John Wiley.

WALLACE, M. (1978) Black Macho and the Myth of the Superwoman. New York: Warner Books.

WALUM, L. R. (1977) The Dynamics of Sex and Gender: A Sociological Perspective. Chicago: Rand McNally.

WILBER, C. G. [ed.] (1975) Contemporary Violence. Springfield, IL: Charles C Thomas.

YOUNG, V. (1970) "Family and childhood in a southern Negro community." American Anthropologist 72: 262-288.

12

WOMEN'S VALUES REGARDING
MARRIAGE AND THE FAMILY

JEROLD HEISS

After a number of years of sociological investigation, it is now clear that the distributions of several family variables are different for blacks and whites. Black families, for example, tend to be somewhat larger, they are more likely to be female-headed, they are more likely to be extended in form, and so forth (Jackson, 1973; Baughman, 1971; Heiss, 1975). However, the reasons for this racial variation remain unclear. Some authors argue that there are important differences in family values, and they see the differences in family behavior as a reflection of these psychological differences. Others deny the existence of attitudinal differences. They contend, for example, that blacks and whites are equal in their acceptance of the values contained in what is often called the "mainstream family model." These authors believe that variation by race occurs primarily because the situations of blacks and whites differ in ways which produce differential access to the resources that are required if one is to live by that model.

Ladner (1972: 247) expresses the "attitude difference" view when she says that many of the girls in her study of the lower-class "reject larger societal expectations of them and *realistically* adapt to as well as create their own alternatives and norms." Peters and de Ford (1978: 193) express a similar sentiment when they list three family values that they say black families subscribe to, "unlike most families in the dominant culture." And, of course, the value difference view is held by those who place the sources of the contemporary black family in Africa and/or slavery (see, for example, Nobles, 1978; Herskovits, 1941).

Scanzoni (1971: 3), by denying attitudinal differences, is stating part of the "situational" view when he argues that "the *dominant* family form throughout western society at the level of values . . . is what the majority of adults (black and white) prefer." Along the same lines, Hannerz (1969: 71) suggests, in speaking of lower-class blacks, that "there is an idealization of the mainstream model of marriage. People get married and hope to make a go of it largely along its lines." And, similarly, "no ghetto-specific model for a male-female union has anything close to the normative validity which the mainstream model enjoys in the ghetto as well as outside it" (Hannerz, 1969: 102).

According to these authors, the differences in family form emerge from situational differences. Hannerz contends, for example, that conflict arises in lower-class black families because "the rights and duties prescribed in the mainstream model are applied to the situation so that facts of limited access to resources are transformed into ambiguities and deviations in the definition of the conjugal relationship. . . . In such cases the influence of the mainstream model prevents a stable settlement on the basis of ghetto-specific macrostructural conditons" (1969: 89; see also Rainwater, 1970; Schulz, 1969; Liebow, 1967; Staples, 1978; Ladner, 1972).

Cutting across the lines drawn by the two positions just described is a difference of opinion that relates to the contribution of socioeconomic status (SES) to the differences between the races. Some of those who posit the existence of attitudinal differences see them as a function of the differential distribution of SES. Their view is that SES is the major factor affecting these attitudes, and they believe that the racial difference is due to the fact that the races differ in SES. Others suggest that the racial differences would remain even if the races were equal on SES. They argue that the experiences that cause the supposed attitudinal differences are associated with racial status at all SES levels, though perhaps to different degrees. Similarly, those who focus on situational factors may claim that the situations of blacks tend to differ from those of whites regardless of social class, or they may posit that racial differences reflect social status differences between the races (see Udry, 1966; Billingsley, 1968; Frazier, 1939; Jackson, 1973).

The goal of this chapter is to cast some light on these matters by considering data drawn from a national sample of women. It will not be possible to settle the issue completely, but we will be able to test the "attitude-difference" theory by directly comparing the attitudes of women of the two races. Furthermore, when such differences are found, we will be able to estimate the degree to which they are a function of SES by comparing the attitudes of the racial groups with SES held constant.[1]

In addition, we will attempt to push the matter somewhat further by determining the independent effect of race, SES, and other variables[2] upon the variation in attitudes. By comparing the magnitude of these various effects we will be able to determine the relative significance of the racial effect. In sum, and more specifically, the research to be reported here is intended to provide answers to the following questions:

(1) Is there an association between racial status and attitudes on family-related issues?
(2) When there are racial differences on these issues, are they a function of the differential distribution of SES between the races?
(3) Are the SES or racial effects greater?
(4) If the racial groups showed the same distribution on SES, and other variables (age, religion, current marital status, number of children, and work status), would they differ in their responses?
(5) Are the racial differences that remain after the effects of other independent variables are ruled out greater or less than the SES differences that remain when the other independent variables are controlled?
(6) How much do other variables add to the variance explained by SES and race?

The answers to these questions will allow us to estimate the independent effects of racial status and will provide us with standards by which to judge the relative significance of these effects. In addition, the data will permit us to determine the relationship between SES and the dependent variables for each race separately. This will allow us to discover if the patterning of responses is the same in the two races; if variables which affect attitudes in one race have similar effects in the other. If this is the case, it would suggest that if the races become more similar in social status, they would probably become more similar in family attitudes. Also, since we have available surveys conducted in 1974 and 1979 which asked some of the same questions, it will be possible to determine whether the attitudes of the races are converging or diverging.

HYPOTHESES

Our basic hypothesis is that the attitude differences between the races are of minor significance. We expect that they will be rather small in absolute size, that they will be no larger than those associated with SES and the other demographic variables, and that they are at least partially a function of the differential distribution of SES and the other variables to be considered.

It is our belief that the family values held by an individual are a result of his or her particular socialization experiences, and that the relevant experiences are not strongly affected by race and the other demographic variables that are used in this study. This view is based, to begin with, on a rejection of the "Africanist" and "slavery" positions. Certainly, African ancestry and the experience of slavery represent two major differences between blacks and whites. We believe, however, that these differences have relatively little direct impact on the family attitudes that are taught contemporary blacks. Further, we assume, consistent with recent research (Gutman, 1976), that if there is any remaining effect of slavery, it does not push in the direction of a markedly distinctive family value set.

This is not to deny that there are relevant differences in the *recent* histories of blacks and whites. Racial status is a significant element in the lives of people in this society, and it is quite probable that race has an effect on the family attitudes that people encounter and on the choices they make among the attitudes presented to them. At the same time, however, we would note that both races are constantly exposed to the general American culture, and this would serve to reduce the difference between them.

It also seems likely that some of the differences in the experiences of blacks and whites are as much a function of differences in SES and other demographic variables as they are of racial status, per se. Thus we would expect that when SES and the other demographic variables are controlled, the differences between the races would be reduced. Given this, and the known relevance of some of the other variables—for example age and marital status—we would expect that the *independent* effect of racial status would prove to be no greater than the independent effects of the other factors.

We further assume that SES is related to family attitudes in a similar manner in both races. This hypothesis rests on the assumption that the situations of blacks and whites are sufficiently alike to ensure that the implications of possessing a particular trait are the same in both races—even if the magnitude of the effect is not the same in all cases. For example, regardless of race, people who are well educated are likely to have important socialization experiences that differ from those of the less well educated. The former are, for one thing, more likely to be economically secure. Such differences may very well be reflected in similar intraracial SES effects.

Finally, we expect to find that the races have come closer together on family attitudes over the last few years. This prediction is based on the assumption that recent societal events have brought many additional blacks into the mainstream of American life. This would have had the effect of further reducing the influence of the relevant parts of black culture, it would have increased blacks' exposure to the secondary agencies of socialization, and it would have reduced the differences between their life experiences and those of the typical white. All of these would lead to a convergence in attitudes over time.

METHODS

The data to be considered in this study were obtained from surveys of national samples conducted in 1974 and 1979 under the sponsorship of Virginia

Slims cigarettes. A multistage, stratified, probability design was used to choose sampling units to the level of blocks, and beyond this level there was a combination of random and quota methods. (The quotas were for sex, age level, and employment status.) The subjects of this study are the 2566 white women and the 318 black women of the 1974 survey and the 2607 white women and 296 black women questioned in 1979.

The SES scale is a factor-analytic score using respondents' education, family income, and a complex occupational prestige code. This code used the respondent's occupation if she was unmarried and employed, husband's occupation for married women not in the labor force, and a composite of husband's and respondent's occupation for married women who held outside employment. The factor analysis and scoring were done separately for the 1974 and 1979 samples so that changes in the distribution of socioeconomic characteristics in the society would not produce a higher set of scores for the 1979 respondents.

RESULTS

The first set of questions bears on motivations for marrying. The respondents' views were determined by giving them a list of ten possible reasons for marrying and asking them to choose the two or three they considered the most important. The responses were analyzed by means of factor analysis, and a clear expressive-instrumental factor emerged. Those who scored high on this factor tended to choose items which referred to instrumental concerns related to responsibilities, income, and the quality of life. On the other hand, high scorers were less likely than other respondents to choose the expressive reasons which related to being in love, liking and wanting to be with a particular person, having children, and so forth.

The respondents were also asked to rate 13 marital outcomes in terms of their importance "for a good marriage,"[3] and their responses provide us with an index of their motivations for marriage. When these responses were factor analyzed, two useful factors were found; an expressive factor, which had its major impact on the items that had to do with sexual relationships and the survival of love; and a companionship factor indexed by items dealing with understanding the spouse's life, sharing the humorous side of things, and the sharing of feelings. The analysis which follows utilizes these factors plus two items which did not weight heavily on either factor; the necessity of financial security and children for a good marriage.

The goal of this section is to test the general validity of Ladner's (1972) conclusion that the motivations that led the lower-class black women in her sample to marry differ from those of whites. She states that the former enter marriage after "a more realistic cold assessment of the chances of its succeeding. . . . Love, emotional security, etc. are actually 'luxury' reasons for getting married. Thus, Black females . . . are using more sophisticated and rational reasons for entering the marriage contract" (Ladner, 1972: 247).

Our data bearing on this issue are presented in Table 12.1. Since they are complex and presented in a somewhat unusual format, I will begin with a detailed reading of the data bearing on the first dependent variable to ensure that the reader will be able to follow the argument in the later sections despite the use of cursory references to the tables.

Section 1 of the table presents Pearson correlations between race, SES, and the dependent variables. The figures in column A show that race and SES are both weakly related to the number of instrumental reasons for marriage chosen by the respondent. Blacks are more likely than whites to choose such reasons (r = .18), and the higher the SES, the smaller the number of instrumental reasons chosen (r = −.13).

The numbers in Section 2 are the standardized regression coefficients (Betas) for race and the dependent variable controlling for SES, and for SES

TABLE 12.1 Analysis of Responses to Questions Bearing on Marital Motivations and Goals

Statistic: Variable; Constants	Motives and Goals				
	(A) Instru-mental[1]	(B) Expres-sive[1]	(C) Companion-ship[1]	(D) Financial Security[2]	(E) Having a Child[2]
1. Correlation: race	.18	−.01	−.10	.12	.02
SES	−.13	−.01	.06	−.13	−.16
2. Beta: race; SES constant	.16	−.01	−.09	.10	−.02
SES; race constant	−.09	−.02	.04	−.11	−.16
3. Final Beta: race	.15	−.03	−.11	.10	.00
SES	−.07	−.03	.04	−.10	−.13
4. R: race + SES	.20	.02	.11	.17	.16
R added by 5 other variables	.04	.09	.04	.01	.12
5. b: SES, no variables constant					
Black	−.10	−.03	−.04	.01	−.09
White	−.09	−.01	.04	−.07	−.10
6. b: SES; 5 variables constant					
Black	−.04	−.06	−.06	.05	−.06
White	−.06	−.02	.04	−.06	−.08
7. Trend, 1974-1979[3]					
Black	−.14	−.11	−.11	+1.8%	−6.9%
White	−.03	−.06	−.08	+8.3%	−5.2%

[1] For numerical scores a positive sign indicates that blacks or higher-status persons tended to get the higher scores.

[2] For nonnumerical variables a positive sign means that blacks or high-status respondents were more likely to say the goal was important.

[3] A positive sign means that people in the 1979 study had higher scores or a greater likelihood of saying the goal was important.

and the dependent variable controlling on race. In column A we see that race and SES are related to instrumental score independently of each other, though some of the original SES relation is due to the association of SES and race.

The figures in the third section are the Betas for race and SES when they and age, religion, marital status, number of children, and employment status are all in the equation. For instrumental score these Betas are approximately equal to the SES and race betas without the other variables held constant. This means that the "other" variables do not explain the effects of SES and race on the dependent variable.

The first row of Section 4 presents the multiple correlation of race and SES with the dependent variable. In the case of instrumental score, the multiple correlation is quite small. When taken together, race and SES explain only a small amount of the variation in instrumental scores.[4] The second row of Section 4 shows how much the other five variables add to the multiple correlation if they are put into the equation after race and SES have been entered. In this case, the addition of the other variables does not raise the multiple R very much. The other variables do not increase our ability to explain variations in the dependent variable.

In summary, none of the variables is strongly related to variations in response to the measure of instrumental motivations, but race has a somewhat stronger effect than SES, and the other five variables do not increase the correlation by any significant amount.

Sections 5 and 6 present *unstandardized* regression coefficients (b's) for SES for each race separately, with and without the other variables held constant. These figures tell us how SES affects the dependent variables in each race, another way of judging the extent to which the races are similar or different.

The data in column A suggest that for instrumental scores the patterning is similar in the two races. The coefficient for SES and instrumental score is in the same direction for whites and blacks, and it is about the same magnitude. Controlling the other variables reduces the coefficient more for blacks, but the end result is that the b's for SES are about the same size for both races.

The trends from 1974 to 1979 are presented in Section 7. As is indicated by the negative signs, both races had lower instrumental scores in 1979 than they had in 1974. Importantly, however, the change is somewhat greater for blacks. Since in the 1974 study the blacks had higher scores than the whites, this means that there has been a small convergence of the races between 1974 and 1979.

The items bearing on the criteria for a good marriage show a variety of patterns. Section 1 indicates that neither SES nor race is related to choosing expressive criteria (column B). In fact, none of the independent variables shows a substantial association with this dependent variable. As compared with whites, however, blacks do show a tendency to give less importance to companionships (column C), and they emphasize financial security more than whites (column D), even when other variables are held constant. The racial effect on the rating of companionship is stronger than the SES effect; for financial security it is the same strength. And the ratings on the importance of children for a good marriage (column 3) are related to SES but not to race.

This diversity makes it difficult to present a general conclusion, but it does seem that there are small racial differences on some marital goals and motivations. And, just as Ladner (1972) suggested, blacks tend to be more instrumental. The differences are small, to be sure, and they are not found on all variables, but they do seem to exist and, importantly, none of them is a reflection of racial differences in SES or the other variables being considered here.

In general, the social status patterns are about the same in the two races. For two of the variables, the signs of the b's are different, but the effects are so small that they may be considered to be practically zero.

The time trends are all in the same direction for the two races, and generally they do not differ much in magnitude. This suggests that there is neither convergence nor divergence. The financial security item is an exception, however. Both races rated this higher in 1979 than in 1974, but the increase was greater for whites. This caused the races to converge on this matter, since in 1974 the blacks were more likely to respond that financial security was important.

Turning now to other matters, we note that many authors have reported that the structural patterns prescribed by the mainstream model are followed less often by blacks than they are by whites.[5] For example, maternal employment outside the home is more common for blacks (Nye, 1974); the black rate for extramarital parenthood is higher (White, 1979); black families are more likely to be female-headed (Rodgers-Rose, 1980); and there is a greater likelihood that the household will contain people who are not members of the nuclear family (Hill and Shackleford, 1978). The purpose of this section is to determine if there are attitudinal differences behind such structural differences.

Column A of Table 12.2 analyzes the responses to an item which asked the respondents to choose among a variety of family forms. For our purposes the item was dichotomized into "mainstream" and "nonmainstream" categories. The former is comprised of those who chose the option of a nuclear family with a "traditional" division of labor. The second category was comprised primarily of people who preferred a nuclear family with an equal sharing of responsibilities for housework, children, and "breadwinning".[6] The item considered in Column B asks the respondents whether they would respect a man who stayed home and did the housework while his wife worked, more, less, or about the same as a man who was a wage earner. The remaining two variables also deal with variant family forms; cohabitation without marriage (for one's child), and parenthood without marriage.[7]

TABLE 12.2   Analysis of Responses to Questions Bearing on Acceptance of
"Nonmainstream" Family Forms

Statistic: Variable; Constants	Family Forms Accepted			
	(A) Accepts Nontrad. Form[1]	(B) Respects House Husband[1]	(C) Kids w/o Marriage[2]	(D) Accepts Child Who Cohabits[1]
1. Correlation: race	.04	−.10	.07	−.04
SES	.15	.23	.11	−.14
2. Beta: race; SES constant	.08	−.05	.11	−.08
SES; race constant	.17	.22	.14	−.16
3. Final Beta: race	.06	−.05	.08	−.05
SES	.10	.21	.10	−.10
4. R: race + SES	.17	.24	.15	.16
R added by 5 other variables	.20	.02	.14	.16
5. b: SES, no variables constant				
Black	.12	.16	.13	−.06
White	.09	.12	.08	−.16
6. b: SES; 5 variables constant				
Black	.11	.18	.08	−.01
White	.05	.12	.06	−.11
7. Trend, 1974-1979[3]				
Black	+3.0%	—[4]	.16	+13.7%
White	+7.6%	—[4]	.04	+12.2%

[1] For nonnumerical variables a positive sign means that blacks or high-status respondents were more likely to say the form was acceptable.
[2] For numerical scores a positive sign indicates that blacks or higher-status persons tended to get the higher scores.
[3] A positive sign means that people in the 1979 study had higher scores or a greater likelihood of saying the form was acceptable.
[4] The question was not asked in 1974.

Despite the behavioral differences that exist, the races show very little difference on these attitude items. None of the racial correlations is above .10, which indicates that blacks are not *substantially* more accepting of these "nonmainstream" family forms.[8] It is also clear that this failure to find racial differences is not due to a lack of patterned variation. The SES differences are all .10 or above, even when other variables are held constant. In addition, the demographic factors, particularly age, add a reasonable amount to the multiple R's for three of the variables.

The patterns of response are generally the same for both races (Sections 5 and 6). The only notable difference is that SES has less of an independent effect on attitudes toward cohabitation for blacks than for whites. This notwithstanding, these data give further evidence of the similarity of the races.

The data for trends over time show that for two of the three items for which there are data, the movement is in the same direction at about the same speed. Blacks, however, increased their acceptance of parenthood without marriage to a greater degree than did whites. Since blacks were originally more accepting, this produces a small widening of the gap between the races.

With the exceptions noted, it may be concluded that the hypotheses of this study are generally supported by the data on acceptance of "nonmainstream" family forms.

Finally, we turn to the subject of divorce, a matter about which there has been considerable controversy. That blacks have higher divorce rates than whites is beyond dispute by now (see Ross and Sawhill, 1975; Heiss, 1975), but we still do not know if this is due to a greater acceptance of divorce by blacks or to situational factors which make it more difficult for blacks to achieve a stable marriage (Hannerz, 1969; Liebow, 1967; Heiss, 1975; Ross and Sawhill, 1975).

The first matter to be considered is responses to a general item that asked the respondents whether they would favor or oppose divorce as a solution to a marriage which was "not working out." The second variable is the number of reasons the respondent accepted as valid reasons for divorce. (The list given the respondents contained items that referred to such things as the loss of love, different ideas about how children should be raised, and a severe drinking problem.) Thus, we can determine whether the races differ in their general willingness to resort to divorce if a marriage is defined as bad, and we can also determine their reactions to particular kinds of problems. The final two variables are factor-analytic scores which group the reasons into an expressive group which included such reasons as feeling the romance has gone out of the marriage, and a conflict group which contained items dealing with matters such as conflict over how money should be spent.

Our discussion of Table 12.3, which contains the relevant data, is brief, for the races show no differences on any of the items. Thus, several of the other questions lose their relevance. We simply note that SES differences are also quite trivial, though they are generally larger than the race differences; that the races are quite similar in their patterning of responses; and that from 1974 to 1979 there is essentially no change in acceptance of divorce for whites or blacks.

SUMMARY AND CONCLUSION

The data suggest the following answers to the questions that were posed at the beginning.[9]

1. Though there are differences between the family attitudes of black and white women, the evidence of this study suggests that they are trivial in size,

TABLE 12.3   Analysis of Responses to Questions Bearing on Attitudes
              Toward Divorce

Statistic: Variable; Constants	Divorce Attitudes			
	(A)	(B)	(C)	(D)
		Number of		
	Accepts	Reasons	Expressive	Conflict
	Divorce[1]	Accepted[2]	Reasons[2]	Reasons[2]
1. Correlation: race	−.02	.01	.06	.01
SES	−.05	.09	.01	.13
2. Beta: race; SES constant	−.03	.03	.06	.05
SES; race constant	−.06	.10	.02	.14
3. Final Beta: race	−.01	.01	.05	.03
SES	−.05	.09	−.01	.14
4. R: race + SES	.06	.10	.06	.14
R added by 5 other variables	.10	.09	.10	.06
5. b: SES, no variables constant				
Black	−.02	.29	.01	.14
White	−.03	.29	.03	.13
6. b: SES; 5 variables constant				
Black	.01	.39	.03	.14
White	−.03	.25	−.01	.13
7. Trend, 1974-1979[3]				
Black	+3.0%	—[4]	—[4]	—[4]
White	−0.1%	—[4]	—[4]	—[4]

[1] For nonnumerical variables a positive sign means that blacks or high-status respondents were more likely to
say the reason was acceptable.
[2] For numerical scores a positive sign indicates that blacks or higher-status persons tended to get the
higher scores.
[3] A positive sign means that people in the 1979 study had higher scores or a greater likelihood of saying
the reason was acceptable.
[4] The question was not asked in 1979.

more often than not. The prime exception to this generalization seems to be that
black women are more instrumental in their motivations for marriage and in
their marital goals. Even here, however, the racial correlations are not large.

2. The differences that were found do *not* seem to be a reflection of SES
differences. The control for SES does not typically reduce the race-attitude
correlations, even though race and SES are correlated.[10]

3. There is not much difference in the magnitude of the race and SES
differences; race is certainly not more important than SES. In fact, in most
cases the SES betas are somewhat larger.

4. As noted before, the racial differences are quite small, but in almost no
case are they made significantly smaller by controlling for the other variables
considered in this study. The racial differences are not due to differences in
these social characteristics.

5. When the other variables are controlled, SES still seems to have a some-what greater independent effect than race.

6. In general, the other variables do not add much to the multiple correlations obtained by using only SES and race. Variations in the dependent variables are not strongly related to any of the independent variables for which there is information in these surveys.

In addition, we conclude that SES tends to show similar relations to the dependent variables in both races, and between 1974 and 1979 the races have not changed their relative positions very much. However, there is more evidence for convergence that there is for divergence.

The major general conclusion is that the differences in the history and present experiences of blacks and whites have not produced major differences in their attitudes toward the family matters considered here. The common core of experience they share because of their exposure to the "mainstream model" seems to be more important than the differences that separate them. Certainly, race does not seem to hold the key to family attitudes. In some cases, for example, the SES differences within each race are considerably larger than the difference between the races. Undoubtedly, racial differences in family attitudes are neither as large nor as important as some have claimed.

Finally, it does not seem likely that attitudinal differences of the size we have found could account for the differences in family behavior that have been reported in other studies. It seems extremely likely that much of the racial variance in family behavior is a function of situational and resource differences rather than attitude differences.

NOTES

1. There is, of course, a basic problem involved in the attempt to control for SES when racial comparisons are being made, for people of different race who are equal on *objective* indicators of SES do not necessarily occupy comparable positions in the status hierarchy (see Dodson, this volume; Heiss, 1975; Jackson, 1973). There does not seem to be an adequate operational solution to this problem, though the use of a composite indicator such as is used here does reduce its magnitude. The reader should keep in mind that when we speak of comparisons with SES controlled, we are not in fact dealing with groups that are equal in social status, broadly conceived.

2. The "other" variables are age, religion, current marital status, number of children, and work status.

3. For these questions, the subjects were asked to rate the importance of each item. They were not asked to choose the few they considered most important, as in the previous set.

4. To make the figures in the table more comparable, R rather than R^2 is presented. The increase in variance explained is, of course, indicated by R^2.

5. No value judgment is implied by this statement. We do not believe that it is necessarily desirable for a group to live by the mainstream model (see Heiss, 1975).

6. This category also includes those who choose other forms such as the communal family. However, over 90 percent of the subjects chose one of the responses that involved a nuclear family unit.

7. The latter variable was a factor-analytic scale. Some of the items which loaded heavily on this factor referred to single people having children, and others asked about them raising children. A question that asked if a couple should marry for the sake of the child if the woman was pregnant did *not* load heavily on this factor.

8. The strongest correlation is found for the item that asks about respect for a man who keeps house. It is negative, which means that blacks are a little less favorable to this variant form.

9. It should be emphasized that these conclusions should not be generalized to aspects of family life not covered here. Even within the areas we have considered we have found that the findings are not totally consistent.

10. The reductions do not occur because in most cases when there is a correlation between race and attitude, the correlation of SES and the attitude is quite small.

REFERENCES

BAUGHMAN, E. E. (1971) Black Americans. New York: Academic Press.
BILLINGSLEY, A. (1968) Black Families in White America. Englewood Cliffs, NJ: Prentice-Hall.
FRAZIER, E. F. (1939) The Negro Family in the United States. Chicago: University of Chicago Press.
GUTMAN, H. G. (1976) The Black Family in Slavery and Freedom. New York: Pantheon.
HANNERZ, U. (1969) Soulside. New York: Columbia University Press.
HEISS, J. (1975) The Case of the Black Family. New York: Columbia University Press.
HERSKOVITS, M. J. (1941) The Myth of the Negro Past. New York: Harper & Row.
HILL, R. B. and L. SHACKLEFORD (1978) "The Black extended family revisited," pp. 201-206 in R. Staples (ed.) The Black Family: Essays and Studies. Belmont, CA: Wadsworth.
JACKSON, J. J. (1973) "Family organization and ideology," pp. 405-445 in K. S. Miller and R. M. Dreger (eds.) Comparative Studies of Blacks and Whites in the United States. New York: Seminar Press.
LADNER, J. A. (1972) Tomorrow's Tomorrow: The Black Woman. Garden City, NY: Anchor.
LIEBOW, E. (1967) Tally's Corner. Boston: Little, Brown.
NOBLES, W. (1978) "Africanity: its role in Black families," pp. 19-26 in R. Staples (ed.) The Black Family: Essays and Studies. Belmont, CA: Wadsworth.
NYE, F. I. (1974) "Sociocultural context," pp. 1-31 in L. W. Hoffman and F. I. Nye (eds.) Working Mothers. San Francisco: Jossey-Bass.
PETERS, M. and C. de FORD (1978) "The solo mother," pp. 192-200 in R. Staples (ed.) The Black Family: Essays and Studies. Belmont, CA: Wadsworth.
RAINWATER, L. (1970) Behind Ghetto Walls. Chicago: AVC.
RODGERS-ROSE, L. F. (1980) "Some demographic characteristics of the Black woman: 1940 to 1975," pp. 29-41 in L. F. Rodgers-Rose (ed.) The Black Woman. Beverly Hills, CA: Sage.
ROSS, H. L. and V. SAWHILL (1975) Time of Transition. Washington, DC: Urban Institute.
SCANZONI, J. H. (1971) The Black Family in Modern Society. Boston: Allyn & Bacon.
SCHULZ, D. (1969) Coming Up Black. Englewood Cliffs, NJ: Prentice-Hall.
STAPLES, R. (1978) "The Black family revisited," pp. 13-18 in R. Staples (ed.) The Black Family: Essays and Studies. Belmont, CA: Wadsworth.
UDRY, J. R. (1966) "Marital instability by race, sex, education and occupation using 1960 census data." American Journal of Sociology 72: 203-209.
WHITE, L. K. (1979) "The correlates of urban illegitimacy in the United States, 1960-1970." Journal of Marriage and the Family 41: 715-720.

13

ATTITUDES TOWARD PROCREATION
AMONG BLACK ADULTS

ALGEA HARRISON

The purpose of this discussion is to examine the attitudes toward procreation among black adults. The attitudes were examined by reviewing the literature on family planning, specifically fertility rates and birth control practices. It was assumed that an important indicator of attitudes toward procreation was fertility rate figures and that planned family size reflected attitudes toward incorporating parenting into a lifestyle. In addition, behavior in parental roles was considered another indicator of one's attitude toward procreation. Hence, studies and investigations that examined paternal and maternal roles among black adults were reviewed. Importantly, the black community was not viewed as monolithic; instead, important demographic differences were delineated and noted. The discussion of these issues is pertinent, since improvements in scientific technology and health care delivery systems have increased opportunities for blacks to consider the options of childlessness or limiting the number of offspring.

FAMILY PLANNING

FERTILITY RATES

Between 1959 and 1967 there was a 30 percent decline in the general fertility rates for nonwhites (Farley, 1970). This decline in average number of births continued during the decade between 1967 to 1977 among black women, who expect to have fewer children in the future. There was a decline in births from 3191 in 1967 to 2364 in 1977 among black wives in the 18-39 age range. (All figures are based per 1000 women.) At the same time, there was a decline in birth rates for women of all races 18-39 from 2427 in 1967 to 1860 in 1977 (U.S. Bureau of the Census, 1977). Hence, there has been a consistent decline in fertility rates among black wives and wives of all races.

When examining levels of fertility in the black community, socio-economic and regional characteristics should be considered (Sly, 1970). In 1977, black women 18 to 34 years old accounted for 69.9 percent of lifetime births of children already born. Among this group, 81.9 percent were born to women who were not high school graduates, and 50.2 percent were born to women with one or more years of college (U.S. Bureau of the Census, 1977). Furthermore, in this age group of black women, 68.5 were residents of a metropolitan area, as compared to 73.6 percent women residing in a nonmetropolitan area. Moreover, the variations in region of residence in terms of percentage of lifetime births already born were not dramatically different between Northeast (66.3 percent), South (69.3 percent), and West (66.9 percent). The area with the largest percentage of births for black women was North Central, 75.8 percent. When data for future births of this age group were examined, of those who were childless to date, 29.5 percent expected to remain so and the largest percentage (38.7) of the women expected to have only two children in the future (U.S. Bureau of the Census, 1977). Thus, further decline in fertility rates can be predicted, and birth control practices among blacks to accomplish this goal were reviewed.

BIRTH CONTROL PRACTICES

Population studies indicated that before World War II relatively few black women used birth control. After World War II, increased health and medical services, urbanization, and improved general living conditions had an impact on birth control usage among the black population (Farley, 1970). There were, however, demographic differences with more favorable attitudes reported by urban than rural females and more positive orientations the higher the educational levels (Furstenberg et al., 1969; Ladner, 1972; Valien and Fitzgerald, 1949). Nevertheless, urban black middle-class females preferred smaller families, used the most effective available birth control methods—pills and IUD—and had lower fertility rates. In contrast, urban and rural poor females also preferred smaller families, yet were using less effective birth control methods—preparations available at drug stores and condoms—and as a result had higher fertility rates than they desired (Furstenberg et al., 1969; Linn et al., 1978; Westoff, 1970).

Moreover, there was evidence that both partners wanted to use some type of contraceptive and felt the decision should not be the sole responsibility of either partner (Johnson and Staples, 1979; Vadies and Hale, 1977). Yet there were sex differences in motives to act to control family size patterns among blacks. Data indicated that feelings of powerlessness, value of children, and fear of racial genocide were important variables in explaining and predicting birth control usage among black males (Bauman and Udry, 1972; Treadwell, 1972; Tobin et al., 1975). In contrast to black males, poor black females in 17 cities failed to support the idea that high feelings of powerlessness lead to selection of poor or no contraceptive methods (Morris and Sison, 1974). Furthermore, among black females, the most frequently cited reasons for wanting to limit family size were economics and desire to control their lives (Cochrane et al., 1973; Gustavos and Mammen, 1973; Treadwell, 1972). The best predictors of birth control usage among black females were information about contraceptives, past experiences of failure with birth control methods, and intention to act (Haney et al., 1974; Kothandapani, 1971; Linn et al., 1978). Hence, there were sex differences among blacks in motivations to practice birth control.

Nevertheless, although black adults wanted to control for the probability of pregnancy, the role of parent was considered a significant indicator of adulthood (Scott, 1976). Therefore, a review of literature on behavior of black adults in parental roles follows.

PARENTAL ROLES

PATERNAL ROLE

Historically, the role of black males as fathers has been controversial (Cross, 1978; Elkins, 1959; Frazier, 1939; Herskovits, 1958; Hill, 1971; Moynihan, 1965; Staples, 1971b; Wilkinson and Taylor, 1977). Moreover, it has been suggested that lover and sexual partner were the most salient interpersonal adult roles for black males, and paternity was viewed as a mark of masculinity and not an adult role to implement (Buckhout, 1971; Staples, 1978). This lack of understanding and knowledge about the contributions of fathers to the socialization process has been true also for white fathers (Lamb, 1976). In contrast to black fathers, however, it was assumed that white fathers functioned in their role and the reason there was limited scientific evidence concerning their influence was the fault of social scientists, who frequently used mothers as subjects in investigating parental roles (Lamb, 1976).

Subsequently, in recent years there were attempts to fill this void in scientific knowledge concerning white fathers (for example, *The Family Coordinator*, 1979) as a result of inquiries into the social affectional systems of infants and changes in the family structure in contemporary society (Lamb, 1976). In the same manner, there was an increase in investigations of the role of black fathers, but these studies were generated for different reasons. Research projects and articles were initially reactions to the reported matriarchal black family structure (Moynihan, 1965). Later explorations continued as a result of the shortcomings in the literature and limited knowledge regarding demographic differences among black fathers.

The major shortcomings in the body of scientific knowledge were that researchers (a) failed to recognize the existence of a black culture and the antecedent African experience and examine social roles in that context (Nobles, 1980; Peters, 1974); (b) neglected to interview black fathers and observe father-child interactions for demographic differences (J. McAdoo, 1979); (c) observed and investigated black family life using the very poorest families as subjects and generalized the findings to all black families (Billingsley, 1968); and (d) used theoretical models limited to Western cultural lifestyles (Nobles, 1980).

Indeed, the devaluing of black fathers in data analysis and policies implemented by social agencies was not lost on black males. Studies revealed that they resented being treated as absent and ineffectual fathers and viewed themselves as salient figures in the lives of their children and active participants in the child-rearing process (Cazenave, 1977; Coles, 1977; Hopkins, 1977; J. McAdoo, 1979). In addition, consistent with the customs of their culture, black males have assumed the paternal role in the status of boyfriend and as members of a kinship network system (Schulz, 1971; Stack, 1984). Importantly, because black males were thwarted in their role as economic provider—one aspect of the father role—did not preclude failure in all aspects of the father role.

In the socialization process, parents function as models, socializing agents, and figures for identification. Several reports of black family life indicated that black males fulfilled these psychological aspects of the father role (Aseltine, 1978; Billingsley, 1968; Blassingame, 1972; Gutman, 1976; Hill, 1971; H. McAdoo, 1978; J. McAdoo, 1979). Indeed, highly mobile, as compared to lowly mobile, black males reported strong attempts to identify with their fathers and pressure from their mothers to be like him (Moulton and Stewart, 1971). In contrast, there were reported findings of failures of black males in the father role (Frazier, 1939; Rainwater, 1970). It is difficult to ascertain, however, whether these and similar studies were reporting that black fathers had no impact or influence, or whether their reported values and behaviors were inconsistent with white middle-class and Western theoretical models of parenting and thus were negative and ineffectual.

From the start, research investigations of black parental roles were more concerned with effects of father absence rather than presence. Psychoanalytic theoretical discussions suggested that the combination of absent fathers and mother-dominated household structures among black families would have a negative impact on the socialization of black children (Thomas and Sillen, 1972). The subsequent studies of black family life were criticized for several reasons (Billingsley, 1971; Breyer and May, 1970; Gary, 1974; Scott, 1976). Notably social scientists generally compared children from poor black families with multiproblems, one of which was father absence, to children from white middle-class families, with fathers present, on a number of child behavioral variables. The negative findings for black children were attributed directly to the effect of father absence or mother-dominated households, and there were no attempts to control for the effects of confounding of variables.

In the same manner, critics noted how investigations failed to acknowledge the impact of the wider black community, culture differences in role prescriptions, and importance of kinship systems which were documented and postulated as important mediating variables (Barnes, 1980; H. McAdoo, 1978; Stack, 1974). Furthermore, the accumulated evidence on the impact of father absence reflected an inconsistency in findings (Badaines, 1976; D'Andrade, 1973; Earl and Lohmann, 1978; Keller and Murray, 1973; Longebaugh, 1973; Rubin, 1974). This inconsistency may be explained by the criticisms discussed previously. This position does not dismiss father absence as inconsequential; rather, it states what scientific data are needed for more definite statements of effects and how black culture and lifestyle might mitigate the impact on the socialization process. Besides, there was evidence that black mothers functioned in an instrumental and expressive manner (Beckett, 1976; Hannerz, 1977), and father absence was shown to alter the mother-child relationship (D'Andrade, 1973; Longebaugh, 1973). Hence, a discussion of the maternal role of black females follows.

MATERNAL ROLE

The contributions of black women in their role as mother in Africa and America was acknowledged and described (Billingsley, 1968; Blassingame, 1972; Herskovits, 1958; Gutman, 1976; Staples, 1971a, 1971b, 1973). Interestingly, performance of black women in their role of mother has generated myths and stereotypes that have dominated the research literature on black families for the past decade. Data generated from numerous studies were most critical of the behavior of black mothers as reinforcing agents. Generally, mother-child interactions were viewed as detrimental to sex-role socialization, cognitive development, and a variety of personality traits in black children (D'Andrade, 1973; Lott and Lott, 1963; Thomas and Sillen, 1972). As noted previously, these studies of black family life were subsequently criticized. Consequently, research projects were designed and discussions initiated to note the limitations of previous studies and view the parenting style of black mothers from the perspective of their own culture (Banks et al., 1979; Boykin, 1979; Gary, 1974;

Franklin, 1979; Willie, 1974). Data indicated and discussions suggested that black mothers were reinforcing behavior that facilitated the coping skills of black children in dealing with a dualism in their lives, being black in a racist society and acquiring the necessary skills to advance in the dominant culture.

Similarly, performance evaluations of black mothers as role models and figures of identification were inconsistent (Halpern, 1973; Peters, 1974; Scott, 1976). Interestingly, research investigations have found, when black and white children were compared, that blacks had less sexual dimorphism of expression of pleasure (Balkwell et al., 1978), more androgynous attitudes (Johnson, 1977; Klienke and Nicholson, 1979), and less stereotypic view of sex roles (Gold and St. Ange, 1974). In short, data suggested that the feminine behavior model black mothers presented shaped the sex-role perceptions of black children toward a more androgynous view. Still, more investigations are needed. Mothers were presenting behaviors of a more active involvement in their world that contributed to the androgynous attitudes that were being formulated by the children. Indeed, there is evidence on the implementation of the maternal role among black mothers for clarification and correction of criticisms noted earlier.

Black women have consistently indicated that they value the role of mother and consider it an important aspect of their sex-role identity (Harrison, 1977). Indeed, there was evidence that black women sometimes prioritized the mother role over wife and worker roles (Blood and Wolfe, 1971; Harrison and Minor, 1978). In other words, it is evident that conflict will arise between these social roles because of personal time and energy constraints. Whenever interrole conflicts emerge, some black women attempt to resolve the conflict by putting their children's needs before their husband's or employer's demands. In addition, black women generally have internalized the black community's perceptions of them as strong, independent, and resourceful persons (Ladner, 1972; Watson, 1974). Thus, black mothers have placed a high value on their role as mothers.

SUMMARY

There has been a decline in fertility rates among blacks for the past two decades; however, there were demographic differences. Indeed, sex differences in motivation for birth control usage were evident. Yet it was predicted that fertility rates among all blacks will decline further in the future. Nevertheless, black adults have not concurrently devalued parental roles.

Implementations of the paternal role by black males were controversal in the research literature, and the need for further scientific investigations was discussed. Black fathers valued their role, yet few studies have revealed their perspective of role prescriptions. The reasons for this lack of knowledge can be attributed to several criticisms of studies of black family life.

In the past decade, studies of parental roles were dominated by investigations of the performance of black females in their role as mother. Theoretical postulations and data from several studies were critical of their performance as reinforcing agents, models, and figures of identification. The reactions to this negative portrayal have resulted in critical examinations of the body of scientific knowledge and creation of innovative and sensitive approaches to the study of parental roles among blacks.

REFERENCES

ASELTINE, G. (1978) "Family socialization perceptions among black and white high school students." Journal of Negro Education 47 (Summer): 256-266.

BADAINES, J. (1976) "Identification, imitation, and sex-role preference in father-present and father-absent black and chicano boys." Journal of Psychology 92 (January): 15-24.

BALKWELL, C., J. BALSWICK and J. BALKWELL (1978) "On black and white family patterns in America: their impact on the expressive aspect of sex-role socialization." Journal of Marriage and the Family 40 (4): 743-747.

BANKS, W. C., McQUATER, and J. L. HUBBARD (1979) "Toward a reconceptualization of the social-cognitive bases of achievement orientations in blacks," pp. 294-311 in A. W. Boykin, A. J. Franklin, and J. F. Yates (eds.) Research Directions of Black Psychologists. New York: Russell Sage.

BARNES, E. (1980) "The black community as the source of positive self-concept for black children: a theoretical perspective," pp. 106-130 in R. L. Jones (ed.) Black Psychology. New York: Harper & Row.

BAUMAN, K. and R. UDRY (1972) "Powerlessness and regularity of contraception in an urban negro male sample: a research note." Journal of Marriage and the Family 34 (1): 112-114.

BECKETT, J. O. (1976) "Working wives: a racial comparison." Social Work 21 (November): 463-471.

BILLINGSLEY, A. (1968) Black Families in White America. Englewood Cliffs, NJ: Prentice-Hall.

——— (1971) "The treatment of negro families in American scholarship," in R. Staples (ed.) Black Families in America: Essays and Studies. Belmont, CA: Wadsworth.

BLASSINGAME, J. (1972) The Slave Community. New York: Oxford Press.

BLOOD, R. O. and D. M. WOLFE (1971) "Negro-white differences in blue-collar marriages in a northern metropolis," pp. 171-177 in R. Staples (ed.) The Black Family: Essays and Studies. Belmont, CA: Wadsworth.

BOYKIN, A. W. (1979) "Black psychology and the research process: keeping the baby but throwing out the bath water," pp. 85-103 in A. W. Boykin, A. J. Franklin, and J. F. Yates (eds.) Research Directions of Black Psychologists. New York: Russell Sage.

BREYER, N. L. and J. C. MAY (1970) "Effect of sex and race of the observer and model on imitative learning." Psychological Reports 27 (2): 639-646.

BUCKHOUT, R. (1971) "The war on people: a scenario for population control." Environment and Behavior 3 (September): 322-344.

CAZENAVE, N. (1977) "Middle-income black fathers: an analysis of the prouder role." The Family Coordinator 28 (October): 583-593.

COCHRANE, C., C. VINCENT, C. HANEY, and R. MICHIELATTE (1973) "Motivational determinants of family planning clinic attendance." Journal of Psychology 84 (May): 33-43.

COLES, R. (1977) "Black fathers," pp. 85-101 in D. Wilkinson and R. Taylor (eds.) The Black Male in America. Chicago: Nelson-Hall.

CROSS, W. E. (1978) "Black family and black identity: a literature review." Western Journal of Black Studies 2 (Summer): 111-124.

D'ANDRADE, R. (1973) "Father absence, identification, and identity." Ethos 1 (Winter): 440-455.

EARL, L. and N. LOHMANN (1978) "Absent fathers and black male children." Social Work 23 (September): 413-415.

ELKINS, S. (1959) Slavery. Chicago: University of Chicago Press.

ENTWISTLE, D. and E. GREENBERGER (1972) "Adolescents' views of women's work roles." American Journal of Orthopsychiatry 42 (July): 648-656.

FARLEY, R. (1970) Growth of the Black Population. Chicago: Markham.

FRANKLIN, A. J. (1979) "Recall and memory organization from variations in list content: a test of the culture-specific hypothesis," pp. 241-252 in A. W. Boykin, A. J. Franklin, and J. F. Yates (eds.) Research Directions of Black Psychologists. New York: Russell Sage.

FRAZIER, E. F. (1939) The Negro Family in the United States. Chicago: University of Chicago Press.

FURSTENBERG, F., L. GORDIS, and M. MARKOWITZ (1969) "Birth control knowledge and attitude among unmarried pregnant adolescents." Journal of Marriage and the Family 31 (1): 34-42.

GARY, L. E. [ed.] (1974) Social Research in the Black Community. Washington, DC: Howard University.

GOLD, A. and C. St. ANGE (1974) "Development of sex-role stereotypes in black and white elementary school girls." Developmental Psychology 10 (3): 461.

GUSTAVOS, S. and K. MAMMEN (1973) "Black-white differentials in the family size preferences among youth." Pacific Sociological Review 16: 107-119.

GUTMAN, H. (1976) The Black Family in Slavery and Freedom, 1750-1925. New York: Pantheon.

HALPERN, F. (1973) Survival: Black/White. New York: Pergamon.

HANEY, C., R. MICHIELUTTE, C. VINCENT, and C. COCHRANE (1974) "Factors associated with the poverty of black women." Sociology and Social Research 59 (1): 40-49.

HANNERZ, V. (1977) "Growing up male," pp. 33-59 in D. Wilkinson and R. Taylor (eds.) The Black Male in America. Chicago: Nelson-Hall.

HARRISON, A. (1977) "Black women," pp. 131-146 in V. O'Leary, Toward Understanding Women. Monterey, CA: Brooks/Cole.

———— and J. MINOR (1978) "Interrole conflict, coping strategies, and satisfaction among black working wives." Journal of Marriage and the Family 40 (November): 799-805.

HERSKOVITS, M. J. (1958) The Myth of the Negro Past. Boston: Beacon Press.

HILL, R. B. (1971) The Strengths of Black Families. New York: Emerson Hall.

HOPKINS, T. (1977) "The role of community agencies as viewed by black fathers." American Journal of Orthopsychiatry 42 (April): 508-516.

JOHNSON, J. (1977) "Androgyny and the maternal principle." School Review 86 (1): 50-69.

JOHNSON, L. and R. STAPLES (1979) "Family planning and the young minority male: a pilot project." The Family Coordinator 28 (October): 535-543.

KELLER, P. and E. MURRAY (1973) "Imitative aggression with adult male and female models in father absent and father present negro boys." Journal of Genetic Psychology 122 (June): 217-221.

KLEINKE, C. L. and T. NICHOLSON (1979) "Black and white children's awareness of de facto race and sex difference." Developmental Psychology 15 (2): 84-86.

KOTHANDAPANI, V. (1971) "Validation of feeling, belief, and intention to act as three components of attitude and their contribution to prediction of contraceptive behavior." Journal of Personality and Social Psychology 19 (September): 321-333.

LADNER, J. (1972) Tomorrow's Tomorrow. Garden City, NY: Doubleday.

LAMB, M. E. (1976) The Role of the Father in Child Development. New York: John Wiley.

LINN, M., J. CARMICHAEL, P. KLITENICK and N. WEBB (1978) "Fertility related attitudes of minority mothers with large and small families." Journal of Applied Social Psychology 8 (January-March): 1-14.

LONGEBAUGH, R. (1973) "Mother behavior as a variable moderating the effects of father absence." Ethos 1 (Winter): 456-465.

LOTT, A. and B. LOTT (1963) Negro and White Youth: A Psychological Study in a Border-State Community. New York: Holt, Rinehart & Winston.

McADOO, H. (1978) "Factors related to stability in upwardly mobile black families." Journal of Marriage and the Family 40 (November): 761-776.

McADOO, J. (1979) "Father-child interaction patterns and self-esteem in black preschool children." Young Children 34 (January): 46-53.

MORRIS, N. and B. SISON (1974) "Correlates of female powerlessness: parity, methods of birth control pregnancy." Journal of Marriage and the Family 36 (4): 708-713.

MOULTON, R. and L. STEWART (1971) "Parents as models for mobile and low-mobile black males." Vocational Guidance Quarterly 19 (June): 247-253.

MOYNIHAN, D. P. (1965) The Negro Family: The Case for National Action. Washington, DC: U.S. Department of Labor.

NOBLES, W. (1980) "African philosophy: foundations for Black psychology," pp. 23-36 in R. L. Jones (ed.) Black Psychology. New York: Harper & Row.

PETERS, M. F. (1974) "The Black family-perpetuating the myths: an analysis of family sociology textbook treatment of Black families." The Family Coordinator 23 (October): 349-357.

RAINWATER, L. (1970) Behind Ghetto Walls. Chicago: AVC.

RUBIN, R. (1974) "Adult male absence and the self-attitudes of black children." Child Study Journal 4 (1): 33-46.

SCHULZ, D. (1971) "The role of the boyfriend," pp. 94-100 in R. Staples (ed.) The Black Family: Essays and Studies. Belmont, CA: Wadsworth.

SCOTT, P. B. (1976) "A critical overview of sex roles research on black families." Women Studies Abstracts: 1-13.

SLY, D. (1970) "Minority group status and fertility." American Journal of Sociology 76 (3): 443-450.

STACK, C. B. (1974) All Our Kin: Strategies for Survival in a Black Community. New York: Harper & Row.

———— (1973) The Black Woman in America. Chicago: Nelson-Hall.

———— (1978)"Masculinity and race: the dual dilemma of black men." Journal of Social Issues 34 Social Issues 34 (Winter): 169-183.

The Family Coordinator (1979) "Men's Roles in the Family." Special issue, Vol. 28 (October).

THOMAS, A. and S. SILLEN (1972) Racism and Psychiatry. New York: Brunner/Mazel.

TOBIN, P., W. CLIFFORD, R. MUSTIAN, and A. DAVIS (1975) "Value of children and fertility behavior in a tri-racial, rural county." Journal of Comparative Family Studies 6 (Spring): 46-55.

TREADWELL, J. (1972) "Is abortion black genocide?" Family Planning Perspectives 4 (1): 4-5.

U.S. Bureau of the Census (1977) Population Reports. Washington, DC: Government Printing Office.

VADIES, E. and D. HALE (1977) "Attitudes of adolescent males towards abortion, contraception, and sexuality." Social Work in Health Care 3 (Winter): 169-174.

VALIEN, P. and A. FITZGERALD (1949) "Attitudes of the negro mother toward birth control." American Journal of Sociology 55 (3): 279-283.

WATSON, V. (1974) "Self-concept formation and the Afro-American women." Journal of Afro-American Issues 2 (3): 226-236.

WESTOFF, C. (1970) "Contraceptive practice among urban blacks in the United States, 1965." Milbank Memorial Fund Quarterly 48 (2): 215-233.

WILKINSON, D. and R. TAYLOR [eds.] (1977) The Black Male inAmerica. Chicago: Nelson-Hall.

WILLIE, C. (1974) A New Look at Black Families. Englewood Cliffs, NJ: Prentice-Hall.

PART IV

SOCIALIZATION IN BLACK FAMILIES

Marie Peters begins this section with a historical overview of the Black family socialization literature. She shows how the early works were descriptive and used the comparative deficit-oriented approach, finally becoming more value free in the ecological approach. In her excellent review, she points out the major contributions made by the various studies and gives a critique of the weaknesses of several of the noted studies. For instance, many studies did not mention race; others focused only on the mother-child relationship and no other or used simplistic correlation and excluded possible influences of other factors. There are critiques also of the different intervention methods and of the questionable research methodology used in earlier studies. Peters traces the literature through the early stages on through the war on poverty to the present. Several key variables are then detailed: protectiveness, discipline, idiosyncratic rearing practices, and changes in parental values. Her examination brings light to some of the dim concepts commonly held about socialization, while the blurring of sex-typed roles in family tasks and child-caring of both parents and children is mentioned. There have been changes in parental values of those who are upwardly mobile or who prepare their children for mobility through "anticipatory socialization." The differences that do exist in Black lifestyles are presented within the context of the family's attempt to shield the child from a hostile environment as long as possible.

John McAdoo describes the limited literature available on the father's involvement in his child's development. An extensive review is given of father stereotypes, the differential role he plays, his influence on the mother, his involvement in child-related decision making, and the interaction patterns and expectations he holds for his children. The earlier, exclusive reliance on his instrumental role has changed to one of greater involvement. Fathers themselves rate the companionship of the child as primary and not their instrumental roles. As fathers gain more economic security, they tend to become more involved with their children.

Decision making has moved from dominance to a greater egalitarian sharing between father and mother. The chapter gives a delineation between authoritarian and authoritative fathering, and shows that the father-child interactions of Blacks have tended to be more supportive for the achievement and independence of girls rather than boys. The parent-child interaction is not unidirectional but circular. The Black father's role is still not clearly understood. Fathers of all races have similar expectations for their children, but may use different approaches. Little ethnic differences have been found in actual parenting style. The reciprocal relationship between father and child has yet to be adequately researched.

Wilhelmina Manns discusses the roles played by significant others in the lives of Black families. These are the persons that one would like to hold one in high esteem and are influential in one's life. These significant others are those persons who have been found to be the components of the extended family support networks, both kin and nonkin, who enable families to survive under continuing adversity. Nonrelatives were often found to be as influential as relatives, highlighting the elasticity of the extended family. Those of lower status and with few financial resources have been found to have more people who are significant kin. Blacks of lower incomes have been found to have a greater number of significant others, to offset their negative life experiences. Black parents were important in relation to achievement. Lower-income parents mandated achievement, and middle-income parents provided an achievement-oriented atmosphere. However, neither group was extensively involved in teaching as a component of their support. The parental influence lasted throughout the life cycle, with more Blacks having parents who were significant in these dimensions well into adulthood. The other relatives who were supportive tended to do this by providing models, while the nonrelative supporters tended to be members of the structured institutions such as the church or community center.

James Jackson, Wayne McCullough, and Gerald Gurin extend the discussion of significant components of family life by examining the roles the family plays in the development of the child's group identity and consciousness. The family forms a buffer within the home that protects the child and then gradually introduces him or her into the heterogenous, often hostile society, and remains a refuge for the child, as pointed out by Peters. An extensive review is given of the differences found in the pre- and post-civil rights literature. The earlier studies related a negative effect of Black identification, and all accepted the premise of self-hatred. Yet they did not measure the racial attitude and self-concept variables separately. The post-civil rights research looked at the positive psychological effect of a strong Black identification and went beyond simple measures of association. The racial homogeneity of the home is felt to aid in the personal identification of race, to assist the child in the compartmentalization of their private and public selves, and to filter the impact of the nonsupportive environment. The child then is able to go out in the heterogenous environment and be successful. The family is seen as the mediating link between the individual's self-concept and the individual's racial group. The call is made for the refinement of group identity theories.

14

PARENTING IN BLACK FAMILIES WITH YOUNG CHILDREN
A Historical Perspective

MARIE F. PETERS

Most Black parents, as do most parents in every society, socialize their children to become self-sufficient, competent adults as defined by the society in which they live. For Black families in the United States, socialization occurs within the ambiguities of a cultural heritage that is both Afro-American and Euro-American and a social system that espouses both democratic equality for all citizens and caste-like status for its Black citizens. Although social scientists have appreciated the uniqueness of Blacks, research on Black children and their families has generally been simplistic and often pejorative in approach (Allen, 1978; Mathis, 1978).

Today, many social scientists are moving beyond the comparative, pathological approach of much of the research of the sixties and early seventies and are beginning to study Black families from a perspective that recognizes the cultural variations, functionality, and validity of Black family lifestyles. This research has begun to provide basic information about parenting in Black families. The purpose of this chapter is to describe briefly the history of research on the behaviors and attitudes of Black parents and to summarize the major findings concerning child rearing and the parent-child relationships that many families with young Black children share.

Because the topics social scientists choose to research and the scientific research methodologies they use reflect the prevailing philosophies and concerns of the time, research which has focused on Black mothers and fathers has changed through the years. Early research was descriptive. It was generally replaced by comparative deficit-oriented research. Currently, much research on Black parenting and parent-child interaction employs ecologically oriented and culturally relevant approaches.

CRITIQUE OF RESEARCH APPROACHES

For those interested in parent-child relationships in Black or other minority families, a search of the literature reveals many methodological weaknesses and problems in many of the available studies. The most prevalent shortcomings include the following: (1) Many studies do not specify the race of the participants. Culture-specific influences are thus ignored. (2) Research is often unidirectional: The focus is typically on mother's influence on child and does not observe child's influence on mother. (3) When the research population involves both Black and white parents, the research design, typically, compares Blacks to whites and comparative statistics are used. Rarely is the research ethnomethodological and descriptive. (4) Simplistic correlations often exclude the possible influences of other environmental forces. For example, in the Radin and Kamii study (1965), it was assumed that if a child identified with a warm mother, the child's intellectual development would be positive. Yet teacher warmth was not measured, nor was the child's relationship with other adults in the family considered. The influence of kin in the lives of Black children has been well documented (McAdoo, 1978; Nobles, 1977; Stack, 1974). (5) Researchers tend to view Black families as monolithic. Few studies incorporate both lower-class and middle-class Black families in the study population. Consequently, the accessibility of lower-class families in welfare agencies or urban schools (and their concomitant absence in college communities) generally influences researchers to use the all-inclusive category of race as a monolithic variable. (6) When Blacks are studied, so-called problem populations are often the focus of research—single parents; parents of emotionally disturbed, mentally retarded, or academically nonachieving or delinquent children, and/or youths; or low-income families. The majority of Blacks are ordinary American citizens not in special trouble categories, but are typically not included in these research studies. (7) The research design used to study an all-Black population often differs from that used to study whites. When a white population is used, an investigation may be concerned with process, examining how various influences affect the subjects in the study. This central concern shifts subtly to one of intervention when a Black population is involved. The focus of research becomes *changing* the target subject to conform to the abilities and behaviors of white parents and children, and investigators are concerned with the achievement or nonachievement of this goal. (8) Studies that examine parent-child interaction and include Blacks in their sample are often conducted in an unfamiliar, intimidating experiment room. Data are often correlated with IQ or SES and are typically based on but one or two observations. We know parent-child interaction is much higher in a laboratory setting than in the natural setting of the home. (9) The presence of an outside "expert" is often an unmeasured influence. Studies have shown that when the research study or intervention program requires visiting homes with a bag of toys and books and observing or recording parent-child interaction with these special toys/books only, mothers talk to their child more than they normally do every day. (10) The research methodology may incorporate subjective measures of the quality of home environments—based on the researcher's personal unarticulated values, such as organization versus disorganization or "quiet" home environment believed to be conducive to study versus high noise level and activity, presumed to be distracting and confusing to a child.

DESCRIPTIVE APPROACHES

Systematic research on Black families was first approached within a descriptive framework which recognized the pressures, demands, and extreme constraints of the environment in which Blacks lived. This research essentially provided facts about Blacks and described aspects of the lives of Black families. Publishing the first sociological study of Black families in America in 1908, W. E. B. Du Bois described the social conditions of Afro-American families living in Philadelphia at the beginning of this century. He accounted for the influences of Africa and of slavery on the development of Black people. However, Du Bois said little about child rearing. Some years later, social scientists such as Charles S. Johnson, in his books *Shadow of the Plantation* and *Growing Up in the Black Belt,* provided insightful descriptions of family life among Blacks in the South, including child rearing and socialization practices. The publications of social scientists before World War II, such as historian Carter G. Woodson, together with the slave narratives collected during the thirties have provided a rich source of descriptive data essential to understanding Black family life today. However, during and after World War II, descriptive approaches to research on the Black family began to be eclipsed by more sophisticated research methodologies patterned after the physical sciences (see Lewin, 1935). This approach reflected changing perspectives in this country regarding race.

COMPARATIVE DEFICIT APPROACHES

During the forties and fifties research was highly stimulated by the assimila-
tion theories of two outstanding sociologists, Robert Park of the University of
Chicago and Gunnar Myrdal, author of *An American Dilemma*. The theories of
Park and the writings of Myrdal, in assuming that assimilation of Blacks into
American society was possible and probable, helped to provide a scientific
basis for research which investigated why Blacks were not assimilating into
American society (Lyman, 1972). They articulated a rationale for comparative
deficit approaches which assume Blacks are culturally deprived and view differences found between white mainstream Americans and Black Americans as
deficits. Behaviors, abilities, or attitudes observed in Black mothers, it was
assumed, "needed to be changed" (see Mathis, 1978).

The perspectives of sociologists studying Black families, in shifting from
descriptive research to comparative deficit approaches, reported findings about
Black families within a Black/white comparative framework. For example,
Davis and Dollard (1940), two of the first researchers to describe in detail the
socialization of Black children, analyzed Black families according to class,
structure, and parental roles. Comparing Black families to white families, they
reported Black mothers were more restrictive than white mothers in toilet
training and more likely to employ physical punishment in disciplining their
young children. Twenty-five years later, Radin and Kamii (1965), whose innovative methodology has served as a model for much parent-child observational
research, similarly provides an example of this approach. In the Radin and
Kamii study a small group (45) of "culturally deprived" Black mothers, over
half of whom received public assistance, and a small group (50) of middle-class
white mothers were observed in a laboratory play room. Their behaviors in
interacting with their preschool child were compared. The finding that Black
mothers often shield children from problems was interpreted by these researchers as "overprotective." Neither the importance of varying influences of
environmental differences in the home situations nor the differential effects of
the laboratory observations on the mothers was acknowledged in this interpretation of the research findings.

In many similar studies, if white mothers participated, Black mothers were
compared to whites directly; if white mothers were not part of the study, the
Black mothers were compared to whites indirectly and by assumption. In either
case, the Black mothers were viewed negatively, as generally inferior and as
unable to fulfill their responsibilities adequately.

Frazier's classic study, *The Negro Family in the United States*, a major
source of information about Black families, provides a dramatic illustration of
the comparative deficit approach. In this and other works (Frazier, 1933, 1950)
Frazier accurately reported findings, descriptive of Black families, but inter-

preted the behaviors of Blacks pejoratively. He supplied a model for the study of Blacks which emphasized family disorganization and dysfunction—an approach that directly influenced subsequent research of the sixties and early seventies. The influential government-sponsored Moynihan report (1965) viewed differences between Blacks and whites as deficits and identified Black "matriarchal" mothers as responsible for the "breakdown" and "pathology" of Black families (who, he claimed, were responsible for high rates of illegitimacy, delinquency, and unemployment). The deficit perspective of Moynihan spawned more than a decade of research that focused on improving the child-rearing practices of Black mothers, and it influenced many of the programs and policies subsequently developed for Black children and their parents.

In response to the government's "war on poverty" efforts, a number of sociologists and psychologists turned their research interests to low-income Black families who received public assistance and who lived in public housing or in inner-city ghettoes. These findings on low-income families, although about a minority of the Black population, became generally accepted as descriptive of the family life of all Blacks in America (Hannerz, 1969; Liebow, 1966; Rainwater, 1966; Schulz, 1969). In much research Black families were viewed as monolithic and were conceptually linked to data regarding low-income families. Socioeconomic differences were often assumed to be the same as Black/white differences. This methodological weakness made it difficult, if not impossible, to unravel the "packaged variable" of class and race in much of this research (Whiting, 1973). The comparative deficit perspective of most Black parent-Black child studies of this period influenced family sociology textbooks which similarly incorporated the cultural deprivation deficit approach (Peters, 1974).

ECOLOGICAL APPROACHES

Perhaps in reaction to the negativism of the comparative deficit approach and the criticisms of many social scientists of this research emphasis (Richardson, 1980), in the past decade much research on parenting in Black families shifted to an ecological approach. Similar to the earlier descriptive research, but incorporating the more sophisticated social science theories, methodologies, and techniques of the present, the ecological approach observes parental and child behavior within the environment in which it occurs and analyzes behavior according to the value system of a family's indigenous culture or subculture.

By providing a theoretical framework for ecologically oriented research, the writings of Lewin (1935) and Kuhn (1963) had an important influence on many researchers concerned with understanding the sociological and psychological factors involved. Black families and parent-child interaction were now examined from a culture-specific or functional perspective, and the Black family's socialization of its children was considered in terms of the values and realities of its Afro-American culture.

Research findings of ecologically oriented studies have dramatically changed the picture of parenting and child behaviors of Blacks and are providing interesting, myth-destroying information. It is assumed that Black families encourage the development of the skills, abilities, and behaviors necessary to survive as competent adults in a racially oppressive society (Willie, 1976), and a number of studies have investigated the characteristic, often culture-specific, child-rearing behaviors and survival mechanisms which enable Black parents to cope with everyday exigencies or with crisis situations (Gutman, 1976; Hill, 1971; Stack, 1974).

In general, Black families are reported to be strong, functional, and flexible (Aschenbrenner, 1973; Billingsley, 1968; Hill, 1972; Martin and Martin, 1978; Scanzoni, 1971, 1975; Stack, 1974). They provide a home environment that is culturally different from that of Euro-American families in a number of ways (Abrahams, 1970; Gay, 1975; Ladner, 1971; D. Lewis, 1975; Nobles, 1974a; Young, 1970). The environment of Black children is described as including not only the special stress of poverty or of discrimination but the ambiguity and marginality of living simultaneously in two worlds—the world of the Black community and the world of mainstream society, a phenomenon unique to Blacks (Willie, 1976). This perspective views Black children as socialized into a dual but normal existence of being both Afro-American and Euro-American, and many ambiguities and inconsistencies are reconciled without surprise or conflict (Dixon, 1971).

APPROACH TO DISCIPLINE

Discipline techniques of Black parents have often been noted by observers of Black parent-child interaction. Although definitive studies of discipline in Black families have yet to be done, many researchers have described the Black parent's more direct, physical form of discipline that differs from the psychologically oriented approach preferred by mainstream families, such as withdrawal of love or making approval or affection contingent on the child's behavior or accomplishment. The strict, no-nonsense discipline of Black parents—often characterized as "harsh" or "rigid" or "egocentrically motivated" by mainstream-oriented observers (Chilman, 1966)—has been shown to be functional, appropriate discipline of caring parents (Peters, 1976; Young, 1970).

A recent study of discipline techniques in a sample of working-class Black families reported that mothers became more dynamic in their disciplining as their young children began to understand the appropriate behavior parents expected. Most parents emphasized obedience. However, obedience was not viewed negatively; it was an important issue, often of special significance to a parent. Parents said that they believed obedience "will make life easier for my child," "means respect," "is equated with my love," or "is necessary if my child is to achieve in school" (Peters, 1981).

SOCIALIZATION TOWARD ENCOURAGEMENT OF NONCOMPETITIVE INDIVIDUALISM

A number of researchers have commented on the high value placed on personal uniqueness in Afro-American culture. Young (1970), who studied parental behavior and child-rearing practices of Black families in a southern community during the late sixties, noted the highly idiosyncratic interactions of mothers in the preparation of food, feeding, and toilet training of young children. Others (such as D. Lewis, 1975; H. Lewis, 1955) have described individualism within great interpersonal involvement of infants, children, and adults with one another. This individualism is often expressed in the way Black men and women as well as young Black boys and girls have been observed to interact with and respond to the infants and young children in the family (D. Lewis, 1975; Young, 1970).

SEX/AGE ROLES

Within many Black families more importance is attached to getting a job done than to the sex of the child for a task. Children's behaviors are viewed more in terms of the child's competency and age than the child's gender. The first-born, for example, whether boy or girl, is expected to become nurse-child to a younger child in many Black families (Young, 1970), and a high positive valuation is placed on "mothering," whether the person is male or female (D. Lewis, 1975).

COMPARATIVE RELEVANT APPROACHES

Concomitant with ecologically oriented research, comparative relevant studies have examined the child-rearing patterns of both Black and white parents with young children. This research perspective espouses cultural pluralism and uses the nonevaluative cultural variant model (Allen, 1978). The comparative relevant approach observes differences in behaviors but attempts to avoid enthnocentric judgments by focusing on process and through empirical research which attempts to link parental behaviors with child outcomes. Ethnicity, race, education, and social class indicators are typically controlled.

PARENT-CHILD COMMUNICATION

There have been many studies of parent-child communication patterns of Black and white parents and of differences in the verbalization of Black children compared to white children. Investigators have analyzed the grammar and language patterns of Black and white parents and their children. Although it has been found that Black parents talk to young children less than do white parents, the significance placed on race may be misleading. Schacter's (1979) review of this literature emphasizes the importance of social class. Studies show verbal stimulation to be a major factor in distinguishing between the environments of young children from economically advantaged and from economically disadvantaged homes. However, Schacter's research reported that "differences in total verbal production are related to maternal educational level and not to race. . . . Black mothers with educational and economic advantages speak just as much to their toddlers as do whites with similar advantages" (p. 155).

PARENTAL TEACHING STYLES

Black mothers, according to Hess et al. (1968), appear to prefer two types of teaching styles, both of which have an influence on the cognitive competence of four-year-old Black children. One style, which Hess et al. describe as the "personal-subjective" style, is responsive to the child—its needs, preferences, interests, moods, stage of development. The mothers who employ this style are concerned about the orientation and preparation a child needs in a new situation and try to make a task rewarding to their child. A second style is identified by Hess et al. as the "status-normative" teaching style. Mothers using this style tend to teach their child a task or insist on a certain behavior because it is the "correct" way or because it conforms to a rule or regulation. They do not generally consider the child's preferences. The differences between these two parenting behaviors appear to be quite similar to the differences between authoritative and authoritarian parenting styles identified by Baumrind (1972).

Hess's findings have been supported by other studies. For example, Schacter (1979: 65) reported that educated mothers "appear to adopt a responsive communication style." Similarly, Carew et al. (1976) found that the intellectual quality of the play activities created or encouraged by the mothers of toddlers correlated with their children's IQ at age three. Clarke-Stewart's (1973) study of Black/white working-class children age nine to eighteen months also reported that a relationship existed between parental behaviors and their child's academic abilities. The quantity of a mother's verbalization, the responsiveness, warmth, and stimulation of her interactions with her young child, significantly affected the child's intellectual development and linguistic performance.

A study of Black infants and preschool children by Andrews et al. (1975) reported that parents differed in their interactions with their children and that their children's subsequent social and cognitive behaviors reflected this difference. A series of studies conducted by Bradley and Caldwell (1976a, 1976b, 1978) and Elardo et al. (1975, 1977) found that measures of the child's home learning environment predicted IQ scores significantly better than did socioeconomic status (SES) variables typically used in studies of achievement or IQ. Slaughter (1978) examined linkages between parental teachings styles and children's cognitive development and play behaviors. Her findings, supporting the observations of Hess, Carew, Clarke-Stewart, and others, also show a relationship between specific maternal behaviors and children's abilities and behavioral styles. Mothers in Slaughter's study were supportive and nondirective with their children. White et al. (1977) reported that one- and two-year-old children whose caregivers talked to them a lot were developing better than children raised in a less verbal environment. Zegiob and Forehand (1975) investigated interactions of mothers and their children, ages four to six, in an experimental room equipped with toys. They found that the most significant factor in determining maternal interactive behavior was the socioeconomic status of the family. Other studies have reported similar findings.

PARENTAL ATTITUDES

Zegiob and Forehand (1975) observed that many Black parents were in the process of changing their values and attitudes. As they became upwardly mobile, many began to adopt middle-class values concerning child rearing. Scanzoni (1971) described how lower-class Black families prepare their children to be upwardly mobile via "anticipatory socialization." Thus parenting behavioral styles among Blacks may be in a state of flux. Many identify with middle-class value systems, especially when their own family is upwardly mobile.

These studies of parent-child interactions in their natural home environment provide the most reliable information available about childhood socialization. Although this research can only involve small samples, the rich descriptive data, often facilitated by audiovisual recordings, can enable us to view socialization processes in families with young children—to see what parents do, to understand why they do it, and to see the behavioral outcomes of their children.

THE IMPACT OF RACE ON PARENTING

An inescapable aspect of the socialization of Black children is that it prepares them for survival in an environment that is hostile, racist, and discrimina-

tory against Blacks (Bernard, 1966). According to Harvard psychiatrist Pierce
(1969), Black Americans live in a unique but mundane extreme environment of
subtle to overt racism. Oppressive environmental forces influence how Black
families live and raise their children (Peters, 1980). Research on the socialization of Black children supports these observations.

Daniel (1975) in a study of 25 Black fathers of preschool sons reported that
19 of the fathers mentioned specifically that race had an impact on their fathering. Renne (1970: 62) found that in Black families of all income levels, racial
identity had a strong impact on the amount of protection a Black parent could
provide a child. Even families with adequate income, wrote Renne, cannot
protect their children completely from the "irrational restrictions, insults, and
degradation black people encounter in this society." Renne further suggests that
rearing children in a white-dominated society places special pressures on the
black parent. However, as Harrison-Ross (Harrison-Ross and Wyden, 1973:
xx-xxi) wrote in her manual on child rearing for Black parents, Black parents
want "to bring their children up to be comfortable with their blackness, to be
secure, to be proud, to be able to love. . . . [They] want their children to grow up
being and feeling equal, comfortable, responsible, effective, and at home in the
world they live in."

Peters and Massey (in press) describe how Black families have developed
coping behaviors that enable them to deal with the racism they and their children may encounter. Black parents recognize that their children must be accepted in the Black community in order to have friends, and they must be
accepted in the white community in order to survive. Parents understand the
stress placed on their children when forced to perform better than whites in
order to be recognized. Black parents, Peters and Massey summarized, "have
internally developed patterns of coping with racial oppression, strategies
proven to be effective in the past that are incorporated into their own socialization process" (p. 3).

In her study of Black mothers of young children, Richardson (1981: 154-
164) reported that most parents believed "this society places more limitations on
Blacks' life chances and opportunities than on any other group of people within
the society" because of racism. They agreed that "being black in this country
full of anti-black feelings and/or actions (racism) presents real problems."
Their own experiences influence their decisions about how they will raise their
children. In preparation for expected encounters with racism, the mothers in
Richardson's study felt that it was necessary to develop high self-esteem and
self-confidence in their children. Other studies of Black parenting have also
reported the high priority Black parents give to developing self-esteem in their
children (Peters, 1976; Peters and Massey, in press).

A number of parents decide not to discuss racism or discrimination with their
children because they do not want them to feel bitter, resentful, or prejudiced

against others (H. Lewis, 1955). These protective parents expect that their children will discover institutional or individual racism some day, and they are prepared to help children cope with this reality as necessary (Peters, 1976, 1981). Black parents provide a buffer for the negative messages that may be transmitted to their children by a society which perpetuates stereotypic images of Black people (Ogbu, 1978; Scanzoni, 1971).

SUMMARY

Researchers are beginning to learn about the socialization of young Black children and to explore how they grow and develop to become self-sufficient, competent adults in the face of the real constraints American society places on Black Americans. The lives of Black parents and their child-rearing approaches are embedded in the racial, cultural, and economic situations of Blacks in America. Research on parenting in Black families must reflect this reality.

Research on Black families overwhelmingly shows that the behaviors and lifestyles of Black people are different from those of whites. Their child-rearing priorities, attitudes, and patterns of behavior have developed out of the exigencies of the unique economic, cultural, and racial circumstances in which they have lived. However, because of the pervasive belief that Blacks can and should eventually assimilate into mainstream society once they learn the "ways" of white mainstream Americans, social scientists often have not recognized or been interested in the validity and functionality of the parenting behaviors Black families have developed based on the realities of survival in a continuing, hostile environment. Instead, social scientists have frequently viewed the adaptations of Black families to the circumstances of poverty and discrimination and the subtle behavioral aspects that reflect their African heritage, where they differed from the behaviors and living patterns of whites, as the source of "their problem." Research priorities, therefore, have often emphasized educating Blacks to conform to the values and behaviors of mainstream white Americans.

Recently, however, researchers are describing the child-rearing patterns and socialization practices of Black parents from the perspective of their effectiveness as relevant, supportive, or practical strategies appropriate to the social realities Black people face. Mainstream America and its social scientists are becoming aware of a reality in American life that Blacks cannot, for long, forget—that this is a cultural pluralistic country and the historical roots of its multiethnic peoples are varying, valuable, and strong. As Richardson has observed (1981: 100-101), the cultural styles and child-rearing approaches unique to Black families have enabled them "to provide supportive and effective environments for the development of black children." Research into the parenting and socialization of Black children promises to provide rich data essential for developing social and educational policies by local, state, or federal governing agencies which determine and support programs directed at Black families and Black children.

REFERENCES

ABRAHAMS, R. D. (1970) Deep Down in the Jungle. Chicago: AVC.

ALLEN, W. R. (1978) "The search for applicable theories in Black family life." Journal of Marriage and the Family 40 (February): 117-129.

ANDREWS, S., J. BLUMENTHAL, W. BACHE, and G. WIENER (1975) "Parents as early childhood educators: the New Orleans model." Paper presented at the Society for Research for Child Development, Denver, Colorado.

ASCHENBRENNER, J. (1973) Lifelines: Black Families in Chicago. New York: Holt, Rinehart & Winston.

BAUMRIND, D. (1972) "An exploratory study of socialization effects on Black children: some Black-White comparisons." Child Development 43: 261-267.

BERNARD, J. (1966) Marriage and Family Among Negroes. Englewood Cliffs, NJ: Prentice-Hall.

BILLINGSLEY, A. (1968) Black Families in White America. Englewood Cliffs, NJ: Prentice-Hall.

BRADLEY, R. and B. CALDWELL (1976a) "Early home environment and changes in mental test performance in children from 6 to 36 months." Developmental Psychology 12: 93-97.

———— (1976b) "The relation of infants' home environments to mental test performance at 54 months: a follow-up study." Child Development 47: 1172-1174.

———— (1978) Home Environment, Social Status, and Mental Test Performance. (unpublished)

CAREW, J. V. with I. CHAN and C. HALFAR (1976) Observing Intelligence in Young Children. Englewood Cliffs, NJ: Prentice-Hall.

CHILMAN, C. S. (1966) Growing Up Poor. Dept. of H.E.W. Welfare Administration Publication, No. 13. Washington, DC: Government Printing Office.

CLARKE-STEWART, K. A. (1973) "Interactions between mothers and their young children: characteristics and consequences." Monographs of the Society for Research in Child Development 38 (6-7, Serial No. 153).

DANIEL, J. (1975) "A definition of fatherhood as expressed by Black fathers." Ph.D. dissertation, University of Pittsburgh.

DAVIS, A. and J. DOLLARD (1940) Children of Bondage. New York: Harper & Row.

DIXON, V. (1971) "Two approaches to Black-White relations," in V. J. Dixon and B. G. Foster (eds.) Beyond Black or White: An Alternate America. Boston: Little, Brown.

DU BOIS, W. E. B. (1908) The Negro American Family. Atlanta: Atlanta University Press.

ELARDO, R., R. BRADLEY, and B. CALDWELL (1975) "The relations of infants' home environments to mental test performance from six to thirty-six months: a longitudinal analysis." Child Development 46: 68-74.

———— (1977) "A longitudinal study of the relation of infants' home environments to language development at age three." Child Development 48: 595-603.

FRAZIER, E. F. (1933) "Children in black and mulatto families." American Journal of Sociology 39: 12-29.

_____ (1939) The Negro Family in the United States. Chicago: University of Chicago Press.

_____ (1950) "Problems and needs of Negro children and youth resulting from family disorganization." Journal of Negro Education 19: 269-277.

GAY, G. (1975) "Cultural differences important in education of Black children." Momentum (October): 30-33.

GUTMAN, H.G. (1976) The Black Family in Slavery and Freedom: 1750-1925. New York: Random House.

HANNERZ, U. (1969) Soulside: Inquires into Ghetto Culture and Community. New York: Columbia University Press.

HARRISON-ROSS, P. and B. WYDEN (1973) The Black Child—A Parents' Guide. New York: Peter H. Wyden.

HESS, R.D. (1970) "Social class and ethnic influences on socialization," in P. Mussen (ed.) Carmichael's Manual of Child Psychology. New York: John Wiley.

_____ et al. (1968) The Cognitive Environments of Urban Preschool Children. Report to the Children's Bureau, U.S. Department of Health, Education, and Welfare. Washington, DC: Government Printing Office.

HILL, R. (1971) The Strengths of Black Families. New York: National Urban League.

JOHNSON, C.S. (1934) Shadow of the Plantation. Chicago: University of Chicago Press.

_____ (1941) Growing Up in the Black Belt. Washington, DC: American Council on Education.

KUHN, T. (1963) The Structure of Scientific Revolutions. Chicago: University of Chicago Press.

LADNER, J. (1971) Tomorrow's Tomorrow: The Black Woman. Garden City, Doubleday.

LEWIN, K. (1935) A Dynamic Theory of Personality. New York: McGraw-Hill.

LEWIS, D. (1975) "The Black family: socialization and sex roles." Phylon 26 (Fall): 471-480.

LEWIS, H. (1955) Blackways of Kent. Chapel Hill: University of North Carolina Press.

LIEBOW, E. (1966) Tally's Corner. Boston: Little, Brown.

LYMAN, S.M. (1972) The Black American in Sociological Thought. New York: Capricorn Books.

McADOO, H.P. (1978) "Factors related to stability in upwardly mobile Black families." Journal of Marriage and the Family 40 (November): 761-778.

MARTIN, E.P. and J.M. MARTIN (1978) The Black Extended Family. Chicago: University of Chicago Press.

MATHIS, A. (1978) "Contrasting approaches to the study of Black families." Journal of Marriage and the Family 40 (November): 667-678.

MOYNIHAN, D.P. (1965) The Negro Family: A Case for National Action. Washington, DC: Government Printing Office.

MYRDAL, G. (1944) An American Dilemma. New York: Harper & Row.

NOBLES, W.W. (1974a) "African root and American fruit: the Black family." Journal of Social and Behavioral Sciences 20 (Spring): 66-77.

_____ (1974b) "Africanity: its role in Black families." The Black Scholar (June): 10-17.

_____ (1978) "Toward an empirical and theoretical framework for defining Black families." Journal of Marriage and the Family 40 (November): 679-690.

OGBU, J. (1978) Minority Education and Caste: The American System in Cross-Cultural Perspective. New York: Academic Press.

PETERS, M.F. (1974) "The black family: perpetuating the myths: an analysis of family sociology textbook treatment of black families." Family Coordinator 23 (October): 349-357.

_____ (1976) "Nine Black families: a study of household management and childrearing in Black families with working mothers." Ph.D. dissertation, Harvard University.

_____ (1980) "Childrearing in Black families: potential continuities and discontinuities between home and school." Paper presented at annual meeting of National Council on Family Relations, Portland, Oregon, October.

_____ (1981) "Childrearing patterns in a sample of Black parents of children age 1 to 3." Paper presented at Annual Meeting of Society for Research in Child Development.

———— and G. C. MASSEY (in press) "Chronic vs. mundane stress in family stress theories: the case of Black families in White America."

PIERCE, C. (1969) "The effects of racism." Paper presented at the American Medical Association AMA 15th Annual Conference of State Mental Health Representatives, Chicago, Illinois.

RADIN, N. and C. KAMII (1965) "The child-rearing attitudes of disadvantaged Negro mothers and some educational implications." Journal of Negro Education 34 (2): 138-146.

RAINWATER, L. (1966) "Crucible of identity: the Negro lower-class family," pp. 160-204 in The Negro American. Boston: Beacon Press.

RENNE, K. R. (1970) "Correlates of dissatisfaction in marriage." Journal of Marriage and the Family 32: 54-67.

RICHARDSON, B. B. (1981) "Racism and child-rearing: a study of Black mothers." Ph.D. dissertation, Claremont Graduate School.

SCANZONI, J. (1971) The Black Family in Modern Society. Boston: Allyn & Bacon.

———— (1975) "Sex roles, economic factors, and marital solidarity in Black and white marriages." Journal of Marriage and the Family 37 (February): 130-144.

SCHACTER, F. F. (1979) Everyday Mother Talk to Toddlers: Early Intervention. New York: Academic Press.

SCHULZ, D. (1969) Coming Up Black. Englewood Cliffs, NJ: Prentice-Hall.

SLAUGHTER, D. (1978) "Modernization through education of mother-child dyads." Final Report I to the National Institute of Child Health and Human Development. Evanston, IL: Northwestern University.

STACK, C. B. (1974) All Our Kin: Strategies for Survival in a Black Community. New York: Harper & Row.

WHITE, B. L., B. KABAN, B. SHAPIRO, and J. ATTANMUCCI (1977) "Competence and experience," in I. C. Uzgiris and F. Weizman (eds.) The Structuring of Experience. New York: Plenum Press.

WHITING, B. (1973) "The problem of the packaged variable." Paper presented at the Biennial International Conference on Behavioral Development, Ann Arbor, Michigan, August.

WILLIE, C. V. (1976) A New Look at Black Families. New Bayside, NY: General Hall.

YOUNG, V. (1970) "Family and childhood in a southern Negro community." American Anthropologist 72 (April): 269-288.

ZEGIOB, L. and R. FOREHAND (1975) "Maternal interactive behavior as a function of race: socioeconomic status and sex of the child." Child Development 46: 564-568.

15

INVOLVEMENT OF FATHERS IN THE SOCIALIZATION OF BLACK CHILDREN

JOHN L. McADOO

Sociological and psychological research related to the socialization of the child has been described as matricentric in character (Lamb, 1976; Rapaport et al., 1977). Rapaport et al., (1977) have even suggested that the matrifocal parenting paradigm for parenting in our society is in need of revision, while most researchers feel that the role of the father in the socialization of their children is only beginning to be understood (Lamb, 1976; Biller, 1974). We find that the exploration of the Black father's role in the socialization of his children is almost nonexistent in social science literature. From the matricentric researcher's point of view, the Black father is usually seen as an invisible man who is not active in and has no power, control, or interest in the socialization of his children (McAdoo, 1979). There is a need, then, to describe some of the research findings related to Black fatherhood.

The objectives of this chapter are to present some of the literature related to the parenting styles of Black fathers in the socialization of their children, to examine some of the trends in father-child research, and to indicate some of the implications of these trends to the stereotyping of the Black father's role in the socialization of his children. We will be examining a variety of roles: that of provider; the father's influence in decisions related to child rearing, nurturing, and control functions; the father's expectations of his children; and interaction patterns between father and child.

PROVIDER ROLE

Most of the sociological literature relating to the provider role of the father follows Parsons and Bales's (1955) description of the instrumental and expressive modes of family process. The father was described as playing only an instrumental role. That is, he was seen as being primarily a provider who both protected the family from the outside world and was the conduit of information and resources between the family and the outside world. The mother-child relationship was the key expressive relationship until the child had passed the preschool stage. While Parsons and Bales's theories have served as a theoretical model in early family socialization literature, the literature does not provide clear-cut support for their thesis. At least one researcher has provided evidence suggesting that fathers are engaged in expressive socialization functions (Cazenave, 1979).

Price-Bonham and Skeen (1979) noted that the effectiveness of the Black father in his role as a provider is viewed as dependent on his ability to aid in supporting his family and to share the provider role with his wife, thus legitimizing his authority within the family and allowing him to serve as a model of responsible behavior to his children. Tausch (1952) noted that Black fathers and fathers of other racial and ethnic groups saw themselves as more than just economic providers to their families, and they valued companionship with their children more than the provider role. The role of provider for these fathers may have presented a dilemma for them, since the amount of time fathers spent with their children was partially controlled by employment pressures.

In analyzing the research of Maxwell (1976) and others (Cafritz, 1974; Fasteneau, 1976), Cazenave (1979) found that they overemphasized the provider role as a parenting style in focusing exclusively on the lack of paternal participation, involvement, and expressiveness in white middle- and upper-middle-income classes. In his research with middle-income Black fathers, Cazenave notes that the greater the economic security, the more active the father becomes in the child-rearing function. His findings on 54 mailmen seem to support this conclusion, as these fathers were found to be more active in child-rearing activities than their fathers had been.

In summary, while many researchers appear to use Parsons's theory as a guide, it now appears evident from Cazenave's and others' data relating to paternal nurturance (McAdoo, 1979; Radin, 1972; Radin and Epstein, 1975) that Parsons may have overemphasized the instrumental or provider role of the father. It is safe to assume that the American father plays many roles in the family—that of provider, decision maker, nurturer, husband, and father. Research that isolates or focuses on any of these roles may provide misinformation about his role in the nurturing of his children. While this evaluation analyzes each of the roles of fathers separately, it is important to recognize the interrelationship of the roles the father plays and the reciprocity of father/mother, sibling/child roles in the socialization process.

DECISION MAKING

Several authors have described the Black family as equalitarian in their decision-making patterns (Dietrich, 1975; Hill, 1971; Lewis, 1975; Reuben, 1978; Staples, 1976; Tenhouten, 1970; Willie and Greenblatt, 1978). Much of this literature was in reaction to social scientists' assertions that the Black family was matriarchal in structure (Moynihan, 1965). Willie and Greenblatt (1978), in reviewing the power relationship literature, found that Black families appear to be more equalitarian than white families, with the middle-class Black family being more equalitarian than any other type. McDonald (1980), in an extensive review of the family power literature, suggests that because of theoretical and methodological problems inherent in family power research, we have not moved much beyond the original finding of Blood and Wolfe (1960) on this issue.

Blood and Wolfe (1960) and others have demonstrated that American fathers are moving toward an egalitarian relationship in the decision-making and power relationship in the home. Jackson (1978) reported that lower-class Black fathers tended to be more patriarchal in their decision-making patterns than lower-class white fathers and Black and white middle-income fathers. Her review of selected literature on Black and white families noted that wife-dominant families (matriarchal) were more characteristic of white professional families with unemployed wives. Mack (1978) found that regardless of race or class, fathers perceived themselves as the dominant decision makers.

The studies related to child-rearing decision making in Black and white families indicate that the predominant pattern is egalitarian. That is, fathers share equally in the decisions about the child's needs (McAdoo, 1980). McAdoo (1979) had previously found that middle-income Black fathers shared equally with their wives in decisions on child-rearing activities. However, the Cromwells' (1978) analysis of husbands' and wives' reports of dominance on child-rearing decision making revealed conflicts in Black and Chicano homes on this issue. This points up the need to develop theoretical and methodological frameworks that allow researchers to look at both process and outcomes of decision making in child-rearing practices. The reports by either father, mother, or both about the father's role in this process may be limited without some actual observational data in conflictual and nonconflictual situations (McDonald, 1980).

Our conclusions, given the previous assertions, are that both Black and white middle-income fathers' involvement in decision making regarding child-rearing practices appears to be changing in the same general pattern found by Bronfenbrenner's (1958) analysis of the literature 23 years ago. He found the predominant child-rearing decision-making pattern to be equalitarian and attributed the change to the influence of professional child development practitioners. These changes perhaps were also due to the addition of mothers to the work force and the use of television in getting child development practitioners' message to more people.

More systematic study is needed on the impact sharing of the provider's role has on child-rearing decision making within Black and other families. While the sharing of the provider's role has led in most cases to greater economic and educational resources in Black families, there is some need to understand what this change has meant for other family processes and functioning in addition to decision-making processes. A question may be raised as to the impact on paternal attitudes and parenting style.

PARENTING STYLE

Very few studies related to father's expectations and parenting style were found. In a review of the literature, Bartz and Levine (1978), in a study of 455 parents of different ethnic groups, noted that fathers of all socioeconomic classes shared similar expectations of their children's behavior. Ethnic differences in fathers' expectations of their children's behavior were a matter of degree and not kind. Working-class fathers of all ethnic groups and races believed that children should help formulate rules and have the right to express their own ideas within the family. Black fathers and fathers belonging to other ethnic groups think parents earn the respect of their children by being fair, not by imposing parental will or authority.

While Bartz's data seem to suggest that lower socioeconomic Black fathers may be changing their traditional values to meet the new demands for socialization in society, it is clear from other literature (Staples, 1978; Taylor, 1978; Coles, 1978; Schulz, 1978) that many of them retain and support the values of their socioeconomic status. These men see themselves as the head of the family, and they believe they are expected to provide punishment to their children for transgressing externally imposed rules and regulations. They describe themselves as strict, using physical as opposed to verbal punishment liberally. The child's punishment is related to the transgression's consequence rather than the intent of the child's actions.

Cazenave (1979), reviewing the changes in child-rearing activities in two generations of Black fathers, found that middle-income fathers reported being more actively involved than their fathers in child-caring activities. This sample was more actively involved in changing their children's diapers, in babysitting, and in playing with their children than their fathers had been. They reported spending more time with their children and claimed to punish their children physically less often than their fathers had punished them.

Black middle-income fathers in McAdoo's (1979) study resembled those in Cazenave's study, in that they were equally involved in making child-rearing decisions. Most of these fathers could be described as traditional (Duvall, 1946) in their values toward child rearing. They expected their child to respond immediately to their commands, would almost never allow angry temper tantrums from their child, and perceived themselves and their attitudes toward child rearing as moderate to very strict. These fathers expected good behavior from their children as opposed to assertive and independent behavior. They were more likely to tell the child that they approved of his good behavior as opposed to hugging and kissing him. Their attitudes appeared to be like Baumrind's (1968) authoritarian fathers.

Baumrind (1966, 1967, 1973), in a series of research studies, has described three parenting styles that cut across all ethnic groups. The permissive, authoritarian, and authoritative parents have different child-rearing values and different expectations for their own role behaviors. The permissive father was described as the father who responds to his child's impulses, desires, and actions in a nonpunitive, accepting, and affirmative manner. This father made very few demands on his child for orderly behavior or doing household chores. He sees himself as a consultant to be used as the child desires and not as an agent responsible for shaping the child's ongoing or future behavior.

In contrast, the authoritarian father attempts to shape, control and evaluate his child's behavior and attitudes in accordance with a set standard of conduct. He values and expects obedience as a virtue and believes in punitive, forceful measures to control the child's behavior when it is in conflict with what the father believes is right. There are few give-and-take discussions, and the child is expected to accept the father's view of what is right.

The authoritative father seems to be a composite of the best points of the authoritarian and permissive fathers. This parent, according to Baumrind's findings, also attempts to direct the child's activities but in a more rational, issue-oriented manner. The authoritative father is able to encourage give-and-take discussions and gives reasons for his rules and expectations. The authoritative father tends to value both expressive and instrumental attributes, both autonomous self-will and disciplined authority. The father provides firm control with explanations when the child violates family policy. He believes in the use of reasoning as well as power in achieving his objectives with the child.

Baumrind's (1971) series of observational studies demonstrated that authoritative fathers promoted purposive and dominant behavior in boys and girls. Authoritative paternal control was associated with the development of social responsibility in boys and with achievement (but not friendly, cooperative behavior) in girls. Fathers who were either authoritarian or permissive in their child-rearing styles had children who were either markedly high or markedly low on overall competence (Baumrind, 1971).

In a comparative exploratory study observing Black and white fathers and their preschool children, Baumrind (1973) found sex differences in the fathers' expectations and the behavior of the children. There were few significant differences in Black and white fathers' expectations of their sons' behavior. Black sons were expected to behave in a more mature fashion, and the fathers were likely to encourage independent behavior. While no significant differences were observed in the behavior of the children, Black boys appeared to be less achievement oriented and more aggressive than white boys. Fathers of Black girls appeared to be significantly different from fathers of white girls in their parenting styles and child-rearing practices. The Black fathers did not encourage individuality and independence or provide enrichment of their daughter's environment. Black fathers did not promote nonconformity and were authoritarian in their practices.

The conclusion drawn by Baumrind was that socialization practices which would characterize Black families as authoritarian by white social science standards, and therefore in need of change, actually benefit Black daughters. In comparing Black and white girls Baumrind found that Black daughters of authoritarian parents were exceptionally independent and at ease in the nursery school setting where the observations took place. The study provides us with an interesting observation which needs to be verified and clarified in future research. Black authoritarian fathers and families differ significantly from white authoritarian families in the degree to which they adhere to rigid standards. White fathers who were found to be authoritarian in Baumrind's studies were more likely to be seen as having an authoritarian personality syndrome (Adorno et al., 1950)—that is, dogmatic and intolerant attitudes being motivated by repressed anger, emotional coldness, and a sense of impotence.

In summary to this section on parenting styles, it would appear that Black fathers socialize their children differently than white fathers, and the impact of that process may lead to the development of high competence in girls. There appears to be a need for more research related to the Black father's attitude toward child rearing, some observational validation of his behavior in relationship to his expressed values, and some validation through data gathering from significant others in the family. There is a need to evaluate the three types of parenting styles in more depth to determine whether cultural, ethnic, or racial differences influence our particular parenting style and its relationship to child outcome variables. Finally, there is a need to determine how the particular parenting style a father adopts influences his relationship to his son and/or daughter.

PARENT-CHILD RELATIONSHIPS

Walters and his associates (Walters and Stinnett, 1971; Walters and Walters, 1980) have done the most consistent reviews of the research related to parent-child relationship issues. Their latest work focused on the emerging research trends of physiological influences, parent-infant relationships, divorce, fathering, stepparenting, child abuse and neglect, values of the child, methodological issues, and intervention strategies.

Some of their conclusions were that patterns of parent-child relationships are influenced by parenting models which fathers and mothers provide to each other. To understand the concurrent contributions of parents to each other and to their children, research studies should focus on the mother-father-child relationship and on the mother-father-sibling-child relationship rather than on the father-child, mother-child relationship.

Walters believes that a clearer picture or conceptualization is emerging from the research literature on the reciprocal effects of relationships between parents and children. Family researchers are moving away from a unidirectional model, which sees the relationship going from parent to child, toward one which emphasizes a reciprocal model of relationships between parent and child. Children not only influence their parents' behavior but are also important determiners of their own behavior patterns (Walters and Walters, 1980).

While Walters's review emphasizes the need for research on parent-child interactions and reciprocal relationships, it is also clear from his review and that of others (Lamb, 1977; Price-Bonham and Skeen, 1979) that the role of the father in the parent-child relationship studies is not clearly understood. Studies of father-child relationships tend to emphasize the relationship between fathers and sons and leave the impact on daughters virtually unexplored (Walters and Stinnett, 1971). Further, as Staples (1970) notes, the role of the Black father in these studies is not explored very well. He concludes that the Black male may be more difficult to reach, the implication being that social science researchers select other sources for their information on Black fathers.

Price-Bonham and Skeen, (1979), in their review of the literature, agree with Staples's assessment and suggest that studies of Black father-child relationships suffer from the same deficiencies as do studies of other ethnic groups. Most researchers doing family relationship studies generally collect data on fathers from mothers and/or wives (Walters and Stinnett, 1971; McAdoo, 1979), neglect to control for social class (Busse and Busse, 1972), and focus on the impact of absent fathers.

In summary to this section on father-child relationships, what seems lacking from the various literature reviews is a theory which describes how these relationships differ over the life span of the child's development within the family. This theory should address racial, ethnic, and social class differences within the father-child relationship. More descriptive research methodologies need to be developed using both questionnaire and observational techniques to generate data bases related to the general concept of parent-child relationships and to particular aspects of that relationship. For Black father-child relationships, given socioeconomic class and other variables, there is a need to develop the boundaries, quality, and quantity of the parent-child relationship over time.

Once the relationships between fathers and children are identified, more sophisticated research designs can be used to determine the impact of mothers, siblings, and the kin network system on the development and changes in the parent-child relationship process. This would suggest the use of multitraits and multimethod approaches with more complex research designs (Walters and Walters, 1980). Using such approaches, researchers could begin to measure the impact of the child on the relationship and move away from linear models to curvilinear or other models that are appropriate.

FATHER-CHILD INTERACTION

The observations of father-child interaction patterns and their effect on the preschool child's social and cognitive growth are relatively new phenomena for social science researchers. The two most studied interaction patterns are nurturance and control. Nurturance may be defined as the expression of warmth and positive feelings of the father toward the attitudes and behaviors of his child.

Several researchers (Radin, 1972; Radin and Epstein, 1975; Baumrind, 1971) have suggested that maternal warmth (nurturance) facilitates the child's identification with the mother, particularly the female child. Radin (1972) has suggested that paternal nurturance facilitates the male child's identification with the father. Identification with either parent should lead to an incorporation by the child of the parent's ideas, attitudes, beliefs, and feelings about the child. The parent communicates to the child a positive acceptance of the child as a person. Nurturance is one of the patterns of interaction that is important in the development of social competence in preschool children.

Nurturance (warmth) is used most by parents who recognize and respond to their child's needs, who communicate acceptance, and who are available for interaction than by parents who are inaccessible and insensitive. Warmth is seen as a characteristic of both parent roles (Newman and Newman, 1978). Newman notes that warmth is usually expressed in praise or approval in nonverbal interactions including patting, touching, stroking, hugging, kissing, and in playful activities. Rodman (in Newman and Newman, 1978) suggests evidence that warmth and rejection can be observed across a variety of cultural groups.

Parental control is another dimension of father-child interaction patterns. Control refers to the parent's insistence that the child carry out important directions and adhere to rules that the parent feels are important. Control and

nurturance are seen as necessary ingredients in authoritative parents' socialization patterns (Baumrind, 1973). Authoritarian fathers usually use restrictive
control interaction patterns in socializing their children. These fathers' verbal
interaction patterns with their preschool children are described in the literature
as being restrictive, rather cold, unfeeling and aloof, and therefore represent an
expression of the authoritarian father's negative feelings toward his child's
attitudes and behavior within the family (Radin, 1972).

Parental restrictiveness does not facilitate positive communication and identification (Radin, 1972) between the child and his parent. Restrictive behaviors
are those behaviors that are not warm, loving, and supportive of the child.
Nonsupporting behaviors are usually in criticism or expressed disapproval and
may also include grabbing, pushing, or restraining the child from some event or
activity without explanation. It may be viewed as a negative reaction by the
parent to the child's attitude, behavior, and beliefs. Nonsupport may also lead
the parent to handle the symptoms of the problem and not the needs of the child,
or to control behavior and cut off the usual patterns of identification and
communication of the child. Restrictiveness in the parents could lead the child
to develop a negative image of himself and his worth as a human being, as well
as having negative feelings about those around him.

Radin and her associates (Radin, 1972; Radin and Epstein, 1975; Jordan et
al., 1975) observed white lower- and middle-income fathers interacting with
their preschool children. She found the predominant pattern of interaction to be
nurturance. The fathers were warm and loving toward their children. She
hypothesized that children of nurturant fathers would do well on cognitive tasks
in kindergarten. They were able to support the hypothesis for boys of middle
income fathers but not for boys of lower-class fathers. Her studies also found
that the relationship between paternal nurturance and the child's intellectual
functioning was higher for boys than for girls. It was suggested that the fathers
of girls may be sending mixed messages to their daughters and this may lead to a
reduction in intellectual performance (Radin and Epstein, 1975).

McAdoo (1979) partially replicated Radin's work with Black middle-income
fathers. He hypothesized that the predominant pattern of verbal interaction
between Black fathers and their sons and daughters would be nurturance. He
was able to support the hypothesis: 75 percent of the Black middle-income
fathers were found to be nurturant toward their children. Fathers were equally
nurturant toward their sons and daughters. One unanticipated finding was that
children of restrictive parents initiated the interaction between them and their
fathers significantly more often than children of nurturant parents. This finding
supports the Walterses' (1980) suggestion that there needs to be an examination
of the impact of the reciprocal nature of the pattern of interaction between
parent and child.

McAdoo was not able to find any relationship between a father's interaction
patterns and his sons' and daughters' self-esteem. The children's positive self-

esteem lead McAdoo to suggest that the relationship between father-child interaction and self-esteem may be indirect. Walters and Stinnett (1971), in their decade review of parent-child relationships, noted that the research results converge in suggesting that parental acceptance, warmth, and support are positively related to favorable emotional, social, and intellectual development of children. They further found that extreme restrictiveness, authoritarianism, and punitiveness without acceptance, warmth, and love tend to be negatively related to a child's positive self-concept and emotional and social development. The studies they reviewed also indicate that parental attitudes and behaviors vary according to sex and behavior of the child.

Mackey and Day (1979), in one of the most comprehensive cross-cultural observational studies involving father figures in the United States, Ireland, Spain, Japan, and Mexico, found that American father figures did not interact much differently than father figures of other nations. They noted that father figures interacted more nonverbally with younger children and were closer to them. American men were as nurturant to their children as were American women. No differences in intensity of interaction level between men and women were observed in American families.

SUMMARY

Selected literature related to the roles Black fathers play in the socialization of their children were reviewed. It was noted that when economic sufficiency rises within Black families, an increase in the active participation of the Black fathers in the socialization of his children was observed. Black fathers, like fathers of all ethnic groups, take an equal part in the child-rearing decisions in the family. Their expectations for their child's behavior in the home also appear to be similar given socioeconomic status patterns. Unlike other fathers who are authoritarian, Black fathers appear to be socializing their daughters to be more competent and independent at an early age. His predominant relationship and interaction pattern appears to be nurturant, warm, and loving toward his children. Finally, as Lamb (1976) has suggested, the father's socialization role is defined by his position within the family system.

The implications of these findings appear to be that research should now move beyond the ethnocentric studies of the past that focus on the most problematic, economically devastated Black families, sometimes inappropriately comparing them to families of college professors, and study the various roles the Black father plays in the socialization of his children. More studies are needed which describe the father's attitudes, expectations, values, and beliefs about the roles he plays in both problematic and nonproblematic or both stressful and nonstressful situations. There needs to be more observational research related to the kinds of socialization activities and interaction patterns that take place between the father and his child in the home and community.

Theoretical frameworks and methodologies are needed that examine all the reciprocal socialization relationships of the total family system. We need to describe and evaluate reciprocal interaction and relationship patterns between father, mother, child, siblings, and kin. There is a need to go beyond the dyadic models and linear relationships to a more dynamic interaction model which looks at the family interaction processes in a developmental way and evaluate these processes in terms of social, emotional, and cognitive development of the child and his family members over time.

REFERENCES

ADORNO, T. W., E. FENKEL-BRUNSWICK, D. J. LEVINSON, and R. N. SANFORD (1950) The Authoritarian Personality. New York: Harper & Row.

BARTZ, K. W. and B. S. LEVINE (1978) "Child rearing by Black parents: a description and comparison to Anglo and Chicano parents." Journal of Marriage and the Family 40 (4): 709-720.

BAUMRIND, D. (1966) "Effects of authoritative parental control on child behavior." Child Development 37 (4): 887-907.

_____ (1967) "Child care practices anteceding three patterns of preschool behavior." Genetic Psychology Monographs 75: 43-88.

_____ (1968) "An exploratory study of socialization effects on Black children: some black-white comparisons." Child Development 43: 261-267.

_____ (1971) "Current patterns of paternal authority." Developmental Psychology Monographs 4 (1) Part 2.

_____ (1973) "Authoritarian vs authoritative parental control," in M. Scarr-Salapatek and P. Salapatek (eds.) Socialization. Columbus, OH: Charles Merrill.

_____ and A. E. BLOCK (1967) "Socialization practices associated with dimensions of competence in preschool boys and girls." Child Development 38 (2): 291-327.

BILLER, H. B. (1972) Parental Deprivation. Lexington, MA: Heath.

BLOOD, R. and D. WOLFE (1960) Husbands and Wives. New York: Free Press.

BRONFENBRENNER, U. (1958) "Socialization through time and space," in E. E. Maccoby, T. M. Newcomb, and E. L. Hartley (eds.) Readings in Social Psychology. New York: Holt, Rinehart & Winston.

BUSSE, T. and P. BUSSE (1972) "Negro parental behavior and social class variables." Journal of Genetic Psychology 120: 289-291.

CAFRITZ, J. S. (1974) Masculine/Feminine or Human? Itasca, IL: F. E. Peacock.

CAZENAVE, N. (1979) "Middle income Black fathers: an analysis of the provider's role." Family Coordinator 28 (November).

COLES, R. (1978) "Black fathers," in D. Wilkerson and R. Taylor (eds.) The Black Male in America. Chicago: Nelson-Hall.

CROMWELL, V. L. and R. E. CROMWELL (1978) "Perceived dominance and conflict resolution among Anglo, Black and Chicano couples." Journal of Marriage and the Family 42 (4): 749-759.

DIETRICH, K. T. (1975) "A reexamination of the myth of Black matriarchy." Journal of Marriage and the Family 37 (May): 367-374.

DUVALL, E. (1946) "Conceptions of parenthood." Journal of Sociology 52 (November): 193-203.

FASTENEAU, M. (1976) The Male Machine. New York: Macmillan.

JACKSON, J. (1978) "Ordinary Black husbands: the truly hidden men," pp. 139-144 in M. E. Lamb (ed.) The Role of the Father in Child Development. New York: John Wiley.

JORDAN, B. E., N. RADIN, and A. EPSTEIN (1975) "Paternal behavior and intellectual functioning in preschool boys and girls." Developmental Psychology 11: 407-408.

LAMB, M. E. (1976) "Interactions between eight-month old children and their fathers and mothers," in M. E. Lamb (ed.) The Role of the Father in Child Development. New York: John Wiley.

———— (1977) "The role of the father: an overview," in M. E. Lamb (ed.) The Role of the Father in Child Development. New York: John Wiley.

LEWIS, D. K. (1975) "The Black family: socialization and sex roles." Phylon 36 (Fall): 221-237.

McADOO, J. (1979) "A study of father-child interaction patterns and self-esteem in Black preschool children." Young Children 34 (1): 46-53.

———— (1980) "Socializing the preschool child." Government grant funded by the National Institutes of Mental Health, Contract No. 1 R01 MH25838-01.

McDONALD, G. W. (1980) "Family power: the assessment of a decade of theory and research 1970-1979." Journal of Marriage and the Family 42 (4): 881-854.

MACK, D. E. (1978) "Power relationships in Black families." Journal of Personality and Social Psychology 30 (September): 409-413.

MACKEY, C. W. and R. O. DAY (1979) "Some indicators of fathering behaviors in the United States: a cross-cultural examination of the adult male interactions." Journal of Marriage and the Family 41 (2): 287-298.

MAXWELL, J. (1976) "The keeping of fathers in America." The Family Coordinator 25: 387-392.

MOYNIHAN, D. (1965) The Negro Family: The Case for National Action. Washington, DC: Department of Labor, Office of Planning and Research.

NEWMAN, B. M. and P. R. NEWMAN (1978) Infancy and Childhood Development and its Contents. New York: John Wiley.

PARSONS, T. and R. F. BALES (1955) Family Socialization and Interaction Process. New York: Free Press.

PRICE-BONHAM, S. and P. SKEEN (1979) "A comparison of Black and white fathers with implications for parents' education." The Family Coordinator 28 (1): 53-59.

RADIN, N. (1972) "Father-child interaction and the intellectual functioning of four-year old boys." Developmental Psychology 8: 369-376.

———— (1973) "Observed paternal behaviors as antecedents of intellectual functioning in young boys." Developmental Psychology 6: 353-361.

———— and A. EPSTEIN (1975) "Observed paternal behavior and intellectual functioning of preschool boys and girls." Paper presented at the Society for Research in Child Development, Denver.

RAPAPORT, R., R. N. RAPAPORT, and Z. STRELITZ (1977) Fathers, Mothers and Society. New York: Basic Books.

REUBEN, R. H. (1978) "Matriarchal themes in Black literature: implications for family life education." Family Coordinator 27 (January): 33-41.

SCHULZ, D. A. (1978) "Coming up as a boy in the ghetto," pp. 7-32 in D. Y. Wilkerson and R. L. Taylor (eds.) The Black Male in America. Chicago: Nelson-Hall.

STAPLES, R. (1970) "Educating the Black male at various class levels for marital roles." The Family Coordinator 20: 164-167.

———— (1976) "The Black American family," in C. H. Mindell and R. W. Haberstein (eds.) Ethnic Families in America. New York: Elsevier.

———— (1978) "The myth of the Black matriarchy," in D. Y. Wilkerson and R. L. Taylor (eds.) The Black Male in America. Chicago: Nelson-Hall.

TAYLOR, R. L. (1978) "Socialization to the Black male role," pp. 1-7 in D. Y. Wilkerson and R. L. Taylor (eds.) The Black Male in America. Chicago: Nelson-Hall.

TAUSCH, R. J. (1952) "The role of the father in the family." Journal of Experimental Education 20: 319-361.

TENHOUTEN, W. (1970) "The Black family: myth or reality." Psychiatry 2 (May): 145-173.

WALTERS, J. and N. STINNETT (1971) "Parent-child relationships: a decade of research," in C. B. Broderick (ed.) A Decade of Family Research and Action. Minneapolis: National Council on Family Relations.

WALTERS, J. and L. H. WALTERS (1980) "Parent-child relationships: a review 1970-1979." Journal of Marriage and the Family 42 (4) November: 807-824.

WILLIE, C. V. and S. L. GREENBLATT (1978) "Four classic studies of power relationships in Black families: a review and look to the future." Journal of Marriage and the Family 40 (4): 691-696.

16

SUPPORT SYSTEMS OF
SIGNIFICANT OTHERS IN BLACK FAMILIES

WILHELMINA MANNS

INTRODUCTION

Many persons, performing a variety of roles and functions within individual lives, contribute to the socialization process of members of the family. Moreover, such persons are often significant others. Examining the influence of the significant other in the life of individual blacks, therefore, increases knowledge about selected aspects of the socialization process of the black family.

The concept of the significant other developed from the formulations of Cooley (1902/1964) and later Mead (1934/1962), who suggested that the self-concept develops out of social interaction and that the individual assumed the viewpoint (reflected appraisal) of the "other" and "generalized other" of the general society of which he is a member. Expanding on these earlier formulations, Sullivan (as cited by Kuhn, 1972) described a specific "significant other" later defined by Denzin (1970) as a person "whose evaluations of his behavior and attitudes, the individual, holds in high esteem." These evaluations and/or reflected appraisals from both the "generalized other" (the community) and a specific significant other can be either positive or negative and thus may influence the individual's self-concept accordingly.

For the past 25 years, investigators have examined various factors in the sphere of the significant other influence. Among these studies is the work of

Haller and Woelfel (1972), who concentrated on developing an instrument that would identify significant others and measure their influence, simultaneously examining the influence of the significant other on the educational and occupational aspirations of high school students. They concluded that their findings supported earlier formulations by Mead and Sullivan that stressed the role of the expectation of other persons in determining the goal orientations of the individual, and that "significant other" is a precise and flexible concept currently available "for use in assessing interpersonal influence on orientation variables" (p. 591).

The significant other as a factor in the lives of black people has received attention in both theoretical formulations and empirical research. In suggesting reasons for his finding that black people, despite minority racial status, managed to achieve stability and social status, Billingsley (1968) included reference to the influence of the significant others—from not only the individual's family but also all segments of the wider community, the latter of whom functioned primarily as social supports. Whereas Billingsley's sample for the most part concentrated on blacks from established achieving families, Manns (1974) examined the autobiographies of blacks from low socioeconomic background and found that parents, other relatives, and nonrelatives were identified as significant others and that they influenced the individual in several ways. Other empirical research included the work of Shade (1978), who examined the significant other influence of "disadvantaged Afro-American freshmen" and found that although both family and nonfamily members were identified, the nonfamily significant others were more prevalent. There were questions, nevertheless, that persisted about the influence of the significant other. Accordingly, this chapter will share selected findings from an intensive study that focused on two areas: (1) identification of the type of significant other, and (2) delineation of the manner of the influence of the significant other.

The study participants included 20 black adult respondents, purposively selected according to: education, minimum master's degree in social work; socioeconomic status of the family of origin as determined by a modified version of the Hollingshead-Redlich SES scale; age between 40 and 65; and sex. The influence of the significant other was examined in terms of the respondent's educational and occupational achievement in order to anchor the influence to an observable event. In addition, because the perceived response of others is more important than the actual response (Quarantelli and Cooper, 1966/1972), the perception of the influenced individual was a perspective selected for identifying the significant other.

NUMBER OF SIGNIFICANT OTHERS

The respondents identified a large number of significant others—212, approximately ten per person. A persistent pattern in the data suggested that there is an association between the respondent's societal status, as determined by race and socioeconomic background, and the number of significant others. In a larger comparative study that examined race and socioeconomic status as variables, it was found that there was a tendency for blacks to have more significant others than whites, and also for the lower class to have more than the middle class (Table 16.1). In addition, the low variability of the black middle class indicated group stability that supports the notion that minority racial status accounts for the difference between blacks and whites (Table 16.1). Finally, an accumulative effect was observed in the black lower class which, confronted with both minority racial status and low socioeconomic status, tended to have more significant others than the black middle class (Table 16.1).

The observed pattern implies that groups which are viewed as low status (blacks and the lower class) by the larger society tend to have more significant others than higher-status groups (whites and the middle class). In order for low-status groups to achieve, they may require more specific significant others than high-status groups.

Black people, as a minority group, experience negative appraisals from the overall society (the "generalized other"). When individuals experience negative appraisals from the "generalized other," the specific significant other may take on special meaning. It is suggested that a sizable number of specific significant others compensate, in part, for the negative aspects of the minority experience. However, in order to achieve, lower-class blacks may require even more significant others than middle-class blacks, because they are confronted with negative life experiences from both minority racial status and low socioeconomic status.

TYPE OF SIGNIFICANT OTHER
AND MODE OF INFLUENCE

An initial grouping of the type of significant other as caretaker or parent, relative and nonrelative was followed up with a more precise specification of both the relative and the nonrelative.

TABLE 16.1   Frequency, Mean and Standard Deviation of the Number of Significant Others by the Race and Socioeconomic Status of the Respondents (N = 20 black, 20 white)

Respondent Groups				
Race	SES	f	M	S.D.
White	middle	84	8.4	5.31
White	lower	93	9.3	6.37
Black	middle	98	9.8	3.32
Black	lower	114	11.4	6.43

As a result of analyzing the manner in which almost 400 significant others influenced, eight modes of influence categories were established: modeling, validation of self, emotional support, achievement socialization, learning elicitation, providing, disconfirmation of self, and negative modeling.

The pattern in which individual significant others used these modes varied. A specific significant other, for instance, may have influenced through validation, or through validation and modeling—in other words, through two or more modes.

CARETAKING SIGNIFICANT OTHER

Of 212 significant others identified by the black respondents, 15 percent were caretakers or parents. This percentage must be considered within the context of the parent pool generally limited to two parents per individual. Actually, parent significant others were prominent among the respondents, especially the middle class. Eighty percent of the middle-class respondents designated both parents as significant others, as opposed to only 50 percent reported by lower class respondents.

The majority of the parents influenced respondents through the mode of achievement socialization (Table 16.2) in which the significant other inculcates an achievement orientation in the individual, either by establishing an achievement atmosphere or by mandating achievement. The former was described by a middle-class male whose parents were both college graduates. "It was just something I grew up with. There was always the idea that I was to go to college and achieve something. I cannot break it down, further. It was just a way of life."

In contrast, a mandate to achieve is a clear and explicit requirement. Directives of this nature sometimes were attributed to the family reputation. A middle-class mother told her son that "you have come from a family who has

TABLE 16.2 Percentage Distributions of Type of Significant Other of Black Respondents by Mode of Influence (N = 20)

Mode of Influence	*Type of Significant Other %*		
	Parent	*Relative*	*Nonrelative*
Modeling	39	52	35
Validation of self	6	13	33
Emotional support	23	17	12
Achievement socialization	71	22	13
Providing	19	17	21
Learning elicitation	6	15	18
Disconfirmation of self	0	7	15
Negative modeling	3	2	7
	N = 31	46	135

achieved . . . and you will be expected to achieve also." Another rationale was attributed to racism in society and can be seen through the statement of a female respondent who was an only child in a middle-class home. The mother had three years of college but added to the family income by taking in sewing. She "always said that 'as a black person, you really have to go to college and get an education in order to get a job.' I grew up with the idea." Although mandates to achieve appeared in both classes, the middle-class parents were more likely to establish an achievement atmosphere, while the lower-class parents were inclined to mandate achievement.

Historically, both middle-class and lower-class black parents have extolled achievement as the means of combating the negative aspects of minority status. The class difference found in the achievement socialization mode, however, is probably a function of the difference between the interpersonal environments. Middle-class parents are able to establish achievement atmospheres (even casual ones) because of the inherent support from the interpersonal environment: parents and other significant persons are more likely to be educated than significant persons in the interpersonal world of the lower class. Therefore, lower-class parents, who may be achievement-oriented but are usually uneducated and lack support from the interpersonal environment, rely to a greater extent on mandating achievement. Irrespective of this class distinction, the parental emphasis on achievement was persistent and relenting.

Almost 40 percent of the parents influenced respondents through the mode of modeling (Table 16.2), in which the significant other projects a quality and/or performs in a manner that inspires the individual to emulate and/or to adopt the said quality and/or performance. A middle-class female described the exemplary life of her father, a physician:

> My father was extremely committed to anything he did; to his family, to the community, and to the institution that he served for many, many years. There was always the expectation that you would go to school, that you would develop a skill and thus prepare to be of service to others.

Accordingly, she selected social work as her life's work.

Parents exerted influence through the other modes of influence, to a lesser extent (Table 16.2). Through emotional support, significant others sustained, supported, and/or nurtured. Interestingly, the parent significant others were described as sustaining and supportive but they were not described as nurturing, a usual caretaking or parental function. (Since the sample consisted of achievers only, it is assumed that a foundation of self had been established in early life and thus it is probable that nurturing on the part of the parents was either "lost in the unconscious" of the respondent or taken for granted (and consequently not designated as significant). The fact, however, that parents were not described as nurturing merits further study.

Through providing, the significant other gives or makes available to the individual a concrete item, a service, and/or an opportunity. Of those using this mode, the lower-class parents were more prevalent than the middle class. A lower-class male offers a clue to the reason for this class difference. He described his father as a significant other because he "worked hard in a dirty job at the steel mill, but he always stuck with us and provided food, clothing, and a roof over our heads. He wanted me not to give up or quit." Lower-class respondents credited their parents for items that the middle-class parents, undoubtedly, also provided their offspring. It is surmised that in the middle-class these items—basic to life—were taken for granted and hence were not designated as significant.

Learning elicitation involves a couple of subcategories, one of which is teaching—the significant other facilitates the acquisition of specific knowledge and skills. Very few of the parents influenced through teaching, although this finding is not supported by Jones (1981), who, in a study on a current group of low-income black mothers, identified a "range of teaching styles as characterizing [their] interaction with their children."

None of the respondents described his or her parents as influencing through disconfirmation of self, a mode in which the significant other manifests disapproval and/or a rejection of the individual. More than likely, already confronted with minority racial status, blacks who also experience a disconfirmation by a parent find the dual stress an intolerable trauma and tend to disappear from the achievement structure. Other findings indicated that this notion may be especially applicable to the black lower class, which faces both minority and low socioeconomic status.

Almost all of the parents exerted influence during the respondents' early childhood and adolescent years, but a majority continued to influence during a large part of the respondents' adult life cycle. (In fact, in the larger study it was found that black parents were more likely than white parents to influence during the respondents' adult years of 18 to 40, at a significant level.) In this group of achievers, black parents remained an important factor in their offsprings' transition to adulthood and during many of the years that followed.

RELATIVE SIGNIFICANT OTHER

Twenty-one percent of the significant others were relatives. As with the percentage of parents designated significant others, this finding must be considered along with the recognition that there is a limit to the number of relatives one can have. Other findings, nonetheless, clarify the extent of relative involvement. Eighty percent of the respondents mentioned at least one relative as a significant other. From another perspective, some of the respondents (30 percent), who did not mention a specific significant other, referred to a number of their relatives as a group influence. Thus, although the majority of the respondents mentioned at least one relative signficant other, only a few mentioned a number of them.

The array of relative significant other types that were found is extensive: aunt/uncle, sibling, grandparent, spouse, cousin, great-relative and even the in-law. The sibling, aunt/uncle, and grandparent were more likely to be named a significant other than the latter four types. Thus, although most relatives had the potential for being a significant other, those who were close in blood relationship were more likely to be viewed as a significant other.

The majority of the relative significant others influenced by serving as models (Table 16.2). There were various aspects to the manner of the influence of the modeling, but whether the influence was through a projected quality and/or a performance on the part of the significant other, almost all incidents of modeling (irrespective of the type of the significant other) reflected one major theme; the effort, planning, personal quality and/or lifestyle which culminated in achievement (as measured by education and occupation). This proneness can be observed in the following description of an older brother.

> He was a kind of great guy; I really admired his ability to lead. When I was eleven, I became a tenderfoot because he was the scout master. He managed to pass the civil service exam in 1939 and get a job in the postal service. He could have been a doctor, but it was during the Depression. Still, he did manage two years of junior college. Quite a feat for a poor black then.

There were a few instances of what might be called structural kinds of modeling such as pairing. This occurred when cousins of the same age paired up and formulated mutual achievement goals and/or agreed to follow family expectations, as with two cousins who "went off to college together." The family "expected it because she was my pair." Pairing is characterized by friendly competition, reciprocal modeling, and a prolonged relationship. Also observed was a pairing that was not mutual (one-sided pairing) and, in fact, the significant other was unaware of its existence. Such cousins were not intimately close, and usually the significant other cousin "came from the side of the family that was better off financially." These respondents were often from the lower class and used the opportunity to observe that "it was possible within the family" to achieve and were inspired "to keep up."

The family ghost model was another instance of special modeling. These were family members who had achieved—sometimes a first for the family, or even the race. They related peripherally, if at all, to the respondents. Their deeds were known through family lore passed around to extended family members and down to succeeding generations. "Aunt _____ was important in my life. She always worked into every conversation that Poppa (her father and my grandfather) had gone to _____ College; had not graduated but had just 'gone.' But his children were all so proud." Hearing the story, "reinforced my desire to get an education." No one had ever clarified how long "Poppa" had attended the college; it didn't matter, it was enough that he had "gone."

Although relatives influenced the respondents primarily through modeling, to some extent, they also influenced through other modes of influence (Table 16.2).

A wise and persistent grandmother exerted influence through validation of self as she set forth her expectations.

> My grandmother . . . conveyed to me that she had high expectations, and she saw me fulfilling aspirations for the family that other members of the family, like my father, had not been able to achieve. She talked to me about the importance of an education, the importance of staying in school. I was devoted to her.

And through her efforts, family "dreams deferred" were finally realized. This illustration calls attention also to the "grandparent factor" in black life (Manns, 1977) which has been sensitively depicted in autobiographies (for example, Waters, 1978; Angelou, 1969) and fiction (for example, Walker, 1970).

Older siblings sometimes influenced younger brothers and sisters through emotional support; some often really parented. A middle-class male whose father was dead and whose mother took a second teaching job in the evening spoke of his brother.

> My oldest brother was wonderful, just the end of the world for me; he was responsible for getting my sister and me our evening meal. At dinner, and after dinner while doing the dishes, he had a game of whistling. He would whistle songs and my sister and I had to guess the name. He read everything and retained everything; but in those hours together, we read everything, too. I still love to read and cannot go into a store without buying a book.

How nourishing this must have been during crucial growth and development years. And what a beautiful way in which to learn to appreciate a basic achievement tool—the book. The older sibling has been more critical to black family life than has been recognized in either research or literature, and merits study.

The majority of the relative significant others influenced the respondents when they were between the ages of six and seventeen. Some, however, continued their influence during the youth and adult years that followed, although at a decreasing rate. Nevertheless, 22 percent of the relatives influenced respondents when they (the respondents) were in their forties.

Occasionally, a "great significant other factor" manifested itself. These were relatives who were described in superlatives, served as models in several ways (in contrast to the usual one-dimensional modeling of most significant others), and profoundly influenced the lives of the respondents. Thus, the relative significant other, through modeling, represented sources of inspiration for other family members in their quest for achievement.

The black family, for some time, has been described as a vital force in its members' overall efforts to survive and cope, as well as in their efforts toward achievement (Billingsley, 1968; Hill, 1971). Recent studies, whether reporting on the middle-class family (McAdoo, 1977) or perhaps less solvent families (Martin and Martin, 1978), also delineated the support by the black family's kinship network.

The findings in this study generally support the notion of a black family support system, but further clarify specific dynamics of the system. Relative significant others who influenced the achievement of the respondents were not as prevalent as the large, extensive kinship network that has been described as supporting overall survival and coping efforts. (However, in comparison to whites, the black relative significant other was more prevalent, at a significant level.) In addition, it was found that although almost all relative types were identified as being significant others, those closest in blood relationship were more likely to be so designated; and that although relative significant others influenced the respondents through a variety of modes of influence, they tended to influence through modeling.

NONRELATIVE SIGNIFICANT OTHER

More than half (64 percent) of the significant others were nonrelatives, suggesting that, in addition to the parent and the relative, the nonrelative is greatly involved in the achievement of black family members. Furthermore, these nonrelatives were found in almost every segment of the respondents' lives.

The largest group of nonrelatives was the education significant other (47 percent), of which the majority were teachers and professors from grade school through graduate school. Other institutional personnel responsible for different aspects of the educational experience (counselors, administrators, and others) were described, pointing out that the source of the education significant other extended beyond that of the teacher-learner configuration.

The work significant other included administrators, supervisors, and work colleagues from the respondents' job. The appearance of this significant other (18 percent) focuses attention on the role of the work environment in its influence on the individual. It also indicates that the influence occurs during the adult years—a part of the life cycle frequently overlooked in discussions of the significant other—and has implications for adult development theory that is emerging.

Mental health significant others included a playground instructor and a boy scout leader. Characterized as professionals and other helpers who relate to individuals around life coping efforts, these significant others were not prevalent (2 percent) among the respondents.

The religion significant others (8 percent) were ministers for the most part, but included persons outside the church leadership, such as the minister's wife. Half of the respondents also mentioned that black ministers, as a group, influenced their achievement.

Thus, 75 percent of the nonrelatives were from education, work, mental health, and religion—which underscores the importance of the structured institutional environment in the socialization process. Outside the family, such institutional arrangements reflect most of the areas of living. In addition, and particularly germane to black life, is the fact that many of these institutions are white dominated. Thus, their potentiality as a source for significant others is a critical issue.

Close nonkin (11 percent) included peers, family friends, and sweethearts who shared a relationship qualitatively near to that intimacy usually ascribed to caretakers and close relatives. The majority were family friends and were found primarily in the middle class.

Three other types of significant others were categorized: the neighborhood (4 percent), community (4 percent), and the world-at-large (6 percent) significant other. Although only representing 14 percent of all nonrelatives, these types are noteworthy because, along with the significant others from the institutional settings, their presence speaks to the extensiveness of the sources of possible significant others. The neighborhood and one of the subtypes of the world-at-large (the chance encounter) were found only in the lower class, indicating that lower-class respondents "required" significant others from a broader base than the middle class.

Unlike the parent and the relative, the nonrelative significant other did not tend to influence primarily through one mode (Table 16.2). Nonetheless, more than one-third influenced through modeling and/or validation (Table 16.2). Pairing and one-sided pairing, special kinds of modeling described earlier as being characteristic of some cousins, also appeared with a nonrelative—the peer. Pioneering was another instance of modeling in which the significant other penetrated educational and occupational areas previously closed to blacks and "showed that it could be done." After overcoming many obstacles, a lower-class male entered college but worried about job possibilities. One day he heard a black male social worker address a public forum. "He became a role model for job possibilities and opportunities open to blacks. So I switched to social work." A necessary condition for pioneering is a situation in which the significant other—a member of one's own group—can be observed achieving.

The cultural or lofty hero was another instance of modeling and were persons of renown—gracious Marian Anderson of the concert stage and Joe Louis beloved by his people for both his skill and his integrity. The element of pioneering was present also, because the lofty hero was often one of the first blacks to achieve distinction in his or her field and thus opened up a new possibility for other blacks.

There were several nuances of the validation of self mode. The most frequently observed was that of positive defining, in which the significant other articulated a direct positive definition of the respondent. A teacher told a respondent's mother that "'she was very bright and that she should attend college'; it reaffirmed that I was somebody." Along class lines an interesting difference was noted in the manifestations of positive defining. In the middle class there was a tendency for the positive definition, although appreciated, to serve as reinforcement of information already known to the respondent. In the lower class the significant other, in contrast, often offered information that was either unknown and/or not quite believed by the respondent. In the following episode, the respondent's father was dead and the mother, burdened with a large family, worked long, hard hours as a farm laborer. An interested high school teacher "raked me over for considering giving up a scholarship to college. It finally got through to me that I was getting information about myself, and it made me feel important. Maybe, I was worth something."

Another nuance of validation was heritage-reminding, in which the significant other advised the respondent of his or her racial background. One respondent recalled the first time a teacher who happened to be black "taught us black history. It inspired all of us. We really got a sense of what it was like really being black." Although heritage-reminding appeared infrequently as a nuance of validation of self, it was observed as an aspect of other modes. For example, modeling significant others, in demonstrating achievement, sometimes projected a sense of pride in black roots and the need to appreciate it.

More than a third of the nonrelatives influenced through validation of self, indicating that the nonrelative (Table 2) was important in meeting a human need—the need for positive appraisals (Rogers in Maddi, 1968).

It is recalled that the parent exerted influence through the achievement socialization mode either by *establishing* an achievement atmosphere or by *mandating* it. In contrast, the nonrelative influenced through achievement socialization by *stipulating* educational and occupational goals. Such incidents occurred primarily in the lower class, which indicates that they may have required information on the options available to them from others outside the family.

Nonrelatives also influenced through one of the subcategories of learning elicitation: teaching. A respondent recalled her first boss, who "taught me administrative skills and how to handle budgets, committees, and boards." In addition to knowledge and skills, teaching sometimes emphasized the rudiments of everyday living. For example, a significant other articulated thoughts on living in the form of a proverb, such as the one provided by a librarian who employed a respondent as teenager, after school. "'If anything is worth doing, it is worth doing well.' It helped me to incorporate a certain thoroughness in my work." The black elderly was found to use a similar teaching tool the "maxim" in interactions with younger family members (Martin and Martin, 1978).

Most of the family friends (close nonkin) performed supplemental parenting roles—nurturing—through the mode of emotional support. A middle-class female, though loved by her two busy and task-oriented partners, remembered a close family friend who was uneducated but

> who saw me as a child always. She was one of those very good people who always give tender, loving care. She had the capacity to give and the capacity to love. She nurtured me; my mother did not. She gave me something to fall back on; somebody who was always there.

However, the respondent also described her mother as important in her life and as a significant other, but for mandating achievement. This combined input of parent and nonrelative significant other illustrates a kind of partnership in parenting that may characterize some black families.

Numerous nonrelatives, persons outside the family system, influenced the respondents' achievement. Thus, these findings support earlier references to the influence of the nonrelative significant other in the achievement of various groups of black individuals (Billingsley, 1968; Manns, 1974; Shade, 1978). However, the findings additionally indicated that the nonrelative was proportionally more prevalent than the relative and parent, combined, irrespective of class; that although nonrelative significant others were from almost all of the life areas, they were most likely to be from the instructured institutional environment, especially education and to some extent the work arena; and that although they concentrated in influencing through modeling and validation of self, they were more inclined than the parent and the relative to influence in all of the categories of the mode of influence. It is concluded that the nonrelative significant other was an important and necessary presence in the achievement of the respondents.

A profile of the nonrelative significant other was developed. For the most part, the nonrelative significant other tended to be like the respondent on ascribed characteristics, race and sex. Although nonrelative significant others were of both races—black and white—they tended to be black. Since relative and parent significant others were also black, the majority of all significant others who influenced the achievement of the respondents were black. For influence on achievement, members of these black families were dependent primarily, but not exclusively, on their own race.

On achieved characteristics, nonrelative significant others were at a higher educational, income, and community level than the respondents. In a sense, this finding supports an accepted definition of significant other as "someone the individual holds in esteem." Yet is also raises a question. To what extent are potential significant others who influence achievement available to the black lower socioeconomic class, often surrounded by people who are of the *same* or *lower* educational, income, and community levels? This question is particularly relevant to growing attention to the locked-in plight of a special group of the black lower class, the *underclass* (Glasgow, 1980; Wilson, 1980).

Nonrelative significant others were older in age than the respondents. Although nonrelative significant others appeared throughout a large part of the respondents' life cycle, they concentrated during the respondents' childhood, adolescence, and young adulthood, which underscores the importance of the black adult in black life.

This concentration on the influence of the significant other is not intended to negate the role of the black individual's inner resources or self-directiveness, which is also a factor in achievement. Rather, the discussion focused on examining the influence of the many persons who contributed to that achievement and thereby participated in the socialization process of these black families.

REFERENCES

ANGELOU, M. (1969) I Know Why the Caged Bird Sings. New York: Random House.

BILLINGSLEY, A. (1968) Black Families in White America. Englewood Cliffs, NJ: Prentice-Hall.

COOLEY, C. H. (1964) Human Nature and the Social Order. New York: Schocken. (Originally published, 1902)

DENZIN, N. K. (1970) The Research Act. Chicago: AVC.

GLASGOW, D. G. (1980) The Black Underclass. San Francisco: Jossey-Bass.

HALLER, A. O. and J. WOELFEL (1972) "Significant others and their expectations, concepts and instruments to measure interpersonal influence on status aspirations." Rural Sociology 35 (December): 591-621.

HILL, R. B. (1971) The Strengths of Black Families. New York: Emerson Hall.

JONES, R. L. (1981) "The effects of person-environment fit, locus of control and the mother's perception of the teaching behaviors of the significant other on the teaching behaviors of low income Black mothers." Ph.D. dissertation, Case Western University.

KUHN, M. H. (1972) "Major trends in symbolic interaction theory in the past twenty-five years," in J. Manis and B. N. Meltzer (eds.) Symbolic Interaction: A Reader in Social Psychology. Boston: Allyn & Bacon.

McADOO, H. P. (1977) "The impact of extended family variables upon the upward mobility of black families." Final report to Department of Health, Education and Welfare. Washington, DC: Office of Child Development.

MADDI, S. R. (1972) Personality Theories: A Comparative Analysis. Homewood, IL: Dorsey Press.

MANNS, W. (1974) "Significant others in black autobiographies: an exploration." (unpublished)

———— (1977) "Significant others in black autobiographies." Paper presented at conference on

Black Families: A Source of National Strength, sponsored by National Urban League's Project Thrive. Chicago, November.

MARTIN, E. P. and J. M. MARTIN (1978) The Black Extended Family. Chicago: University of Chicago Press.

MEAD, G. H. (1962) Mind, Self and Society, vol. 1 (C. W. Morris, ed.). Chicago: University of Chicago Press. (Originally published, 1934)

QUARANTELLI, E. L. and J. COOPER (1966) "Self-conceptions and others: a further test of Meadian hypotheses." Sociological Quarterly 7 (Summer). Reprinted in J. G. Manis and B. N. Meltzer (eds.) Symbolic Interaction: A Reader in Social Psychology. Boston: Allyn & Bacon, 1972.

SHADE, O. (1978) "Significant other influences on the educational and occupational goals of disadvantaged Afro-American college freshmen." Dissertation Abstracts International, Vol. 38 7200-A.

WALKER, A. (1970) The Third Life of Grange Copeland. New York: Harcourt Brace Jovanovich.

WATERS. E. (1978) His Eye is on the Sparrow: An Autobiography. Westport, CT: Greenwood Press. (Originally published, 1951)

WILSON, W. J. (1980) The Declining Significance of Race. Chicago: University of Chicago Press.

17

GROUP IDENTITY DEVELOPMENT
WITHIN BLACK FAMILIES

JAMES S. JACKSON, WAYNE R. McCULLOUGH,
and GERALD GURIN

INTRODUCTION

Much of the social and psychological literature over the last 40 years on black Americans has dealt, directly or indirectly, with issues of group identification and consciousness. This interest in group identity derives largely from the minority status of blacks in our society. In any minority experiencing discrimination, a central issue becomes how individual group members relate to the group, to its history of discrimination, and, in the case of blacks, to the current active collective struggle to confront a racist system. And *how* they deal with their minority status has been viewed as a critical determinant of their general psychic health and functioning. Writers have differed in whether they focused on the pathological consequences of discrimination or the strength and coping in the face of it. But all have agreed on the central significance of this psychic relationship to the group, the individual's group identity.

AUTHORS' NOTE: We wish to particularly acknowledge Phillip Bowman, Belinda Tucker, and Shirley Hatchett, our collaborators on our ongoing research. They help us formulate our ideas on group identity and consciousness and made major contributions to other substantive and theoretical areas as well. Support for the preparation of this chapter was provided, in part, by the Ford Foundation, the Center for the Study of Minority Group Mental Health, the National Institute of Mental Health, and the National Institute on Aging.

Despite the universal unquestioned assumption of the tie between group identity and psychic health, it is surprising that the actual documentation of this relationship is ambiguous, overly simplistic, and ill-defined (Cross, 1980). Most studies in this area have had serious conceptual and measurement limitations (Banks, 1979). There has been conceptual confusion in the definition of personal and group identity and consciousness, as well as inadequate formulation of the conceptual links between the two sets of concepts. Measurement problems have followed largely, although not entirely, from these conceptual confusions.

The failure of empirical research to confirm a strong and consistently positive relationship between personally held group and self-images suggests strongly that the conceptualization which views images of self and group as inextricably tied may be seriously in error (Cross, 1980; McAdoo, 1976). We argue in the present chapter that the group and personal identity are separate and separable phenomena and may be only tied under certain, specifiable conditions.

Within our conceptualization, the rudiments of the self are conceived as emerging initially in infancy and early childhood and affected primarily by the socialization practices of the family and small insulated community in which the family resides (Young, 1970). Similarly, group identity is conceived to be developed through the person's perceptions, filtered by the family and other primary groups, of the relationships and cleavages which exist in the larger society between and among various social, economic, and political groups. Both personal and group identity development are viewed as essentially cognitive phenomena—one as the self-placement of the individual in relationship to the primary group and local community (who am I); and the other, as the recognition by the individual of the societal placement of the group(s) to which he or she belongs within the stratification system that characterizes a particular society (who are we; who are they). Related to these essential cognitive processes are the affective loadings that become attached to one's individuality and to one's group belongingness.

There is little systematic evidence regarding the buffering and insulating functions and the identity nurturant roles served by the black family in fostering a functional group or personal identity (Taylor, 1976). Similarly, the coping strategies and situational adaptations derived from this identity and fostered in the familial context have not been empirically examined in any detail (Lipscomb, 1975).

The minority family is the important agent of socialization, for it is within the family context that the individual first becomes aware of and begins to grapple with the significance of racism and discrimination (Washington, 1976). The intrafamilial socialization of group and personal identity has considerable bearing on personal functioning in a society which cultivates negative conceptions of minority group members through direct interaction, the media, and institutional barriers. An important social structural factor discussed in this chapter is racial homogeneity or heterogeneity of the socialization environment. How do such environments differentially affect the development and compartmentalization of group and personal identity? Our focus is not only on the degree of racial homogeneity of the socialization environment, but also the timing of socialization and the elements of group and personal identity which are transmitted across generations.

In the remainder of this chapter we will briefly review the major previous literature in this area, discuss some of the conceptual and measurement issues, and note some preliminary thoughts on the role of the family and other selected socialization influences on the development of personal and group identity.

GROUP AND PERSONAL IDENTITY

The literature on black identification and personal functioning can be divided into two distinct periods demarcated by the civil rights movement of the sixties. The studies antedating the civil rights movement focused almost exclusively on supposedly negative effects of black identification. Identifying as black was seen as a "problem," because it meant identifying with an oppressed group and internalizing the negative group image from the dominant white society. Two types of studies predominated in this period: those based on intensive clinical material (Kardiner and Ovesey, 1951), and the empirical studies with young children, mostly around their choices and reactions to black and white dolls. These latter studies were particularly influential in promoting the view that black identity implied self-hatred. Following the early work of the Clarks, a number of these studies showed that, given one choice, a majority of black children tended to choose a white rather than a black doll and saw the white doll as "nice" and the black doll as "bad" (Clark and Clark, 1947; Radke and Trager, 1950; Goodman, 1952; Landreth and Johnson, 1953; Stevenson and Stewart, 1958; Moreland, 1962). These choices were viewed as reflecting rejection of the group and self-hatred.

A critical characterization of these doll studies should be noted: They did not measure group identification and self-feeling as *separate* sets of variables. Rather, the choice of the white doll was seen both as group rejection and self-rejection. The relationship between group rejection and self-rejection was an unquestioned assumption rather than a hypothesis to be empirically tested. This assumption was not peculiar to views of the psychic consequences of black identification; it was applied to the supposed internalization of negative group images held by the majority of individuals belonging to any minority group which experienced discrimination. Many of the writers on black identification and self-rejection referred to Lewin's (1948) classic statement about Jewish

identification. Rejection of one's Jewishness was seen as automatically imply-
ing "self-hatred."

Literature on black identification published during the second period reflects
the influence of the civil rights movement. It differs from the earlier writings in
two major ways. First, although some writers still stress negative black identity
(for example, Gitter et al., 1972), the majority of studies focus on the positive
psychic effects of black identification. This emphasis predominates in the
speculative writings on the psychological impact of the movement, as well as in
the empirical research (Hraba and Grant, 1970; Thomas, 1971; Barnes, 1972;
Hall et al., 1972; Ward and Braun, 1972; Wyne et al., 1974; McAdoo, 1976;
Cross, 1979, 1980). While obviously different in tone, this literature nonetheless shares important conceptual similarities with the work conducted prior to
the civil rights movement. Like the studies that tied negative group identity to
self-rejection and other negative psychological consequences, the newer
studies tie positive identity to high self-esteem and other positive psychological
consequences. Both assume a simple, direct relationship between group identification and psychic outcomes.

A second departure from premovement thinking about black identification is
that recently some writers have directly attacked the assumption of this simple
relationship (Cross, 1980; McAdoo, 1976). For example, Barnes (1972) has
indicated that earlier work that projected a negative identity and a negative
self-image as almost automatic consequences of a powerless minority status
neglects the role family and community can play in mediating the impact of the
wider society on the developing child. The assumption that discrimination is
internalized as self-hatred (rather than as hatred of the oppressing group, for
example) represents the majority group's perspective (and wish). Zavalloni
(1973) stresses this and further argues that the relationship between a particular
group identification and self-attitudes cannot be automatically assumed because any given group identification is only one aspect of a person's social
identity. McAdoo (1976) has also made this point, noting that very few studies
have measured separately racial identification and self-feelings. When measured separately, the two have not consistently been related to each other. While
some empirical studies suggest a positive relationship between black identification and positive self-concepts (Ward and Braun, 1972; Mobley, 1973) other
empirical studies have found no such consistent relationships (Sacks, 1973;
McAdoo, 1976). This inconsistency in the empirical findings has been noted in
three recent reviews of this issue (Cross, 1979, 1980; Porter and Washington,
1979).[1]

This selective review of the literature suggests that we need studies that more
adequately conceptualize the relationship of black identification and consciousness to psychic outcomes, and then subject these conceptualizations to systematic empirical test. A major limitation in existing conceptualizations of group

identification and consciousness has been the tendency to view them simplisti-
cally in "either-or" terms: a person identifies or does not identify, feels pride in
or rejection of the group. This has been true in the writings on group identification and consciousness generally, not just in the literature specific to blacks.
With few exceptions (such as Zavalloni, 1971, 1973), the empirical literature
has not dealt with the fact that the feelings toward the group are usually a
complicated mixture of positive and negative, and the process of identification
usually involves identifying with some aspects of the group and attempting to
disassociate oneself from others (McAdoo, 1976). This is probably particularly
true for minority group members who, no matter the degree of their positive
identification, have to psychologically confront the negative images of their
group found in the majority culture. By overlooking these issues of ambiva-
lence and selective identification, the empirical literature has not only distorted
the phenomena being studied but has also ignored the truly interesting issues in
the relationship between group identity and personal functioning. The critical
issue is not the simple one of positive identity leading to positive personal
effects and negative identity having pathological psychic consequences.
Rather, the critical issue is how the individual balances the negative and positive images of and feelings toward the group, and the extent to which the
individual connects the self to the positive rather than to the negative group
images.

In general, the relationship between group orientations and self-orientation
has been viewed as self-evident. It has seemed an obvious assumption, not
requiring testing, that disassociating oneself from one's blackness implied some
rejection of the self, that feeling pride about black people implied feeling pride
in the self, that blaming blacks for their life conditions implied inappropriate
blaming of the self. The literature has assumed a high degree of permeability
between the boundaries of the group and the boundaries of the self, so that the
view of the group automatically fuses with the view of the self. But, as we have
already indicated, we have not found the empirical evidence to support this
seemingly self-evident assumption (Cross, 1980; McAdoo, 1976). Cross, in a
recent review of this literature, is particularly eloquent on this issue. "It is
disconcerting but true that an entire people have been burdened with an image
of their children as filled with self-hate even though social scientists have never
really empirically demonstrated the link between racial preference behavior and
direct measures of low self-esteem." (Cross, 1979: 30). A recent review by
Porter and Washington (1979) also makes this point.

Why is this true? Why have we not found consistent empirical support for
assumptions that to many seem self-evident and obvious? As we have indicated, we believe the major problem is a conceptual one. The thinking in this
area has been overly simplistic.[2] We need a more complex view of the nature of
an individual's relationship to the group, and of the processes, such as the

family and other major socialization influences, that make this relationship to the group relevant to an individual's self-concepts and personal functioning. In the following pages we turn to a discussion of some of these family and socialization processes.

THE FAMILY AND SOCIALIZATION ENVIRONMENT

FUNCTIONAL SEPARATION OF SELF FROM GROUP MEMBERSHIP

The compartmentalization of group and personal identity, as alluded to earlier, is viewed as psychically functional and allowing for adaptations to the variety of environmental situations confronting the individual. Simmons (1978) describes the possible psychic separation of self from minority group status:

> It is very possible that an individual may rate the black race as less good in general than the white without feeling that he, himself, is less deserving as a total human being. While other minority members may be seen as deserving of societal prejudice, one may view oneself as an exception. . . . At some fantasy level, a person might prefer to be white or lighter skinned without feeling dissatisfied with himself as a total human being. Such fantasies may assume less significance than the fact that he is well-regarded by parents, teachers, and peers (most of whom are also black), or that he is skilled at highly valued activities [1978: 55].

Simmons's statement, relative to personal psychic functioning, suggests several things. First, there is a distinction between personal identity and esteem and group identity, which has important implications for psychological functioning. Second, the individual can actually identify with the outgroup while still maintaining highly valued self-worth. And third, self-worth (personal identity) evolves out of the interaction with the primary group, family, peers, and possibly teachers. If these conditions are likely, as much of the earlier evidence leads us to believe, how is it possible that the compartmentalized identities develop and foster such development?

The suggestion that the socialization environment may have a bearing on the development of identity has some empirical grounding. The optimal environments which foster independent identity development are suggested by several studies (Wellman, 1970; McAdoo, 1976; Porter and Washington, 1979). Hare (1977), in delineating general self-esteem from area-specific self-esteem (school, peer, and home), analyzed data collected from fifth-grade black and white students for the effects of socioeconomic status, race, and sex. He found that home and peer self-esteem were not significantly different by racial group; however, school self-esteem was significantly higher among whites. These findings suggest that the typical racially homogeneous settings (home and peer group) have nurturant effects on self-esteem development. For blacks, only home area-specific esteem accounted for a significant amount of variance in general self-esteem. These data suggest not only a disjunctive development of group and personal identity, but also that the environment may differentially affect their development.

FAMILY AND SOCIALIZATION ENVIRONMENT

As intimated earlier, self-esteem and other aspects of personal functioning are mainly developed in the context of an individual's immediate personal relationships—particularly those involved in early socialization in the family, but also peer relationships and those in the immediate community (Young, 1970). For most blacks in our society this has meant an all-black setting for these formative personal relationships. Self-evaluations develop almost totally with other blacks as the comparative reference group. In contrast, group identification and consciousness develop out of the relationships of blacks to a broader set of influences and referents, those in which the white majority, blacks' relationships with whites, and their experiences in the white-dominated world play the major role. These differences in influences and reference points lead to different and possibly unrelated consequences in self and group orientations. Porter and Washington (1979) point out that this may explain the suggestive findings in the literature antedating the civil rights movement that middle-class blacks were higher in personal self-esteem (where they were comparing themselves predominantly with blacks as a group) but lower in racial esteem (where they were using the majority world as their comparative referent). Cross (1979, 1980) also draws on this difference to explain the findings that the civil rights movement seems to have wrought a great increase in black identification and consciousness but no apparent change in the personal self-esteem of black Americans.

The evidence previously cited suggests that the racial composition, degree, and quality of intergroup contacts may affect the positiveness of personal identity development and its compartmentalization from group identity. If we presume that personal identity development (who am I) temporally precedes the internalization of group identity, the family serves at least two important functions in this early development. First, there is the development of self-worth and the personal frame of reference for achievement and other behaviors in this society. Second, the insulating function of the family serves to lessen the negative and often deleterious consequences of minority group status—for both personal and group identity.

It has been suggested that the racially homogeneous home environment may also serve an insulating or buffering role with regard to personal identity development (Hare, 1977; McAdoo, 1976; Simmons, 1978; Lipscomb, 1975; Porter and Washington, 1979). Self-worth and self-conceptions are formed under the auspices of the family/primary group. In the homogeneous racial environment there are fewer occasions than in the heterogenous environment for negative messages regarding group membership to directly impinge on personal identity development. Thus, the homogeneous environment can help to foster a high degree of individual compartmentalization. Once the development of self is established, integrating conceptions of one's relationship to the group and understanding the group's status in society can be achieved through exposure to images such as art, stories, history, and culture.

Introduction to more racially heterogeneous environments (for example, school or camp) consequently leads to a reduction of the buffering or insulating role played by the family. The family's filtering of input from the larger society is reduced as a broader range of experiences is encountered. As the minority individual gains more intergroup experience, however, the family has an increasing role in interpreting these experiences. This particular role is critical for maintaining the integrity of the already developed early personal identity as well as the developing conceptions of group identity.

In comparison to the homogeneous environment, the racially heterogeneous environment may serve to hasten the development of the individual's group identity (McCullough, 1981). Because most interactions with the dominant culture do not take place until after the establishment of personal identity (Simmons, 1978; Porter and Washington, 1979), the intergroup comparisons which are made help the individual to establish the timber of the individual's relationship to the group, gain an appreciation of the group's status vis-à-vis the dominant group, and examine the overlap of characteristics shared with the group.

The categorical treatment minority individuals receive (as distinct from interpersonal treatment based on individual traits or characteristics) helps to place them within the bounds of the minority group and to discern their group's status with regard to the dominant group (who are we/who are they). Other intragroup and intergroup comparisons help to define further boundaries, commonalities, and other discrepancies between groups. It should also be pointed out that in a nonhostile, nonsegregated, and nondiscriminatory intergroup environment, the development of even a meager sense of belonging to a minority group would undoubtedly be difficult to foster.

Little has been mentioned to this point relative to the role which family ideology about the society serves in identity development. We believe that it is through the enactment of parental ideologies that the external world is buffered and filtered through to the developing individual (Lipscomb, 1975). It is not very likely that individuals socialized to a strong sense of compartmentalized personal identity and a thorough understanding of their minority group status, in addition to the historical cultural underpinnings of their group, will hate themselves because they are black. Possibilities do exist for significant influences outside the family (for example, the peer group) to affect the relative valences of personal and group identities (Hare, 1977). This is plausible in those circumstances where parental ideologies are neither communicated nor grounded in the socialization which transpires. It is also conceivable that minority group members, regardless of the racial homogeneity or heterogeneity of the environment, evolve with an incorporation of group and personal identities which are undifferentiated. Individuals reared in family and environmental settings devoid of an emphasis on separateness may develop an orientation in which their fate is inextricably linked to that of the group. The individual internalizes all images, characteristics, and treatments of the group as statements of his or her individual nature. This fatalism entails a total dependence on the group for "individual definition." The lack of differentiating socialization by the primary group in the racial homogeneous setting or the unbuffered press (categorical treatment and characterizations) by the dominant majority may accentuate this effect.

Related to both conceptual and measurement issues in the role of family ideology, another possibility exists which may account for the differentially observed lack of relationship between group and self-images (Cross, 1980). It is possible that the strong inculcation of black pride and a sense of common fate with other blacks, strong components of group identification and consciousness, may serve to mitigate observed relationships with frequently used measures of self-esteem. In fact, some work suggests that negative relationships are most often demonstrated when group identity is related to highly individualistic, achievement-oriented, and Western-value-dominated measures of self-esteem (Gordon, 1976; Nobles, 1973; Adam, 1978; Taylor and Walsh, 1979). In a recent study of third graders (Rasheed, 1981), it was found that the most highly positively identified black youngsters demonstrated the most negative levels of self-esteem. This relationship was also found in experimental conditions with manipulations designed to increase the level of group identification. Close examination of these data revealed that the most negative relationships existed in those youngsters socialized in the highest and most positive black consciousness situations. We believe a thorough examination of previous studies that have included more academic and individual-achievement-oriented measures of self-esteem (such as the Piers-Harris) have probably obtained similar results. Certainly many of the previous findings in the literature are consistent with this view (Cross, 1980; McAdoo, 1976). In addition to the studies done within the United States that support this interpretation, the findings of some cross-cultural research are also consistent with this position (Brofenbrenner, 1970). Succinctly, we believe that if socialization attempts of parents to inculcate a strong sense of black group identity and consciousness are successful, then we might consistently observe either a negative relationship or no relationship with traditional measures of self-esteem, particularly those that are the most individually achievement-oriented.

CONCLUSIONS

In this chapter we have attempted to review some of the basic literature regarding the meaning, definition, and complexity of group and personal identity. In so doing we directed our attention to the observed relationships between group identification and personal functioning, most often operationalized as self-identity or self-esteem. Some of the problems in the relationships between these concepts were noted, most notably conceptual and methodological problems and the failure of researchers to consider other major factors that may have an important role in the development of both personal and group identity in blacks. Although somewhat speculative because of the lack of strong empirical research, we argued that the family and racial environment may be two important factors in mediating the link between individually held conceptions of the individual and racial group. The role of the racial environment in buffering, insulating, or confronting group membership was briefly reviewed; the functions of the family as a filtering, supportive agent were also mentioned.

Finally, we briefly discussed a possible reason why group and personal identity, as currently conceptualized and measured, might logically and consistently demonstrate a negative relationship with one another. Though highly speculative, some support is available in the literature for a view that the inculcation of black pride and strongly held group images of survival is antithetical to Western-dominated conceptions and measures of self-esteem that are most often used in empirical studies. Under these circumstances, we would predict that blacks who hold the strongest conceptions of group identification may be loath to endorse self-esteem items which stress highly individualistically oriented conceptions of self.

In conclusion, we feel that empirical research is needed on those conditions that affect both group and individual orientations, and that make the group a salient element in the formation of personal identity. Special emphasis should be placed on the study of family relationships and socialization patterns since, as we have argued, the black family is the purveyor of both group and personal identity. Given the simplistic nature of the state of theory in this area, we see the need for more refined and specified theory, rather than the testing of existing theoretical speculations. As we have attempted to argue in this chapter, despite over 40 years of studies and speculations on the relationship between black group and personal identity, we are only beginning to recognize and conceptualize the complexities in this area.

NOTES

1. In addition to these two theoretical reformulations, some recent writings have also raised methodological questions about the earlier work on negative black identity and self-concept. In a review of the studies on preference behavior in blacks, Banks (1979) points out that most of the studies indicate that preferences do not depart from chance; he also questions whether they have demonstrated self-rejection and indicates the need to appreciate the complexity of the issues. In a similar vein, Brand et al. (1974), in their very extensive review of studies of ethnic identification and preference, point up the questionable state of our knowledge in this area. They note that results vary according to method and nine other situational, contextual, and individual variables.

2. An engagement of personal values may also provide some explanation of this simplistic view. Cross makes an interesting comment on how difficult it is to challenge the assumption that there is a direct relationship between group identity and psychological functioning. After noting that we have not been able to demonstrate empirically a direct relationship between RGO (reference group orientations) and PI (personal identity), Cross (1979) comments: "During several recent lectures, this observer has found it difficult to even present the idea that RGO and PI may not be related, so emotional was the response of students and faculty in the audience" (p. 30).

REFERENCES

ADAMS, B. A. (1978) "Inferiorization and self-esteem." Social Psychology 41: 47-53.

BANKS, W. C. (1979) "White preference in blacks: a paradigm in search of a phenomenon." Psychological Bulletin 83 (6): 1179-1186.

BARNES, E. J. (1972) "The black community as the source of positive self-concept for black children: a theoretical perspective," in R. L. Jones (ed.) Black Psychology. New York: Harper & Row.

BRAND, E. S., R. A. RUIZ, and A. M. PADILLA (1974) "Ethnic identification and preference: a review." Psychological Review 81: 860-890.

BROFENBRENNER, U. (1970) Two Worlds of Childhood: U.S. & U.S.S.R. New York: Russell Sage.

CLARK, K. B. and M. P. CLARK (1947) "Racial identification and preference in Negro children," pp. 169-178 in T. M. Newcomb and E. L. Hartley (eds.) Readings in Social Psychology. New York: Holt, Rinehart & Winston.

CROSS, W. E., Jr. (1980) "Black identity: rediscovering the distinction between personal identity and reference group orientation." Presented for Research in Child Development, Study Group, Atlanta, Georgia, December.

CROSS, W. E. (1979) "Black families and black identity development: rediscovering the distinctions between self-esteem and reference group orientations." Presented at the International Seminar on The Child and the Family, Gustovus Adolphus College, St. Peter, Minnesota, August.

GITTER, A. G., D. J. MASTOPHY, and Y. SATOW (1972) "The effect of skin color and physiognomy on racial misidentification." Journal of Social Psychology 88 (October): 139-143.

GOODMAN, M. E. (1952) Race Awareness in Young Children. Reading, MA: Addison-Wesley.

GORDON, V. V. (1976) "Methodologies of black self-concept research: a critique." Journal of Afro-American Issues 4 (3): 373-381.

HALL, W. S., W. E. CROSS, and R. FREEDLE (1972) "Stages in the development of black awareness: an exploratory investigation," in R. L. Jones (ed.) Black Psychology. New York: Harper & Row.

HARE, B. R. (1977) "Racial and socioeconomic variations in preadolescent area-specific and general self-esteem." International Journal of Intercultural Relations 1 (3): 31-59.

HRABA, J. and G. GRANT (1970) "Black is beautiful: a reexamination of racial preference and identification." Journal of Personality and Social Psychology 16: 398-402.

KARDINER, A. and L. OVESEY (1951) The Mark of Oppression. Cleveland, OH: World.

LANDRETH, C. and B. C. JOHNSON (1953) "Young children's responses to a picture and inset test designed to reveal reactions to persons of different skin color." Child Development 24: 63-79.

LEWIN, K. (1948) Resolving Social Conflicts. New York: Harper & Row.

LIPSCOMB, L. (1975) "Socialization factors in the development of black children's racial self-esteem." Presented at the annual meeting of the American Sociological Association.

McADOO, H. P. (1976) "The development of self concept and race attitudes of young black children over time." Presented at Third Conference on Empirical Research in Black Psychology, Cornell University, October.

McCULLOUGH, W. R. (1981) "The development of group identification in Black Americans." Ph.D. dissertation, University of Michigan, Ann Arbor.

MOBLEY, B. (1973) "Self concept and conceptualization of ethnic identity: the black experience." Ph.D. dissertation, Purdue University.

MORELAND, J. K. (1962) "Racial acceptance and preference of nursery school children in a southern city." Merrill Palmer Quarterly 8: 271-280.

NOBLES, W. W. (1973) "Psychological research and the black self-concept: a critical review." Journal of Social Issues 29: 11-31.

PORTER, J. R. and R. E. WASHINGTON (1979) "Black identity and self-esteem: a review of studies of black self-concept." Annual Review of Sociology 5: 53-74.

RADKE, M. J. and H. G. TRAGER (1950) "Children's perceptions of the social roles of Negroes and whites." Journal of Psychology 29: 3-33.

RASHEED, S. (1981) "The development of ethnic identity and self-esteem in Bilalian (black) children." Ph.D. dissertation, University of Michigan, Ann Arbor.

SACKS, S. (1973) "Self-identity and academic achievement of black adolescent males: a study of racial identification, locus of control, self-attitudes, and academic performance." Ph.D. dissertation, Columbia University.

SIMMONS, R. B. (1978) "Blacks and high self-esteem." Social Psychology 41: 54-57.

STEVENSON, H. W. and E. C. STEWART (1958) "A developmental study of race awareness in young children." Child Development 29: 399-409.

TAYLOR, R. L. (1976) "Black youth and psychosocial development: a conceptual framework." Journal of Black Studies 6 (4): 353-372.

TAYLOR, M. C. and E. J. WALSH (1979) "Explanations of black self-esteem: some empirical tests." Social Psychology Quarterly 42 (3): 253-261.

THOMAS, C. (1971) "Boys no more: a black psychologist's view of community." Encino, CA: Glencoe Press.

WARD, S. and J. BRAUN (1972) "Self-esteem and racial preference." American Journal of Orthopsychiatry 42: 644-647.

WASHINGTON, V. (1976) "Learning racial identity," in R. C. Granger & J. C. Young (eds.) Demythologizing the Inner-City Child. Silver Springs, MD: National Association for the Education of Young Children.

WELLMAN, B. (1970) "Social identities in black and white." Sociological Inquiry 41: 57-66.

WYNE, M. D., K. P. WHITE, and R. H. COOP (1974) The Black Self. Englewood Cliffs, NJ: Prentice-Hall.

YOUNG, V. H. (1970) "Family and childhood in a southern Negro community." American Anthropologist 72: 269-288.

ZAVALLONI, M. (1971) "Cognitive processes and social identity through focused introspection." European Journal of Social Psychology 1, (2): 235-260.

ZAVALLONI, M. (1973) "Social identity: perspectives and prospects." Social Science Information 12 (3): 65-91.

PART V

BLACK FAMILY POLICIES AND ADVOCACY

A volume such as this could have concentrated only on the conceptual and empirical literature and be considered complete. However, it was felt that this was a luxury that could not be afforded. As so many of the authors emphasized, the economic plight of the Black family is depreciating rapidly. For that reason, three authors who are actively involved in the field of policy analysis and advocacy were invited to combine their skills as a complement to those of the more academic scholars in other sections of the book. They were asked to share their perceptions of the present situation during this time of flux and what avenues are open to parents and family members if they want to attempt to improve their family and community's economic situation.

Robert Hill, formerly of the Urban League, discusses two kinds of income support programs that have existed for almost a half-century. He explains the extent to which poverty has come to exist within the Black community and the forces that are increasing the need for governmental transfer payments of different kinds. He highlights the fact that much of the payments that are budgeted do not actually go to the poor, but to providers and vendors who are becoming wealthy on programs designed to aid the poor. There is a need for a coordinated examination of the impact of these programs, for most evaluations are made piecemeal on one program at a time. This chapter effectively refutes the claims of those who believe the war on poverty has been "won." The analyses of benefits point to the need for strong action, outlined at the end of Hill's chapter and included in Moore's and Edelman's chapters.

Evelyn Moore, of the National Black Child Development Institute, continues the examination of the policies that are affecting the status of children and their families. She addresses the narrow restrictions that deny assistance to many worthy poor. The children suffer the most from these gaps. Infant mortality is twice as high for Black babies, and the number of Black children in foster care is substantial. There seems to exist a pervasive sensitivity to Black family needs.

Concerns are addressed only when they also become a problem for white families. The welfare system, youth unemployment, the problems related to child care and the tragic lack of health care are all detailed. The statistics on education echo Ogbu's chapter precisely in Blacks' limited education and their inability to pass the minimum competency exams. The need for action is starkly evident. Moore and Edelman both outline efforts that must be made if the situations outlined by Hill and Moore are to be changed in any way.

Marian Wright Edelman, of the Children's Defense Fund, ends the section on an upbeat with positive steps that can and should be taken. Whenever lists are made of all that ails the Black family, the tendency is to become depressed and to feel powerless. Instead, this section gives positive, manageable, but definitive, actions that are within the ability of all families. The premises for effective advocacy are presented in a form that could be disseminated to local parent and community groups. The major premise is that nothing will be done for Black families except what they do for themselves. Both Edelman and Moore outline the ground rules of each institution that must be mastered and then used to advantage, with an effective focus of energy. Family members should not expect rapid change, for they must be prepared to fight a long battle for what they want. The need for unity and focus on real enemies is emphasized.

This section ends where the volume began, with the recognition that the cultural history must be taught to Black children so that they will not take the few gains for granted.

18

MULTIPLE PUBLIC BENEFITS AND
POOR BLACK FAMILIES

ROBERT B. HILL

Millions of Americans experienced extreme social and economic hardships during the Great Depression of the 1930s because of the lack of adequate economic supports to "cushion" its impact. In order to prevent such widespread suffering in the future, a broad range of programs was instituted to provide individuals with some social and economic security against unemployment, poverty, old age, or physical disability. Thus, the Social Security Act of 1935 was passed and has continued to serve as the conerstone of social welfare policies and programs in this nation for almost half a century.

Two kinds of income support programs were established by this legislation—public assistance and social insurance. Public assistance (or "welfare") programs were designed to aid the poor and needy, while social insurance programs were designed to provide benefits to individuals, regardless of economic need, based partly on their own financial contributions to the system. Thus, programs for the poor, such as Aid to Families with Dependent Children (AFDC) and Old Age Assistance (OAA), were instituted at the same time as were key social insurance programs, such as social security and unemployment compensation. The public assistance programs expanded sharply during the War on Poverty era of the 1960s, resulting in a greater mix of *in-kind* (that is Medicaid, food stamps, day care, and so on) and *direct cash* benefits. At the same time, with Americans living longer and longer, social insurance income transfer programs also expanded.

Between 1960 and 1977, social welfare expenditures rose from $53 to $362 billion. Payments for public assistance programs for the poor rose from $8 to $74 billion, while payments for social insurance programs spiraled from $44 to $239 billion from 1960 to 1977. Thus, by 1977, total expenditures for all types of income transfer programs comprised about one-fifth of the nation's gross national product (GNP) (McMillan, 1979).

Because of the wide range of economic support programs, many observers began to claim that poverty had been virtually "abolished" in the United States, since anyone who was hungry, sick, or jobless could "easily" avail themselves of the benefits of some program to reduce their hardship. However, while they "felt" that poverty had been abolished, the official government figures on poverty continued to reveal that the poor were still very much with us. According to the Census Bureau's figures, the proportion of all persons who were poor in the United States remained virtually unchanged (at about 12 percent) between 1968 and 1975. Moreover, these figures also revealed that there were 500,000 *more* poor people in 1975 than there were in 1968 (Anderson, 1980).

Such official poverty figures were especially distressing to proponents of "balanced budgets" and "fiscal austerity," who could not understand how the number of poor people could be increasing at the same time that expenditures for the poor were at record levels. It never occurred to many of them that one reason why there were more poor people in 1975 than in 1968 was because this nation was in the depths of the most devastating recession since the Depression. And this recession occurred only about five years later than another serious economic downturn (during 1969-1971). Consequently, two recessions took place during that interval and resulted in a doubling of the number of unemployed persons between 1968 and 1975. Many of the "poverty has been abolished" proponents find it hard to believe that poverty actually increases when unemployment soars! Furthermore, they fail to take account of the fact that, concurrently, double-digit inflation is vastly outstripping the rate of increase in governmental expenditures for the poor. Many recent analyses have revealed that the "real" benefits to the poor (in constant dollars) are in fact less today than they were five years ago.

But to such proponents, the real villain is not recession or inflation, but the inaccurate statistics of the U.S. Census Bureau. They argue, correctly, that the official poverty statistics are based primarily on *cash* income (that is, from earnings, social security, welfare, interest, dividends, pensions, rents, and so on) and do not take account of *in-kind* benefits to the poor (such as Medicaid, food stamps, free school lunches, day care, and public housing). They argue, incorrectly, that since these in-kind benefits are "universally" available to the poor, when they are "cashed out" in dollar value, the "real" incomes of the poor take most of them far above the official poverty level.

One research arm of Congress, the Congressional Budget Office (CBO), undertook an analysis of the impact of in-kind benefits to the poor in 1977.

Consequently, using various assumptions and techniques, it cashed out the in-kind benefits to the poor and succeeded in reducing the official poverty figures to half—from 12 to 6 percent. Other economists were able to reduce the proportion even further—to 3.6 percent. None of these analyses, however, attempted to cash out the wide range of in-kind benefits available to the nonpoor—such as employer-paid health insurance, sick leave, paid vacations, maternity leave, free college tuition for children of alumni, free or sharply reduced air or rail travel, perquisites as a result of private club memberships, and fraternal associations—as well as noncash assets and liberal tax loopholes and benefits. It is invalid to cash out only the in-kind benefits of the poor and attempt to depict the poor relative to the nonpoor in this nation. An accurate description of the economic well-being of the poor relative to the nonpoor requires the cashing out of in-kind benefits, noncash assets and tax payments, as well as tax benefits among *both* groups (U.S. Congress, Congressional Budget Office, 1977).

Furthermore, such across-the-board cashing out of in-kind benefits for the poor are based on the unproven assumption that most of the poor actually receive most of these benefits. In fact, studies that were based on the "actual" benefits received by the poor, rather than on simulations of "potential" benefits, have found that most of the poor do not in fact receive most of these in-kind benefits. In addition, certain in-kind benefits (such as Medicaid, which is paid to the vendor and not to the poor recipient) are much more difficult to cash out than other kinds of in-kind benefits (such as food stamps). Based on the cashing out mentality, the sicker the poor get, the richer they become. And, as Mollie Orshansky has often chided, the poor who die in the hospital after an extended period of hospitalization are the "wealthiest" of all—for they have clearly benefited the most from their Medicaid entitlements (Orshansky et al., 1978).

Yet the issue of the actual extent of poverty in this nation is not merely a debate among statisticians and economists. Major cutbacks in expenditures to the poor are occurring daily throughout the nation—there is a widespread belief that severe economic hardships are not extensive in the United States today because:

(a) existing economic support programs, such as unemployment insurance, welfare, and food stamps, provide adequate levels of benefits to the poor, jobless, help-less, and infirm; and

(b) these income cushions are easily available to virtually all who are in acute economic distress.

Consequently, many policymakers sincerely believe that (1) most unem-ployed persons are receiving unemployment compensation; (2) almost all poor families are receiving either AFDC, SSI, or General Assistance (GA); and (3) all AFDC recipients are benefiting from Medicaid and food stamps. They find it difficult to concede the possibility that most of these programs and benefits may not in fact be reaching most of those who need them, especially among blacks and other minorities.

Unfortunately, no studies have been conducted to determine the extent to which the minority poor have benefited from the *broad* range of governmental economic support programs. Most studies have usually focused on the participation of minorities in only one income transfer program at a time; they have not systematically assessed the extent to which multiple benefit participation occurs among the minority poor and jobless. The primary purpose of this chapter is to make such an assessment. It is vital that policymakers and social action groups be provided with empirical data in place of speculations concerning the "universality" of income cushions for the poor, especially among minorities.

The NUL Black Pulse Survey will provide the primary data base for this report. The Black Pulse is a nationwide survey of 3000 black households conducted by the National Urban League and its affiliates in the fall and winter of 1979. It was designed to (a) assess the needs and status of blacks in such areas as employment, housing, child care, education, health, crime, political participation, family patterns, and discrimination; and (b) attempt to determine the extent to which major governmental policies, programs, and services were in fact reaching blacks and meeting their needs. Thus, it provides a unique opportunity to systematically determine the extent to which major government economic support programs are indeed "cushions" for blacks who are poor and jobless.

IMPACT OF INCOME CUSHIONS ON BLACKS

Because of the sharp increase in the level of spending for both social insurance and public assistance programs over the past decade, many commentators, such as Martin Anderson, are declaring that the "war on poverty has been won" and that "poverty has been virtually eliminated in the U.S.":

> The key criteria by which to judge the efficacy of welfare programs are two: the extent of coverage and the adequacy of support.
>
> Coverage of the eligible welfare population is now almost universal—if one is sick, or is hungry, or cannot work, or is blind, or has small children to care for, or is physically disabled, or is old—then there are dozens of welfare programs whose sole purpose is to provide help.
>
> And the level of help is substantial. Virtually all people who are eligible qualify for government checks and government-provided services that automatically left them out of the offical ranks of poverty. . . .
>
> There will be isolated instances where a person is unaware of being eligible, or is unjustly denied aid by a welfare bureaucrat or simply chooses not to accept the

social stigma of being on welfare. But these cases are the exceptions. In fact, just the opposite concern—those getting welfare who have no right to it—is the one that seems to be growing [Anderson, 1980].

Several studies of income transfer programs strongly challenge Anderson's assumption about the "universality" of coverage of the eligible poor population. Moreover, we contend that among certain segments of the poor, especially blacks and other minorities, the unjust denial of aid is not "isolated instances" or "exceptions."

Unfortunately, although there appears to be widespread consensus concerning the easy availability of public assistance benefits to minorities, there have been few systematic studies of the extent of participation of minorities in the various income transfer programs—both cash and in-kind. Moreover, surprisingly, there have been even fewer studies of the extent of multiple benefit participation of the poor—whether black or white. Most observers merely assume that all welfare families *automatically* receive Medicaid, food stamps, free lunches, housing subsidies, and so on without systematically verifying the extent to which this is the case.

Perhaps the most comprehensive attempt to determine the incidence of multiple benefits in income transfer programs on a nationwide basis was undertaken in the early 1970s by the U.S. Congress Joint Economic Committee's Subcommittee on Fiscal Policy under the chairmanship of Martha Griffiths. Based primarily on samples drawn from administrative case records in selected areas across the nation, estimates were derived concerning the extent of program overlap by beneficiaries of cash and in-kind income transfers. Attempts also made to estimate the value of in-kind benefits to participants (U.S. Congress Joint Economic Committee, 1974).

This congressional committee study revealed that sizable proportions of the poor did not receive most of the multiple benefits for which they were "automatically" eligible. For example, although most all AFDC recipients were supposed to be covered by food stamps or food distribution programs, it estimated that only about two-thirds of them participated in either one of those food programs. Moreover, it estimated that only 50 percent of AFDC children benefited from free or reduced-price school lunches, while only 13 percent of AFDC benefited from publicly subsidized housing. Since this analysis did not present its data by race, it was not possible to determine whether or not there were racial differentials regarding participation in multiple income transfer programs.

Government agencies tend to conduct special studies and surveys to determine the extent of participation in only the income transfer programs funded by those agencies. For example, the Agriculture Department periodically conducts studies of characteristics of food stamps households; HUD's Annual Housing Survey obtains data on extent of participation in public housing units; HEW conducts a survey every two years on the characteristics of AFDC families; and the Labor Department conducts its own studies of the characteristics of participants in employment and training programs. Consequently, there is no *one* government survey that periodically obtains information on the nature and extent of participation in income transfer programs that cut across various agencies. It is for this reason that most of the assumptions about "universal coverage" and "multiple benefits" of the poor are based more on speculation than on systematic examination of actual program participation.

One government effort that should significantly enhance this nation's knowledge concerning the nature and extent of participation in various cash and in-kind income transfer programs is the proposed Survey of Income and Program Participation (SIPP) under the direction of the Department of Health and Human Services (HHS; formerly HEW). This SIPP survey is currently in its pilot phase, but once fully operational, it may eventually obtain program participation data from as many as 100,000 households. Although this effort is being sponsored by HHS, it is envisioned that information relating to income transfer programs funded by other government agencies would also be incorporated in this survey.

However, in order to obtain current information on the extent of participation of blacks in the various income transfer programs, the National Urban League included questions related to this area in its nationwide survey (the "Black Pulse") of 3000 black households conducted during the fall and winter of 1979.

The Black Pulse asked *only* the heads of household (either a husband or wife or an unmarried adult head) about the extent to which members of that household had received income or other benefits from the following "means-tested" sources over the past year:

(1) public assistance or welfare
(2) Supplemental Security Income (SSI)
(3) Medicaid
(4) Food Stamps
(5) Free school lunches
(6) Public housing
(7) Rent subsidy.

Information was also obtained concerning receipt of income or benefits from non-income-based social insurance programs, such as social security, Medicare, workmen's compensation, government pensions, and veterans benefits. In order to keep the face-to-face interviews within a manageable length of time, no information was sought concerning the amount of income households received from these various sources.

In order to determine the extent of multiple participation of blacks in income transfer programs for the poor, an index was developed consisting of the seven income-based benefits listed above. This was scaled from 0-7 and indicated only the *number* of different income benefits received. In later studies, we intend to examine these multiple benefits patterns according to the various types of combinations (welfare and SSI; food stamps, SSI, and welfare; public housing, welfare, free lunches, and Medicaid, and so on).

UNEMPLOYMENT INSURANCE

The Black Pulse survey revealed that the overwhelming majority (70 percent) of unemployed black household heads received no income from unemployment compensation. Only one-tenth (11 percent of the unemployed black household heads were currently receiving jobless benefits, while 18 percent had exhausted their benefits because of their extended periods of unemployment.

But these findings are not too surprising, since the majority of the unemployed are not eligible for unemployment insurance, because they have not been laid off. Therefore, we examined the extent to which blacks who had been laid off received jobless benefits. Once again, the Black Pulse Survey revealed that even the majority (56 percent) of laid-off unemployed black household heads had not received any jobless benefits. Only 20 percent were currently receiving benefits, while one-fourth (24 percent) had used up their benefits.

Although only a small fraction of the unemployed received unemployment benefits, one should not conclude that they did not receive any income support. In fact, about half (52 percent) of all the unemployed black household heads were on welfare. Dependence on public assistance was especially significant among the unemployed who had used up their jobless benefits (58 percent) or who had never had any unemployment benefits (53 percent). Only one-fourth (26 percent) of the unemployed who were currently receiving unemployment compensation also received public assistance. Thus, since unemployment insurance is less available to jobless blacks, there is a greater need for them to rely on public assistance to meet their family needs during extended periods of unemployment, especially in times of recession.

PUBLIC ASSISTANCE

Although about half of unemployed blacks receive public assistance, one should not infer that a similar proportion of *all* black households are on welfare. On the contrary, only about one-fourth (24 percent) of all black households received some public assistance. The Current Population Surveys conducted by the Census Bureau have also regularly revealed that about one-fourth of all black families were on welfare.

Interestingly, however, over half of all low-income black households are *not* on welfare. The Black Pulse Survey revealed that 56 percent of all black households with income under $6000 receive no income from public assistance. Moreover, 60 percent of all black households with no income from wages also did not receive any income from welfare benefits. Thus, contrary to popular belief, over half of all poor black households receive no income from welfare.

MULTIPLE BENEFITS

Since it is widely believed that welfare families are automatically eligible for virtually all of the other income transfer programs for the poor, we decided to determine the extent to which this was the case among blacks. In the Black Pulse Survey, except for food stamps, a significant majority of black households on welfare did not receive most of the other benefits. For example, although all welfare households are supposed to be eligible for Medicaid, only half (51 percent) of black welfare families reported that they had Medicaid coverage. Moreover, only one-third (32 percent) of welfare families were in public housing units, and only one-fourth (25 percent) received rent subsidies. And, only 45 percent of black welfare households received free school lunch benefits, while 72 percent of them participated in the food stamp program.

The extent of participation of low-income black households in general in income assistance programs for the poor was lower than that of households on welfare. For example, among black households with income under $6000 only 51 percent received food stamps; 39 percent were covered by Medicaid; 33 percent were in public housing; one-fourth had rent subsidies (25 percent) and free school lunches (25 percent); and only 22 percent had SSI. Thus, it is apparent that large segments of the "eligible" poor black population are not in fact receiving most of the so-called universal benefits for the poor.

These findings further underscore the need to distinguish "potential" and "actual" benefits from income transfer programs. Two past studies that made significant contributions in this area were a later study by the Joint Economic Committee, "How Public Welfare Benefits are Distributed in Low-Income Areas," which used actual case records from various administrative agencies of recipients in six poverty areas across the nation, and a Rand Corporation study, *Multiple Welfare Benefits in New York City* (1976), which used agency records in New York City to examine the actual multiple benefit participation of 42,450 AFDC recipients. Both studies found that actual participation of low-income groups in various income transfer programs was much lower than revealed by simulation research studies of "potential" participation based on categorical eligibility. In addition, both studies revealed quite a wide range of combinations of benefits received by the poor—depending on their individual circumstances. The findings from these and related studies of actual participation patterns were reinforced by results from the Black Pulse Survey when key means-tested income transfer were combined into an Index of Economic Benefits for the Poor (U.S. Congress, Joint Economic Committee, 1974; Rand Corporation, 1976).

INDEX OF ECONOMIC BENEFITS FOR THE POOR

As we observed previously, an Index of Economic Benefits for the Poor was developed by combining seven income-based public assistance programs— welfare, SSI, Medicaid, public housing, rent subsidy, food stamps, and free school lunches. Although the index was scored 0-7, none of the 3000 Black Pulse households received all seven of the benefits. Therefore, the results actually ranged from 0 to 6.

First, contrary to the popular image of most black families being dependent on public assistance programs, the Black Pulse Survey revealed that almost half (45 percent) of all black households did not receive benefits from any of the seven best-known income support programs for low-income persons. And only 20 percent benefited from one of the seven low-income programs. In other words, about two-thirds (65 percent) of all black households participated in only one or none of these seven income programs for low-income persons.

However, these results may not be too surprising for those who believe that the majority of black families are already "middle-class" and have no need to participate in income support programs for the poor. But one would expect the overwhelming majority of *low-income* black households to receive most of these governmental benefits for the poor.

On the contrary, the Black Pulse Survey also revealed that the majority of low-income black households are also *not* recipients of most of these "universal" income cushions for the poor. In fact, one-fifth (20 percent) of all black households with incomes under $6000 participated in none of the seven income programs for the poor, and another 20 percent received benefits from only one of the seven programs. Similarly, one-fourth (24 percent) of the black households with no income from wages also received no benefits from any of the seven programs, while 18 percent benefited from only one of the seven programs. In short, about two-fifths of all poor black households received benefits from only one or none of the seven most popular and heavily funded income transfer programs for the poor. Clearly, these results suggest that the billions of dollars in expenditures for those programs are not being effectively targeted to the black poor across the nation.

But what about multiple participation among black households that are already receiving at least one of these benefits? Certainly, there should be a high level of multiple use among low-income families that have been reached by one of these programs for the poor.

Results from the Black Pulse Survey do reveal, as might be expected, that recipients of one of these benefit programs are more likely than low-income persons who are not recipients to participate in other income transfer programs from the poor—but not to the extent that simulation studies of potential benefit participation suggest.

For example, only 7 percent of the welfare recipients benefit from none of the other six programs. But 19 percent benefit from only one of the remaining six programs for the poor, while one-third (32 percent) benefit from only two additional income support programs. In other words, more than half (58 percent) of all black welfare recipients benefit from two or less of the six remaining programs. These findings are quite startling, since most policymakers (as well as the general public) believe that welfare recipients are "automatically" eligible for Medicaid, food stamps, free school lunches, rent subsidies, and public housing.

But eligibility should not be equated with participation. Although further in-depth analysis will be made of the Black Pulse data in order to be more definitive about the "eligibility" of households based specifically on their household size and other attributes, these preliminary findings strongly suggest that even the majority of black welfare households are not benefiting from most of the major government income programs for the poor.

If the majority of welfare households are not receiving benefits from most of these economic support programs, it is not surprising to note that multiple participation is even lower among recipients of other programs. For example, one-fifth (18 percent) of SSI recipients receive benefits from only that program, while 27 percent benefit from only one additional program. Similarly, 16 percent of Medicaid recipients benefit from none of the remaining six programs, while 19 percent benefit from only one additional program. One-fourth (23 percent) of public housing recipients receive no benefits from any of the other six programs, while 19 percent benefit from only one additional programs. Likewise, 47 percent of free school lunch recipients either get no benefits (29 percent) from any of the remaining six programs or only one (18 percent) additional benefit. But while 22 percent of food stamps recipients benefit from only one of the remaining six programs, 11 percent receive benefits only from the food stamps program. In short, excluding welfare recipients, between one-third and one-half of the recipients of other public assistance programs receive only one or no benefits from the remaining six income transfer programs for the poor.

In sum, these preliminary findings from the Black Pulse Survey revealed the following:

(1) Only one-fifth of all unemployed blacks who have been laid off their jobs currently receive unemployment benefits.
(2) About two-fifths of all low-income black households received benefits from only one or none of the seven most popular income support programs for the poor.

(3) About one-fourth (26 percent) of all blacks on welfare benefited from only one or none of the other six income transfer programs for the poor.
(4) Between one-third and one-half of the nonwelfare public assistance recipients received benefits from only one or none of the other six income support programs.
(5) Two-thirds (65 percent) of all black households received benefits from only one or none of the seven income support programs for the poor.

CONCLUSIONS

These findings strongly suggest that large segments of the low-income black population in this nation are not being reached by most of the major government income transfer programs for the poor and jobless. Why these "universal" income cushions are not readily available to most low-income blacks has not been revealed by this study. Some of the black poor may be unaware of these programs; some may be aware but, because of pride, may refuse to apply for their benefits; some may be unjustly denied benefits for both racial and nonracial reasons; and many may not be "eligible" based on unique regulations of their states. And, most significantly, many of them may have been former recipients in one or more of these programs but were removed from the rolls as a result of more stringent eligibility criteria due to budget-cutting and budget-balancing efforts at the federal, state, and local levels.

Moreover, these results also indicate that it is erroneous to cash out all the *potential* benefits to the poor, since they do not receive most of them. And, that, if the benefits they actually received were cashed out, most of them would still probably remain *below* the official poverty level!

Furthermore, these data indicate that the black community was already in a state of economic depression before the onset of the current recession during the first half of 1980. Thus, this recession, which was deliberately induced by the government as a primary means of fighting inflation, clearly is being borne disproportionately by blacks across the nation. This fact was especially highlighted in an earlier Black Pulse report that revealed that one-fourth of all black heads of households were unemployed during the last quarter of 1979.

Based on these results, we feel that some of the following actions should be taken by major policymakers:

(1) Efforts to insure full employment for *all* groups in this nation should be mounted as a number one priority—especially during this current recession.
(2) There should be more effective targeting of economic support programs to the poor and jobless in the black community.
(3) Insensitive and punitive eligibility criteria for economic support employment and income programs should be removed.

(4) Intensive efforts should be made to eliminate or reduce racially discriminatory practices in the administration of economic support programs at the federal, state, county, and city levels.

(5) Surveys of the needs of minority and low-income groups should be conducted periodically in order to determine systematically the extent to which government programs are in fact reaching those most in need of them.

REFERENCES

ANDERSON, M. (1980) How to Think About Welfare for the 1980's. Testimony before the U.S. Senate Committee on Finance, Subcommittee on Public Assistance; Senior Fellow, Hoover Institution, Stanford University. Washington, D.C.

McMILLAN, A. (1979) "Social welfare expenditures under public programs, fiscal year 1977." Social Security Bulletin 42(6). 3-13.

ORSHANSKY, M., H. WATTS, B. SCHILLER, and J. KORKEL (1978) "Measuring poverty: a debate." Public Welfare (Spring): 46-55.

Rand Corporation (1976) Multiple Welfare Benefits in New York City. Santa Monica, CA: Rand Corporation.

U.S. Congress, Congressional Budget Office (1977) Expenditures for Health Care: Federal Programs and their Effects. Washington, DC: Government Printing Office.

U.S. Congress, Joint Economic Committee, Subcommittee on Fiscal Policy (1974) "National survey of food stamp and food distribution program recipients: a summary of findings on income sources and amounts and incidence of multiple benefits." Studies in Public Welfare, Paper No. 17. Washington, DC: Government Printing Office.

U.S. Congress, Joint Economic Committee, Subcommittee on Fiscal Policy (1973) "How public welfare benefits are distributed in low-income areas." Studies in Public Welfare, Paper No. 6. Washington, DC: Government Printing Office.

19

POLICIES AFFECTING THE STATUS OF
BLACK CHILDREN AND FAMILIES

EVELYN K. MOORE

INTRODUCTION

Black families join other minority groups in America in being disproportionately impacted by the decisions of public policymakers at state, national, and local levels. For those families whose incomes are low enough to qualify, an array of programs are available to help meet needs that range from housing to health. Far too often, however, while many programs constructively assist some Black families, others fail to reach adequately the targeted population or else view their client families with such a negative slant that their effect tends to be minimal. Equally as important, many Black families do not qualify for government programs because of narrow eligibility restrictions ranging from family income to such arbitrary restrictions as family structure. The consequences of such unresponsive public policy often fall heaviest on children, many of whom must forever shoulder the ultimate burdens of unfair labeling, classification, and stigmatization. In every sphere—public education, child welfare, and health—Black children face enormous public policy barriers which impede their opportunity for healthy development. Because children can neither vote nor lobby for themselves, they have received low priority on the family advocacy scale. Hence, this chapter on family advocacy will focus on the critical effect public policy has on children.

Misdirected or inadequate services pervade nearly every facet of the policy arena. Beginning with research, which undergirds subsequent policy development, the Black family is often examined from such a negative framework that usually only the most disadvantaged families are given concerted attention. Most early childhood development studies, for instance, consider only extremely poor children who seem to need a drastic "rescue," even though children slightly better off would probably benefit just as well from a similar program. When translated into public policy, positive findings have led to strong federal support for Head Start, an outstanding program aimed at the very poor, but relatively little backing for any child development programs targeted at a wider population. Ironically, then, the government often limits its successful programs only to those families it deems "inadequate." Yet, when other programs, such as those in the child welfare system, destructively intervene in Black family life, the government displays few such inhibitions. Whether they are inadequate in scope or excessive in their zeal to affect families, many individual programs often do not incorporate Black leadership in either planning or administration, thus permitting some services to merely "treat" Black families rather than constructively support them.

To eliminate stereotyping, inappropriate interventionism, and even indifference in public policy will require concerted cooperation from the Black community and support from allies. Yet before a constructive response to the problems facing many Black families will ever be instituted, an advocacy campaign must be waged simply to erase negative and damaging views. Books, reports, and speeches can only begin to cut into such deeply rooted and strongly protected perspectives; ultimately, only the involvement of families themselves in the public arena will awaken the most intransigent of policymakers to a positive view toward Black families. Without such a change in attitude, the efforts to reform public policy will continue to stumble.

SPECIFIC ISSUES

It will not be easy to erode the pervasive insensitivity toward Black family needs. Historically, Black concerns have infiltrated public awareness only when they have either affected white families to a similar magnitude or else reached such epidemic proportions among Black families that the national conscience cannot help but be touched. Child care, to cite just one of the countless examples, has always been a major concern for Black women, who have traditionally worked to meet their families' most essential economic needs; in 1978, for instance, 66 percent of all married Black mothers worked or sought work (Waldman et al., 1979). From 1970 to 1978, the participation of married white mothers in the labor force jumped from 30 to 49 percent (Waldman et al., 1979). With this recent acceleration of white mothers into the labor force, child care has become such a significant issue as to merit a national debate and a national response. Alternately, with an issue such as infant mortality, which occurs at twice the rate for Black babies as it does for white (National Center for Health Statistics, 1980), public policy at best offers a token acknowledgement of the problem. Indeed, despite the startling fact that Black infants die at the same rate that white infants did over 20 years ago, existing programs proven effective at reducing infant mortality are severely underfunded, while new legislative initiatives, such as the Child Health Assurance Plan, have repeatedly failed to pass Congress. In each of the following areas, then, the inadequacy of public policy at least partially derives from an inherent insensitivity to Black concerns in general.

INCOME MAINTENANCE

Upon the enactment of the Social Security Act of 1935, the United States openly acknowledged that families and individuals are entitled to some minimum floor of support from the public sector when their general welfare is in jeopardy. Many poor Black families have found, however, that even as their numbers and their relative distance from the American mainstream have increased over the past decade (Hill, 1980), government policies have not responded with an effectively consistent or constructive program. Unfortunately, the welfare system of 1981 remains a fragmented structure that minimally supports families up to the point that they do not qualify for assistance, but it does not provide them with the resources necessary for genuine self-sufficiency. Hundreds of thousands of low-income working families (the "working poor") are therefore trapped with earnings too high to qualify for public assistance and jobs too menial and low-paying to raise them out of poverty. Children, who receive more than two-thirds of all federal welfare payments, are the true victims of this inadequate scope.

As the principal federal vehicle of public assistance, the Aid to Families with Dependent Children (AFDC) program has provided basic economic support to countless families. Nevertheless, due to serious deficiencies in its structure, the program has yet to reach all needy families, while those who are served receive vastly differing benefits depending on their state. Slightly less than half of all states do not, for instance, extend AFDC coverage to families with unemployed fathers, no matter how low their annual income. For two-parent families whose incomes are below state AFDC eligibility levels, such a restriction either condemns them to a marginal income of less than $4000 per year or forces the father to leave his family in order to make his family eligible for aid. Even beyond such an unrealistic approach to family structures, individual payments vary to such a degree from state to state and region to region that benefits in the Northeast are more than double those in the South, where eight states pay less than $40 per month per recipient. At that low a base and without quality training and other services, most families may well leave the welfare rolls, but many will not escape poverty and even fewer will achieve a "marginal" standard of living.

The inadequacies of American welfare policy certainly affect a wide variety of families and children, well under half of whom are Black. Nevertheless, by sheer virtue of the fact that 42 percent of all Black children live in poverty (U.S. Bureau of the Census, 1980), the issue holds particular significance for many Black families. If 42 percent of all white children lived in poverty, the country would undoubtedly demand drastic and immediate action to counter a clear national emergency. Indeed, even if the mass media or influential policymakers just acknowledged and promoted the fact that the majority of AFDC recipients are white, welfare reform would probably be a much more popular and less divisive issue. Sadly, then, so long as poverty is perceived as a peripheral concern for most white families, public policy will continue to provide only the barest of cushions for Black children.

CHILD WELFARE

The child welfare system is but one example of a well-intentioned, yet frequently destructive, program with an inappropriate approach toward Black families. Originally developed to protect and nurture children when their families were no longer capable of such functions, the child welfare system now, in fact, often inappropriately removes children from their natural homes and locks them in long-term foster care. Unfortunately, the negative perspectives are pervasive in the system—in order to save children, families must be dissolved regardless of the long-term consequences. Once taught to work within this system, many social workers consequently remove children without first considering the needs of the family within a cultural context; they fail to explore viable alternatives to foster care, such as supporting the natural family unit through a crisis or utilizing relatives, and they often deny poor parents the opportunity to overcome a particular stressful situation, such as unemployment. No individual can be blamed for such actions, however, when the entire system places such an emphasis on saving children from even a remote possibility of abuse or neglect that few supportive services to prevent family disruption are made available by states and localities.

For Black children, who are disproportionately likely to live in poverty, often under extreme duress, such practices have had extreme consequences. Anywhere from 28 to 40 percent of the 500,000 children estimated to live currently in foster care are Black, and these children are much more likely to be inappropriately placed, to have long-term placements, and to be denied equitable services than are their white counterparts (National Black Child Development Institute, 1980). Again, because of an underlying structural insensitivity toward Black families, Black children in foster care face inordinate obstacles that prevent them from either returning home or finding new permanent placements through adoption. Ironically, then, the very system that was created to help children and their families eventually fractures Black families and deprives Black children of a permanent supportive home.

How does this deplorable situation reflect on public policy? Put simply, when a child welfare policy is established to separate families if their problems become insurmountable, Black families will suffer most, since—almost by definition—the system does not view Black families in a positive, constructive light. Those strengths within Black families and communities that could be utilized to avoid family disruption, such as the extended family network (Hill, 1977), are ignored, while potentially helpful and cost-effective services, like family advocacy, day care, and homemakers, are unavailable. One recent reform of the system, Public Law 96-272, does address many of these problems, but ultimately its success will also depend on whether the institutions and practitioners that judge Black families start to acknowledge family strengths before they weigh family problems.

YOUTH UNEMPLOYMENT

Although the pervasive unemployment of Black youths is not necessarily a family issue per se, its magnitude is so pandemic, and the public response so inadequate, that its ramifications for Black families are severe and unavoidable. To examine how public policy has responded to the frightening 39 percent unemployment rate for Black youths (U.S. Bureau of Labor Statistics, 1979), it is more instructive to examine a government effort to prevent youth unemployment than to discuss any of the current programs which only "treat" the current crisis.

As a service specifically intended to train youths with the skills they will need for useful employment, vocational education holds a great promise for reducing at least some of the impediments to assimilating Black teenagers into the work force. Despite its vast potential as a preventive program, vocational education in practice, has failed to provide its Black students with the same progressive training accorded to their white counterparts. According to recent survey data, Black students enrolled in vocational training programs are vastly overrepresented in those courses geared toward low wage, low upward mobility, and low demand occupations (U.S. Office of Civil Rights, 1979b). It is not a coincidence, then, that less than 15 percent of those students enrolled in electronics classes are Black, in contrast to 65 percent of the textile production students; that Black students are more likely to be enrolled as clerk-typists than as secretaries; and that only 8 percent of vocational education teachers and 6 percent of all supervisors are Black (U.S. Office of Civil Rights, 1979b). Again, the mere provision of minimal assistance seems sufficient to mollify any public concern for training and unemployment prevention.

It is a further demonstration of the basic indifference of public policy that a program intended to help Black youths step into productive, meaningful positions in the work force should instead prove only to give token benefits to those students with the greatest needs. Apparently, most local supervisors are more than content that Blacks receive minimal vocational training; the purpose and the quality are irrelevant. In this instance, as in many others, unless Blacks begin to design, administer, and provide actual services, the program will probably never meet the real needs of its federally targeted population.

CHILD CARE

As a simultaneous source of early childhood education and necessary support for working Black parents, child care holds particular importance for Black families. Considering this doubly crucial role of child care, it is especially tragic that quality child care options are mostly limited either to "comfortable" families with incomes high enough to afford the steep price of quality care, or to extremely poor families, who can receive federal subsidies. "Working poor" families whose incomes are too high to qualify for subsidies must therefore forego quality care to preserve their economic independence; again, government neglects many deserving Black families even though their child care needs are as urgent as those of the most impoverished families.

The present child care system in the United States is largely an uncoordinated patchwork that varies from Head Start and other comprehensive preschool programs to licensed day care to care by neighbors. Title XX, a federally funded block grant program for social services, subsidizes licensed child care for approximately 850,000 low-income children, 40 percent of whom are Black, but many more families who need child care assistance lie beyond its scope. Although the program was originally intended to help families make a successful and permanent transition from welfare to self-sufficiency, the presence of rigid cutoff levels for eligibility (often at 60 percent of a state's median income) actually impede, if not prevent, parents from leaving welfare or even obtaining a second job (Hosni, 1979). In other words, many families must remain poor if they are to obtain quality care for their children.

Such an ironic "Catch-22" situation is especially painful in light of the proven benefits that quality care can hold for children (Ruopp et al., 1979), the rising number of Black families headed by single mothers (39 percent, according to the U.S. Bureau of the Census, 1979), and the still disproportionately large numbers of Black working married mothers (Waldman et al., 1979). Recent longitudinal studies have shown that early childhood programs can hold lasting benefits for children by reducing special education placements, improving academic achievement and school attendance, and even lowering the incidence of juvenile delinquency (Consortium for Longitudinal Studies, 1979), yet a large segment of Black families have no access to such care.

That the largest single federal expenditure for child care, an income tax credit for child care expenses, should almost exclusively help middle- and upper-income families (Congressional Budget Office, 1978) amplifies an already unfair public policy. By denying equitable access to quality care for so many Black working families, government indirectly discriminates against struggling but self-sufficient families. Unfortunately, the ultimate victims of this bias are the countless Black children who are losing the invaluable opportunity to enhance their development.

HEALTH

Restrictive eligibilities, inadequate supports, and misdirected services are perhaps most damaging to Black families when they affect basic health needs. Above all other factors, health prevention and treatment most determine family well-being and, ironically, are often the least manageable by the family itself. It is an extremely powerful indictment against American family policy that many Blacks are more likely to suffer from poor health than are their white counterparts.

Black families face a dual threat to their health. Poverty, unsafe housing, and poor nutrition make illness much more probable for low-income Black families, who at the same time have less access to competent health care. From such a combination, the consequences are particularly grim. Blacks have lower life expectancies, infant mortality rates nearly twice as high, greater incidences of hypertension and cancer, plus more child fatalities (Health Resources Administration, 1979). The coupling of harmful environments and inadequate health care probably takes its greatest toll on Black children, almost half of whom have never been inoculated against measles (Center for Disease Control, 1979) and 13 percent of whom are born with low birth weights often associated with infant mortality, prematurity, mental retardation, and malnutrition (National Center for Health Statistics, 1979). When given both the greater susceptibility of Black families to poor health and the facts that over 40 percent of all Black children do not see a single physician each year and that as many as 16 percent are not covered by Medicaid or private insurance (National Center for Health Statistics, 1979), it becomes distressingly obvious that the public and private health systems are failing many American families.

While government has enacted some programs to address the health problems of Black children, again restrictive eligibilities and misapplications have limited their effectiveness. The Early Periodic Screening, Diagnosis and Treatment (EPSDT) program, which makes available commendable preventive health care to low-income children, nevertheless fails to serve more than nine million eligible children (Children's Defense Fund, 1977). Furthermore, since EPSDT eligibility is restricted to Medicaid recipients, an additional five million poor children who live in two-parent families that are ineligible for Medicaid similarly do not qualify for EPSDT. Again, by creating an artificial and arbitrary linkage between access to health care and family structure, government policy keeps hundreds of thousands of Black children from receiving demonstrably effective and efficient health care.

The drastic consequences of our shortsighted health policy are best illustrated by the insufficient availability of prenatal care. Black mothers are twice as likely never to have had prenatal care, while for each month of pregnancy Black women, again, are twice as likely as whites to not receive prenatal care (National Center for Health Statistics, 1979). That the mortality rate for Black infants during the first month after birth actually rose in the seventies (National Center for Health Statistics, 1980) is therefore not a coincidence; more than any other statistic, it proves that a health policy which directs 99 percent of all health expenditures away from health prevention and education (Dellums, 1979) has fatal implications for Black families.

EDUCATION

Among all basic family functions, education is the one prerogative that has been freely surrendered to government. Consequently, the failure of many public school systems to educate properly substantial numbers of Black children is a direct affront to Black families, causing perhaps more severe damage than any other aspect of public policy. Many Black children are cruelly subjected to a unique double jeopardy: Not only do many receive poor education, but once the system fails Black children, it then labels and stigmatizes them.

Even despite notable progress throughout the decade, many Black students still lag behind their white counterparts in many educational categories ranging from achievement to graduation. Black children are more than twice as likely as white students to have their education delayed by two or more years (National Center for Education Statistics, 1979), so that the average Black sixteen-year-old has a 30 percent probability of being enrolled at least one grade below normal (M-L Group, 1978). On national standardized tests, Black children of varying ages generally score more than 10 percent below the national mean (National Center for Education Statistics, 1979), a clear demonstration that many schools simply do not educate Black children and that parents are unable to reinforce needed achievement motivations (see Ogbu in this volume).

While the problems of schools are certainly intricate and multifaceted, one overriding characteristic of most programs is the inclination to condemn Black students for the failures of the educational system itself. In one especially deplorable example, Black students are disproportionately referred to special educational programs, where Blacks are three times as likely as whites to be assigned to classes for the Educable Mentally Retarded (EMR) than to Special Learning Disability (SLD) programs. Nationally, Black students constitute 41 percent of the total EMR enrollment (U.S. Office of Civil Rights, 1979a), and the proportion has increased by 8 percent in only two years. By comparing placement patterns in different states and regions, discrimination and poor assessment clearly emerge as the decisive factors of the disparity in classifications, but few schools have done much to correct the tragic labeling of Black children despite two laws enacted since 1973.

Equally as frightening a trend, 36 states have initiated minimum competency testing to determine eligibility for graduation, but few have instituted the courses and training necessary to prepare children equitably for the examination. For Black children, the consequences of competency testing are becoming increasingly severe; in Florida, for instance, where Black students were found by a court to be tested for subjects they were never taught, only 23 percent of all Black students passed the math exam, in contrast to 76 percent of all whites (Frahm and Covington, 1979). Originally conceived as a vehicle for introducing accountability into schools, minimum competency testing in practice only punishes Black students without first assessing whether the school in fact taught them the required skills. When one then considers that many states hold competency testing as the best response to the malaise of their school systems, and yet simultaneously deny those schools the funds necessary to educate children, it is clear that educational policy will negatively judge Black children before it will condemn its own systems. Rather than constructively address the deplorable failure of many public schools, public policy has ironically developed a program which undermines Black children merely to support their already successful peers. Tragically, as the previous examples demonstrate, this response to a deep concern of Black families is not atypical.

SOLUTIONS

Given both the complexity of the difficulties that burden Black families and the traditional intransigence of white-controlled public policy to those concerns, only a massive and concerted effort will ever successfully address—and redress—the inadequacies of programs and policies. Virtually every individual and institution concerned about Black families must take stock of Black needs and then voice those issues to representatives in the power structure on the national, state, and local levels. Increasingly, political and social battles are being won by those interests which have mobilized a sophisticated and diverse cadre of advocates who promote their cause on every possible front. The future progress of Black families will depend on our ability to do the same.

BLACK PARENTS MUST STEP OUT AND CONFRONT THE FORCES THAT SHAPE THE LIVES OF THEIR FAMILIES

No grass-roots advocacy effort can be effectively waged today without the vigorous support and participation of the individuals most affected by the issue. In the case of Black families, then, parents themselves must learn the issues and master the facts of public policy. Much can be accomplished by locating and organizing like-minded parents, friends, and local resources so that Black families can develop a collective voice to amplify their views. With such mutual support, Black parents can overcome any fear of confronting the spectrum of policymakers and institutions, ranging from local school boards to congressmen to media executives, who may ultimately impede Black families from social and economic progress.

The media, in particular, especially need to learn from Black families that the images portrayed in music, cinema, and television have played an important role in the current disillusionment of so many Black youths. For, despite their critical effect on Black families and their equally as vital potential for helping to strengthen many Black communities, most decision makers in the media rarely hear, and even less frequently heed, the complaints of their Black viewers. They and all other policymakers must at least be confronted with the choice of eroding or promoting Black family life.

COMMUNITY AGENCIES MUST ENSURE THAT THEIR POLICIES AND PROGRAMS ARE DESIGNED TO STRENGTHEN BLACK FAMILIES TO WHATEVER EXTENT POSSIBLE

As the institutions which directly affect troubled families, local service organizations have a particular responsibility to determine whether their structure, their philosophy, and their practices are in conflict with the true needs of their clients. Individual workers must receive specific training and guidelines expressly devoted to eliminating the commonly misperceived correlation between a family's status and its ethnicity. Ultimately, however, dramatic institutional changes may occur only when agencies integrate their policy, administrative, and service structures to the extent that Blacks are fully represented at every level of decision making, be it in the board room or on a child welfare case review panel.

PROFESSIONALS WHO WORK WITH BLACK FAMILIES AND CHILDREN MUST APPLY THEIR SERVICE EXPERIENCES TOWARD PUBLIC POLICY ADVOCACY

Social workers, teachers, and other practitioners are the "tools" of public policy; they implement programs and policy directives with relatively little voice in their formulation and even less of a role in deciding their long-range consequences. Since, however, such professionals actually work with family members and can witness the true effects of programs, they have an especially vital responsibility to report their observations and experiences back to the policymakers who originally designed their jobs. As the cutting edge of policy, every professional worker must examine his/her own personal and institutional attitude toward Black clients; if any prejudgment based on ethnicity does occur, then that worker must both modify his/her own behavior and then work to reform the policies that promote and perpetuate such roles.

POLICY ANALYSTS AND NATIONAL ORGANIZATIONS MUST INCORPORATE THE VIEWS OF BLACK PARENTS INTO THEIR POLICY RECOMMENDATIONS AND MOBILIZE AND TRAIN PARENTS IN POLICY ADVOCACY

Groups and individuals with a national presence or voice have a prime responsibility to develop, define, and articulate a coherent and relevant philosophy that both answers the needs of Black families and can be expressed convincingly to policymakers on all levels. Advocates for Black families must be able to demonstrate clearly that their agenda does in fact reflect and answer widespread local concerns. To best achieve this goal, national groups must serve a coordinating role by informing and training local advocates on issues and targets while simultaneously channeling local concerns to national policymakers. The National Black Child Development Institute has, for instance, found particular success by organizing parents, teachers, academicians, social workers, and other professionals into local affiliates that can address policy issues on a variety of fronts. Finally, above all else it is imperative that national advocates remain steadfast. Since the passage of major policy reforms can take years to effect, advocates must steadily and consistently advocate the needed reforms even if no outward signs of progress emerge.

CONCLUSION:
POLICY CHANGES TO SUPPORT BLACK FAMILIES

In light of the still unmet needs of Black families, some effort must be made to collate these issues into consistent and understandable principles. Each principle can then be utilized to develop a national and cohesive public policy in individual subjects that affect Black families.

First, the availability of individual services should be based on a family's genuine need, not by an arbitrary determination of such artificial boundaries as family structure or income. Concerns such as child care, health, and housing transcend any arbitrary restrictions. All families have the right to receive these services; yet, with the exception of education, few policies observe those needs, let alone recognize them as rights.

Second, the principle that those services should be available to all families in need cannot justify any sacrifice in quality as a tradeoff for wider coverage. Policies must acknowledge that all families, regardless of their structure or income, need quality programs in child care, education, health, and every other policy area.

Finally, those programs targeted at primarily low-income families, such as child welfare, public assistance, and housing, must be restructured and better coordinated to support family strengths and promote family self-sufficiency. When structured to react merely to immediate problems, as many educational, vocational, welfare, and other programs currently do, services both fail to prevent the recurrence of problems and often allow discriminatory practices to develop and flourish. That Black social service agencies have demonstrated their ability to assist Black families effectively only underscores the need for greater institutional reform of agency and school practices.

Such policy reforms play a particularly important role for Black families, inasmuch as the severity and extensive misperception of these problems often disproportionately affect Black communities. Due to the consistent combination of outright discrimination with the high frequency of povery and marginal incomes, the strengths of Black families are all but ignored by the public while their needs are often painted as indications of pathological weaknesses. Indeed, as Black experiences with the 1980 White House Conference on Families have demonstrated, only when Black family needs are framed within the context of cross-cutting social issues will the white majority recognize those concerns as valid and sincere. Our challenge, then, is to persuade America that the survival of our families is more than sufficient justification for the long overdue reforms.

REFERENCES

Center for Disease Control (1979) U.S. Immunization Survey: 1978. Washington, DC: U.S. Department of Health, Education and Welfare.

Children's Defense Fund (1977) EPSDT: Does It Spell Good Health Care for Children? Washington, DC: Washington Research Project.

Congressional Budget Office (1978) Child Care and Preschool: Options for Federal Support. Washington, DC: Government Printing Office.

Consortium for Longitudinal Studies (1979) Lasting Effects After Preschool. Washington, DC: Government Printing Office.

DELLUMS, R. V. (1979) Speech at "A National Conference on Health Policy, Planning, and Financing the Future of Health Care for Blacks in America." Washington, DC: U.S. Department of Health, Education and Welfare.

FRAHM, R. and J. COVINGTON (1979) What's Happening in Minimum Competency Testing? Bloomington, Indiana: Phi Delta Kappa.

Health Resources Administration (1979) Health Status of Minorities and Low-Income Groups. Washington, DC: Government Printing Office.

HILL, R. (1977) Informal Adoptions Among Black Families. Washington, DC: National Urban League Research Department.

_____ (1980) "Black families in the 70's," pp. 29-58 in J. Williams (ed.) The State of Black America 1980. New York: National Urban League, Inc.

HOSNI, D. (1979) An Economic Analysis of Child Care Support to Low-Income Mothers. University of Central Florida.

M-L Group (1978) Minority Education, 1960-1972: Grounds, Gains, and Gaps. Chicago: CEMREL, Inc.

National Black Child Development Institute (1980) "The Status of Black Children in 1980." Washington, DC: National Black Child Development Institute, Inc.

National Center for Education Statistics (1979) The Condition of Education, 1979 Edition. Washington, DC: Government Printing Office.

National Center for Health Statistics (1979) Health, United States 1979. Washington, DC: Government Printing Office.

_____ (1980) Health, United States 1980. Washington, DC: Government Printing Office.

RUOPP, R., J. TRAVERS, F. GLANTZ, and G. COELEN (1979) Children at the Center. Cambridge, MA: Abt Associates.

U.S. Bureau of the Census (1979) Current Population Reports, Series P-23, No. 80. Washington, DC: Government Printing Office.

_____ (1980) Current Population Reports, Series P-60, No. 125. Washington, DC: Government Printing Office.

U.S. Bureau of Labor Statistics (1979) Special Labor Force Report No. 218. Washington, DC: Government Printing Office.

U.S. Office of Civil Rights (1979a) Statistical Report: Enrollment in Special Education Programs. Washington, DC: U.S. Department of Health, Education and Welfare.

_____ (1979b) Vocational Education Survey. Washington, DC: U.S. Department of Health, Education and Welfare.

WALDMAN, E., A.S. GROSSMAN, H. HAYGHE, and B.L. JOHNSON (1979) "Working mothers in the 1970's: a Look at the Statistics," in Special Labor Force Report No. 233. Washington, DC: Government Printing Office.

20

AN ADVOCACY AGENDA FOR
BLACK FAMILIES AND CHILDREN

MARIAN WRIGHT EDELMAN

A PORTRAIT OF INEQUALITY

A Black child still lacks a fair chance to live, learn, thrive, and contribute in America.

A Black baby is three times as likely as a white baby to have a mother who dies in childbirth and is twice as likely to be born to a mother who has had no prenatal care at all. A Black infant is twice as likely as a white infant to die during the first year of life. The Black infant mortality rate in 1978 was about the same as the white infant mortality rate in 1950.

Black teenagers die from heart and congenital defects at twice the rate of white teenagers, and Black teenage girls die from heart disease at three times the rate of white teenage girls. There are five times as many newly detected tuberculosis cases among Black as among white children.

Black children are more likely to be sick because they are more likely to be poor. They are twice as likely as white children to have no regular source of health care, are likely to be more seriously ill when they finally do see a doctor,

AUTHOR'S NOTE: Sections reprinted from *Portrait of Inequality: Black and White Children in America* by permission of the Children's Defense Fund, 1520 New Hampshire Avenue, N.W., Washington, D.C. 20036.

and are five times as likely to have to rely on hospital emergency rooms or outpatient clinics.

A Black baby today has nearly one chance in two of being born into poverty and faces a losing struggle to escape poverty throughout childhood. A Black child is more than two and one-half times as likely as a white child to live in dilapidated housing and is twice as likely to be on welfare. A Black child's mother is more likely to go out to work sooner, to work longer hours, and to make less money than a white child's mother. As a result, young Black children are far more dependent on full-time day care arrangements than are white children.

A Black child's father is 70 percent more likely than a white child's father to be unemployed, and when Black fathers find work, they bring home $70 a week less than white fathers. When both parents work, they earn only half what a white father earns.

A Black child is twice as likely as a white child to live with neither parent, three times as likely to be born to a teenage mother, seven times as likely to have parents who separate, and three times as likely to see his or her father die.

A Black child is three times as likely as a white child to live in a single-parent home. A Black preschool child is three times as likely to depend solely on a mother's earnings. Because the Black woman still faces discrimination as a Black and as a woman, she is the lowest paid among workers and the family she heads alone is the poorest in the nation.

A Black child is twice as likely as a white child to grow up in a family whose head did not finish high school and is four times less likely than a white child to grow up in a family whose head graduated from college.

In school, a Black child faces one chance in three of being in a racially isolated school and is twice as likely as a white child to be suspended, expelled, or given corporal punishment. A Black child is twice as likely as a white child to drop out of school, almost twice as likely to be behind grade level, three times as likely to be labeled educable mentally retarded, but only half as likely to be labeled gifted. The longer a Black child is in school, the farther behind he or she falls.

A Black youth is three times as likely as a white youth to be unemployed. A Black student who graduates from high school has a greater chance of being unemployed than a white student who dropped out of elementary school. A Black college graduate faces about the same odds of unemployment as a white high school dropout.

Between the ages of 11 and 17, a Black teenager has a better than one in ten chance of getting into trouble, is seven times as likely as a white youth to be arrested for violent crimes, and is twice as likely to be arrested for serious property crimes. A Black male teenager is five times as likely as a white male teenager to be a victim of homicide and is twice as likely to be detained in a juvenile or adult correctional facility—the conclusion of a winding, uphill struggle to beat the odds against success.

ELEVEN PREMISES FOR EFFECTIVE ADVOCACY

Become an active and effective advocate for Black and poor children. We all must take a stronger, more systematic, and more programmatic interest in alleviating the problems that affect Black children. No one has a greater stake than we do in whether our children read, write, think, survive, and grow up healthy. If the widespread nutrition, health, child care, education, and employment needs described are to be met, Black parents and leaders must constantly raise them in public, organize to challenge them, and vote for leaders who will do something about them.[1]

Become well informed about the needs of Black children and families in your area and nationally. We will not help Black children if we are uninformed. We must argue with facts as well as with emotion. We must teach as well as preach. Homework is a key to effective change. We must take the time to define specifically the problems facing children in our communities. We must then analyze and seek a range of appropriate remedies within our own families and institutions and through appropriate policy changes in other institutions. Those who care about Black children and families should hold study groups in churches and in women's, civic, and social clubs; invite speakers knowledgeable about and active on behalf of children; and find out how to achieve specific positive policies for children.[2]

Don't give or accept excuses for doing nothing. Too many of us hide behind excuses:

"Whatever I do won't make a difference anyway."

"I've already done my bit or paid my dues. Now I'm going to get mine."

"It'll just get me and my child into trouble."

These and other do-nothing excuses are an abnegation of personal responsibility for one another and for our children. We are not out of the woods because some of us have two cars, a big mortgage, and several charge accounts. Any Black person who thinks this way is courting danger and jeopardizing our children's future.

The Black community today stands poised between progress and regression. We should heed Frederick Douglass's warning about how fragile change is:

I know that from the acorn evolves the oak, but I know also that the commonest accident may destroy its potential character and defeat its natural destiny. One wave brings its treasure from the briny deep, but another sweeps it back to its primal depths. The saying that revolutions never go back must be taken with limitations [1972: 284].

The hard-earned progress of the 1950s and 1960s is not a keepsake that can be taken for granted. Indeed, it is threatened daily. There is a growing resistance to affirmative action, programs targeted for the poor, increased government spending, and strong federal regulations. There is a defense budget that is regarded by many as a tradeoff for children's futures. And there is a national impatience that resents the fact that the effects of centuries of segregation and discrimination did not disappear quietly and cheaply in a decade or two. The revival of Ku Klux Klan activity, increasing clashes between the police and Black communities, and threatened retrenchment of Black political power through restrictive judicial interpretation of the Voting Rights Act of 1965 are all causes for concern.

The Black community must be constantly vigilant lest our rights and our children's futures are undermined by subtle and not-so-subtle means. Today's atmosphere, against the end of the Reconstruction era and the backsliding on equal opportunity during the Nixon and Ford administrations, should be adequate warning.

Understand clearly that nobody is going to give us or our children anything. Frederick Douglass put it bluntly: "Men may not get all they pay for in this world, but they must certainly pay for all they get" (1972: 200). Whatever we achieve for Black children and families will depend more on what we do with our votes and political power than on what those in power do on their own. We must vote strategically and intelligently and, through our example and leadership, encourage Black youths to participate in the political process.[3]

Even as we seek additional resources and laws, we must constantly monitor the enforcement of laws already on the books, help weed out those that do not work, and see how existing money can be used better to reach the children intended to be served. For example, only one-sixth of the children eligible for Medicaid get the Early and Periodic Screening, Diagnosis and Treatment (EPSDT) services to which they are entitled (U.S. Department of Health, Education and Welfare, 1979). These children are disproportionately Black. Tens of thousands more children could receive needed health services *now* if their families knew of the program's availability and if Black organizations demanded better enforcement of that law by states and the federal government.

Recognize that the ground rules for achieving change are different now than they were five or ten years ago. The resource pie is contracting. The burden of proof and the level of competency required of groups seeking social change have increased. We cannot represent the interests of children and families effectively simply by asserting that what we want is morally right. We cannot look at children's or poor people's or civil rights programs and simply ask for more money.

We must gain greater technical proficiency in how bureaucracies work; how programs are administered; how services are delivered; and how budget decisions are made at the federal, state, and local levels. We must be aware of and learn to influence the complicated tradeoffs that are made by those in power. "Whoever controls the budget controls policy and will have a critical impact on jobs and services for Black families in the decade to come" (Children's Defense Fund, 1981).

Focus attention and energies. We should always maintain our vision and work toward longer-range goals for Black children and the Black community. But we must break down our big goals into manageable, practical pieces for action. Too much of our current effort is diluted by our failure to set priorities and stick with them until they are accomplished. Too many possible, incremental gains are overlooked while we focus on long-term agendas we cannot accomplish in the foreseeable future. We must act now to deal with our children's immediate needs for adequate nutrition, education, child care, health care, and family stability. They only grow up once. Another generation should not be sacrificed while we work toward ideal solutions. A child health bill that we can help pass now, for instance, is worth a lot more than a national health insurance program that may or may not pass in the next five years or at all.[4] We must set specific immediate, intermediate, and long-range goals and go systematically, step by step, until we achieve them.

Expend energy on real issues, not symbolic ones. We must not be bought off by appeals to vanity or status. We must avoid a treadmill of endless consultations and meetings that result in little or no action. Consultations, conferences, and commissions are not substitutes for programs and money. We must set substantive goals, think about how to achieve them, and choose the means that get us there.

There is another, more important dimension to this substance versus symbolism issue for the Black community. Nannie Burroughs, a leading Black churchwoman, spoke of the need for Black people to organize "inside" and to teach our children

> the internals and eternals rather than the externals. Be more concerned with putting in than getting on. We have been too bothered about the externals— clothes or money. What we need are mental and spiritual giants who are aflame with a purpose [1972: 522-553].

In the 1980s, we must focus more on what is in our children's heads and hearts and less on what is on their backs and feet. Black people have always brought a special dimension to our nation because of our struggle for freedom and equality. We must not squander it by buying into the materialistic values of the culture and abandoning the commitment to serve others that our past has dictated. We have not come so far to seize so little.

Persist and dig in for a long fight. Recognize that a major agenda for Black children and families is possible and essential—but will not be achieved overnight. There are no miracles on the horizon to make the dream of equal opportunity a reality for Black children. There are no Moseses or Kings in the wings to lead us to light. We must each take the responsibility for lifting ourselves and bringing along others. Everything we have earned as a people—even that which is our own by right—has come out of long struggle. The latest civil rights movement did not start in the 1950s. It started in the 1930s with a small band of brave parents and lawyers plotting to challenge legal segregation. As in past decades, nothing is more likely to bring about change now for our children than determination and persistence.

Use what you have to do what you must. Don't hide behind lack of education or wealth as a reason for inactivity or despair. To do so is to betray a central quality of our history and key to our futures. Our attitude must be like the father on a plantation in Issaquena County, Mississippi, when his child's Head Start center did not appear to have any chance of being refunded: "If there is no way, we'll find a way anyway" (Greenberg, 1969: 1). And they did.

Sojourner Truth, a woman who could neither read nor write, pointed the way for us. She never gave up talking or fighting against slavery and the mistreatment of women, not even against odds far worse than those we and our children face today. Once a heckler told Sojourner that he cared no more for her talk "than for a fleabite." "Maybe not," was her answer, "but the Lord willing, I'll keep you scratching" (Lerner, 1972: 524).

Her retort should be ours today and tomorrow to a nation that keeps turning its back on our children. Although many politicians, voters, schoolteachers, corporations, and unions do not really want to hear or act on the problems of our families and children, Black parents and leaders have got to "make them scratch" all over the nation. Every single person can be a flea and can bite. However poor, however unlearned, everybody can stand up for a child who is mistreated. Enough fleas for children can make even the biggest dogs mighty uncomfortable. If they flick some of us off and others of us keep coming back, we will begin to get our children's needs heard and attended to.

Attack the right enemy. Stand united. We remain our own worst enemies. Some Black people spend more time fighting and picking at each other than at the real opponents of Black children and families. Too many of us are forever looking over our shoulders to see who else is doing something. People who always look over their shoulders are not looking ahead. The facts make plain that there is plenty for all of us to do without stepping on each other's toes. Let us pull together. It is Black children who lose from our ego-tripping and fragmentation. How can we expect other people to place our children's needs higher than their own interests if we ourselves do not? And how can we ask others to invest more time, energy, and service than we do? Our ideas will not work unless we do.

Teach our children our history so that they can gain confidence, self-reliance, and courage. I recall hearing Mary McLeod Bethune, who founded Bethune-Cookman College, talking about the need to arm ourselves with the facts of our past so that we and our children could face the future with clear eyes and sure vision. Yet there are some Black youngsters in our urban schools who have never heard of Martin Luther King, Jr. There are talented Black students in Ivy League universities who complain about how tough it is to get an education. There are Black youths who neither know who Benjamin Mays is nor what he went through to get from the town of Ninety Six, South Carolina, to Bates College, to become the president of Morehouse College (see Mays, 1971). Too many Black students in Black colleges today do not know the debt they owe John Lewis or that Andrew Young earned his way to fame by way of the jailhouse and billyclub. They have not basked in the eloquence of Frederick Douglass, Countee Cullen, or James Weldon Johnson or escaped slavery and death with Harriet Tubman. They do not know the Negro national anthem, "Lift Every Voice and Sing," that many Black adults learned before "The Star Spangled Banner." They have not flared up indignantly against discrimination with Sojourner Truth or laughed with Langston Hughes's "Simple" or raged with Claude McKay (see, for example, Hughes, 1965). They are unaware of the contributions Charles Drew and Ralph Bunche made to world health and peace. Too many of our children are not anchored in the faith of a Bethune, who could envision and start a college on a dump heap and promised down payment of $5.00 that she did not have. They do not sense or share deeply enough the sorrowful despair channeled into song and sermon that allowed our grandparents, fathers, and mothers to keep going when times were so tough. They are missing the pride, confidence, and purpose of a Nanny Burroughs, who boasted about specializing "in the wholly impossible" (Lerner, 1972: 132).

More critically, too many of our middle-class children do not know the dangers of taking anything for granted in America or what remains to be done to achieve justice because we adults are not sufficiently teaching them and leading the way. That is the task before us now if the portrait of inequality drawn here is to develop into a portrait of hope.

The 1980s may look complex and bleak. But not as complex and bleak as what the Tubmans, Truths, Douglasses, Bethunes, DuBoises, Everses, Parkses, and Kings faced when they began to stand up for our children and for the justice to which the Black community is entitled. That is what each of us must do now: Find the ways to help those of our Black—and white and brown and red—children still left behind and to guide the nation away from the moral shame, the ongoing toll of dependency, lost talent, foregone productivity, and unrealized promise that ignoring our children brings.

AN ACTION AGENDA FOR
BLACK CHILDREN AND FAMILIES

This agenda is by no means all-inclusive. It focuses on specific goals to help Black children that are critically important and that can be accomplished immediately or in the near future. It calls not only for new legislation and more resources, but also for better enforcement of laws and more efficient administration of programs already on the books. It calls for improving some programs, like the EPSDT program, that are not working well. It calls for expanding others, like Head Start, that are successful. It also calls for the enforcement of new laws—such as the Adoption Assistance and Child Welfare Act of 1980, which holds promise of getting Black and other children out of costly, long-term, and discontinuous foster and institutional care. In sum, we must analyze what we have, eliminate practices and programs that do not work, build on those that do, and improve or redirect those that could be made to work better.

In looking at specific problems of and programs for children, we do not ignore the overarching importance of adequate jobs and income to Black family stability and to Black children's well-being. We will continue to lend our support to civil rights, labor, and other proponents addressing these important issues.[5] But jobs and income alone are not enough to meet children's needs. We must, in addition, find specific remedies to alleviate the education, health, child welfare, child care, and housing problems daily facing millions of Black children and families. Equally important, we must change the negative attitudes and expectations that so many who teach and come into contact with Black children hold and transmit to them.

No one institution—the family, Black churches, corporations, the government—has all of the power and responsibility to meet all the needs of Black children and families. To blame or place responsibility on government or business alone would be as much a mistake as blaming parents or communities for all the problems their children face in schools, health clinics, and a range of other institutions over which they can exercise little or no control (see, for example, Keniston, 1977; National Academy of Sciences, 1976). Rather, we call for the primacy of Black parents in making decisions affecting their children. They can and must exercise responsibility for their children. But public and private officials and institutions must be more sensitive to Black children and families. They must ensure that their policies and practices are fairly administered and implemented and help rather than hurt, strengthen rather than undercut, parental roles and children's well-being.

Included in this agenda are two kinds of activities: those that can be undertaken by local organizations (often using existing resources) and those that require changing the policies and practices of other institutions. Both are critically important.

Do not be overwhelmed by all that needs to be done. Take one issue or set of problems that are most pressing in your community or that most concerns your church or organization. Make a plan and begin to learn who can help you. Reach out to friends, neighbors, and local groups for support. Call CDF for assistance.

NOTES

1. For a step-by-step description of how parents and others can become more effective child advocates, see Children's Defense Fund (1979).

2. For sources and pointers to help you do research on the needs of children in your community, see Children's Defense Fund (1980). In addition, facts about children's needs and strategies for addressing them appear in other CDF publications and in our monthly newsletter, *CDF Reports*. For information, call our toll-free number: (800) 424-9602.

3. Only 27.7 percent of Black youths aged 18-20 are registered to vote. Black voter participation rates for this age group are 30 percent below white voter participation rates. Current efforts by a number of Black organizations to register young voters and get them to vote must be continued and strengthened (see U.S. Department of Commerce, 1979).

4. Therefore, one of CDF's top 1980 legislative priorities was passage of the Child Health Assurance Program (CHAP, S. 1204 and H.R. 4962), even as we work toward national health insurance.

5. For discussion of the effects of structural unemployment and inflation on children and families, see Keniston and Carnegie Council on Children (1977). For a series of recommendations pertaining to jobs, inflation, and economic policy, see Joint Center for Political Studies (1980).

REFERENCES

BURROUGHS, N.H. (1972) "Unload your Uncle Toms," in G. Lerner (ed.) Black Women in White America: A Documentary History. New York: Vintage.

Children's Defense Fund (1979) It's Time to Stand Up for Your Children: A Parent's Guide to Child Advocacy. Washington, DC: Children's Defense Fund.

_____ (1980) Where Do You Look? Whom Do You Ask? How Do You Know? Information Resources for Child Advocates. Washington, DC: Children's Defense Fund.

_____ (1981) Children and the Federal Budget. Washington, DC: Children's Defense Fund.

DOUGLASS, F. (1972) "The mission of war" and "If there is no struggle, there is no progress," in The Voice of Black America (P. Foner, ed.). New York: Simon & Schuster.

GREENBERG, P. (1969) The Devil Has Slippery Shoes. Toronto: Macmillan.

HUGHES, L. (1965) Simple's Uncle Sam. New York: Hill and Whang.

Joint Center for Political Studies (1980) The National Black Agenda for the 80's: Richmond Conference Recommendations. Washington, DC: Joint Center for Political Studies.

KENISTON, K. and Carnegie Council on Children (1977) All Our Children: The American Family under Pressure. New York: Harcourt Brace Jovanovich.

LERNER, G. (1972) Black Women in White America: A Documentary History. New York: Vintage.

MAYS, B. E. (1971) Born to Rebel: An Autobiography. New York: Scribners.

National Academy of Sciences (1976) Toward a National Policy for Children and Families. Washington, DC: National Academy of Sciences.

U.S. Department of Commerce, Bureau of the Census (1979) "Voting and registration in the election of November 1978." Current Population Reports, Series P-20, No. 344. Washington, DC: Government Printing Office.

U.S. Department of Health, Education and Welfare (1979) Data on the Medicaid Program: Eligibility/Services/Expenditures. Baltimore, MD: Health Care Financing Administration.

CONTRIBUTORS

Noel A. Cazenave is Assistant Professor of Sociology at Temple University. He recently edited a special issue of *Alternative Lifestyles* on Black alternative lifestyles, and has conducted research on battered elders, Black fathers, and male sex roles. Cazenave received his Ph.D. at Tulane University and has done postdoctoral research at the University of New Hampshire. He and his wife have one child.

Frank G. Davis, Graduate Professor, Department of Economics, Howard University, earned his Ph.D. at the State University of Iowa. He is the author of *The Economics of Black Community Development* and *The Black Community's Social Security*. He is married and has three grown children.

Jualynne Dodson is Associate Professor at the Graduate School of Social Work, Atlanta University, Atlanta, Georgia. She was founder and Director of the school's Research Center, whose emphasis was curriculum-related research on Black families. She is married and the mother of two children. She is completing her Ph.D. at the University of California, Berkeley.

Marian Wright Edelman, President and Founder, Children's Defense Fund, received her B.A. at Spelman and her LL.D. from Yale. She directed the Harvard Center for Law and Education and the Legal Defense and Education Fund of the NAACP. She wrote *Portrait of Inequality, Black and White Children in America*. She is married and the mother of three boys.

Paul C. Glick served as the Census Bureau's Senior Demographer from 1972-1981. His research interest is family demography. In 1938 he received his doctorate in sociology at the University of Wisconsin and married his present wife, Joy, the mother of Paul (junior) and David. He was President of the National Council on Family Relations in 1978-1979.

Gerald Gurin received his Ph.D. in social psychology from the University of Michigan in 1956. He is currently a research scientist at the Institute for Social Research and Professor of Higher Education. He has worked and published extensively in the area of group identity and consciousness. He is married and has three children.

Algea Harrison received her Ph.D. at the University of Michigan. She is Associate Professor of Psychology at Oakland University in Rochester, Michigan. Harrison's research interests center on inter-role conflict among Black women and the socialization process among Black families. She is the mother of two children.

Jerold Heiss received his Ph.D. from Indiana University and is currently Professor of Sociology at the University of Connecticut. His books include *The Case of the Black Family: A Sociological Inquiry* and *The Social Psychology of Interaction*. He is married and the father of daughters.

Robert B. Hill, formerly Research Director, National Urban League, received his B.A. from the City College of the City University of New York and his Ph.D. from Columbia University. He is the author of *Strengths of Black Families, Informal Adoption Among Black Families*, and *Illusions of Black Progress*. He is the father of two children.

James S. Jackson received his Ph.D. in social psychology from Wayne State University in 1972. He is Associate Professor in the Department of Psychology and Faculty Associate at the Institute for Social Research at the University of Michigan. He is Director of a nationwide, three-generation study on Black families. He is married and is expecting a child.

Leanor B. Johnson, Research Associate, The Urban Institute, received her Ph.D. from Purdue University and formerly taught at Florida State University. She has published on marriage and family and human sexuality. She is married and the mother of two children.

Wilhelmina Manns is Associate Professor of Social Work at Howard University where she coordinates and teaches Family and Child Services and also teaches Direct Services. She received a B.A. from Ohio State University, a M.S.W. from Case Western Reserve University, and a Ph.D. from the University of Chicago. She has four grown children.

Harriette Pipes McAdoo, Professor, School of Social Work, Howard University and Research Associate, Columbia Research Systems, received her Ph.D. from the University of Michigan with postgraduate work at Harvard. She has published on racial attitudes and self-esteem in Black children, mobility patterns of Blacks and support networks of single mothers. She is a Director of the National Council on Family Relations and the Society for Research in Child Development.

John L. McAdoo, Associate Professor, University of Maryland, received his Ph.D. from the University of Michigan and did postgraduate work at Harvard and John Hopkins University. He has published on parent-child interactions, fear of crime in the Black elderly, and evaluation of social services. John and Harriette are married and are the parents of four children.

Wayne R. McCullough has an A.B. from Princeton University and an A.M. from the University of Michigan, where he is currently completing his Ph.D. in social psychology. McCullough has been involved with identity research issues since the early 1970s. Married, he is joining IBM's Personnel Research Division.

Evelyn K. Moore is Executive Director and Founder of the National Black Child Development Institute, a national advocacy organization which conducts research and mobilizes Black communities in policy areas that affect Black children and their families. Before coming to NBCDI, she taught at the School of Education at the University of Michigan.

Wade W. Nobles, President of the Urban Institute for Human Services, received his Ph.D. from Stanford University. He was Director of the Black Family Research Project at Westside Community Mental Health Center. He has written widely on the Black family and the African-American continuities. He is married and the father of five children.

John U. Ogbu, a native of Nigeria, is Professor of Anthropology at the University of California, Berkeley, where he received his Ph.D. in anthropology. He was a research associate with the Carnegie Council on Children and a distinguished visiting professor at the University of Delaware. His major publications include *The Next Generation: An Ethnography of Education in an Urban Neighborhood* and *Minority Education and Caste: The American System in Cross-Cultural Perspective*. He is married and has four children.

Marie F. Peters, Associate Professor, Human Development and Family Relations at the University of Connecticut and P.I., Toddler and Infant Experiences Studies, received an Ed.D. from Harvard. She is Secretary of the National Council on Family Relations, Director of the Groves Conference on Marriage and the Family, and edited the Black family issue of *Journal of Marriage and the Family*. She conducts research on socialization, stress, and development of children in Black families. She is married with three grown children.

William Harrison Pipes, Professor Emeritus, American Thought and Language, Michigan State University, was the author of *Say Amen, Brother, Is God Dead?* and *Death of an Uncle Tom*. His B.A. was earned at Tuskegee Institute, his M.A. at Atlanta University, and his Ph.D. at the University of Michigan, the first U.S. Black to attain this degree in speech. He was formerly President of Alcorn State University and Dean of Philander Smith College. Married, he was the father of three children, five grandchildren, and one great-grandchild.

Robert Staples, Associate Professor of Sociology, University of California, San Francisco, received his Ph.D. from the University of Minnesota. He is the author of *The Black Woman in America, Introduction to Black Sociology, The Lower Income Negro Family in St. Paul, The Black Family: Essays and Studies*, and *The World of Black Singles, Changing Patterns of Male/Female Relations*.

Niara Sudarkasa (formerly Gloria A. Marshall) is Professor of Anthropology and Director of the Center for Afroamerican and African Studies at the University of Michigan. She has published extensively on women, trade, and family organization among the Yoruba of Nigeria and other parts of West Africa. Her Ph.D. was from Columbia, and she is married and has one son.

DATE DUE

AP 19'83			